Tibetan Historical Literature

A. I. VOSTRIKOV (1904–1937)

TIBETAN HISTORICAL LITERATURE

A. I. Vostrikov

Translated from the Russian by
Harish Chandra Gupta

LONDON AND NEW YORK

First published 1994 by
RoutledgeCurzon Press Ltd.

Published 2014 by Routledge
2 Park Square, Milton Park, Abingdon, Oxfordshire OX14 4RN
711 Third Avenue, New York, NY 10017

First issued in paperback 2014
Routledge is an imprint of the Taylor & Francis Group, an informa business

Transferred to Digital Printing 2006

ISBN 978-0-700-70267-1 (hbk)
ISBN 978-1-138-86227-2 (pbk)

British Library Cataloguing-in-Publication Data
A CIP record for this title is available from the British Library

CONTENTS

TRANSLATOR'S NOTE

The present work was taken up for translation at the suggestion and request of Dr. Alaka Chattopadhyaya. The Tibetan language being almost Greek to me, the work of steering me safe through the complex Tibetan jargon of this brilliant work obviously fell on her shoulders.

However, despite all care, certain discrepancies have still crept in into the present publication, some of these having been reproduced in toto from the original Russian edition.

Two different Russian words—*kuritsa* (lit. "hen", "chicken") and *ptitsa* (lit. "bird", "fowl")—have been used for the animal "Hen" of the Tibetan sexagenary cycle [for example : *god zheleza-ptitsa* (Iron-Hen year ; A.D. 1681) on p. 113, but *god zemli-kuritsy* (Earth-Hen year ; A.D. 1729) on p. 317, etc.].

Certain obvious misprints, when detected, were "silently" corrected : "bsTan-pa-tshe-rin (b. 1678)" in place of "bsTan-pa-tshe-rin (b. 1668)"; "Fire-Mouse year (A.D. 1696)" in place of "Fire-Hen year (A.D. 1696)" in f. n. 553 ; "336 years" in place of "396 years" in f. n. 608 ; "fols. 236^b 4..." in place of "fols. 263^b 4 . " in f. n. 298 ; "544 years B.C." in place of "554 years B.C." in f. n. 342 ; "1928" in place of "1927" in f. n. 673, etc. etc.

As will be seen, the work abounds in footnotes, and the footnote numbers follow each other so closely that, in certain cases, I had no choice but to retain the very syntax of the original sentence.

I would also like to take this opportunity of expressing gratitude to my friend Professor Debiprasad Chattopadhyaya (the editor of the series in which the present translation has been published), for constantly putting me on the rails and literally making me move whenever and wherever I got stuck up.

To my friends Shri Ramakrishna Maitra,. Professor Haridas Sinharay and Professor Mrinalkanti Gangopadhyaya, I am greatly indebted for kindly assisting me in seeing this book through the press.

November 7, 1970 *Harish C. Gupta*

INTRODUCTORY NOTE

Professor Andrei Ivanovich Vostrikov was one of the distinguished representatives of the Russian scholars of Oriental studies. He made an enormous contribution to the study of the history and philosophy of Tibet and India, though his untimely death put an abrupt end to this creative academic life.

In 1931, Professor Vostrikov prepared for publication his work *O filosofii Darmakirti* [On the philosophy of Dharmakīrti]. In 1933, he translated from Sanskrit Kauṭilya's political and economic treatise—the *Arthaśāstra*—jointly with Academician Shcherbatskoi, Academician Ol'denburg, Professor Obermiller and B. V. Semichov, and also compiled a terminological lexicon to it.

In 1934, Vostrikov published the article *Logical Works of Vasubandhu,* and the next year he completed the monograph *Logic of Vasubandhu* which is a comprehensive treatment of the problem on the basis of all available sources. In 1934, he also published in the "Indian Historical Quarterly" (vol. xi, No. 1, March 1935) his article *The Nyāyavārtika of Uddyotakara and the Vādanyāya of Dharmakīrti.*

Towards the end of his life, Professor A. I. Vostrikov was engaged in the study and translation of the ancient Sanskrit philosophical monument *Kālacakra.* He prepared for the press a composite text of the *Kālacakra* frcm two manuscripts (one preserved in London and the other the southern edition of the *Kālacakra* ; the latter was brought from India by Professor I. P. Minaev) and a Tibetan translation. He was also translating this work into Russian and writing a commentary on it, but he could not complete these.

A. I. Vostrikov paid great attention to Tibetan studies. He worked on the compilation of a scientific grammar of the Tibetan language, which was completed by Shcherbatskoi in 1941. However, the problems of the Tibetan historical literature held a greater attraction for Vostrikov. In 1934 was published his article *Bibliografiya tibetskoi literatury* [Bibliography of Tibetetan Literature] in the journal "Bibliografiya Vostoka" (Nos. 2-4).

This article contains a critical analysis of the article of van Manen (*Contribution to the Bibliography of Tibet*) and some new valuable information on Tibetan historical literature. In 1936, this article was published in English (*Some Corrections and Critical Remarks on Dr. J. van Manen's "Contribution to the Bibliography of Tibet*",—"Bulletin of the School of Oriental Studies", London, vol. viii, 1935, pp 51-76) when it attracted a most lively attention of the Tibetologists of the whole world.

Of the remaining works of A. I. Vostrikov, mention must be made of the *Letopis' barguzinskikh buryat* [Annals of the Barguzinsk Buryats] and the article *S. F. Ol'denburg i izuchenie Tibeta* [S. F. Ol'denburg and the Study of Tibet],—which gives an outline of the history of Tibetan study in Russia and of the history of the formation of the collection of Tibetan manuscripts and xylographs (the largest in the world) in the Leningrad Branch of the Institute of Peoples of Asia (Academy of Sciences, USSR).

The present monograph on *Tibetan Historical Literature* is the result of all that Vostrikov could do for a systematization and description of the vast and multifarious literature of Tibet, which till then had not been much studied. To this work is also appended a special table compiled by him for the conversion of the dates of Tibetan sexagenary cycle into European calendar.

14th June, 1958 *N. P. Vostrikova*

EDITOR'S NOTE

The Russian original of the present work was posthumously published in 1962 in the revived *Bibliotheca Buddhica* series and edited by G. N. Roerich.

On two points, the English publication differs from the Russian original. First, in the Russian original the notes and references are given at the end of the book while in the present translation these are rearranged page-wise. Secondly, all the Tibetan words are given here in Roman transliteration and this based on the principles followed in the *Tibetan-English Dictionary* by S. C. Das.

To Dr. I. D. Serebryakov of the Institute of the Peoples of Asia (now Institute of Oriental Studies), Academy of Sciences, USSR, we are indebted for the copy of the Russian original and for very much else besides.

—D. C.

TIBETAN HISTORICAL LITERATURE

A. I. Vostrikov

Translated from the Russian by

Harish C. Gupta

Vos. 1

AUTHOR'S PREFACE

The main theme of the work *Tibetan Historical Literature* was expounded by me in March, 1935, at a session of the Academy of Sciences, USSR. The attention which my communication received and the offer of the Academy to publish this work with all the relevant materials in the *Trudy Instituta narodov Azii* [Transactions of the Institute of Peoples of Asia] encouraged me to enlarge considerably my original brief work. I specifically endeavoured to study, though briefly, the most important and interesting monuments of Tibetan historiography available in the collections of the Institute of Peoples of Asia. Nevertheless, even in this enlarged and revised form, my work has no pretensions to being exhaustive. It is intended to serve only as an introduction of its kind to the study of Tibetan historical literature.

In preparing this work for publication, I was very shaky in the matter of transcription of the Tibetan words. At first, I thought it possible to restrict myself to writing the Tibetan words in Tibetan characters only. But this would have made the present work totally obscure to a non-Tibetologist. The use of Roman transcription, though simpler, would have been inadequate ; for the wide divergence between the Tibetan words as written and pronounced would still have rendered the transliterated names unreadable to the non-specialists. It would, of course, have been most natural to put such words in Tibetan script and also to give the transcription of their Lhasa pronunciation. But this pronunciation has not so far been used in the Russian scientific literature ; its use, therefore, would have made many known names unrecognizable. Besides, this would have necessitated the use and hence explanation of a number of diacritical marks, which would have taken much space and diverted us from our immediate task. Therefore, on the advice of my teacher, Academician F. I. Shcherbatskoi [Th. Stcherbatsky], I decided to retain the Mongolian pronunciation of Tibetan words with its conventional simplified Russian transcription as heretofore followed in our literature, bearing in mind that it is only this pronunciation (with some variations) that is known in Mongolia and Buryatia. To avoid any misunderstanding, the words have also been written in Tibetan alongside this transcription of the Mongolian pronunciation.

The notes in the present work mostly supplement and further the main theme of the text and are often fairly large. These have, therefore, been put separately at the end of the book for the sake of convenience. Unfortunately, the distribution of material between the text and the notes is not always consistent enough. There are notes which could well have been put in the text, and there are, on the other hand, materials in the text which could have safely gone as notes. The extremely short time that I got for giving final shape to this enlarged work prevented me from making these changes. It is hoped that the presence of indexes will obviate these shortcomings for the readers.

I consider it my duty to express my deep gratitude to F. I. Shcherbatskoi for the constant attention with which he followed my work from the very beginning, and to N. P. Vostrikova for her suggestions and selfless help in my work and in the compilation of the indexes.

Leningrad
October, 1936

A. Vostrikov

INTRODUCTION

The history of Tibet is one of the least studied fields of science. It is only the history of Western Tibet, or, to put it more precisely, the history of Ladakh, that can be considered comparatively better studied at present. Much work has been done in this regard by A. Cunningham[1], E. Schlagintweit[2], K. Marx[3], and specially by A. Francke, who is responsible for the best and most complete edition of the *Ladakh Chronicle* (*La-dwags-rgyal-rabs*), the publication of a number of small historical texts and for a general study of the history of Western Tibet[4]. The

1. A. Cunningham, *Ladak: Physical, Statistical and Historical, with Notices of the Surrounding Countries*, London, 1854.
2. E. Schlagintweit, *Die Konige von Tibet, von der Entstehung koniglicher Macht in Yarlung bis zum Erloschen in Ladak*,—Abhandlungen der k. bayer. Akademie der Wissenschaften, I Cl, X Bd, iii Abt., München, 1866.
3. K. Marx, *Three Documents Relating to the History of Ladakh. Tibetan text, Translation and Notes*,—JASB, vol. lx. 1891, pt. i, N 3, pp.97-135 ; vol. lxiii, 1894, N 2, pp. 94-107 ; vol. lxxi, 1902, pt.I, N I, pp.21-34.
4. A. Francke has devoted a number of his works—mainly articles scattered in various journals—to the study of Tibetan monuments. Professor N. V. Kyuner [Kuehner] who, after many years of persistent work, compiled a comprehensive bibliography of Russian and foreign works in the field of Tibetology published before 1935, has kindly supplied me with the alphabetical list of A. Francke's historical works given below. For this, I express my deep gratitude to him.

   Antiquities of Indian Tibet, pt. i : *Personal Narrative*, Calcutta, 1914 (*Archaeological Survey of India, New Imperial Series*, vol. xxxviii).

   Antiquities of Indian Tibet, pt. ii : *The Chronicles of Ladakh and Minor Chronicles. Tibetan Texts and Translations with Notes and Maps.* Edited with foreword by F. W. Thomas, Calcutta,' 1926 (*Archaeological Survey of India, New Imperial Series*, vol. I).

   Archaeological Notes on Balu-mkhar in Western Tibet. Introduction by Jane E. Duncan,—"Indian Antiquary", vol. xxxiv, 1905, pp. 203-210.

   Archaeology in Western Tibet, "Indian Antiquary", vol. xxxv, 1906, pp. 237-241, 325-333 ; vol. xxxvi, 1907, pp. 85-98, 148.

   Ein Dokument aus Turfan in tibetischer Schrift, aber unbekannter Sprache,—"Sitzungsberichte der Preussischen Akademie der Wissenschaften, Philos.-hist. Klasse", 1927, N 12, SS. 124-130.

   Dritte Sammlung von Felszeichnungen aus Unter-Ladakh. Leh, 1902 (lithogr).

   Erste und Zweite Sammlung tibetischer historischer Inschriften, 1906 (Selbstverlag).

history, ancient as well as modern, of Tibet proper has not been studied much. It is true that there have been some sporadic attempts in this direction. Apart from

---

Felsinschriften in Ladakh,—"Sitzungsberichte der Preussischen Akademie der Wissenschaften, Philos.-hist. Klasse", 1925, SS. 366-370.

Die Geschichte des Dogra-Krieges. Nach dem Manuscript C des Ladvags rgyalrabs,—ZDMG, Bd. lxiv, 1910, SS. 537-552.

Historical Documents from the Borders of Tibet,—"Archaeological Survey of India", Annual Report, 1909/1910, Calcutta, 1914, pp. 104-112.

Historische Dokumente von Khalatse in West Tibet (Ladakh),—ZDMG, Bd lxi, 1907, SS. 583-614.

Die historischen und mythologischen Erinnerungen der Lahouler, Kye-lang, 1907.

A History of Western Tibet. One of the unknown empires, London, 1907.

The Kingdom of gNya khri btsanpo, the First King of Tibet,—JASB, 1911, vol. vi, N 3, pp. 93-99.

Kleine archaeologische Ertrage einer Missionsreise nach Zangskar in Westtibet,—ZDMG BD lx, 1906, SS. 645-661, Bd lxi, , 1907, pp. 645-647.

Konigsnamen von Khotan (A-ma-ca) auf tibetischen Dokumenten der Turkestan-sammlungen von London und Berlin,—"Sitzungsberichte der Preussischen Akademie der Wissenschaften, Phil.-hist. Klasse", 1928, SS. 671-676.

List of Ministers' Names Found in the Tibetan Inscription in Front of the Ta-chao-ssu Temple (Jo-khang) in Lhasa, 822, A.D.,—"Epigraphia Indica", vol. xi, 1912, pt. vi, pp. 272-276.

Notes on Rock-Carvings from Lower Ladakh,—"Indian Antiquary", xxxi, 1902, pp. 398-401.

Notes on Sir Aurel Stein's Collection of Tibetan Documents from Chinese Turkestan,—JRAS, 1914, pp. 37-59.

References to the Bhottas in the Rājataraṅgiṇī,—"Indian Antiquary", vol. xxxvii, 1908, pp. 181-192.

Remarks on a Photograph, near Ating, taken by the Hon. Eric Upton, during a Tour in Zangskar in 1907,—"Indian Antiquary", vol. xxxvii, 1908, pp. 332-333.

The Rock Inscriptions at Mulbe,—"Indian Antiquary", vol.xxxv, 1906, pp. 72-81.

Some More Rock-Carvings from Lower Ladakh,—"Indian Antiquary", vol. xxxii, 1903, pp.. 361-363.

Ten Ancient Historical Songs from Western Tibet,—"Indian Antiquary", xxxviii, 1909, pp. 57-68.

Tibetan Inscription on the Darkot Pass. (In : A. Stein, *Innermost Asia,* vol. ii, pp. 1050-1051).

the works of E. Schlagintweit and A. Francke, which also deal with the history of Tibet on the whole, the Tibetan historical monuments have been studied, published and translated with varying success by A. Csoma de Koros[5], Sarat Chandra Das[6],

---

Tibetan Inscription on the Stone Monument in front of the Ta-chao-ssu Temple in Lhasa, 822, A. D.,—"Epigraphia Indica", vol. x, (1909-1910), part iv, pp. 89-93.

Tibetische Handschriftenfunde aus Turfan,—"Sitzungsberichte der Preussischen Akademie der Wissenschaften", 1924, iii, SS. 5-20.

Vorbuddhistische Religion Tibets, Allgemeine Mission,—"Zeitschrift", xxviii, SS. 879-884.

5. A. Csoma de Koros, *A Grammar of the Tibetan Language in English*, Calcutta, 1834, pp. 181-198 (*Appendix iv, Chronological Table*). This *table* was published later in an abridged form in the work : Prinsep, *Useful Tables, pt. ii*, Calcutta, 1836, pp. 129-131 : *Table LIV, Buddhist chronology of Tibet.* This work also contains (pp. 131-132, *Table LV*) a list entitled *Kings of Tibet, to the Sub-Division of the Country in the Tenth Century* compiled by Csoma de Koros on the basis of *Deb-ther-sňon-po.*
6. Though the works of Sarat Chandra Das, as we shall see later, suffer from many errors and inaccuracies, we cannot and must not forget that it is precisely to him that the world of Tibetology is indebted for its first familiarity with the contents of a number of important historical texts which heretofore were totally unknown or were known only by title. And in this lies his great and indisputable service to scholarship. Even till today, many texts used by S. C. Das (often without naming them) remain unpublished, untranslated and uninvestigated.

The most outstanding work of S. C. Das in the field of Tibetan historiography is the publication of the first two parts of the Tibetan text of *dPag-bsam-ljon-bzaň*—see S. C. Das, *Pag Sam Jon Zang*, pt. i : *History of the Rise, Progress and Downfall of Buddhism in India*, pt. ii : *History of Tibet from Early Times to 1745 A. D., by Sumpa Khan-po Yeśe Pal Jor*, Calcutta, 1908. He also published an interesting Bon chronicle (see *rGyal-Rab Bon Kyi Jung-Nas*, ed. by Sri Sarat Chandra Das, Calcutta, 1915) and some other texts. Besides, he published a number of articles on Tibetan history which mostly are simple translations or adaptations of Tibetan sources. These include *Contributions on the Religion, History etc. of Tibet*, JASB, vol. l, 1881, pt. i, pp. 187-251; vol. li, 1882, pt. i, pp. 1-75, 87-128 ; *Life of Sum-pa-Khan-po*, also styled Ye-śes dPal-'byor, the author of the *Re'umig* (Chronological table), JASB, vol. lviii, 1889, pt. i, pp. 37-84 ; *Indian Pandits in Tibet*, JBTS, vol. i, 1893, pt. i, pp. 1-31 ; *A short note on the origin of the Tibetans and their division into clans, ibid.*, vol. v, pt. i, pp. 1-4 ; *The Hierarchy of the Dalai Lama* (1406-1745),—

F. W. Thomas[7], L. Waddell[8], E. E. Obermiller[9], and other scholars. Besides, Iakinf Bichurin[10] and later Bushell[11] translated very valuable Chinese documents

JASB, vol. lxxiii, 1904, pt. I, Extra, pp. 80-93 ; *Tibet under the Tartar Emperors of China in the 13th Century A. D.*,—*ibid.*, pp. 94-102 ; *The Monasteries of Tibet*,—JASB, New Series, vol. i, 1905, pp. 106-116 ; *Tibet, a dependency of Mongolia* (1643-1716 A. D.),—*ibid.* pp. 152-155 ; *Tibet under her last Kings* (1434-1642 A.D.),—*ibid.*, pp. 165-167; *A short history of the house of Phagdu, which ruled over Tibet on the decline of Sakya till 1432 A.D.*,—*ibid.*, pp. 202-207 etc.

7. Professor F. Thomas rendered outstanding service in the study of Tibetan documents and narrative sources about Sinkiang. See F. W. Thomas, *Tibetan Documents Concerning Chinese Ṭurkestan*, pt. i : *the Ha-za*,—JRAS, 1927, pp. 51-85 ; pt. ii : *the Sa-cu Region*,—JRAS, 1927, pp. 807-844 ; JRAS, 1928, pp. 63-98 ; pt. iii : *The Nob Region*,—JRAS, 1928, pp. 555-595. See also F. W. Thomas and Sten Konow, *Two Medieval Documents from Tun-huang*,—"Royal Frederik University Publications of the Indian Institute", 1, 3, Oslo, 1929, pp. 121-160. One may also mention his *The Language of Ancient Khotan*,—"Asia Major", 1925, vol. ii, pp. 251-271 and *Notes on the Tibetan Manuscripts illustrated in Plates cxxx-cxxxiii* (printed as an *Appendix* to : A. Stein, *Innermost Asia*, vol. ii, pp. 1084-1090). Recently, F. Thomas published *Tibetan Literary Texts and Documents Concerning Chinese Turkestan*, pt. i, *Literary Texts*, London, 1935 (*Oriental Translation Fund, New Series*, vol. xxxii . See also his article *Law of Theft in Chinese Kan-su* : *A IX-X Century Fragment from Tun-huang*,—"Zeitschrift fur vergleichende Rechtswizzenschaft", L Bd, 1936, 3 Hft., SS. 275-287 etc.
8. See L. A. Waddell, *Ancient Historical Edicts at Lhasa*, JRAS, 1909, pp. 923-952,—JRAS, 1910, pp. 1247-1282, JRAS, 1911, pp. 389-435 ; *Chinese Imperial Edict of 1808 A.D. on the Origin and Transmigrations of the Grand Lamas of Tibet*,—JRAS, 1910, pp. 69-86 ; *Tibetan Invasion of India in 647 A.D. and Its Results*,—"The Imperial and Asiatic Quarterly and Oriental and Colonial Record", vol. xxxi, 1911, pp. 37-65 (cf. also JRAS, 1911, p. 203) and other works.
9. E. Obermiller, *History of Buddhism* (chos-'byuṅ) by Bu-ston, pt. I : *The Jewelry of Scripture*, Heidelberg, 1931 (*Materialen zur Kunde des Buddhismus*, 18 Heft), pt. ii : *The History of Buddhism in India and Tibet*, Heidelberg, 1932,—*ibid.*, 19 Heft.
10. *Istoriya Tibeta i Khukhunora s 2282 goda do R. Kh. do 1227 goda po R. Kh.* [History of Tibet and Kokonor from 2282 B. C. to A.D. 1227] with a map on various periods of this history. Translated from the Chinese by monk Iakinf Bichurin, pt. i & ii, St. Petersburg, 1833.
11. S. W. Bushell, *The Early History of Tibet. From Chinese Sources*,—JRAS, 1880,

on the early history of Tibet. Finally, W. Rockhill[12] published the translation of extracts from Chinese sources concerning the contemporary history of Tibet. However, these rare publications are far from adequate for any idea of the history of Tibet, particularly when compared with the material which is still totally unstudied and unused.

The immediate task in the field of study of Tibetan history is undoubtedly the publication and translation of historical texts. But the main hurdle here is the lack of any clear and accurate idea of the volume, nature and type of the Tibetan historical literature. Unfortunately, one has to accept that the historical works of Tibet are little known to the academic world—and that too not always in the very best specimens. In a majority of cases, even the names of these works continue to remain unknown.

Nevertheless, the study of Tibetan historical texts is of interest not to the research student of Tibet alone. The history of the Tibetans is so closely linked to the fate of a number of peoples of Asia that its study is necessary for any research in the history of the Mongols, the Oirats, the Tangut kingdom, Khotan, and even India and China on the whole. Besides, for a fairly long time, Tibet was the spiritual centre for several peoples of Asia. In the course of the last three centuries, the Tibetan literary language had acquired almost the same significance among the Mongols, Oirats, Tanguts and other peoples, as Latin in medieval Europe, for, as the language of the sovereign Buddhist order, it became a pre-requisite for feudal scholastic education and the language of religion, philosophy and science[13]. Therefore, in creating an extensive

pp. 435-541. An attempt to compare Chinese and Tibetan sources on the early history of Tibet was made by Herbert Müller in his article *Tibet in seiner geschichtlichen Entwicklung*,—"Zeitschrift fur vergleichende Rechtswissenschaft", xx Bd, Hft 2-3, SS. 279-344.

12. W. W. Rockhill, *The Dalai Lamas of Lhasa and Their Relations with the Manchu Emperors of China 1644-1908*,—"T'oung Pao", vol. xi, 1910, pp. 1-104. See also an earlier work : E. H. Parker, *Manchu Relations with Tibet or Si-tsang*, —JRAS, N Ch. B., 1886, pp. 289-304.
13. For the significance of Tibetan language, say in Mongolia, see : B. Ya. Vladimirtsov, *Mongol'skii sbornik rasskazov iz Pañcatantra* [Mongolian Collection of Tales from Pañcatantra], Petrograd, 1921, pp. 50-51. "Tibetan language", wrote B. Ya. Vladimirtsov, "is like a second literary language of the Mongols of the 18th and 19th centuries, throwing Mongolian literary language to a secondary position. In Mongolia, it is not the members of the Buddhist Order alone who are beginning to study Tibetan language, write and conduct theological disputes in it, the secular society too is now taking up

and multifarious literature in Tibetan language including also the historical literature, a big role was played not only by the Tibetans themselves but also by the representatives of other peoples who often achieved exceptional fame and authority[14]. The Tibetan language was so widely spread that various Tangut, Mongol and other non-Tibetan scholars wrote even the histories of their own countries in full or in part in Tibetan. Such works certainly deserve most careful study even in cases where they co-exist with the highly developed historical literature in their national language. This is so in respect of the sources for the history of Mongolia, for they can really give some additional information[15].

this language. The Mongolian princes and officials—in fact, everyone trying to become literate—are beginning to study Tibetan language" (*Ibid.*, p. 51). Cf. a similar report of G. N. Potanin (*Ocherki Severo-Zapadnoi Mongolii* [Essays on North-Western Mongolia], i, pp. vi-vii, St. Petersburg, 1881). See also M. I. Tubyansky, *Nekotorye problemy mongol'skoi literatury dorevolyutsionnogo perioda* [Some Problems of Mongolian Literature of Pre-revolutionary Period],—"Sovremennaya Mongoliya", Ulan Bator, 1935, No. 5 (12), pp. 13-15.

14. As, for instance, Dandar Lha-rampa (bsTan-dar Lha-rams-pa) (b. 1759)—an Alashan Mongol—who has left two volumes of works in Tibetan language published in sKu-'bum and a Tibetan-Mongolian dictionary (compiled in 1838) entitled *brDa'-yig-miṅ-don-gsal-bar-byed-pa'i-zla-ba'i-'od-snaṅ* (107 fols.). Brief information on this author and his works has been given by Acad. F. I. Shcherbatskoi in his Tibetan translation of Dharmakīrti's *Santānāntarasiddhi* and Vinītadeva's *Santānāntarasiadhi-ṭīkā* published by him together with a Tibetan commentary by Ṅag-dbaṅ bsTan-dar Lha-rams-pa, Petrograd, 1916, pp. iii-xii (*Bibliotheca Buddhica*, xix). Another author that can be mentioned is Cha-har-dge-bśes bLo-bzaṅ-tshul-khrims—also a Mongol—who has left 10 volumes of works in Tibetan language, published in Peking. This author is so famous that he is sometimes called second Tsoṅ-kha-pa. Besides, one can mention the famous Urgin scholar Lama mKhas-grub mKhan-po and his equally well-known pupil, dPal-ldan Chos-rje, who have bequeathed to us many interesting works, including a detailed commentary entitled *Grub-mtha'-chen-mo'i-mchan-'grel-dka'-gnad-mdud-grol-blo-gsal-gces-nor* (in three volumes) on the well-known work on Indian philosophical systems, compiled by 'Jam-dbyaṅs-bshad-pa-ṅag-dbaṅ-brtson-'grus (1648-1722) in 1846. Another such Urgin scholar is Lama bsTan-dar sṅAgs-rams-pa.
15. For instance, in his work *Obshchestvennyi stroi mongolov* [Social Order of the Mongols], Leningrad, 1934, p. 19, note 1, Academician B. Ya. Vladimirtsov regrets the inadequate study of Tibetan sources on the history of the Mongols.

Since these works are not Tibetan in respect of either their origin or their subject-matter, they cannot, of course, be included in Tibetan historical literature without reservations. In any case, their study has to merit attention in future, not so much of the Tibetologists as of the historians and litterateurs of the respective countries. But now when the historical works in Tibetan language have just been taken up for study, a survey of such works also becomes as much the task of the Tibetologist as that of the Tibetan historical literature itself.

Generally speaking, the literature on the history of other countries is fairly well represented in Tibetan language. The position of Tibet as Buddhist centre and the universal character thus acquired by the Tibetan script among the Buddhists of various countries have often been the reasons for Tibetan authors to study and expound,—in addition to the history of their country,—that of all those countries where, according to their information, Buddhism was widely spread. Besides the works mentioned above on the history of the Mongols and other peoples, and those on the history of Tibet and other individual fields, we find, in Tibetan language, accounts of the history of India and China as a whole. Unfortunately, the Tibetan literature on the history of other peoples is as little known as that on the history of the Tibetan peoples themselves.

The first and the only attempt to give a classified list of Tibetan historical works was made by the founder of scientific Tibetology, A. Csoma de Koros, who published in 1838, his remarkable article *Enumeration of Historical and Grammatical Works to be met with in Tibet*[16]. Some data given in this article (particularly the list of main types of Tibetan historical works) were printed by him even earlier, in 1834[17], and repeated, without any alteration, by Isaac Schmidt in the Russian and German versions of his Tibetan grammar[18].

Of course, this article by A. Csoma de Koros, written almost hundred years back, suffers from serious shortcomings. The list of Tibetan historical works given in it covers only a little more than a score of texts[19]. We find these to include also Tibetan

---

16. JASB, vol. vii, 1838, pp. 147-152.
17. A. Csoma de Koros, *A Grammar of the Tibetan Language*, p. 180.
18. I. J. Schmidt, *Grammatika tibetskogo yazyka* [Grammar of the Tibetan Language], St. Petersburg, 1839, pp. 231-232 ; *Idem.*, *Gramatik der tibetischen Sprache*, St. Petersburg, 1839, SS. 216-217.
19. A. Csoma de Koros does not indicate the sources used by him in compiling his list. It is, however, not difficult to guess them. The main source from which the titles of the historical works figuring in his list have been taken, was obviously the historical treatise—not entirely unknown—entitled *rGyal-rabs gSal-ba'i-me-loṅ* ("Royal Genealogy—A Clear Mirror") (For this work, see Chapter 3, 3). The list of titles given by A. Csoma de Koros under the

translations of Buddhist works in Sanskrit, like the famous poem *Bodhisattvāvadāna-kalpalatā* and the canonical biography of Buddha—*Lalitavistara-sūtra*[20]. With regard to the Tibetan works themselves, nothing more than the brief conventional titles is mentioned. Not to speak of their volume, their dates of compilation and such other information, even the full titles of the works are lacking. The classification

---

heading "Histories" (*lo-rgyus*) has been compiled entirely on the basis of titles mentioned in this treatise. It is from this source only that A. Csoma de Koros has taken such titles as *bKa'-tshigs-chen-mo* and *rGyal-rab-dpag-bsam-ljon-śiṅ* (see *rGyal-rabs-gsal-ba'i-me-loṅ*, sDe-dge edition, 1. 28 ᵃ2) which usually are not even mentioned in other texts and which he could hardly have consulted directly. From this again, he has obviously borrowed such title as *Śes-bya-rab-gsal* (*ibid.* 1. 6 ᵃ4 though the latter is actually not a historical text but a work of encyclopaedic nature, written by 'Phags-pa-bla-ma (for this work, see footnote 537). The information on the Chinese historical treatise *rGya'i-yig-tshaṅ* translated into Tibetan language by Lama Rin-chen-grags-pa has undoubtedly been borrowed by A. Csoma de Koros from this source (*ibid.*, 1. 96ᵇ4-6). Besides, he has drawn on a number of other historical texts. These include *Deb-ther-sṅon-po* (for this work, see footnote 431), from which A. Csoma de Koros has apparently borrowed the information regarding the work on the history of Buddhism—which has not reached us —written by Nel-pa-paṇḍita (see *Deb-ther-sṅon-po*, Amdo edition, 1. 28ᵇ6), and *Śa-mbha-la'i-rnam-bśad-'phags-yul-gyi-rtogs-brjod* (for this work, see footnote 334), from the colophon of which A. Csoma de Koros has taken the information on the work on the history of India from Aśoka to Pratītasena entitled *Yig-gshun-chen-mo*, etc. However, his entire information is not from Tibetan literary sources only. He was of course also directly familiar with a number of texts.

20. *Bodhisattvāvadāna-Kalpalatā* (*Byaṅ-chub-sems-dpa'i-rtogs-pa-brjod-pa'i-dpag-bsam-gyi-'khri-śiṅ*) is available in *bsTan-'gyur*, Peking edition, mDo-'grel, vol. xciii (*ge*). The Sanskrit text and the Tibetan translation of this work were published by S. C. Das and Hari Mohan Vidyabhusana in the series *Bibliotheca Indica*. *Lalitavistara-sūtra* (*'Phags-pa-rgya-cher-rol-pa-shes-bya-ba-theg-pa-chen-po'i-mdo*) is available in *bKa'-'gyur*, sDe-dge edition, mDo-sde, vol. ii (*kha*), fols. 1-216. Sanskrit text of this work was published by Rajendralala Mitra in *Bibliotheca Indica* and later by S. Lefmann (see S. Lefmann, *Lalita Vistara*, vol. i : Text, vol. ii : Varianten-, Metren-, und Worterverzeichnis, Halle a S., 1902-1908). The Tibetan text was published by Ph. Foucaux along with a translation into French (see Ph. Ed. Foucaux, *Rgya tch'er rolpa ou Developpement des Yeux, contenent l'histoire du Bouddha Sakyamouni*, i partie —*Texte tibetain* ; ii partie—*Traduction francaise*, Paris, 1847-1848)

given by A. Csoma de Koros is also inadequate and defective. Under the heading "Histories" (*lo-rgyus*), he has put works of legendary nature like *Ma-ṇi-bka'-'bum*—which even the Tibetans themselves do not include in their historical literature—and large historical works of the nature of compilations like *Deb-ther-sṅon-po*, which indeed must be classed under the special group of historical works (separated by Csoma de Koros himself), namely the "History of Religion" (*chos-'byuṅ*).

These and other similar shortcomings, fully explained by the fact that Csoma de Koros was, in the full sense of the word, a pioneer in Tibetology, cannot belittle the epoch-making importance of his article. These cannot make us forget that in the course of a whole century of study of Tibetan literature that has passed since this article first appeared, only very little could really be added to the list of works given in it. In any case, right upto the recent times, this article has served as a guide in this field.

After the article of A. Csoma de Koros, no other serious step was taken to survey and classify the Tibetan historical literature. With the exception of the article by V. P. Vasil'ev, *O nekotorykh knigakh, otnosyashchikhsya k istorii buddizma, v biblioteke Kazanskogo universiteta*[21] [On Some Books Relating to the History of Buddhism in the Library of Kazan University], which gives an illuminating account of some Tibetan historical works and which has not lost its importance even till this day, all the later studies in this direction have merely made a passing reference to individual historical works in the catalogues of Tibetan manuscripts and xylographs[22]. When in 1904, in connection with the impending British intervention in Tibet, Professor

21. *Uchenye zapiski Akademii nauk po pervomu i tret'emu otdeleniyam* [Scientific Transactions of the First and Third Sections of Academy of Sciences], vol. III, St. Petersburg, 1855, pp. 1-33.
22. Johan van Manen gives a complete list of catalogues of Tibetan manuscripts and xylographs in his work *A Contribution to the Bibliography of Tibet*, JASB, New Series, vol. xviii, 1922, N 8, pp. 462-466. See also F. W. Thomas, *Note on the Tibetan Collections of the India Office Library*, pp. 5-6. Later, this number of the catalogues of Tibetan texts (not taking into account the catalogues of *bKa'-'gyur* and *bsTan-'gyur*) was increased with the work of J. Bacot (J. Bacot, *La collection tibetaine Schilling von Constadt a la Bibliotheque de l'Institut*,—JA, t. ccv, Paris, 1924, pp. 321-348.). As I have already mentioned elsewhere (see A. I. Vostrikov, *K bibliografii tibeskoi literatury* [On a Bibliography of Tibetan Literature],—"Bibliografiya Vostoka", 1933, No. 2-4, Leningrad, 1934, p. 21), these catalogues are mostly simple lists of titles. Of these, the more important ones are: I. J. Schmidt und O. Bohtlingk, *Verzeichniss der tibetischen Handschriften und Holzdrucke im Asiatischen Museum*—"Bulletin historico-philologique de l'Academie Imp. de Siences de St. Petersbourg", t. iv, N 6, 7, 8, St. Petersbourg, 1847; A. Schiefner, *Nachtrage zu den von O. Boehtlingk und I. J. Schmidt verfassten Verzeichnissen des*

F. W. Thomas tried to give an exhaustive list of Tibetan historical, biographical, and some other texts known to the European scientific literature[23], he had to be content with the above-mentioned articles of Csoma de Köros and Vasil'ev and the catalogues of various Tibetan collections—,mainly those of the Russian Academy of Sciences. The list compiled by Professor F. Thomas, meant obviously to be a practical manual for the direct quest of the respective literature in Tibet, does not give anything new as such. On the other hand, as I have already mentioned, he has sometimes reproduced the data given in the catalogues so literally that he has also repeated the mistakes occuring in them, taking even such texts as those of collections of prayers and songs etc in some monasteries for historical works[24].

There have, of course, been isolated references to Tibetan historical texts from time to time in various European works on Tibet ; but these are largely restricted only to texts which have already been mentioned by A. Csoma de Koros in his list. We shall not enumerate all these scattered references, but shall mention only B. Baradiin's *Statuya Maitrei v Zolotom khrame v Labrane*[25] [Statue of Maitreya in the

---

auf India und Tibet bezuglichen Handschriften und Halzdrucke im Asiatischen Museum,—ibid., t. v, N 10 ; A. Schiefner, *Bericht uber die neueste Buchersendung aus Peking,—ibid.*, t. viii, N 1, 2 ; *Katalog knig i rukopisei na kitaiskom, manchzhurskom, mongol'skom, tibetskom i sanskritskom yazyke v biblioteke Aziatskogo departamenta* [A Catalogue of Books and Manuscripts in Chinese, Manchurian, Mongolian, Tibetan and Sanskrit Languages in the Library of Asiatic Department], St. Petersburg, 1844 ; G. Tsybikov, *Spisok tibetskim izdaniyam, privezennym Gonbozhapom Tsybikovym v 1902 g. i pozhertvovannym Muzeyu I. R. Geograficheskim obshchestom* [A List of Tibetan Publications, Brought by G. Tsybikov in 1902 and Donated to the Museum of the Russian Imperial Geographical Society],—"Musei Asiatici Petropolitani Notitiae", iv, v, vi, St. Petersburg, 1904, pp. 01-07 ("Izvestiya Akademii nauk", 1904, v. xxi, No. 1) ; E. H. C. Walsh, *A List of Tibetan Books Brought from Lhasa by the Japanese Monk, Mr. Ekai Kawa Gochi*,—JASB, vol. lxxiii, 1904, pt. i, N 2, pp. 118-177 ; L. A. Waddell, *Tibetan Manuscripts and Books, etc. Collected During the Younghusband Mission to Lhasa*,—"The Imperial and Asiatic Quarterly Review and Oriental and Colonial Record", 3rd Series, vol. xxxiv, July-October, 1912, N 67-68, pp. 80-113 etc.

23. See F. W. Thomas, *Note on the Tibetan Collections of the India Office Library.*
24. See A. I. Vostrikov, *K bibliografii tibetskoi literatury* (On a Bibliography of Tibetan Literature],—"Bibliografiya Vostoka", Leningrad, 1934, p. 21.
25. B. Baradiin, *Statuya Maitrei v Zolotom khrame v Labrane* [Statue of Maitreya in the Golden Temple in bLa-brañ], Leningrad, 1924 (*Bibliotheca Buddhica*, xxii). Pages 04-011 give a list of Tibetan literature including a number of historical works.

Golden Temple in bLa-braṅ] and C. Bell's *The Religion of Tibet*[26], which describe, in detail, some of the works and also give general information on Tibetan historiography. However, the works described by C. Bell are largely those which are already known to us from the articles by Csoma de Koros and V. P. Vasii'ev.

Thus, the article of A. Csoma de Koros, written in the light of a scientific study of Tibetan language and literature has not been surpassed even till now either in importance or in the number of texts enumerated ; the classification given by him remains unique even now in spite of all its inadequacy.

Nevertheless, this list of A. Csoma de Koros, with all the additions made by subsequent authors, does not include even one-tenth of the actual wealth of Tibetan historical literature. In such circumstances, neither a choice of monumental works worthy of publication nor a critical attitude to the published material is possible, for each of these works presupposes a basic familiarity with the most important works in this field, if not with all.

A study of the collection—the largest in the world—of Tibetan manuscripts and xylographs in the Institute of Peoples of Asia, Academy of Sciences, U.S.S.R. and extensive travels in Buryatia for studying the Tibetan works available in the monasteries there have shown what an enormous amount of historical and specially biograhical works is available in Tibetan language. Assuming that an expansion of our knowledge in this field is likely to be fruitful, I tried to collect all the accessible materials for having a more or less clear idea of the volume, nature and type of these works.

This task was somewhat facilitated by some very valuable though laconic bibliographical lists of Tibetan authors themselves. These are—

1) a fairly complete though not exhaustive list of Tibetan historical works enumerating more than five-hundred titles—available in the introduction to the voluminous work on the history of Buddhism in Amdo—*Deb-ther-rgya-mtsho* (Sea-book)[27], written in 1865 by Brag-dgon-shabs-druṅ dKon-mchog-bstan-pa-rab-rgyas (b. 1801)[28], the forty-ninth Head of the bLa-braṅ (bLa-braṅ-bkra-śis-'khyil) monastery, and

26. C. Bell, *The Religion of Tibet*, Oxford 1934, pp. 195-219.

27. More details about this text will be found below. Its full title is: *Yul-mdo-smad-kyi-ljoṅs-su-thub-bstan-rin-po-che-ji-ltar-dar-ba'i-tshul-gsal-par-brjod-pa-deb-ther-rgya-mtsho*. It was published in the A-mchog-dga'-ldan-chos-'khor-gliṅ monastery in Amdo. (A list of historical works is available in the first volume, fols. 4a6-19a4).

28. The data of birth of the author has been established on the basis of the colophon which states that the original short edition of the text of *Deb-ther-rgya-mtsho* was written in the Water-Snake year—the thirty-third year of the life of the author (see vol. iii fol. 272a1). Considering that the author was the pupil

2) a list of rare historical texts, comprising the first section of the special "List of Some Rare Books"—*dPe-rgyun-dkon-pa-'ga'-shig-gi-tho-yig-don-gñer-yid-kyi-kunda-bshad-pa'i-zla-'od-'bum-gyi-sñe-ma*[29], compiled by A-khu-rin-po-che Śes-rab-rgya-mtsho (1803-1875).[30]

The latter considerably explains and partly supplements the former.

It is very unfortunate that none of the above two lists follows a strict order (chronological or any other) in enumerating the historical works. Each of them essentially is only a bare list of abridged titles, by which these historical works are known to the learned Lamas of Tibet. The date of their compilation, their size and subject matter are also not indicated. Even the names of the authors have not been given in all the cases. Sometimes, their mere conventional names according to the places where they were born or where they worked are given. No data are given on the authors themselves, so much so that it is simply impossible to form any idea of Tibetan

of dPal-maṅ dKon-mchog-rgyal-mtshan (1764-1853), this date can correspond only to the year 1833. The author was, therefore, born in 1801. For, while mentioning the age, the Tibetans do not state the number of years that have passed from the date of birth ; they mention the year of life that is running. In B. Baradiin's work (*Statue of Maitreya in the Golden Temple in bLa-braṅ*, p. 05) and—taking from him—even in my article (*Some Corrections and Critical Remarks on Dr. Johan von Manen's Contribution to the Bibliography of Tibet*, BSOS, vol. viii, 1935, pt. i, p. 58, n. 2), the data of birth of the author is wrongly given as 1800.

29. This list is included in its author's "Complete Works" (gsuṅ-'bum)—published in the mDsod-dge-dgon-gsar dGa'-ldan-rab-rgyas-gliṅ monastery in Amdo. A copy of this "Complete works" is available in the Institute of Peoples of Asia in the Tibetan xylographs brought from Amdo by B. Baradiin (*Baradiin Collection*, No. 7). The list referred to is in the sixth volume of the Complete Works and covers 63 folios. The list of historical texts occupies fols. 1-9 ^{a} 1.

30. The dates of birth and death of A-hu-rin-po-che-śes-rab-rgya-mtsho have been taken from his biography entitled *bKa'-drin-mtshuṅs-med-rdo-rje-'chaṅ-dbaṅ-rje-btsun-śes-rab-rgya-mtsho'i-shal-sṅa-nas-kyi-rnam-par-thar-pa-thar-'dod-srid-mtsho-che-las-sgrol-ba'i-gru-gziṅs*, compiled in 1886 by sKal-bzaṅ-thub-bstan-dbaṅ-phyug, the fourth 'Jam-dbyaṅs-bshad-pa. The biography, which is in 148 folios, is available in the first volume of the *Collected Works* by A-hu-rin-po-che. As stated in this biography, A-hu-rin-po-che was born in Water-Pig year of the xiii cycle (see fols. 5 ^{b} 4-6) and died in the 73rd year of his life—the Wood-Pig year (see fols. 129 ^{b} 5ff). He is regarded as the incarnation of the famous kLoṅ-rdol-bla-ma-ṅag-dbaṅ-blo-bzaṅ (b. 1719)—see the above-mentioned biography of A-hu-rin-po-che, fol. 4 ^{b} 2.

historical literature on the basis of these lists alone. For this, it is necessary to decipher the conventional titles mentioned, supplement them with necessary details, and above all, of course, to have a first-hand acquaintance with the historical works themselves. But these lists are important, for they serve as excellent material for beginning the study of Tibetan historical literature. They have been compiled by leading and highly authoritative scholars, and are therefore all the more worthy of attention.

Using the list of works given in the *Deb-ther-rgya-mtsho* as a guide for the quest of Tibetan historical literature, and referring to another list for supplementing and explaining the material in this one, I tried to trace the texts mentioned there, record those not included in this list, and examine carefully each of the works that I could discover. At the same time, I endeavoured to gather, from Tibetan sources, all the necessary information on those historical works that are no longer extant—specially about their authors, period, subject-matter etc, so that one may have a rough idea of the chronological sequence of Tibetan historical literature and mark the main features of its classification.

Besides the two lists mentioned above, I have found the following Tibetan sources highly valuable for my present work :

1) the work on the history of Buddhism in India, China (including Tibet), and Mongolia—*'Phags-yul-rgya-nag-chen-po-bod-daṅ-sog-yul-du-dam-pa'i-chos-byuṅ-tshul-dpag-bsam-ljon-bzaṅ*[31], written in 1748 by the well-known scholar Sum-pa-mkhan-po Ye-śes-dpal-'byor (1704-1788)[32]. This work contains a chronological table (which is very important

31. More details on this work will be found below. Since the text, published by S. C. Das is not complete and is full of mistakes, I have referred throughout to the xylograph edition of this work and have also given, in brackets, the corresponding pages of the publication of S. C. Das.

32. A detailed biography of Sum-pa-mkhan-po Ye-śes-dpal-'byor—entitled *mKhan-po-e-rte-ni-paṇḍitar-grags-pa'i-spyod-tshul-brjod-pa-sgra-'dsin-bcud-len* (258+36 folios in volume)—is given in the eighth volume (*na*) of the Complete Works of Sum-pa-mkhan-po, published in Kuku-hoto (?). This biography contains : an autobiography of Sum-pa-mkhan-po upto the 73rd year of his life (fol 1-180 b 1) and a continuation of this biography,—written, on behalf of Sum-pa-mkhan-po, by his pupils,—ending with an account of his death and of his *suburgan* (fol 180 b 1-258 b 6). This continuation is dated as Wood-Tiger year of xiii cycle, which corresponds to A. D. 1794. Originally, this autobiography apparently existed as a fully finished work, for the text is followed by another 36 folios of author's conclusion and colophon. The

for a study of the history of Tibetan literature) and a store of valuable critical and bibliographical information ;

2) the chronological table *bsTan-rtsis-re'u-mig*, compiled in 1716[33] by one of the most distinguished Tibetan scholars 'Jam-dbyaṅs-bshad-pa Ṅag-dbaṅ-brtson-'grus (1648-1722), the founder and the first head of bLa-braṅ monastery[34]—which gives the dates of compilation of some most important historical works ;

---

colophon states (fol 34ᵇ7 onwards) that this autobiography was started and finished in 1776 (Fire-Monkey year of xiii cycle). Brief biographical data on Sum-pa-mkhan-po are available in the *Description of dGon-luṅ Monastery* which was headed by him (see *dGon-luṅ-dkar-chag*, f. 56ᵃ3-65ᵃ1 ; *Deb-ther-rgya-mtsho*, the edition of the A-mchog dGa'-ldan-chos-'khor-gliṅ monastery, v. 1, f. 74ᵃ4-76ᵃ6).

33. For a description of this table, see Chapter 3. The majority of dates given by me have been taken from this *table* and from the *table* given by Sum-pa-mkhan-po. These *tables* are small and follow a strict chronological order. Hereafter, for the sake of economy of space and time, these dates will be quoted by me only after due conversion to European calendar without mentioning every time how these dates appear in Tibetan system of chronology. (Hereafter, these will be referred to as "Chronological Tables"). Regarding the principles of conversion to Christian era and the mistakes committed by a number of scholars from Csoma de Koros onwards, see the remarkable article by P. Pelliot—*Le cycle sexagenaire dans la chronologie tibetaine*, JA, 1913, v. 1, pp, 633-667. See also B. Laufer, *The Application of the Tibetan Sexagenary Cycle*,—"T'oung Pao", vol. xiv, 1913, pp. 569-596 and his supplementary note—*The Sexagenary Cycle, Once More*,—"T'oung Pao", vol. xv, 1914, pp. 277-279. Also see *infra*.

34. A short autobiography of 'Jam-dbyaṅs-bshad-pa'i-rdo-rje Ṅag-dbaṅ-brtson-'grus in verse—entitled *rJe-btsun-'jam-dbyaṅ-bshad-pa'i-rdo-rje'i-rnam-thar-bka'-rtsom-tshigs-bcad-ma* (7 fol)—is available in the first volume of collection of works of Ṅag-dbaṅ-brtson-'grus, published in bLa-braṅ. A detailed biography of his, entitled *mKhas-śiṅ-grub-pa'i-dbaṅ-phyug-kun-mkhyen-'jam-dbyaṅs-bshad-pa'i-rdo-rje'i-rnam-par-thar-ba-ṅo-mtshar-skal-bzaṅ-'jug-ṅogs* (fol 123), belongs to his incarnation dKon-mchog-'jigs-med-dbaṅ-po (1728-1791) and is included in the second volume of the Collection of Works of the latter, published in bLa-braṅ (see the copy of this Collection of Works in the Institute of Peoples of Asia, *Baradiin Collection*, No. 1). It is dated as 1758. The same author has also compiled *Chos-kyi-rje-kun-mkhyen-'jam-dbyaṅs-bshad-pa'i-rdo-rje'i-rnam-par-thar-pa-dad-pa-daṅ-ldan-pa-dag-la-gtam-du-bya-ba-ṅo-mtshar-gaṅga'i-chu-rgyun* (37 fol, *ibid.*)—a collection of biographies of persons, who are regarded as previous incarnations of Ṅag-dbaṅ-brtson-'grus. There

3) the catalogue of collections of works of the teachers of bKa'-gdams-pa and dGe-lugs-pa sects—*bKa'-gdams-pa-dañ-dge-lugs-pa'i-bla-ma-rags-rim-gyi-gsuñ-bum-mtshan--tho*, compiled by kLoñ-rdol-bla-ma Ñag-dbañ-blo-bzañ (b. 1719)[35]; and various other texts.

The work in this direction is still not over. The next step should be a detailed scientific description of all the works including the historical, biographical and historico-geographical ones, available in the collection of the Institute of Peoples of Asia, and publication, with commentaries, of the most important bibliographical lists of historical literature of Tibet.

In the present work, I would like merely to classify some general information on the nature and main types of Tibetan historical works, noted by me in the course of my work on the study of Tibetan collection of the Institute of Peoples of Asia and Tibetan bibliographical literature, and eliminate incidentally the discrepancies found by me in some European works on the authorship, dating and other details of individual historical texts.

---

also exist other biographies. Besides, the biography of Ñag-dbañ-brtson--'grus can be found in *Deb-ther-rgya-mtsho* (v. ii, fol. 1-10 a 4) and in other works which give an account of the history of bLa-brañ monastery founded by him. The dates of birth and death (Earth-Mouse year of xi cycle—Water-Tiger year of xii cycle) are also mentioned in the *Chronological Table* of Sum-pa--mkhan-po. In view of the fact that the translation of this table made by S. C. Das in his article *Life of Sum-pa Khan-po* . (JASB, vol. lviii, 1889, pt. i, pp. 37-84) is absolutely unsuitable for use (see Chapter iii), I have, in this work, always referred to the Tibetan text of this Table.

35. This catalogue is included in the *Complete Works* of kLoñ-rdol-bla-ma published in the Kun-bde-gliñ monastery in Lhasa and in Peking, and comprises the twenty-fifth book (*ra*) of this work. In the publication of the Kun-bde-gliñ monastery, it has 65 folios, but in the Peking edition—60 folios.

The date of birth of kLoñ-rdol-bla-ma (Earth-Pig year of xii cycle) is indicated in his biography *dPal-ldan-bla-ma-dam-pa-kun-spañs-chen-po-ñag-dbañ--blo-bzañ-dpal-bzañ-po'i-rnam-par-thar-pa-dad-pa'i-myu-gu*, compiled by dKon-mchog-'jigs-med-dbañ-po (1728-1791), the second 'Jam-dbyañs-bshad-pa (fol 2 a 3-4). The biography is available in the *Complete Works* of its author, published in bLa-brañ (v. ii, *kha*) and covers 16 folios.

Chapter One

THE EARLIEST HISTORICAL WORKS OF TIBET

Unfortunately, the earliest historical works of the Tibetans are no longer extant. We can only know them to some extent mostly from the works dating from the last five to six centuries. As regards the still older texts, our information about them is far from being adequate.

Except a few specific texts, almost no historical literature of the 11th-13th centuries has come down to us. These were the earlier three centuries of the so-called "period of the later spread of Buddhism in Tibet" (*phyi-dar*), which replaced the period of almost total extinction of Buddhism (*bstan-snubs*) in the reign of gLaṅ-dar-ma (9th cent.), the well-known persecutor of Buddhism in Tibet, and his successors. This period was marked by great progress of translation activity. Nevertheless, the Tibetan sources point to the existence of a number of historical and specially biographical works dating from this period.

Properly speaking, many works of the 14th-16th centuries known to us from various citations and bibliographical references are also not extant. Nevertheless, some individual basic works of this period are available to us. The possibility of discovering other lost works at a later stage is however not ruled out, for some of them have been used by the Tibetan authors in 18th and partly even in the 19th century.

Considerably worse is the case of the still earlier literature—that of the 7th to early-9th centuries—the highly interesting period, when a considerable part of Central Asia was under the sway of Tibet. Whether this is because the historical works of this ancient period—which the Tibetan historians call "the period of early spread of Buddhism in Tibet" (*sṅa-dar*)—were lost in the subsequent years of disintegration of the undivided empire and those of the civil war, or because even originally these were very scanty and little known, is very difficult to say ; the later Tibetan writers themselves had an extremely vague and overtly inadequate idea of them.

In any case, individual historical works in Tibetan language were already existing in this early period. There also existed Tibetan translations of some works of historical significance—particularly such as *Gośṛṅga-vyākaraṇa*[36], *Vimalaprabhā-paripṛcchā*[37] and *Arhat-saṃghavardhana-vyākaraṇa*[38], which give interesting information

---

36. See *bKa'-'gyur*, sDe-dge edition, mDo-sde, vol. xxxii(*A*), fols. 220ᵇ 6-232ᵃ 7.
37. *Ibid.*, vol. xv (*ba*), fols. 211ᵃ 1-259ᵇ 7.
38. See *bsTan-'gyur*, Peking edition, mDo-'grel, vol. xciv (*ne*), fols. 435ᵃ 8-444ᵃ 2.

on the history of Khotan. We find a reference to these translations in one of the earliest catalogues of the Tibetan canon—*sToṅ-thaṅ-ldan-dkar-ma*—compiled towards the end of the 8th century[39]. Of course, these texts cannot be directly reckoned in Tibetan historiography, for they are not original Tibetan works. Their only relation to Tibetan historical literature is that they are the sources of original Tibetan works on the history of Khotan. One such work obviously is the so-called *Prophecy of the Li Country* (*Li-yul-luṅ-bstan-pa*)[40]. This work is included in the Tibetan Buddhist canon *bsTan-'gyur* and consists, as W. Rockhill[41] and Prof. F. Thomas[42] have rightly pointed out, of two different monumental works purely mechanically related to each other. In fact, it contains *Prophecy of the Li Country*[43] proper, which, according to Professor Thomas, exists as an independent work in two manuscripts of the 9th-10th centuries discovered by A. Stein in Tun-Huang,[44] and the outstanding work *Annals of the Li Country* (*Li-yul-gyi-lo-rgyus*).[45] The later catalogues of *bsTan-'gyur* sometimes assume that this work as well as the *Arhat-saṃghavardhana-vyākaraṇa* (mentioned above)—the latter work directly preceding the former in *bsTan-'gyur*—"have been translated from the language of Khotan"[46]; but this is merely an assumption. Professor Thomas rightly remarks that the *Annals of the Li Country* looks like an original Tibetan work and that there are no grounds to regard the *Prophecy of the Li Country*, at least in the form in which it has reached us, as a non-Tibetan work.[47]

The contents of the texts enumerated (except *Vimalaprabhāparipṛcchā*) were briefly expounded by W. Rockhill[48] in 1884 and by Sarat Chandra Das in 1886 in the article *Buddhist and other Legends about Khoten*.[49] Lately, Professor Thomas, who has devoted

---

39. This catalogue entitled *Pho-braṅ-stoṅ-thaṅ-ldan-dkar-gyi-bka'-daṅ-bstan-bcos-'gyur-ro-cog-gi-dkar-chag* is available in *bsTan-'gyur*, mDo-'grel, vol. cxxvi (*cho*), fols. 352^{b} 5-373^{a} 8. The works on the history of Khotan, indicated here, are mentioned in this catalogue on fols. 361^{a} 2, 356^{a} 8 and 371^{b} 1. For details of this catalogue, see *infra*.
40. See *bsTan-'gyur*, mDo-'grel. vol. xciv (*ṇe*), fols. 444^{a} 2-468^{a} 8.
41. W. W. Rockhill, *The Life of the Buddha and the Early History of His Order*, London 1907, p. 231.
42. F. W. Thomas, *Tibetan Literary Texts and Documents Concerning Chinese Turkestan*, pt. i, pp. 73-74.
43. See *bsTan-'gyur*, mDo-'grel, vol. xciv, fols. 444^{a} 2-448^{a} 3.
44. F. W. Thomas, *Tibetan Literary Texts*..., pt. i, p. 41ff., p. 73ff.
45. See *bsTan-'gyur*, mDo-'grel, vol. xciv, fols. 448^{a} 3-468^{a} 8.
46. See P. Cordier, *Catalogue du fond Tibetain de la Bibliotheque Nationale*, iii partie, *Index du Bstan-ḥgyur*, 1915, p. 433.
47. F. W. Thomas, *Tibetan Literary Texts*..., pt. i, pp. 50, 76.
48. W. W. Rockhill, *The Life of the Buddha*, pp. 230-248.
49. JASB, vol. lv, 1886, pt. i, N 3, pp. 193-203.

many years to the analysis and translation of the Tibetan documents and literary sources on Central Asia, has published the first part of his large and highly valuable work *Tibetan Literary Texts and Documents Concerning Chinese Turkestan* (*Part I*: *Literary Texts*), which includes the study and complete translation of all the texts mentioned above in addition to the translations of various excerpts from other works. As an *Appendix* to this excellent work,[50] Professor Thomas gave the translation of another Tibetan work on the history of Khotan, viz. *Annals of the Religion of the Li Country* (*Li-yul-chos-kyi-lo-rgyus*), the manuscript of which was discovered by Professor P. Pelliot in Tun-Huang.

To Professor F. Thomas, we are also indebted for the publication and translation of a most interesting fragment of a Tibetan court chronicle from the finds of A. Stein,[51] and for the information on individual extracts in original and in translation from another comparatively larger Tibetan chronicle, one portion of which was discovered by

---

50. F. W. Thomas, *Tibetan Literary Texts*...The only thing that causes some indignation is the way in which Professor F. Thomas has converted some Tibetan dates into European calendar and vice-versa. According to him, for instance, A.D. 644 and A.D. 740-741 are Hare years (p. 47) in Tibetan system. Actually, A.D. 644 is a Dragon year, A. D. 740 is also a Dragon year, and the year 741 is Snake year (see, for example, the tables appended to P. Pelliot's article cited above). Further, according to F. Thomas (p. 76), the year 1047 corresponds to the Dog year in Tibetan chronology. Actually, this year is the Pig year. Similarly, the Hare year of Tibetan cycle corresponds not to A.D. 646-647 as stated by F. Thomas (p. 69, note 10) but to A.D. 643 (the year 646 is the Horse year and the year 647 the Sheep year). The date of birth of Bu-ston, as given by F. Thomas (p. 4), is also incorrect. Bu-ston was born in 1290 and not in 1288. This date was probably taken by Prof. F. Thomas from the Chronological Table of Csoma de Ķoros (see A. Csoma de Koros, *A Grammar of the Tibetan Language*, pp. 181-198) where—as pointed out by P. Pelliot (P. Pelliot, *Le Cycle Sexagenaire*..., JA, 1913, pt. i, pp. 642-645)—all the dates quoted are two years behind the actual ones.
51. F. W. Thomas, *Tibetan Documents Concerning Chinese Turkestan*. I. The *Ha-za*, —JRAS, 1927, pp. 58-66: This fragment contains an year-wise record of events from 634 (Horse year—wrongly mentioned by F. Thomas as 635) to 643 (the year following the Tiger year, corresponding to A.D. 642) and gives much interesting information. Unfortunately, it is very small (55 lines) and defective; about two-fifths of its width (i.e. 16-17 words in each line) are blank.

A. Stein, and another by Professor P. Pelliot in Tun-Huang, prepared for publication in complete form by Professor Bacot.[52]

However, for the present this is all that we have of the earliest historical texts written in Tibetan language. As I have already said, the later Tibetan historians known to us are almost totally ignorant of the historical literature of Tibet of the 7th-9th centuries. Only future archaeological finds in the Tibetan region itself and in the countries where Tibetan language was wide-spread during this period can throw real light on the ealier historiography of Tibet.

As regards the works, which the Tibetan tradition—oral and written—usually ascribes to this earliest period of Tibetan history, apparently there is only one such work, and that too absolutely conjectural. This is the so-called *Annals of the bSam-yas Monastery* (*bSam-yas-lo-rgyus*) or *Great Record af the bSam-yas Monastery* (*bSam-yas-dkar-chag-chen-mo*) which contains a general account of the history of Tibet and is, therefore, known in Tibetan historical literature under the name of *The Royal Genealogy, Compiled by* (*the Minister from*) *Ba* (*rGyal-rabs sBa-bshed*), or simply *The Work of* (*Minister from*) *Ba* (*sBa-bshed*).[53]

This work is ascribed to the Minister of the King Khri-sroṅ-lde'u-btsan (8th century), the well-known sBa gSal-snaṅ, sBa Saṅ-śi, and others[54] and enjoys great fame and authority in Tibetan historiography. It has been referred to in the works of

52. *Ibid.*, pp. 51-57. The fragment described by Professor F. Thomas contains 254 lines and is an year-wise record of events covering a period of 76 years without break from 672 onwards. This fragment was discovered by A. Stein and its previous part by Professor P. Pelliot.

    The numerous Tibetan documents discovered by Professor P. Pelliot in Tun Huang also include an interesting list of miscellaneous dates which gives the names of some Tibetan kings. This list was very skilfully published, translated and commented upon by Hackin (J. Hackin, *Formulaire Sanscrit-Tibetain du x-e Siecle*, Paris 1924).

53. *sBa-bshed* is mentioned in the "List of Historical Literature" in *Deb-ther-rgya-mtsho* (vol. 1, fol. 4ᵃ 6). Besides the description of *sBa-bshed*, one also finds accounts of *rBa-bshed* (see Bu-ston, *Chos-'byuṅ*, the edition of bKra-śis-lhun-po monastery, fol. 104ᵃ 6 ; *dPag-bsam-ljon-bzaṅ*, fol. 242ᵃ 6 (S. C. Das, *Pag Sam Jon Zang*, p. 383) and even *dPa'-bshed* (see *sKyes-bu-dam-pa-rnams-la-spriṅs-pa'i-yi-ge* included in *Sa-skya-bka'-'bum*, sDe-dge edition, vol. xii, fols. 70-76ᵃ 2, fol. 72ᵇ 4) or *dBa'-bshed* (see *Deb-ther-sṅon-po*, vol. i, fol. 28ᵃ 1).

54. See *dPag-bsam-ljon-bzaṅ*, fol. 101ᵃ 5 (S. C Das, *Pag Sam Jon Zang*, p. 152—here wrongly printed as sPans-si) and "List of Rare Books" (*dPe-rgyun-dkon-pa-'ga'-shig-gi-tho-yig*), fol. 7ᵇ 3.

Sa-skya-paṇḍita Kun-dga'-rgyal-mtshan (1182-1251)[55], Bu-ston Rin-chen-grub (1290-1364),[56] 'Gos-lo-tsā-ba gShon-nu-dpal (1392-1481)[57], the Fifth Dalai Lama Ṅag-dbaṅ-bLo-bzaṅ-rgya-mtsho (1617-1682)[58] and his regent, the well-known scholar sDe-srid Saṅs-rgyas-rgya-mtsho (1653-1705),[59] Sum-pa Ye-śes-dpal-'byor,[60] and other authors. And, in fact, the chronology of the ancient history of Tibet as adopted in *sBa-bshed* has, according to Sum-pa-mkhan-po,[61] served as the basis (*rtsa-ba*) for the chronology of Bu-ston Rin-chen-grub and for a number of other historians as, for instance, dPa'-po gTsug-lag-phreṅ-ba (1504-1566), 'Brug-pa Padma-dkar-po (b. 1527), Maṅ-thos-klu-sgrub (b. 1523),[62] for the author of the historical work *rGyal-rabs-gsal-ba'i-me-loṅ* (15th century), for the author of *Deb-ther-dmar-po* (14th century) etc.

Unfortunately, this work *sBa-bshed* is not at our disposal. Even in the last century, the Tibetan writers considered it a bibliographical rarity. We are, therefore, not in a position to judge specifically about its contents or about the actual

55. See *sKyes-bu-dam-pa-rnams-la-spriṅs-pa'i-yi-ge* (*Sa-skya-bka'-'bum*, vol. xii, fol. 72^{b} 4, which mentions the three "histories" : *rGyal-bshed, dPa'-bshed* and *'Bans-bshed.*
56. See Bu-ston, *Chos-'byuṅ*, fol. 104^{a} 6. In translating this text, E. E. Obermiller did not understand that here the reference was to the work entitled *rBa-bshed* and translated the expression *rBa-bshed-nas* as "According to the opinion of Rba" etc. (see E. Obermiller, *chos-'byuṅ* [History of Buddhism], pt. ii, p. 108).
57. See *Deb-ther-sṅon-po*, vol. i, fols. 22^{a} 4, 28^{a} 1.
58. See his historical work *Gaṅs-can-yul-gyi-sa-la-spyod-pa'i-mtho-ris-kyi-rgyal-blon-gtso-bor-brjod-pa'i-deb-ther* (hereafter *rGyal-ba-lṅa-pa'i-deb-ther*), the 'Bras-spuṅs monastery edition, fols. 32^{a} 3, 33^{a} 2-3, 37^{b} 2, 38^{a} 3, 39^{b} 5, 40^{b} 4. While noting the popularity of *sBa-bshed* among the Tibetan historians, the Fifth Dalai Lama also points out its discrepancies.
59. See his work *bsTan-bcos-bai-dū-rya-dkar-po-las-dris-lan-'khrul-snaṅ-gya'-sel-don-gyi-bshin-ras-ston-byed* (*Bai-dū-rya-gya'-sel* in short), Shol-par-khaṅ edition in Lhasa (473 fol.), fols. 12^{b} 3, 63^{a} 2 etc. As I have already mentioned once (See A. I. Vostrikov, *K bibliografii tibetskoi literatury* [On the Bibliography of Tibetan Literature],—"Bibliografiya Vostoka", No. 2-4, p. 42), this work is the author's reply to objections raised against his famous astronomical treatise known under the title *Bai-du-rya-dkar-po.*
60. See *dPag-bsam-ljon-bzaṅ*, fols. 99^{b} 4, 101^{a} 5, 102^{a} 1, 108^{b} 2, 112^{a} 6-7, 242^{b} 6 etc. (S. C. Das, *Pag Sam Jon Zang*, pp. 153, 155, 157, 166, 172, 383).
61. See *dPag-bsam-ljon-bzaṅ*, fols. 99^{b} 4 and 101^{a} 4 ff. (S. C. Das, *Pag Sam Jon Zang*, pp. 153, 154).
62. All dates given here are taken from the "Chronological Tables".

date of its composition. According to Sum-pa-mkhan-po,[63] this work was written by sBa gSal-snaṅ, sBa Saṅ-śi and others as the chronicle of the bSam-yas monastery and was later subjected to various interpolations and abridgements by the monks, kings and ministers. This gave rise to three versions of the text : *bLa-bshed,* i.e. "The Work of the Monks" ; *rGyal-bshed,* i.e. "The Work of the Kings" ; and *sBa-bshed,* i.e. "The work of (the Minister from) sBa". Thus, we cannot normally expect ever to find the actual original text of this work. But we cannot, of course, assert that it will not turn out to be dating from a period earlier than that ascribed by the Tibetan tradition.

63. See *dPag-bsam-ljon-bzaṅ*, fol. 101ᵃ 5-6 (S. C. Das, *Pag Sam Jon Zang*, pp. 155-156). These three works are also mentioned in *sKyes-bu-dam-pa-rnams-la-spriṅs-pa'i-yi-ge* (*Sa-skya-bka'-'bum*, vol. xii, fol. 72ᵇ 4) and in "List of Rare Books" (*dPe-rgyun-dkon-pa-'ga'-shig-gi-tho-yig*, fol. 7ᵇ 3).

Chapter Two

'BOOKS FROM BURIED TREASURES'

The so-called "*gter-ma* books" or "books from buried treasures" (*gter-chos*) which are usually regarded as the works of the earliest period of Tibetan history, have a special place in Tibetan literature. However Tibetan authors themselves are often very sceptical of these books.

It is quite possible and even certain that the custom of putting books in various sacred installations, as observed in Tibet, existed there even in the hoary antiquity. Such immured works have probably been discovered more than once during a thousand years and odd of Tibetan history. There have also been cases—and more than once—when out-dated and forgotten texts have been discovered in the archives and various libraries. But apart from such actual discoveries and, may be, partly under their influence, there have also been fake discoveries in Tibet when the compilations of later authors have been passed on as works of celebrated men of the past. The "*gter-ma* books" or "books from buried treasures" (*gter-chos*), as quite rightly pointed out by Waddell,[64] are exactly of such nature. Or, at least a majority of them is of such type. Usually, these books are passed on as works of the king Sroṅ-btsan-sgam-po (7th cent.) or of Padmasambhava, and are supposed to have been discovered from buried treasures (*gter*) where they had been kept buried deliberately (*sbas*) for some time. These "*gter-ma* books" are sometimes made to look emphatically mysterious and strange. Thus, for instance, in some of these texts, seals are affixed at the end of the chapters ; a number of seals are enumerated in the end of the whole work. The usual vertical line used in Tibetan script for separating sentences and their parts is found replaced by two vertically arranged circles with a diametrical line drawn between them, etc. That these were hidden in the buried treasures is, as a rule, stated in the works themselves ; sometimes whole chapters in them are devoted to an account of the buried treasures supposed to be hidden in various places. It is probable and even certain that in many cases, these works contain some borrowed materials—and those too without any particular change—from really ancient sources; but for ascertaining what exactly this ancient material is and what material has been styled as old, a special and highly difficult investigation has to be made every time.

The "*gter-ma* books" are quite numerous in Tibet. They belong *en masse* to

---

64. L. A. Waddell, *The Buddhism of Tibet or Lamaism*, London 1895, pp. 56-58, 165-166.

Buddhist religious literature though works of historical nature are also found among them. As a rule, these works are of very little value as historical sources. But in European Tibetology, after Csoma de Koros, some of these are accepted as monuments of Tibetan historical literature—a fact which of course could not but influence their general evaluation. Besides, many other hasty and erroneous judgements have been passed on these works. I, therefore, consider it necessary to examine them at great length.

a) *bKa'-chems-ka-khol-ma*

Of the various apocryphal works, one that is relied upon in Tibetan historiography is the so-called *bKa'-chems-ka-khol-ma* i.e. the "Will" of the king Sroṅ-btsan-sgam-po, supposed to have been preserved (*bkol*) near one of the pillars (*ka-ba*) in the grand temple of Buddha at Lhasa and found there by the famous Atīśa (982-1054).[65] During his stay in the vicinity of sÑe-thaṅ, Atīśa, according to a Tibetan legend, is believed to have been drawn by some supernatural occurrence to the grand temple at Lhasa which, the Tibetans think, was built by the king Sroṅ-btsan-sgam-po and his wife, a Nepali princess. Having expressed a wish to know the history of this temple, and having been instructed by a heavenly fairy who appeared before him in the guise of an old woman, Atīśa is alleged to have discovered three manuscript scrolls, two and a half sagenes from the pillar, with a cap of the shape of a vase (*ka-ba-bum-pa-can*). One of these turned out to be a historical work (*lo-rgyus*) written by the ministers and bearing the title *Zla-ba-'dod-'jo*, i. e. "Moon, the Grantor of Wishes". The second one was also a work of the same type written by the queen and entitled *Dar-dkar-gsal-ba*, i.e. "Shining White Silk". The third was the "Will" (*bKa'-chems*) proper of the king Sroṅ btsan-sgam-po and, at the same time, a biography (*rnam-thar*) of the Bodhisattva Avalokiteśvara, whose incarnation this king was believed to be. To distinguish this work from various other "Wills" attributed to the King Sroṅ-btsan-sgam-po, it was named as "The Will, hidden near the Pillar"—*bKa'-chems ka-khol-ma* This name, however, can be applied some-times even to all the three texts mentioned above, viz. to the "Three wills" (*bKa'-chems-gsum*), as they are together called.

As is clear from the accounts of Tibetan historians themselves, *bKa'-chems-ka-khol-ma* was often subjected to alterations, additions and subtractions, and was known to these historians in various enlarged and abridged editions.

65. Dates of birth and death of Atīśa are given in "Chronological Tables'.

[For details, see notes 66 and 67 below.] But in the nineteenth century it apparently began to go out of circulation, for it is found recorded in the above-mentioned "List of Rare Books".[68]

The manuscript available in the Institute of Peoples of Asia of the Academy of Sciences, USSR, is fairly old and is an abridged version of this work[69]. It is written like a *dpe-yig*, on a white thick glossy Tibetan paper, with six lines to a page, and consists of 83 folios in 7½ X 32 cm. format. The entire text is written in Indian ink, with the chapter headings and some proper names being in red colour. Only one folio—apparently the last one having the colophon—is wanting. This manuscript is entitled *rGyal-rabs-daṅ gser-gyi-lha-śākya-mu-ni-bsheṅs-nas-bod-yul-dbus-su-gdan-draṅs-lugs-daṅ-rigs-gsum-mgon-po-mdsad-spyod rgyal-po-sroṅ-btsan-sgam-po'i-rnam-thar-bsdus-pa-legs-pa-gcig-bshugs-lho.* But in the text itself, in the introduction and in the colophon, it has been called *rGyal-po'i-bka'-thems*, i.e. "King's Behest" and is regarded as the last of the above-mentioned three texts supposed to have been found by Atīśa. At the same time, it repeatedly refers for details to the "Main Behest" and is passed for an abridged account of what is contained in the "Main Behest" and the first two treatises alleged to have been found by Atīśa—viz. *Zla-ba-'dod-'jo* and *Dar-dkar-gsal-ba.* The manuscript contains thirteen chapters besides the introduction, which gives the legend (quoted by us here in brief) as to how Atīśa discovered these three texts. Of these thirteen chapters, the first three are devoted to the myth of Avalokiteśvara, the fourth—to the genealogy of Indian and Tibetan kings, the fifth—to the story of advent of Buddhism in Tibet, and all others—to the legends on the life and exploits of the king Sroṅ-btsan-sgam-po and his two wives, and to an account of how the main temple of Lhasa was got built by them, and finally the conclusion.[70]

---

66. See the manuscript (mentioned below) of the abridged version of this work, *rGyal-po'i-bka'-thems*, fols. 2b3-4a6. See also the *thob-yig—Zab-pa-daṅ-rgya-che-pa'i-dam-pa'i-chos-kyi-thob-yig-gaṅgā'i-chu̥-rgyun*, vol. iii, fol. 176a4-6—compiled by the Fifth Dalai Lama.
67. See *dPag-bsam-ljon-bzaṅ*, fol. 101a6 (S. C. Das, *Pag Sam Jon Zang*, p. 156).
68. *dPe-rgyun-dkon-pa-'ga'-shig-gi-tho-yig*, fol. 7b3.
69. This manuscript was brought from Buryatia in 1935 by S. D. Dylykov.
70. It will not be out of place to give here the table of contents of *rGyal-po'i-bka'-thems*. The general introduction (fols. 1-2b3) and the general account of as to how this work appeared (fols. 2b3-4a6) are followed by :

    1) *'Phags-pa-spyan-ras-gzigs-kyi-rnam-thar-las : Loṅs-sku'i-bkod pa-bstan-pa'i-le'u.* From the biography of Avalokiteśvara : Chapter on his deeds as Sambhogakāya, fols. 4a6-6b4 ;

So far as I can judge from the quotations from *bKa'-chems-ka-khol-ma* found in the works of various Tibetan authors, the version as given in the manuscript mentioned here is considerably different from the usual text of this work. In it, some accounts are totally wanting; others have been stated quite differently.[71] It would therefore

---

2) *'Phags-pa'i-rnam-thar-las* : *sPrul-skus-'dul-ba'i-le'u.* From the life of Avalokiteśvara : Chapter on as to how he preaches living beings after becoming an incarnate, fols. 6b4-16a1 ;

3) *'Phags-pa-spyan-ras-gzigs-kyi-rnam-thar-las* : *Kha-ba-can-gyi-sems-can-snod-du-ma-gyur - pa-rnams-sprul-bas - mir-gyur-nas-de-dag-zaṅ-ziṅ-gis-'dul - ba'i-le'u.* From the life of Avalokiteśvara : Chapter on as to how, because of his incarnation, the inhabitants of Tibet became people and were taught husbandry, fols. 16a1-20b2 ;

4) *bKa'-thems-las Rigs-rgyud-bstan-pa'i-le'u.* From the Will : Chapter on genealogy (of Tibetan kings), fols. 20b3-23a2 ;

5) *rGyal-po'i-bka'-thems-las Bod-du-dam-pa'i-chos-dbu-rñes-pa'i-le'u.* From the Will of the king : Chapter on as to how the Buddhist religion originated in Tibet, fols. 23a2-25a3 ;

6) *rGyal-po'i-bka'-thems-las rGyal-bu-sprul-pa'i-sku-bltams-pa'i-le'u.* From the Will of the king : Chapter on the re-birth of Avalokiteśvara in the form of a prince, fols. 25a3-26a4 ;

7) *'Phags-pa'i-rnam-thar-rgyal-bu-dbaṅ-bskur-ba'i-le'u.* From the life of Avalokiteśvara : Chapter on the accession of the prince to throne, fols. 26a5-27b1 ;

8) *'Phags-pa'i-rnam-thar-daṅ-rGyal-po'i-bka'-thems-las Lha-spyan-draṅs-pa'i-le'u.* From the life of Avalokiteśvara and from the Will of the king : Chapter on the arrival of Buddha's statue in Tibet, fols. 27b2-33b1 ;

9) *Lha-cig-khri-btsun-spyan-draṅs-pa'i-le'u.* On the arrival of a Nepalese princess in Tibet, fols. 33b2-44a1 ;

10) *rGya-mo-'o-co-spyan-draṅs-pa'i-le'u.* On the arrival of a Chinese princess in Tibet, fols. 44a1-60a2 ;

11) *Sa-dpyad-byas-pa'i-le'u.* On selecting a site for the construction of Lhasa temple, fols. 60a2-62a4 ;

12) *Lha-khaṅ-brtsegs-pa'i-le'u.* On the construction of the temple, fols. 62a5-77a4 ;

13) *'Phags-pa'i-rnam-thar-rgyal-po'i-bka'-thems-kyi-yi-ge-las 'Phags-pa-spyan-ras-gzigs-dbaṅ-phyug-daṅ Jo-mo-khro-gñer-can-daṅ Jo-mo-sgrol-ma-gsum-gyi-gtsug-lag-khaṅ-gi-rab-gnas.* From the life of Avalokiteśvara and from the Will of the king : Chapter on consecration of the temple, fols. 77a5-81a2.

These are followed by Conclusion and Colophon.

71. See, for instance, the legend on the origin of Buddha available in the manuscript of *rGyal-po'i-bka'-thems* (fol. 10a4 ff) along with the tale quoted from

be pre-mature to evaluate the historical importance of the main edition of *bKa'-chems-ka-khol-ma* (which I could not manage to get) on the basis of this abridged and variated version. All the same, the latter does no doubt give a general idea of the nature and composition of this interesting monument.

There is no doubt that this monumental work does not belong to the king Sroṅ-btsan-sgam-po, as it is passed for. In fact, it dates from a considerably later period. The work mentions the descendants of this king—Khri-sroṅ-lde'u-btsan and gLaṅ-dar-ma—and also gives information on the latter's persecution of Buddhism and later revival of the teachings of Buddhism.[72] But this is not all. The very nature of the legend of the miraculous discovery of this work calls in question the possibility of dating it even from the time of Atīśa and his pupils, and makes the assumption more probable that it was, like many other similar apocryphal writings, compiled in 13th-14th centuries. Beyond doubt, *bKa'-chems-ka-khol-ma* already existed in the 15th century. For, according to the testimony of Lha-dbaṅ-blo-gros, the well-known Tibetan historian 'Gos-lo-tsā-bagShon-nu-dpal (1392-1481) cites, in his work '*Khrul-sel* written in 1442-1443, the opinion expressed in the "Will" (*bKa'-chems-kyi-yi-ge*) of the king Sroṅ-btsan-sgam-po[73] among the views on the date of *Nirvāṇa*. Here, it is highly interesting to note that these details given by him tally, on many points, with the text of the manuscript described here and differ only partly from the main edition of *bKa'-chems-ka-khol-ma*[74] known to us from the quotations in other works. Moreover,

---

bKa'-chems-ka-khol-ma in *dPag-bsam-ljon-bzaṅ* (fol. 89b1 ff ; S. C. Das, Pag Sam Jon Zang, p. 138). See also the manuscript of *rGyal-po'i-bka'-thems* (fol. 75a5) and *dPag-bsam-ljon-bzaṅ* (fol. 110a5 ff ; S. C. Das, *Pag Sam Jon Zang*, p. 169) etc.

72. See *rGyal-po'i-bka'-thems*, fol. 78b1 ff.

73. E. Schlagintweit, *Die Berechnung der Lehre. Eine Streitschrift zur Berichtigung der buddhistischen Chronologie verfasst im Jahre 1591 von Suresematibhadra,*—"Abhandlungen der philosophisch-philologischen Classe der Konigl. bayerischen Akademie der Wissenschaften" ; XX Bd, III Abt., Munchen 1897, SS. 662, 3 (text), 621-622 (translation).

74. See *rGyal-po'i-bka'-thems*, fol. 13b3 ff which gives an account of how the Lhasa statue of Buddha was raised under the patronage of Bodhisattva Maitreya and consecrated by Buddha himself and how after the *nirvāṇa* of Buddha, it remained with the Gods for 500 years and with the dragons for the same period, in Udyāna, with the *rākṣasa*-s and finally in Magadha. This account may be compared with the above-mentioned work of E. Schlagintweit and the legend of origin of the statue of Buddha in *bKa'-chems-ka-khol-ma*—which is quoted

bKa'-chems-ka-khol-ma is mentioned by name in *rGyal-rabs-gsal-ba'i-me-loṅ*,[75] which also dates from the 15th century.

In Tibetan historical literature, *bKa'-chems-ka-khol-ma* is frequently mentioned and quoted.[76] However, the popularity of this work and the trust that it begets are due not so much to its historical worth, which is not much, as to the fact that the compilation and the discovery of this text are associated with well-known celebrities. The fact that its discovery was attributed to Atīśa, whom the dominant sect of Tibet—dGe-lugs-pa—honours as its fore-runner, has of course especially added much to the authority of this work. It is exactly these circumstances coupled with some real merits of the work that have saved it from the attack of the later Tibetan historiographers inclined to treat the apocryphal *gter-ma* literature very critically.

b) *Padma-bka'-thaṅ*

Of all the "*gter-ma* books" (*gter-chos*), the apocryphal "biographies" of Padmasambhava—the so-called *thaṅ-yig*, or more respectfully *bka'i-thaṅ-yig*, or *bka'-thaṅ*—are highly popular. In the Tibetan literature, we find several such works. In particular, as we see from the title and colophon of one later Tibetan biographical compilation of Padmasambhava[77] published by Professor A. Grünwedel, the term

---

in *dPag-bsam-ljon-bzaṅ* (fol. 89b1 ff; S. C. Das, *Pag Sam Jon Zang*, p. 138) and in B. Baradiin's *Statuya Maitrei v Zolotom khrame v Labrane* [Statue of Maitreya in Golden Temple in bLa-braṅ], pp. 19-21.

75. See *rGyal-rabs-gsal-ba'i-me-loṅ*, 24a, 28a2, 78a3.

76. Apart from the works mentioned, it is also referred to in the biography of Tsoṅ-kha-pa, compiled by Cha-har-dge-bśes bLo-bzaṅ-tshul-khrims (19th century) and entitled *rJe-thams-cad-mkhyen-pa-tsoṅ-kha-pa-chen-pa'i-rnam-thar-go-sla-bar-brjod-pa-bde-legs-kun-gyi-'byuṅ-gnas*, Peking edition, Book vi, fols. 10a5 ff and 10b 6 ff and in various other works.

77. See A. Grünwedel, *Padmasambhava und Verwandtes*—"Baessler Archiv", Bd III, Hft I, S. 3. Anm. 3, 4, which contains the Tibetan text of the title and colophon.

The translation of the colophon made by Professor A. Grünwedel (S. 4) is not at all faithful. The colophon reads :

'Gro-ba-yoṅs-kyi-skabs-nas-rin-po-che o-rgyan-gu-ru-padma-'byuṅ-gnas-kyis rnam-par-thar-ba-mthoṅ-ba-don-ldan-'di saṅs-rgyas-bstan-pa-raṅ-shiṅ-rgyas-pa-daṅ rig-'dsin-padma'i-sku-drin-dran-pa-daṅ Sems-can-rnams-kyi-saṅs-rgyas-thob-phyir-daṅ rjes-'jug-sṅags-'chaṅ-rnams-kyi-don-phyir-du gnas-mchog-yar-luṅ-śel-gyi-brag-phug-nas o-rgyan-gliṅ-pas-zab-gter-gdan-draṅs-pas o-rgyan-chen-po'i-rnam-thar-rgyas-pa-daṅ gter-ston-chen-po-mna'-

bka'-thaṅ sometimes denotes the so-called "Will of Padma" (*Padma-bka'-chems*), which is supposed to have been found by the Tibetan king N̄aṅ-ral (b. 1136). The same term *bka'-thaṅ* is also used for the biography of Padmasambhava, which gives an account of

---

-bdag-n̄aṅ-ral-gyis gter-nas-spyan-draṅs-padma-bka'-chems-daṅ lha-lcam-man-dha-gi-ra-bas-mdsad-pa-yis rnam-thar-mdsad-pa-bshi-bcu-she-lṅa-nas lho-brag-gter-stan-gu-ru-chos-dbaṅ-gis bsdus-pas-rnam-thar-mdsad-pa-bcu-gcig-ma gsum-po-gcig-tu-dril-nas-shu-len-daṅ gdams-ṅag-thor-bu-ma-'oṅs-luṅ-bstan-rnams deṅ-saṅ-dus-na-sṅags-kyi-brgyud-'dsin-ciṅ Padma'i-zab-gter-rnams-la-loṅs-spyod-pas-'od-gsal-rdo-rje-sn̄iṅ-po-rnal-'byor-pas dbaṅ-chen-sprel-zla'i-tshe-bcu-la Yoṅs-su-rdsogs-par-bkod-pa'i-dge-ba'-dis...

The translation as given by Professor A. Grünwedel is : "Jenes allseitig anerkannte kostbare Buch ("Juwel"), dessen Lehrtendenz (darśana) die Entwicklungsgeschichte des Padmasambhava von Udyana ist welches, indem es die Lehre Buddhas fordert, weithin gilt und die Erinnerung wachhalt, and die Segnungen des Vidyadhara Padma Korpers und zu dem Zwecke besteht, dass die Lebewesen zu Buddha gelangen, hat zum Nutzen der angehenden Tantrahalter aus der Kristallhohle von Yar-luṅ, dem erhabenen Orte, Udyanadvipin als tiefen Schatz ("Urquelle") durch Eingebung gefunden : dass diese ausfuhrliche Erzahlung vom grossen Manne von Udyana (rNam-thar rgyas-pa) und ferner die vom grossen Schatzefinder, dem Landesfursten N̄aṅ-ral aus dem Schatze hervorgeholten 40, Geschichten (rdsad-pa) des rNam-thar von 45, namlich Padma bka'-chems, und von den Geschichten der Prinzessin Mandharavā, dass ferner noch die vom Guru thos-dbaṅ, dem Schatzefinder von Lho-brag gesammelten Geschichten des rNam-thar, elf stucke umfassend, nun zu dieser Zeit alle drei in ein Werk verarbeitet wurden : Zu-len, die Avadānas einzeln und die Prophezeiung uber die Zukunft : dies ist das Tugendverdienst Tantrahalters, eines Yogin 'Od-gsal rdo-rje sn̄iṅ-po, welcher sich an den Schatzbuchern Padmas ergotzend, in Wasseraffenjahr, in Affenmonat, am 10 Tage alles zusammengestellt hat".

It is difficult to imagine a more erroneous and obscure translation ! The text is absolutely clear, although the confusion of the particles of genitive and instrumental cases is there even in it. A correct translation of this colophon is :

This biography—"Useful for those, who will see it" (*mThoṅ-ba-don-ldan* is the proper title of the work in question)—of Padmasambhava, the teacher from Udyāna (the word "teacher"—gu-ru—is omitted in Grünwedel's text), the eternal gem for all the living beings, has been compiled in absolutely finished form on the 10th day of Monkey month of the Water-Monkey year

his eleven deeds (*rNam-thar-mdsad-pa-bcu-gcig-ma*). This biography, compiled by Gu-ru Chos-dbaṅ (1212-1273)[78], is a remarkable abridged version of the one that narrates the forty-five deeds of Padmasambhava and is supposed to have been written by Princess Mandaravā (Lha-lcam-mandar-ba). But this term is specially applied for denoting the

---

by the yogi 'Od-gsal-rdo-rje-sñiṅ-po, who has perceived various small sermons, precepts and prophecies and is at present the keeper of succession of *tantra*-s and who revels in the much treasured (books) of Padma. It is compiled by a combination of three books : (1) "A detailed biography of the great scholar from Udyāna" (*O-rgyan-chen-po'i-rnam-thar-rgyas-pa*), discovered by (the treasure-finder) U-rgyan-gliṅ-pa from a deep store in Khrustal'nyi grotto in the highlands of Yar-kluṅs ; (2) "Will of Padma" (*Pama-bka'-chems*), obtained from the treasures by the great treasure-finder, the ruler Ñaṅ-ral and (3) "Biography of 11 deeds" (*rNam-thar-mdsad-pa-bcu-gcig-ma*), taken by Lho-brag treasure-finder Gu-ru Chos-dbaṅ from the "Biography of 45 deeds" (*rNam-thar-mdsad-pa-bshi-bcu-she-lṅa*), written by the princess Mandharavā. It has been compiled so that the Buddhist faith be spread and propagated, the memory of merciful Vidyādhara-Padma be retained, the living beings may attain the state of Buddha and (finally) so that it may do good to the subsequent keepers of mantras.

The title of the text as translated by Professor A. Grünwedel is also not correct. The text is called : *O-rgyan-gu-ru-padma-'byuṅ-gnas-kyi-rnam-par-thar-ba gter-ston-chen-po-o-rgyan-gliṅ-pa mṅa'-gdag-ñaṅ-ral gu-ru-chos-dbaṅ-bcas-nas-gdan-draṅs-pa'i-bka'-thaṅ-gter-kha-gsum-bsgregs-mthoṅ-ba-don-ldan.* A Grünwedel has translated it as : "Ausfuhrliche Geschichte des Guru von Udyāna Padmasambhva in Sinneder (ortodoxen) Belehrung (darśana) zusammengestellt aus den drei Schatzquellen der "Ansprachen" (bka'-thaṅ), welche durch Eingebung herbeigeschaft wurden von (solchen) Mannem wie dem grossen Schatzefinder Udyānadvīpin, dem Landesfursten Ñaṅ-ral und dem Guru Chos-dbaṅ". The correct translation, however, would be : "Biography of Padmasambhava, the teacher from Udyāna,—compiled from the three *bka'-thaṅ*-s, which were discovered by the treasure-finder U-rgyan-gliṅ-pa, the ruler Ñaṅ-ral and Gu-ru Chos-dbaṅ—and entitled "Useful for those who will see it".

78. The dates of birth and death of Ñaṅ-ral and Gu-ru Chos-dbaṅ are available in "Chronological Tables." The date of birth of Ñaṅ-ral, as given in the chronological table of the first 'Jam-dbyaṅs-bshad-pa, is 1124. Professor A. Grünwedel, who borrowed these dates from the article by S. C. Das (*Life of Sum-pa khan-po*,—JASB, vol. lviii, 1. 1889, pt. 1, p. 46,51), has repeated the mistakes of the latter : the date of birth of Ñaṅ-ral has been given as 1134 and that of Gu-ru Chos-dbaṅ as 1211.

two works which are very close to each other—the one in verse, known as *Padma-bka'-thaṅ*, i.e. "The Story of Padma" proper ; and the other in prose, usually called *Thaṅ-yig-gser-'phreṅ*, i.e. "Yellow Rosary Stories".

The full title of the work in verse, which is briefly called *Padma-bka'-thaṅ* is *U-rgyan-gu-ru-padma-'byuṅ-gnas-kyi-skyes-rabs-rnam-par-thar-ba - rgyas - par - bkod-pa* [79]. We come across this title in the head-lines of all its chapters. The title page gives an indistinct title "in Udyāna language (U-rgyan-gliṅ-pa)"—"Ru-akśa-śa-ka-ra-ná"—and another in Tibetan—somewhat abridged as compared with the full title—*Gu-ru-padma-'byuṅ-gnas-kyi-skyes-rabs-rnam-par-thar-ba*. Finally, the colophon gives three other brief titles : *Padma-bka'i-thaṅ-yig* ; *rNam-thar-skyes-rabs-rgyas-pa* ; and *Khri-sroṅ-lde'u-btsan-bka'-chems*.[80] As stated in the colophon, this work was supposed to have been hidden in a treasure and sealed, but was found, in the Water-Dragon year, by the treasure-seeker (*gter-ston*) otherwise known as U-rgyan-gliṅ-pa, in the court of Pho-braṅ-padma-śel-gyi-phug-pa in the fortress of Śel-brag (Śel-gyi-brag-ri'i-rdsoṅ) in the Yar-kluṅs valley[81]. *Padma-bka'-thaṅ* consists of 108 chapters and is extant in many xylographic editions and manuscript copies.[82]

Many European scholars took up this work. In particular, it was used by Waddell who includes it in the sources given by him for a legendary history of the founder of lamaism.[83] E. Schlagintweit published, in Latin transliteration, the eighth (without the introductory part) and the ninth chapters of the Tibetan text together with their German translation. Besides, he also gave an account—partly in brief and partly in detail—of the first fifty-four chapters of this text[84] with some occasional translations. B. Laufer translated and published the colophon of the xylograph of this work[85] issued in Peking

79. There are 258 folios in the copy (brought from Tibet by G. Tsybikov ; *Tsybikov Collection*, No. 38) of this work, published in Shol-par-khaṅ (?) in Lhasa. All subsequent references in this work are to this edition.
80. *Padma-bka'-thaṅ*, fol. 252b1.
81. *Ibid.*. fol. 252b2-4.
82. The most important editions are indicated in the colophon to the Peking edition of 1839, which was published and translated by B. Laufer. See B. Laufer, *Der Roman einer tibetischen Konigin*, Leipzig 1911, S. 240ff. To the editions enumerated in this colophon, B. Laufer adds that of the Kat-kuo monastery discovered by him (*ibid.*, S. 245).
83. L. A. Waddell, *The Buddhism of Tibet...*, p. 379, n. 6.
84. E. Schlagintweit, *Die Lebensbeschreibung vom Padmo Sambhava dem Begrunder des Lamaismus I.T.* ; *Die Vorgeschichte, enthaltend die Herkunft und Familie des Buddha Śākyamuni*, II T. ; *Wirken und Erlebnisse in Indien*,—"Abhandlungen der kaiser. bayer. Akademie der Wissenschaften", I Cl., xxi Bd, II Abt., Ss. 417-444 u xxii Bd, III Abt., Ss. 517-576. Munchen 1899-1905.
85. B. Laufer, *Der Roman einer tibetischen Konigin*, Ss. 239ff.

in 1839. Finally, Toussaint published a complete French translation of this work from the manuscript brought by him from Li-thaṅ.[86] Besides, small individual fragments referring to the places in Central Asia were translated and commented upon by Professor F.W. Thomas.[87]

This work cannot at all serve as a historical source. It is of the nature of a narrative and didactic work which has used historical legends and tradition for preaching distinctive religious views not fully accepted by the predominant Order. And in this respect, of course, it is not devoid of interest.

Waddell dates this monumental work to the 12th or 13th century[88], Schlagintweit —to the 10th century[89], and Laufer—to the 9th-12th century.[90] But these hypotheses have no serious grounds. Waddell's opinion can generally be set aside, for it has been expressed by him in a simple sentence and no grounds therefor have been given. As regards Schlagintweit, his opinion is based on a clear misunderstanding. Presuming wrongly that the Tibetan term *kla-klo* denoting "Muslims" is first met with in the grammatical treatise *Za-ma-tog-bkod-pa* and convinced that B. Laufer was supposed to have studied this treatise and regarded it as having been compiled in the 11th century, Schlagintweit arrived at the conclusion that the absence of this term in *Padma-bka'-thaṅ* and also in the later (according to him) works on post-tenth century events permitted the dating of *Padma-bka'-thaṅ* to the 10th century. This conclusion, entirely resulting from false data, was rightly refuted by B. Laufer in his time. He no longer dated *Za-ma-tog-bkod-pa* to 11th century, but decided to date it to 1513[91] on the basis of the date mentioned in the colophon and other data. It is, therefore, not possible to take Schlagintweit's opinion seriously. Apparently, B. Laufer's opinion seemed more well-founded but after due verification, this too was found to be based on errors and misunderstandings. In trying to determine as to what year of the European calendar the Water-Dragon year

---

86. G. C. Toussaint, *Le dict de Padma. Padma thaṅ yig*. Ms. de Lithang, Paris 1933 (Bibliotheque de l'Institut des hautes etudes chinoises, vol. iii). Individual portions of this translation were published by him earlier in the "Bulletin de L'Ecole Francaise d'Extreme-Orient", xx, 1920, 4, pp. 13-56,—JA, cciii, 1923, pp. 257-328, and in "Etudes Asiatiques", t. ii, 1925, pp. 313-373.
87. F. W. Thomas, *Tibetan Literary Texts*.., pt. 1, pp. 288-292.
88. L. A. Waddell, *The Buddhism of Tibet*..., p. 379, n. 6.
89. E. Schlagintweit, *Lebensbeschreibung vom Padma Sambhava*..., T. ii, SS. 521-522.
90. B. Laufer, *Der Roman einer tibetischen Konigin*, *SS*. 9, 242ff.
91. B. Laufer, *Die Bru-za Sprache und historische Stellung des Padmasambhava*,—"T'oung Pao", Série II, vol. ix, 1908, p. 1, n. 2. See also his *Studien Zur Zprachwissenschaft der Tibeter Zamatog*,—"Sitzungsberichte der philos-philol. und der histor. Classe der k. bayer. Akademie der Wissenschaften", 1898, Hft iii, S. 524.

given in the colophon of ***Padma-bka'-thaṅ*** corresponds, B. Laufer found in Sum-pa-mkhan-po's Chronological Table, so negligently translated by S. C. Das, that the above-mentioned Guru Chos-dbaṅ discovered the book-treasure in gNam-skas-brag in 1231. Though there is no doubt that this information relates to other texts, for both the place where they were found and the name of the treasure-finder are totally different, B. Laufer hastened to date the "discovery" of *Padma-bka'-thaṅ* also to 1231 on the wrong assumption that the year 1231 as mentioned in S. C. Das's translation exactly corresponds to the Water-Dragon year.[92] B. Laufer also tried to find out the date

---

It is necessary to note that B. Laufer erred in regarding the date of compilation of *Za-ma-tog-bkod-pa* as 1513. Actually this text was compiled in 1514 (Wood-Dog year). Again B. Laufer is also wrong in fixing the dates of birth and death of the author of this text—Sha-lu-lo-tsā-ba Chos-skyoṅ-bzaṅ-po. Following S. C. Das (see S. C. Das, *Life of Sum-pa Khan-po*,—JASB, vol. lviii, 1889, pt. 1, p. 66), B. Laufer gives this date as 1439, whereas this should actually be 1441 (see "Chronological Tables"). The date of death of the author of *Za-ma-tog-bkod-pa* given by him is actually the date,—mentioned in the colophon of *Za-ma tog-bkod-pa*,—on which this text had been finally completed for press, namely the *mi-zad-pa* year (*akṣaya*) or in other words the Fire-Dog year, i.e. A. D. 1526 (B. Laufer has wrongly given the corresponding year as A.D. 1525). See the colophon of the manuscript—available in the Institute of Peoples of Asia (see I. J. Schmidt und O. Bohtlingk, *Verzeichiss der tibetischen Handschriften und Holzdrucke*, S. 62, N 31)—of this work entitled *Bod-kyi-brda'i-bstan-bcos-legs-par-bśad-pa-rin-po-che'i-za-ma-tog-bkod-pa* (in Tibetan language with Mongolian translation), fol. 44ᵃ 1-3. Actually, as stated in the "Chronological Tables", the author of this text—the above-mentioned great translator (lo-tsā-ba) from Sha-lu—died in 1527.

92. B. Laufer, *Der Roman einer tibetischen Konigin*, S. 242, Anm. 7, S. 245ff. Regarding, after Csoma de Koros, the initial year of Tibetan calendar as A D. 1026 instead of 1027, B. Laufer assumed that A.D. 1231 in the table of S. C. Das—who followed the same principle for the conversion of Tibetan dates—corresponded to Water-Dragon year. Without checking the conversion made by S. C. Das with the original, B. Laufer could not remark that S. C. Das had erred—even on the basis of the principle that he himself had accepted—in calling A.D. 1231 not the Water-Dragon year but, as could be expected, Water-Snake year (which, according to this principle, should correspond to A.D. 1232). In the Tibetan text, the report on the discovery of the treasure in

of the first xylographic edition of *Padma-bka'-thaṅ*. Depending upon the information of the colophon that this publication was brought out with the help of the minister of the king Phag-mo-gru-pa, B. Laufer decided that this referred to the minister of the well-known Tā'i Si-tu Byaṅ-chub-rgyal-mtshan (b. 1302), the founder of Phag-mo-gru-pa dynasty, and hence dated this xylographic edition to the early fourteenth century.[93] However, this is absolutely incorrect. Actually, the first appearance of *Padma-bka'-thaṅ* and especially of its first xylographic edition both date from a considerably later period.

Besides *Padma-bka'-thaṅ*, the treasure-finder U-rgyan-gliṅ-pa is believed to have discovered a number of "*gter-ma* books", particularly the so-called "Five Legends"—*bKa'-thaṅ-sde-lṅa*[94]—which we shall discuss below. In this connection, it is important to note that one of these "Legends", namely "Legend of Translators and Paṇḍita-s",—*Lo-paṇ-bka'i-thaṅ-yig*—contains a very interesting chronological table, which enables us to determine, with greater or less probability, the time of appearance of this text itself and other works, the discovery of which is attributed to the treasure-finder U-rgyan-gliṅ-pa, including also *Padma-bka'-thaṅ* which we are surveying here. This table covers about two folios and is at the end of Chapter 33, which is an account of "development and fall of Buddhist doctrine" (*Saṅs-rgyas-bstan-pa-dar-nub-bstan-pa'i-le'u*).[95] In this table, the date of events is measured by the number of years that have passed from the *nirvāṇa* of Buddha. And for finding out the date of *nirvāṇa*, as is seen from the whole context, the author follows the traditions of scholars from Sa-skya, according to whom the *nirvāṇa* of Buddha took place in the year which, on conversion to European calendar, comes to 2134 B.C.[96] This table given

gNam-skas-brag is dated as Water-Snake year of the iv cycle. Thus, not only the place of discovery and the name of the treasure-finder but also the very year of discovery is wrong.

93. *Ibid.*, SS. 243, 246ff. The date of birth of Tā'i Si-tu Byaṅ-chub-rgyal-mtshan (A.D. 1302) as mentioned by B. Laufer is correct. See "Chronological Tables".

94. The Institute of Peoples of Asia has a complete collection of this "Five Legends"—*bKa'-thaṅ-sde-lṅa*—published in Shol-par-khaṅ in Lhasa in 1889 at the initiative of the thirteenth Dalai Lama (1876-1934) and De-mo-khutukhta. This collection was brought from Tibet by G. Tsybikov (*Tsybikov Collection*, No. 51). Each "Legend" in this collection has its separate pagination. All subsequent references made in this work are to this edition.

95. *Lo-paṇ-bka'i-thaṅ-yig*, Shol-par-khaṅ monastery edition, fols. 68^b 5-70^b 6.

96. According to this tradition, Buddha was conceived in Fire-Hare year, was born in Earth-Dragon year and attained *nirvāṇa* on the boundry of the Fire-Pig and Earth-Mouse years. It is this Earth-Mouse year that is regarded as the first year after the *nirvāṇa* of Buddha. See the works—mentioned later in this

as a prophecy covers the period upto A.D. 1393[97] quite accurately. This table mentions *inter alia* the names of such well-known persons as rÑog-blo-ldan-śes-rab (1059-1109), Sa-skya-paṇḍita Kun-dga'-rgyal-mtshan (1182-1251), Karma Raṅ-byuṅ-rdo-rje (1284-1339)[98] and some others. It also gives the date of fall of the capital of Mongolian

---

volume (footnote 332)—of the scholars from the Sa-skya monastery: *Chos-la-'jug-pa'i-sgo*, fol. 315ᵇ 5 ff and *bLa-ma-rje-btsun-pa-chen-po'i-rnam-thar*, fol. 297ᵃ 3ff. See also the passages quoted from these works by Bu-ston Rin-chen-grub (Bu-ston, *Chos-'byuṅ*, fol. 103ᵃ 5 ff; E. Obermiller, *History of Buddhism*, pt. ii, p. 106), by Lha-dbaṅ-blo-gros (E. Schlagintweit, *Die Berechnung der Lehre*, text—S. 662; translation—S. 623), and by Sum-pa-mkhan-po (*dPag-bsam-ljon-bzaṅ*, fols. 79ᵇ 2-80ᵃ 2; S. C. Das, *Pag Sam Jon Zang*, pp. 123-124) etc. From the year of the *nirvāṇa* to A.D. 822 (both inclusive) when the peace treaty was concluded between Tibet and China, there is a period of 2955 years; to A.D. 1167 when *Chos-la-'jug-pa'i-sgo* was written—that of 3300 years (see *Chos-la-'jug-pa'i-sgo*, fol. 316ᵇ 5); to 1216 when *bLa-ma-rje-btsun-pa-chen-po'i-rnam-thar* was written—that of 3349 years; to 1322 when Bu-ston Rin-chen-grub wrote his historical work—that of 3455 years (see Bu-ston, *Chos-'byuṅ*, fols. 103ᵇ 5 and 244ᵃ 4); to 1592 when Lha-dbaṅ-blo-gros wrote his works—that of 3725 years (see E. Schlagintweit, *Die Berechnung der Lehre*, S. 670; see also A. Csoma de Koros, *A Grammar of Tibetan Language*, p. 200) etc. Thus, on conversion to our calendar, his date of *nirvāṇa* corresponds to 2134 B.C. This year in the sixteenth cycle is actually the Fire-Pig year [see, for example, the tables appended to the above-mentioned article by P. Pelliot (*Le cycle sexagenaire...*,—JA, 1913, vol. 1, pp. 664-665)].

97. i.e. upto Water-Hen year occuring 3525 years after the *nirvāṇa*; see *Lo-paṇ-bka'i-thaṅ-yig*, fol. 70ᵇ 6.

98. The dates of birth and death of these persons are mentioned in "Chronological Tables". *Lo-paṇ-bka'i-thaṅ-yig* states that in A.D. 1215 (Fire-Mouse year—*me-byi*; it is misprinted as *me-bya* in the xylograph) Sa-skya-paṇḍita Kun-dga'-rgyal-mtshan made his chronological calculations (fol. 70ᵇ 1) set forth in the aforesaid work *bLa-ma-rje-btsun-pa-chen-po'i-rnam-thar*. He also calculated that in A. D. 1332, Karma Ran-byuṅ-rdo-rje hoisted the "corolla" (properly "umbrella", *gdugs*—the upper projected ring of a *suburgan*) and the "rings" (*chos-'khor*—13 rings forming the top, placed one over the other and forming the neck of the *suburgan*) on the *suburgan* called *Zuṅ-mkhar-rdo'i-mchod-rten* (fol. 70ᵇ 2).

Lo-paṇ-bka'i-thaṅ-yig also mentions the date of death of rÑog bLo-ldan-śes-rab (70ᵃ 6) which—as distinct from the *Deb-ther-sṅon-po* (vol. 1, fol. 172ᵃ 3-5)

dynasty in China— Ta'i-du or Peking—which occurred in A.D. 1368.[99] Thus, the "Legend of Translators and Paṇḍita-s" (*Lo-paṅ-bka'i-thaṅ-yig*), at least in the form in which it has come down to us could not have appeared earlier than 1393. On the other hand, there are grounds to assume that it did not also appear later than this date, i.e. later than the end of the 14th century. This assumption is evidenced not only by the fact that the chronological table of this text ends with the year 1393 and that the events

---

and "Chronological Tables"—corresponds not to the Earth-Cow year (A. D. 1109) but to Pig year. To the Pig year date the death of rÑog bLo-ldan-śes-rab and such writers as Sa-skya-pa bSod-nams-rtse-mo (1142-1182) and Sa-skya-paṇḍita Kun-dga'-rgyal-mtshan (1182-1251). (See *Chos-la-'jug-pa'i-sgo*, fol. 316ᵇ 4, and *bLa-ma-rje-btsun-pa-chen-po'i-rnam-thar*, fol. 298ᵃ 2). In the extant xylographs of both these works, the date of death of rÑog bLo ldan-śes-rab has been given as Earth-Pig year (*sa-phag*), but this obviously is a misprint in place of Fire-Pig year (*me-phag*). It is precisely this last date—corresponding to A. D. 1107—that is mentioned in the *bsTan-rtsis-'dod-spyin-gter-'bum* (E. Schlagintweit, *Die Berechung der Lehre*, S. 662, Z. 36) where these works are cited. According to the *Deb-ther-sňon-po* (vol. 1, fols. 170ᵃ 3-4 and 172ᵃ 3) and "Chronological Tables", the Earth-Pig year (1059) is the date of birth of rÑog bLo-ldan-śes-rab.

99. Literally : *Sa-pho-spre'u-lo bSam-yas-bgegs-bsos-rab-gnas-byas Zla-ba-dgu-pa-ñer-dgu'i-nub Hor-yul-pho-braṅ-ta'i-du* (wrongly printed as *tal-du* in the xylograph) *Śol* (*Lo-paṇ-bka'i-thaṅ-yig*, fol. 70ᵇ 5).

Translation : "bSam-yas monastery, reconstructed after its déstruction, will be consecrated in the Earth-Female-Monkey year (1368). Ta'i-du, the capital of the Mongolian country will fall on the 29th day of the 9th month". It must be remarked here that neither the month nor the date mentioned in this communication corresponds to what we know from the Chinese sources about the date of fall of the Yüan dynasty and of the flight of Togon Timur from Peking... This information also does not literally tally with the respective place in the *Hor-chos-'byuṅ*. However, some connection is certainly there between the information of the latter and that of the *Lo-paṇ-bka'i-thaṅ-yig*. According to the *Hor-chos-'byuṅ*, the above mentioned event took place on the 28th day of the 8th month of the Earth-Monkey year—*Sa-sprel-lor-zla-ba-brgyad-pa'i-ñer-brgyad-la* (see G. Huth, *Geschichte des Buddhismus in der Mongolei*, vol. i, *Text*, Strassburg 1892, S. 27, Z. 18 ff). The translation of this portion as given by G. Huth (*ibid.*, vol. ii, *Ubersetzung*, Strassburg 1896, S, 41) is totally incorrect. He has taken the date of the month for the age (!) of the Chinese Ju-ge and has translated : "Im achten Monat des Erde-Affen-Jahres, in seinem 28 Lebensjahre, lud namlich der Chinese Juge..." etc.

and the persons of a period later than this date were apparently totally unknown to its author, but also by the fact that in this table—notwithstanding all its brevity—we find such facts of the second half of 14th century mentioned as the repair and consecration of bSam-yas monastery in 1368 or the famine of 1393[100] which could be significant only in the eyes of a contemporary. This is also confirmed by the direct reference in the table that the treasure-finder, U-rgyan-gliṅ-pa, to whom the discovery of this text is attributed, worked in the second half of the 14th century. This reference states that when U-rgyan-gliṅ-pa, on his visit to the locality of Śel-phug, reckoned the number of years that had passed from the time of *nirvāṇa*, it was found that it was 3500th year corresponding to A.D. 1367[101]. Thus, this table included in the "Legend of Translators and Paṇḍita-s" (*Lo-paṇ-bka'i-thaṅ-yig*) directly testifies that U-rgyan-gliṅ-pa lived in the second half of the 14th century.

All this enables us to determine as to which year of European calendar the Tibetan date of discovery of *Padma-bka'-thaṅ* mentioned in its colophon corresponds. As we already know, the colophon of this work states that it was discovered in Water-Dragon year by the treasure-finder U-rgyan-gliṅ-pa in the locality of Śel-phug,[102] i.e. in the locality in which the latter made his chronological calculations in 1367. As compared with *Lo-paṇ-bka'i-thaṅ-yig*, the *Padma-bka'-thaṅ* is unquestionably an earlier work, for the latter is directly referred to in the former.[103] Under these circumstances, the year Water-Dragon to which the colophon of *Padma-bka'-thaṅ* assigns its discovery can correspond to A.D. 1352 only and not to 1231 as supposed by B. Laufer or to 1412 as claimed, of course without any grounds, by Toussaint.[104]

Of course, the date of the fictitious "discovery" of an apocryphal work might also not tally with that of its actual compilation. The work might actually have been written somewhat earlier than the date when it was "discovered". On the contrary, a work compiled at a later date might be passed on as a find of the earlier period. In the present case, however, the date of "discovery" of *Padma-bka'-thaṅ* is close to the actual date of its compilation, provided it is true that the treasure-finder U-rgyan-gliṅ-pa, who discovered this text, actually lived in the second half of the 14th century. On the other hand, the presence, in *Padma-bka'-thaṅ*, of a long chronological list of treasure-finders (*gter-ston*-s)[105] prior to U-rgyan-gliṅ-pa—which also includes the already

---

100. *Lo-paṇ-bka'i-thaṅ-yig*, fol. 70b 5-6.
101. *U-rgyan-gliṅ-pas-śel-phug-brtsis sum-stoṅ-daṅ-ni-lṅa-brgya-lon* (*ibid.*, fol. 70b 4-5)
102. See *infra.*
103. *Lo-paṇ-bka'i-thaṅ-yig*, fols. 69a 2, 80b 6.
104. G. C. Toussaint, *Le dict de Padma...*, p. 2.
105. This list comprises the 92nd chapter (fols. 196b 4-203a 1) of the text, which bears the heading: *Sa-rtags-gter-gyi-'byuṅ-dus-bstan-pa'i-le'u*, i.e. "Chapter,

familiar names of Guru Chos-dbaṅ (1212-1273)[106] and Rin-chen-gliṅ-pa[107] (who, according to the information of the chronological table given in *Lo-paṇ-bka'i-thaṅ-yig*, had calculated the date of *nirvāṇa* in A.D. 1332[108])—positively eliminates any possibility of the appearance of *Padma-bka'-thaṅ* earlier than the middle of the 14th century.

It is true that there is one fact which can shake the possibility of connecting the text of *Padma-bka'-thaṅ*, which has reached us, with the treasure-finder U-rgyan-gliṅ pa and his period. The chronological list of treasure-finders given in this text as a "prophecy" does not end, as one would have expected, with U-rgyan-gliṅ-pa. It continues further and it has been found that in Tibetan literature, there actually exist such works that are considered to have been discovered by these later treasure-finders in the same places which are mentioned in this list.[109] Therefore, it is possible that the work known to us under the title *Padma-bka'-thaṅ* is a counterfeit of the work bearing the same title, mentioned in *Lo-paṇ-bka'i-thaṅ-yig*. It is, however, more probable that what we have here is simply a later addition. It is also possible that the names of later treasure-finders given in *Padma-bka'-thaṅ* were initially imaginary names which, however, were used later by other authors with a view to pass their works as those discovered by persons "prophesied" in *Padma-bka'-thaṅ*. This assumption seems to me not less likely, particularly if one takes into account the fairly artificial nature of the names of later treasure-finders[110] enumerated in *Padma-bka'-thaṅ*. I do not, for the present, venture to

---

Giving an Account of the Indications of Localities and Time of Appearance of the Treasures". The list of the localities as given in this chapter is also reproduced by S. C. Das (see S. C. Das, *A Tibetan-English Dictionary*, Calcutta 1902, under the word *gter-gnas*).

106. *Padma-bka'-thaṅ*, fol. 199ᵃ 4.
107. *Ibid.*, fol. 201ᵃ 1.
108. *Lo-paṇ-bka'i-thaṅ-yig*, fol. 70ᵇ 3.
109. Thus, for example, in the *thob-yig* of the Fifth Dalai Lama, we find an account of the works studied by him and considered to have been discovered by the treasure-finder Kun-skyoṅ-gliṅ-pa in the white *suburgan* (*mchod-rten-dkar-po*) of the bSam-yas monastery (*Thob-yig-gaṅgā'i-chu-rgyun*, vol. ii, fols. 292ᵃ 6, 294ᵃ 6 ff.), by the treasure-finder Shig-po-gliṅ-pa in the locality of Khyuṅ-tshaṅ-brag (*ibid.*, fol. 215ᵇ ff.) and by others. In the list of treasure-finders given in the *Padma-bka'-thaṅ*, the names of these persons are given after the name of U-rgyan-gliṅ-pa.
110. The fact that the word *U-rgyan* has been added in the beginning of the names of all the later treasure-finders except the two immediately following U-rgyan-gliṅ-pa seems to be rather suspicious. No such thing is observed in the names of the earlier treasure-finders. Similarly we also do not almost observe the use of expression *gliṅ-pa* in the end of their names. Generally, whereas the names

assert any of these assumptions. But I think, we shall hardly be in the wrong if we consider that the main text of *Padma-bka'-thaṅ* appeared about A.D. 1352, i.e. in the year to which its colophon attributes its "discovery".

As regards the time of appearance of the first xylograph edition of *Padma-bka'-thaṅ*, the published colophon of the Peking edition of 1839 (the corresponding part of which was interpreted by B. Laufer quite incorrectly) clearly states that *Editio princeps* was accomplished at the initiative of the treasure-finder Śes-rab-'od-zer with material support from Hor-mi-dbaṅ-bsod-nams-stobs-rgyal, the minister to the Tibetan king Phag-mo-gru-pa.[111] Arbitrarily contrasting the proper name of the patron of the publication Hor-mi-dbaṅ-bsod-nams-stobs-rgyal connected with his family title with the title of the minister of Phag-mo-gru-pa dynasty, B. Laufer assumed that the reference here was to two persons—to the Mongolian prince and to the minister of Tā'i Si-tu Byaṅ-chub-rgyal-mtshan himself (b. 1302), the founder of Phag-mo-gru-pa dynasty. Thus B. Laufer came to the conclusion that the first edition of *Padma-bka'-thaṅ* appeared in the beginning of the 14th century.[112]

Nevertheless, this Hor-mi-dbaṅ-bsod-nams-stobs-rgyal is, in fact, none else but the successor of Hor-gshon-nu-bzaṅ-po, one of the famous vassals of the great Tā'i Si-tu Byaṅ-chub-rgyal-mtshan. Just like his ancestors, he bore the title of minister (*mdun-na-'don*) of Phag-mo-gru-pa dynasty but he lived in the 16th century. The father of Hor-mi-dbaṅ-bsod-nams-stobs-rgyal—Hor-bsod-nams-dar-rgyas—was a patron of the third Dalai Lama, bSod-nams-rgya-mtsho (1543-1588).[113] Hor-mi-dbaṅ-bsod-nams-stobs-rgyal

---

of the earlier treasure-finders are the usual Tibetan names, those of the later ones are absolutely unusual.

111. See B. Laufer, *Der Roman einer tibetischen Konigin*, S. 240. See also the colophon to the xylograph edition of *Padma-bka'-thaṅ* (fol. 255ᵇ 5 ff.) referred here.

112. B. Laufer, *Der Roman einer tibetischen Konigin*, S. 243, 246 ff.

113. The dates of birth and death of the third Dalai Lama have been taken from the "Chronological Tables". In many European works—because of the well-known error of Csoma de Koros (see P. Pelliot, *Le cycle sexagenaire* , —JA, 1913, t. 1, p. 639 *et suiv.*)—the dates of this famous leader of Tibetan Buddhism, who was the first to receive the title of the Dalai Lama, are one or two years behind the actual ones (see, for example, L.A. Waddell, *The Buddhism of Tibet*, p. 577 ; G. Huth, *Geschichte des Buddhismus in der Mongolei*, vol. ii, S. 201 ff. ; S. C. Das, *Life of Sum-pa Khan-po*,—JASB, vol. lviii, 1889, pt. i, pp. 71, 74 etc.) Correct dates have been given by : Klaproth, *Table chronologique des plus celebres patriarches et des evenements remarquables de la religion bouddhique, redigee en 1678* (*traduite du mongol*),—JA, 1831, p. 168 and G. Tsybikov, *Buddist-palomnik u svyatyn' Tibeta. Po dnevnikam, vedennym v 1899-1902 gg.* [A Buddhist Pilgrim in the Holy Places of Tibet. From the Diaries of 1899-1902], Petrograd 1919, pp. 256-257.

is mentioned by his great-grandson, Fifth Dalai Lama Ṅag-dbaṅ bLo-bzaṅ-rgya-mtsho (1617-1682), who in his historical work known under the title *Gaṅs-can-yul-gyi-sa-la-spyod-pa'i-mtho-ris-kyi-rgyal-blon-gtso-bor-brjod-pa'i-deb-ther*—or briefly *rGyal-ba-lṅa-pa'i-deb-ther*—sets several folios apart for the genealogy of the family of Hor-gshon-nu-bzaṅ-po.[114] Here he directly states that this Hor-mi-dbaṅ-bsod-nams-stobs-rgyal together with the treasure-finder Śes-rab-'od-zer brought out some xylograph editions (*par*) including the edition of *Padma-bka'-thaṅ*—or, as he calls it, *Śel-brag-gi-thaṅ-yig*, i.e. "Legends Found in Śel-brag".[115] Thus, *Editio princeps* of this text appeared not in the beginning of the 14th century, as assumed by B. Laufer, but in the end of the 16th century.

---

114. The genealogy of Hor gShon-nu-bzaṅ-po occupies fols. 92^b 6—97^b 2. Information on Hor-mi-dbaṅ-bsod-nams-stobs-rgyal is given on fol. 96^b 2-6. Fols. 96^a 5-96^b 1 give an account of his father, Hor-bsod-nams-dar-rgyas, and of the relations of the latter with the third Dalai Lama. A brief and extremly slip-shod exposition of this genealogy has been given by S. C. Das (see S. C. Das, *Contributions on* ..,—JASB, vol. L, 1881, pt. i, pp. 246-248). This exposition is not complete and ends abruptly with an account of bSod-nams-dar-rgyas and bSod-nams-stobs rgyal. Besides, the name of the latter is distorted. Instead of "Sodnamtobgyal" (as it should be according to the scheme of transliteration followed by him), S. C. Das writes "Sonamtarge", i. e. he wrongly repeats the name of his father. The genealogy ends with an account of the brothers and children of bSod-nams-stobs-rgyal—which S. C. Das totally omits.

    A more detailed account of the genealogy of Hor-gshon-nu-bzaṅ-po is available in the autobiography of the Fifth Dalai Lama (pt. i, fols. 11^a 5-20^a 6 ; see also *infra*). The father of the Fifth Dalai Lama, Hor bDud-'dul-rab-brtan, was a grandson to this Hor bSod-nams-ṣtobs-rgyal. In the autobiography of the Fifth Dalai Lama, the account of Hor bSod-nams-stobs-rgyal is available on fols. 18^b 5-19^a 5 and that of his father, Hor-bsod-nams-dar-rgyas, on fols. 18^a 4-18^b 4.

115. *rGyal-ba-lṅa-pa'i-deb-ther*, fol. 96^b 3-4. This title or a similar title *bKa'-thaṅ-śel-brag* is used by the Tibetans as a short conventional title for this work to distinguish it from its prose version,—which, in short, is called *bKa'-thaṅ-gser-phreṅ*. See, for instance, the list of books—compiled in Tibet at his instance—published by van Manen (J. van Manen, *A Contribution to the Bibliography of Tibet*,—JASB, new series, vol. xviii, 1922, pp. 479, 491). Unfortunately, van Manen did not understand the meaning of this conventional title and, therefore made an absolutely wrong translation : "Crystal Rock of Plain Words" (!).

The second edition was brought out in 1675[116] by the well-known scholar and political leader—the regent of Tibet, sDe-srid Saṅs-rgyas-rgya-mtsho (1653-1705). The colophon to this edition was written by the Fifth Dalai Lama[117] himself. Consecrated by the high authority of the latter, this edition became the basis for a number of other later editions.

The fact that Hor bSod-nams-stobs-rgyal published the *Padma-bka'-thaṅ* is repeated in the autobiography of the Fifth Dalai Lama (pt. i, fols. 18ᵇ 6-19ᵃ 1) ; in this case, however, the work figures under its own tittle : *Padma-bka'-thaṅ*.

116. Wood-Hare year. See the colophon in the *Padma-bka'-thaṅ*, fol. 256ᵃ 5 and B. Laufer, *Der Roman einer tibetischen Konigin*, S. 240. In Laufer's work—as already pointed out by P. Pelliot (see P. Pelliot, *Le cycle sexagenaire...*,—JA, 1913, t. i, p. 658) —this date has been wrongly shown as corresponding to A. D. 1674.

117. The colophon is quoted in full in the edition of the *Padma-bka'-thaṅ* (fols. 253ᵇ 1-256ᵇ 4) referred to above. Besides, it is included as a separate work in the Complete Works (*gsuṅ-'bum*) of the Fifth Dalai Lama published in the 'Bras-spuṅs monastery in Central Tibet. The xylographs of this edition of the Complete Works are available in the Institute of Peoples of Asia, Academy of Sciences, U.S.S.R., in the Tibetan books brought by G. Tsybikov (*Tsybikov Collection*, No. 6) and P. K. Kozlov (*Nova*). In the voluminous compilation, the colophon is available under the title *sKu-gsuṅ-thugs-rten-gsar-bsheṅs-rin-po-che'i-mchod-rdsas-khaṅ-bzaṅ-gi-dkar-chag-daṅ-tham-phud-deb-khrims-yig-gi-'go-rgyaṅs-sde-bshi'i-sgo-'phar-phye-ba'i-skal-bzaṅ-gi-glegs-bam*. The compilation contains, in chronological order, various small works of the Fifth Dalai Lama : prayers made at the time of installation of various objects of the cult and their description (*rgyab-yig* and *dkar-chag*), colophons to the editions of the texts (*par-byaṅ*), precepts (*khrims-yig*) etc. This compilation consists of three books (*glegs-bam*). The first book occupies the entire 16th (*ma*) volume of the Complete Works (312 folios), the second contains whole of the 17th (*tsa*) volume (308 folios) and the third—the first part of the 18th (*tsha*) volume (110 folios). The colophon referred to here is available in the 2nd book (17th volume), fols. 83ᵇ 3-86ᵇ 6.

In the prose part of the colophon of the Peking edition, as published by B. Laufer (see B. Laufer, *Der Roman einer tibetischen Konigin*, SS. 239-241), the first, second and third lines also literally reproduce the second prose part of the colophon of the Fifth Dalai Lama. Only the list of proof readers, engravers, etc. given in the end of the original is wanting. The translation

c) *Thaṅ-yig-gser-'phreṅ*

The full title of the prose version of the legend of Padmasambhava known under the title *Thaṅ-yig-gser-'phreṅ* ("Golden Rosary Tales") or *Thaṅ-yig-gser-'phreṅ thar-lam-gsal-byed* ("Golden Rosary Tales, Illuminating the Path to Salvation") is the same as that of the version in verse discussed by us—viz. *U-rgyan-gu-ru-padma-'byuṅ-gnas-*

---

made by B. Laufer is not correct. B. Laufer obviously did not know that the expression *par-byaṅ* was a technical term meaning "publisher's" or more correctly "xylograph" colophon as distinguished from the term *mdsad-byaṅ*, which means "author's" colophon. He also did not understand that the Fifth Dalai Lama and Za-hor-gyi-rigs-las-sṅags-pa-rgan-po-che mchog-'dus-pa-rtsal-padma-sa-miṅ-btags-rdo-rje-thogs-med-rtsal-du-'bod-pa mentioned in the colophon were one and the same person—the writer of the "publisher's colophon" to the edition of the *Padma-bka'-thaṅ* in the monastery of dGa'-ldan-phun-tshogs-gliṅ.

The fact is that the Fifth Dalai Lama, whose full name was Ṅag-dbaṅ bLo-bzaṅ-rgya-mtsho-'jigs-med-go-cha-thub-bstan-laṅ-'tsho [see, for instance, the colophon to his six-volume biography started by him, but finished by sDe-srid Saṅs-rgyas-rgya-mtsho, vol. vi (*cha*), fol. 377ᵃ 6 ; see also the colophon to the account of the Lhasa temple (*Lha-ldan-sprul-pa'i-gtsug-lag-khaṅ-gi-dkar-chag-śel-dkar-me-loṅ*), fol. 21ᵃ 5-6 etc.] also had a number of other names under which he very frequently wrote his numerous works—particularly the smaller ones. Thus, for example, in the compilation mentioned above, we come across his real name Ṅag-dbaṅ bLo-bzaṅ-rgya-mtsho (pt. ii, fols. 115ᵃ 1, 212ᵃ 2 etc.) and those names which he mentions in the colophon to the *Padma-bka'-thaṅ*, viz. Che-mchog-'dus-pa-rtsal (see pt. ii, fol. 117ᵃ 2—Za-hor-gyi-sṅags-'chaṅ-che-mchog-'dus-pa-rtsal) and rDo-rje-thogs-med-rtsal (see pt. iii, fol. 29ᵃ 6—Za-hor-gyi-sṅags-smyon-rdo-rje-thogs-med-rtsal) and various others like Za-hor-sṅags-smyon-zil-gdon-bshad-pa-rtsal (pt. iii, fol. 28ᵃ 2 etc.), Za-hor-gyi-bande-gdon-drug-bsñems-pa'i-laṅ-tsho (pt. i, fol. 286ᵇ 2), Za-hor-gyi-bande-'jam-dbyaṅs-dga'-ba'i-bśes-gñen (pt. i, fol. 125ᵃ 6 etc.) and Za-hor-gyi-bande-tshaṅs-sras-bshad-pa'i-rdo-rje (pt. ii, fol. 177ᵇ 6, 200ᵃ 5, 266ᵃ 4 etc.). Cf. also the colophon to the above-mentioned historical work of this author—*Gaṅs-can-yul-gyi-sa-la-spyod-pa'i-mtho-ris-kyi-rgyal-blon-gtso-bor-brjod-pa'i-deb-ther* (*rGyal-ba-lṅa-pa'i-deb-ther*, fol. 113ᵃ 2). But the name of the Fifth Dalai Lama is more frequently replaced by his nick-name Za-hor-bande (Vandya from Za-hor). The fact that the same person has so many names is explained by the custom, in Tibet, of adopting new names at the time of ordination into various systems of *tantra*-s etc. Of the additional names of the Fifth Dalai Lama given above, the first three names belong

kyi-skyes-rabs-rnam-thar-rgyas-par-bkod-pa.[118] We also come across this title in the head-lines of the text and in the titles of all its chapters. In addition to this Tibetan title, both the versions—in prose and in verse—bear the title "in Udyāna language". This title in the prose version is *Ru-aksa-śa-ka-ri-ni*, which is clearly identical with the analogous title of the version in verse. According to the colophon, this prose version was supposed to have been discovered in Pu-ri-phug-mo-che by the treasure-finder otherwise known as Saṅs-rgyas-gliṅ-pa.[119]

In the European scientific literature, this work is far less known than the previous one. Besides Waddell, who mentioned it in the sources of the *Legendary History of Founder of Lamaism*[120] compiled by him, this work was used by A. Grünwedel who, while publishing excerpts from the life of Padmasambhava written in Lepcha language, incidentally translated and published a few chapters from the *Thaṅ-yig-gser-'phreṅ.*[121]

---

to the category of tantric names, and the last three—to those adopted by persons studying Sanskrit grammar and poetics.

118. The xylograph of this work is available in the Institute of Peoples of Asia among the books brought by G. Tsybikov from Tibet (*Tsybikov Collection*, No. 62). This xylograph contains 365 folios and bears the title : *U-rgyan-gu-ru-padma-'byuṅ-gnas-kyi-rnam-thar-rgyas-pa-gser-gyi-phreṅ-ba-thar-lam-gsal-byed.* All later references in this work are to this edition of the *Thaṅ-yig-gser-'phreṅ.*

119. *Thaṅ-yig-gser-'phreṅ*, fol. 363ᵃ 1.

120. L. A. Waddell, *The Buddhism of Tibet* . , p. 379, n. 6 ff.

121. See A. Grünwedel, *Ein Kapitel des Ta-she-sung*, "Festschrift für Adolf Bastian", Berlin 1896, SS. 459-482, where chapter xviii (fols. 69ᵇ 3-72ᵃ 6 in the *Thaṅ-yig gser-'phreṅ* edition already referred to) and chapter xix (fols. 72ᵇ 1-73ᵃ 5) of this text have been published in Roman transcription. See also his : *Drei Leptscha Texte mit Auszugen aus dem Padma-thaṅ-yig und Glossar*,—"T'oung Pao", vol. vii, 1896, pp. 526-561, which contains Roman transcription of the text, along with translation, of chapter xliii (fols. 132ᵃ 4-133ᵃ 4 in the *Thaṅ-yig-gser-'phreṅ* edition referred to), last third of chapter xli (fols. 128ᵇ 2-129ᵇ 3) and a portion of chapter xliv (fols. 137ᵃ 1-137ᵇ 3), and *Buddhistische Studien. Excurs* ; *Das Supparadschataka in Padma-sambhava's Legendenbuch*,—"Veroffentlichungen aus dem koniglichen Museum für Volkerkunde", v Bd, Berlin 1897, SS. 105-126, which gives a translation and transcription of chapter xii (fols. 39ᵇ 4-44ᵃ 4) and of chapter xiii (fols. 44ᵃ 4-47ᵃ 4). Besides, A. Grünwedel has also used this text in his other works (see *Mythologie des Buddhismus in Tibet und der Mongolei*, Leipzig 1900, SS. 47, 99 u.s.w.; *Padmasambhava und Mandaravā*,—ZDMG., lii Bd., 1898, SS. 447-461 ; *Padmasambhava und Verwandtes*,—"Baessler-Archiv", iii Bd., 1 Heft, Leipzig und Berlin 1912.

In this connection, Grünwedel's assumption that this work which he often simply calls *Padma-thaṅ-yig* or *Padma-bka'-thaṅ* appeared at the time of Yüan dynasty (1280-1367) or still later[122] is not far from truth.

Without having on them the complete text of *Thaṅ-yig-gser-'phreṅ* and on the basis of the excerpts from it as published by A. Grünwedel, E. Schlagintweit and B. Laufer tried, however, to determine its relation to the version in verse and arrived at totally different results. E. Schlagintweit thinks that the prose text is a revised version of that in verse.[123] B. Laufer, on the other hand, opines that either the version in verse (i.e. *Padma-bka'-thaṅ*) sprang from the prose version (i.e. *Thaṅ-yig-gser-'phreṅ*) or, as seemed to him more probable, both the versions appeared independently—the prose one, however, earlier than the other.[124] In this case, Schlagintweit was found to be right. A careful comparison of both the texts shows that *Thaṅ-yig-gser-'phreṅ* indeed is a prose rendering of the versified *Padma-bka'-thaṅ*. It is true that after the twelfth chapter, this rendering does not observe the order of chapters as given in the versified text. Some chapters have been merged together into one, a few new chapters have been added and, to complicate the matters still further, the prose version has 117 chapters in place of 108 in the versified text. Despite these and other changes, however, the prose version still remains largely a re-narration—that too often totally literal, retaining the whole content, vocabulary and even its title and a great majority of chapter headings. B. Laufer's opinion that the prose text is older cannot be accepted simply because in the versified *Padma-bka'-thaṅ*, we do not find any indication to the existence of its prose version. In the latter, however, there is a direct reference to the text in verse. In *Thaṅ-yig-gser-'phreṅ*, just as in *Padma-bka'-thaṅ*, there is a special chapter which gives, as a "prophecy", the list of "treasure-finders" (*gter-ston*-s), indicating the places of their main finds.[125] The list given in *Padma-bka'-thaṅ* makes no mention of the treasure-finder Saṅs-rgyas-gliṅ-pa. The list in *Thaṅ-yig-gser-'phreṅ*, on the other hand, mentions Saṅs-rgyas-gliṅ-pa to whom the discovery of this text is attributed,[126] and also U-rgyan-gliṅ-pa to whom, as we know, the discovery of the versified text of *Padma-bka'-thaṅ* is attributed. It also names the place where the latter was discovered—Śel-brag.[127] It is interesting to note that this list, which has a chronological order, puts the name of Saṅs-rgyas-gliṅ-pa before that of U-rgyan-gliṅ-pa and even before Rin-chen-gliṅ-pa, the predecessor of the latter. But this should be

---

122. A. Grünwedel, *Drei Leptscha-Texte*,—"T'oung Pao", vol. vii, 1896, S. 529.
123. E. Schlagintweit, *Die Lebensbesehreibung von Padma Sambhava*,—"Abhandl. der K. bayer. Akademie der Wissenschaften", i. Cl., xxi Bd, ii Abt., München, 1899, SS. 420-421.
124. B. Laufer, *Der Roman einer tibetischen Konigin*, SS. 246-248.
125. *Thaṅ yig-gser-'phreṅ*, chapter lxxxix, fols. 284^{b} 5-290^{b} 2.
126. *Ibid.*, fol. 288^{b} 5-6.
127. *Ibid.*, fol. 289^{a} 1-3.

taken to be a subterfuge, by which the author of the latter prose version of the text tried to raise its authority, passing this adaptation for a work discovered earlier than its original in verse.

Being actually a later work than the *Padma-bka'-thaṅ*, this *Thaṅ-yig-gser-'phreṅ* just surveyed by us cannot date from earlier than the 14th century. On the other hand, in the middle of the 17th century, this work as well as *Padma-bka'-thaṅ* were used by the Fifth Dalai Lama who, in his *gsan-yig*, names a number of persons who have subsequently written commentaries on these texts.[128] The exact date of the appearance of *Thaṅ-yig-gser-'phreṅ*, therefore, lies between the 14th and 17th centuries.

d) *bKa'-thaṅ-sde-lṅa*

Apart from the works already mentioned, the name *thaṅ-yig* or *bka'-thaṅ* is also applied to another five texts, the discovery of which is attributed to the same U-rgyan-gliṅ-pa. These texts, which are well known in Tibet and elsewhere, are the so-called "Five Legends"—*Thaṅ-yig-sde-lṅa* or *bKa'-thaṅ-sde-lṅa*.[129] These five legends are : 1) "Legend of Gods and Demons"—*Lha-'dre-bka'i-thaṅ-yig* ; 2) "Legend of Kings"—*rGyal-po-bka'i-thaṅ-yig* ; 3) "Legend of Queens"—*bTsun-mo-bka'i-thaṅ-yig* ; 4) "Legend of Translators and Paṇḍita-s"—*Lo-paṇ-bka'i-thaṅ-yig* ; and 5) "Legend of Ministers —*bLon-po-bka'i-thaṅ-yig*. Of these, "Legend of Kings", "Legend of Ministers" and partly "Legend of Translators and Paṇḍita-s" have some historical value, though even in these only the legendary and didactic materials are predominant. The other two works, namely "Legend of Gods and Demons" and "Legend of Queens", are didactic narratives and have no historical value.

---

128. See *Thob-yig-gaṅgā'i-chu-rgyun*, vol. iii (*ga*), fols. 243ᵃ 1-243ᵇ 4 (which give information on the treasure-finder, U-rgyan-gliṅ-pa, and on the *Padma-bka'-thaṅ* "discovered" by him) and fols. 265ᵇ 4-266ᵃ 1 (giving information on *Thaṅ-yig-gser-'phreṅ* "discovered" by the treasure-finder, Saṅs-rgyas-gliṅ-pa). The data on other works "discovered" by these treasure-finders are also given at the same place.
129. As already mentioned, the Institute of Peoples of Asia (*Tsybikov Collection*, No. 51) has a xylograph copy of the "Five Legends" published in 1889 under the orders of the thirteenth Dalai Lama and De-mo-khutukhta in Shol-par-khaṅ in Lhasa (see the colophon of the last, viz. fifth "Legend"—*bLon-po-bka'i-thaṅ-yig*, fols. 76ᵇ 2-77ᵃ 5). This xylograph copy does not have any general title page. Each "Legend" has its own title page and separate pagination. Our references are to this edition.

In European literature, these works were taken up mainly by B. Laufer who published and translated "Legend of Queens" (*bTsun mo-bka'i-thaṅ-yig*) and gave general information on the other four texts.[130] Besides, Professor F. Thomas translated some excerpts (which were of interest for the history of Central Asia) from "Legend of Kings" (*rGyal-po-bka'i-thaṅ-yig*) and "Legend of Ministers" (*bLon-po-bka'i-thaṅ-yig*).[131]

We are already definite that one of these five works, viz. "Legend of Translators and Paṇḍita-s" (*Lo-paṇ-bka'i-thaṅ-yig*) did not appear earlier than A.D. 1393.[132] As regards the other four, though they appeared earlier than this work, for all of them are mentioned in it,[133] there are no grounds whatsoever to consider that they appeared earlier than the second half of the 14th century. B. Laufer's opinion that like the "Legend of Padma" (*Padma-bka'-thaṅ*), the "Five Legends" (*bKa'-thaṅ-sde-lṅa*) appeared between the 11th and the 12th centuries, is based on a false conception (already discussed by us above) of the date of "discovery" and first edition of *Padma bka'-thaṅ*, and cannot therefore be taken into consideration. It is true that Professor F. Thomas, who shared the opinion of B. Laufer to some extent, stated that the historical, geographical and personal details as given in the two texts studied by him—*rGyal-po-bka'i-thaṅ-yig* and *bLon-po-bka'i-thaṅ-yig*—were such as could not have been described accurately long after the Tibetan king Mu-tig-btsan-po (who was crowned in the 9th century A.D.) and that certain accounts in these "Legends" had been found to agree with the information of Tibetan documents of Central Asia.[134] This fact, however, can only testify that the author of these texts has used—and perhaps without any specific changes—some ancient sources, the originals of which have not come down to us. For, besides the information that is unquestionably ancient in nature, we find, in these texts, accounts of events, persons and places relating clearly to a later period. It is enough to point out that what is given in the *rGyal-po-bka'i-thaṅ-yig* under the pretext of "prophecies" is a reference to the king gLaṅ-dar-ma and his successors,[135] to the subsequent new spread of Buddhism in Tibet, to the founder of 'Bri-guṅ-pa sect—the famous Rin-chen-dpal (1143-1217),[136] better known by the title 'Bri-guṅ-skyob-pa-'jig-rten-mgon-po,[137] etc. In the *bLon-po-bka'i-thaṅ-yig* also, we find

130. B. Laufer, *Der Roman einer tibetischen Konigin.*
131. F. W. Thomas, *Tibetan Literary Texts*..., pt. i, pp. 264-288.
132. See *supra.*
133. *Lo-paṇ-bka'i-thaṅ-yig*, fols. 69ᵃ 2-3, 81ᵃ 1.
134. F. W. Thomas, *Tibetan Literary Texts*..., pt. i, pp. 264-265.
135. *rGyal-po-bka'i-thaṅ-yig*, fol. 82ᵃ 2-3.
136. *Ibid.*, fol. 82ᵇ 2-3.
137. In particular, he is referred to by this title of his in the "Chronological Tables". Biographical data on this eminent figure of Tibetan Buddhism can be found in brief in the *Deb-ther-sṅon-po* (vol. ii, fols. 16ᵃ 6-19ᵃ 1) and in a still more concise form in *Grub-mtha'-śel-gyi-me-loṅ* (book iv, *bKa'-brgyud-pa'i-grub-mtha'-byuṅ-tshul*, fols. 12ᵇ 3-13ᵃ 3).

similar prophecies on the successors of the king gLaṅ-dar-ma,[138] and on such celebrities of Tibetan Buddhism as 'Brog-mi-lo-tsā-ba (993-1074),[139] 'Brom-ston pa (1004-1065),[140] and Po-to-pa (1027-1105),[141] on the leaders of various monasteries Bya-yul-dgon-pa (established in 1113),[142] Tshal-gyi-dgon-pa (estd. 1175),[143] 'Bri-guṅ-dgon-pa (estd. 1179)[144] etc., on the great prince (*dpon-chen*) of the Sa-skya-pa dynasty—Byaṅ-rin[145]—who ruled in the end of the 13th century, etc. The presence in these texts, as also in the *Lo-paṇ-bka'i-thaṅ-yig* and *Padma-bka'-thaṅ*, of such later information, the statements of the colophons that all the "Five Legends" and "Legend of Padma" were discovered by the treasure-finder U-rgyan-gliṅ-pa who, as we have seen, worked in the second half of the 14th century, and finally the obvious unity of language and style of these six texts—all these facts taken together lead us to regard these works as belonging to the same author who may have lived in about the second half of the 14th century. The possibility that this author was the treasure-finder U-rgyan-gliṅ-pa himself is not ruled out.

Of all the apocryphal works connected with Padmasambhava, the works enumerated above are the most popular. There also exist other similar works, which we shall not discuss here, for we know of their existence only from individual citations and bibliographical references in the works of Tibetan writers.

---

138. *bLon-po-bka'i-thaṅ-yig*, fol. 57ª 3.
139. *Ibid.*, fol. 65ª 3. His dates are available in the "Chronological Tables".
140. *Ibid.*, fol. 59ª 6. The dates have been borrowed from the "Chronological Tables".
141. *Ibid.*, fol. 63ª 4. The dates are taken from the "Chronological Tables".
142. *Ibid.*, fol. 59ª 4. The date of establishment of the monastery is given in the "Chronological Tables".
143. *Ibid.*, fol. 29ª 2. This date of establishment of the monastery is given in the "Chronological Tables" and in the *Vaiḍūrya-dkar-po* (fol. 20ª 6). A. Csoma de Koros (see A. Csoma de Koros, *A Grammar of the Tibetan Language*, p. 185) wrongly dates this event—like all others—from A.D. 1173, viz. from two years earlier.
144. *bLon-po-bka'i-thaṅ-yig*, fol. 59ª 2, 6. The date of establishment of the monastery is taken from *Vaiḍūrya-dkar-po* (fol. 20ª 6). A. Csoma de Koros (see A. Csoma de Koros, *A Grammar of the Tibetan Language*, p. 185) wrongly gives this date as A.D. 1177.
145. *bLon-po-bka'i-thaṅ-yig*, fol. 58ª 6. In the *Deb-ther-sṅon-po*,—which gives a list of the great rulers (*dpon-chen*) of the Sa-skya monastery (vol. 1, fols. 112ª 2-113ª 3),—Byaṅ-rin is mentioned as the last ruler appointed on the personal notion of 'Phags-pa-bla-ma (1235-1280). It is also stated here that he earned the favour of the emperor Kublai (1260-1294)—see *Deb-ther-sṅon-po*, vol. 1, fol. 112ª 5-6. Byaṅ-rin has also been referred to by the Fifth Dalai Lama,

e) *Ma-ṇi-bka'-'bum*

Before we end this survey of the so-called "*gter-ma* books"—*gter-chos*—we must mention one more apocryphal work of this type, namely the *Ma-ṇi-bka'-'bum.* This monumental work is exceptionally popular in and outside Tibet.

In the European scientific literature, it was known already in the early 19th century. The credit for this goes to P. S. Pallas who published an account, compiled by the translator Erig, of the first few chapters of the first of the texts included in this work.[146] Enumerating the Tibetan historical texts,[147] Csoma de Koros also mentioned the *Ma-ṇi-bka'-'bum* along with other apocryphal works that we have just discussed. Since then, this work has long enjoyed, in European literature, the undeserved reputation of a historical work.[148] A short analysis of this work was reproduced by E. Schlagintweit[149] from the speech of a Buryat Lama Galsan Gomboev. This analysis, however, cannot be called fully successful, for it represents *Ma-ṇi-bka'-'bum* as one single work, whereas actually this monumental work is a collection of many separate works as is clear from its title itself (viz. *Ma-ṇi-bka'-'bum* or "Collection of the Works of Ma-ṇi" —or rather, *rGyal-po-sroṅ-btsan-sgam-po'i-'bum*, i. e. "Collection of the Works of

---

who gives a list of the rulers of Sa-skya dynasty (see *rGyal-ba-lṅa-pa'i-deb-ther*, fol. 60b 2) in his historical work *Gaṅs-can-yul-gyi-sa-la-spyod-pa'i-mtho-ris-kyi-rgyal-blon-gtso-bor-brjod-pa'i-deb-ther.* Sarat Chandra Das, in the third section of his article (see S. C. Das, *Contributions on...*,—JASB, vol. L, 1881, pp. 211-251)—which mainly is an incomplete and slip-shod exposition of this work—has distorted the name of this ruler. The Tibetan expression *bskos-pa*, —which, in the Tibetan text, stands after the name Byaṅ-rin and means "Elevated",—has been wrongly read by S. C. Das as *bskyos-pa* (see pp. 240-241) with the result that the name of this ruler appears to be Chyan-rin bskyos-pa (!). Nevertheless, the Tibetan text of the work of the Fifth Dalai Lama simply reads : *De-rjes-byaṅ-rin-bskos-pa...*, i.e. "Byaṅ-rin, Elevated (to the rank of the ruler) after him" etc. (see *rGyal-ba-lṅa-pa'i-deb-ther*, fol. 60b 1-2). This ruler is also mentioned by Sum-pa-mkhan-po Ye-śes-dpal-'byor —see *dPag-bsam-ljon-bzaṅ*, fol. 103a 2,4 (S. C. Das, *Pag Sam Jon Zang*, p. 159).

146. See P. S. Pallas, *Sammlungen historischer Nachrichten über die Mongolischen Volkerschaften*, II Theil, St. Petersburg 1801, S S. 396-409.
147. A. Csoma de Koros, *Enumeration of Historical and Grammatical works to be met with in Tibet*,—JASB, vol. vii, 1838, p. 148.
148. See, for instance, E. Schlagintweit, *Buddhism in Tibet*, London 1863, p. 83 ; L. A. Waddell, *The Buddhism of Tibet*, p. x ; F. W. Thomas, *Notes on the Tibetan Collections of the India Office Library*, p. 10.
149. E. Schlagintweit, *Buddhism in Tibet*, pp. 84-88.

the King Sroṅ-btsan-sgam-po".[150] The division of *Ma-ṇi-bka'-'bum* into twelve chapters, as given by E. Schlagintweit, is due to the fact that he has not seen the text itself. What he had on him was only a brief description of this collection given by Lama Gomboev, apparently on the basis of a Mongolian translation in which the whole material of the collection is grouped in eleven separate books.[151]

There exist several editions of this work. So far as I can judge, they are distinguished from each other mainly in their arrangement and in the number of works included in them. Among the various manuscripts and xylograph copies of *Ma-ṇi-bka'-'bum* available in the collections of the Institute of Peoples of Asia, Academy of Sciences, U. S. S. R., the text published in 'Bras-spuṅs monastery and brought from Tibet by G. Tsybikov[152] is the most complete. This text is in two volumes, each of which has separate pagination. The first volume is in 377 folios ; the second has 331 folios of the usual Tibetaṅ format. It also has a Table of Contents in the form of a separate book of 11 folios, which gives the classification of works included in the *Ma-ṇi-bka'-'bum.* This Table of Contents is reproduced in full even in other editions of the *Ma-ṇi-bka'-'bum* known to me.[153]

According to this Table of Contents, the whole *Ma-ṇi-bka'-'bum* falls into three sections (*skor*), namely : 1. *mdo-skor,* i.e. "Section of *Sūtra*-s" ; 2. *sgrub-skor,* i.e. "Section of Magical Accomplishments (*sādhana*)" ; and 3. *shal-gdams-kyi-skor,* i.e. "Section of Personal Precepts".[154]

In the first place, the "Section of *Sūtra*-s" contains the work entitled *Lo-rgyus-chen-mo,* i.e. "Great Chronicle". This work consists of 36 chapters and covers 81 folios

---

150. This latter title appears on the title page of the second volume of this work and on the title page of the table of contents.
151. See *infra.*
152. *Tsybikov Collection,* No. 36. Other copies of this work available in the Institute of Peoples of Asia are : Vol. 1 in the Kokonor edition (*Collection of Asiatic Department,* No. 503), 324 folios ; Volume 2 in the Peking (*Nova,* No. B, 1325) and sDe-dge (Inv. 1914, No. 25) editions. The Peking edition has 229 folios. In the copy of the sDe-dge edition, many folios are wanting. These apart, a number of manuscripts of this text is available (see I. J. Schmidt und O. Bohtlingk, *Verzeichniss der tibetischen Handschriften und Holzdrücke im Asiatischen Museum,* 291-295).
153. See the xylograph of Kokonor edition mentioned in the previous note and the editions of Mongolian translation of this work mentioned *infra* in notes 163-167.
154. *Ma-ṇi-bka'-'bum,* 'Bras-spuṅs edition, table of contents (*dkar-chag*), fol. 5 1 ff.

of the first volume of this edition. It deals with the legends on the life and exploits of the Bodhisattva Avalokiteśvara and Buddha Śākyamuni. A summary of the first eight chapters of this work and the beginning of the tenth chapter—published by Pallas[155]—was made by the translator Erig apparently on the basis of a Mongolian translation of the Tibetan text.[156] Besides, the second, third and fourth chapters and the first two-thirds of the thirty-fourth chapter of this work were excellently translated direct from Tibetan by W. Rockhill.[157]

This work is followed by *'Phags-pa-za-ma-tog-bkod-pa-shes-bya-ba-theg-pa-chen-po'i-mdo* (vol. 1, fols. 82ᵃ 1-140ᵇ 4), which is a translation of the Sanskrit text *Kāraṇḍa-vyūhasūtra* ;[158] and *Phyag-stoṅ-spyan-stoṅ-gi-gzuṅs* (vol. 1, fols. 140ᵇ 4-185ᵃ 5), the full title of which is *'Phags-pa-byaṅ-chub-sems-dpa'-spyan-ras-gzigs-dbaṅ-phyug-phyag-stoṅ-spyan-stoṅ-daṅ-ldan-pa-thogs-pa-mi-mṅa'-pa'i-thugs-rje-chen-po'r-sems-rgya-chen-yoṅs-su-rdsogs-pa-shes-bya-ba'i-gzuṅs*. The latter is a translation from Chinese.[159] Both these texts literally reproduce works bearing the same titles in *bKa'-'gyur* ; this is why they are dropped from some editions of *Ma-ṇi-bka'-'bum* and are only referred to the respective chapters in *bKa'-'gyur*.[160] These texts have absolutely no connection with the king Sroṅ-btsan-sgam-po. Their inclusion in the *Ma-ṇi-bka'-'bum* can be explained only by the fact that its compilers did not consider it possible to leave this collection, specially devoted to the cult of Avalokiteśvara and his *avatāra*-s, without these two main canonical texts of the cult of Avalokiteśvara.

The three works enumerated above are regarded as the main content of the "Section of *Sūtra*-s". But in some editions, including the one being surveyed by us, the "Section of *Sūtra*-s" also contains some more works which together comprise a special

155. P. S. Pallas, *Sammlungen historischer Nachrichten* . , vol. ii, SS. 396-407.
156. Erig's exposition corresponds to fols. 1-13ᵃ 2 of the 'Bras-spuṅs edition of the Tibetan text of *Ma-ṇi-bka'-'bum*. It stops at the very beginning of the account of the eighth deed of Buddha. The fact that the proper names in this exposition are given in Mongolian version shows that Erig's source was the Mongolian text and not the Tibetan one.
157. W. W. Rockhill, *The Land of the Lamas*, London 1891, pp. 327-334 (translation of the 2nd, 3rd and 4th chapters, corresponding to fols. 3ᵃ 1-8ᵃ 3 of the Tibetan text of 'Bras-spuṅs edition) and pp. 355-360 (translation of the first two-thirds of chapter 34, fols. 59ᵇ 3-63ᵇ 4 of the Tibetan text).
158. *bKa'-'gyur*, mDo-sde, vol. vii (*na*), fols. 200ᵃ 3-247ᵇ 7.
159. *Ibid.*, rGyud-'bum, vol. xvii (*tsa*), fols. 94ᵃ 1-129ᵇ 6 and gZuṅs-'dus, vol. cxx (*e*), fols. 168ᵃ 6-205ᵃ 5. Cf. B. Nanjio, *A Catalogue of the Chinese Translation of the Buddhist Tripiṭaka*, Oxford 1883, N 318, 319, 320.
160. See *supra* note 152 (Kokonor edition) and all the editions of the Mongolian translation of this work enumerated *infra* (note 206).

"Section of Biographies of the King Sroṅ-btsan-sgam-po" (*Chos-skyoṅ-ba'i-rgyal-po-sroṅ-btsan-sgam-po'i-mdsad-pa-rnam-thar-gyi-skor*).[161] Here, the first biography is that of the king Sroṅ-btsan-sgam-po—though a short one, in sixteen chapters only—bearing the title *Saṅs-rgyas-śā-kya-thub-pa'i-bstan-pa-la-mdsad-pa'i-lo-rgyus* (vol. 1, fols. 185b 2-222b 5). Then follow ten *jātakas* of this king under the general title *Saṅs-rgyas-gshan-gyi-bstan-pa-la-mdsad-pa'i-lo-rgyus* (vol. 1, fols. 222b 5-247b 2), the story of the prince Lokeśvara—*rGyal-bu-'jig-rten-dbaṅ-phyug-gi-skyes-rabs* (vol. 1, fols. 247b 2-261b 6)—which is a highly enlarged version of the first of the ten *jātakas* mentioned ; and finally a biography of the king Sroṅ-btsan-sgam-po under the title *rGyal-po'i-mdsad pa-ñi-śu-rtsa-gcig-pa*, i.e. "*Twenty-One Deeds of the King*" (vol. 1, fols. 261b 6-286a 1). These additional works are, by no means, available in all the editions of *Ma-ṇi-bka'-'bum*. In particular, in the Mongolian translation of this work, only one of them, namely "The Story of the Prince Lokeśvara" is available.

The second section of the *Ma-ṇi-bka'-'bum*, viz. "Section of Magical Accomplishments" (*sgrub-skor*), as the name itself shows, comprises special works *sgrub-thabs* (in Sanskrit, *sādhana*) intended to serve as a guide for calling in oneself or before oneself the image of Avalokiteśvara. They cover the last 92 folios of the first volume of the edition being surveyed here (fols. 286-377).

The third section or "Section of Personal Precepts" (*shal-gdam-sa-kyi-skor*) contains a number of precepts and sermons on a wide range of subjects and covers the whole second volume of the xylograph. The sermons are given by the king Sroṅ-btsan-sgam-po and addressed to various persons. They end up with the dying will of this king to all the Tibetan people—*Bod-'baṅs-spyi-mthun-la-gdams-pa* (vol. ii., fols. 309b 2-330b 1).

Ma-ṇi-bka'-'bum also contains much interesting material from the point of view of studies in literature and folklore. Its fairly frequent deviations from the dominant views of Tibetan Buddhism are of great interest. As a historical source, however, it is of absolutely no value and cannot be classed under historical works. As regards the date of compilation of *Ma-ṇi-bka'-'bum*, I have no grounds to disagree with Rockhill who dated this collection to the 15th century.[162]

Ma-ṇi-bka'-'bum was translated into Mongolian in 1644[163] by the well-known

161. See *Ma-ṇi-bka'-'bum*, vol. i, fol. 185a 5.

162. W. W. Rockhill, *The Land of the Lamas*, p. 327. Also see his *The Life of the Buddha*, pp. 212-213, where he quotes V. P. Vasil'ev's opinion on the dating of *Ma-ṇi-bka'-'bum*.

163. According to the colophon, this translation was started in Water-Sheep year and completed in Iron-Monkey year. Since Dsa-ya-paṇḍita was born in 1599

Oirat scholar Dsa-ya-paṇḍita (1599-1662).[164] The Institute of Peoples of Asia has three different xylographs of this translation, of which one was published in 1712,[165] another—in 1717,[166] and the third—in 1735.[167] As already stated, the Mongolian translation consists of 11 separate books, each having separate pagination. The first book contains the translation of "Great Chronicle", the second and third—"Section of Magical Accomplishments"; the next five books from the fourth to the eighth—"Section of Personal Precepts"; the ninth book—"Story of the Prince Lokeśvara"; the tenth—"The Dying Will to all the Tibetan People"; and the eleventh—the Table of Contents.

As I have already pointed out, Tibetan authors themselves have the tendency of being sceptical of the authenticity of "*gter-ma* books" described above. At the most they are inclined to trust the antiquity of such texts as *Padma-bka'-thaṅ* and *bKa'-thaṅ-sde-lṅa*, but in these texts too, they suspect later additions. As regards the *Ma-ṇi-bka'-'bum*, it is obvious that the Tibetan authors treat it with indifference.

In his small but highly interesting critical and bibliographical work *gSuṅ-rab-rnam-dag-chu'i-dri-ma-sel-byed-nor-bu-ke-ta-ka*, written in 1782,[168] Sum-pa-mkhan-po Ye-śes-dpal-'byor devotes a special section to a survey of "various (texts), falsely attributed to the teacher Padma from Udayāna".[169] Here, he literally says[170]: "We

---

and died in 1662, the former of the two dates mentioned in the colophon can correspond only to A. D. 1643. As regards the date of completion, it is obvious that the "Iron-Monkey year" should be read as "Wood-Monkey year", which corresponds to A. D. 1644. During the life-time of Dsa-ya-paṇḍita, the "Iron-Monkey year" occurred only once, and this corresponded to A. D. 1620. K. F. Golstunsky also mentions that the translation of *Ma-ṇi-bka'-'bum* was made by Dsa-ya-paṇḍita in 1644.

164. The dates of birth and death of Dsa-ya-paṇḍita along with a short biography of his have been given by K. F. Golstunsky (*ibid.*, pp. 121-130).

165. Mong. Xyl. K 8.

166. Mong. Xyl. K 9.

167. Mong. Xyl. J. 85.

168. The date of compilation of this work of Sum-pa-mkhan-po—Water-Tiger year, the 79th (wrongly put as 80th in the text) year of life of the author—is mentioned in the colophon (fol. 13^b 6). This work comprises the fourth volume (*na*) of the Complete Works of Sum-pa-mkhan-po Yes-śes-dpal-'byor and covers 13 folios of large format.

169. *sLob-dpon-u-rgyan-padma-la-rdsun-khag-bkal-ba-sna-tshogs* (fol. 11^a 1).

170. Bod-kyi-bsam-yas- lha-khaṅ- thog-mar- bsheṅs-skabs- su- byon-pa'i-grub- chen-padma-sambha-vas-gaṅs- can-du-bstan-bcos-maṅ-po-brtsams-pa'i-gtam-mi-snaṅ-yaṅ. Padma-thaṅ-yig-daṅ-thaṅ-yig-sde-lṅa-shes-pa-de'i-dus-su-byuṅ-na-yan-deṅ-saṅ-gi-de-la-ltad-shugs-ma-shugs-sos-ñi-mchis. gshan-ma-ṇi-bka' - 'bum - daṅ

have no information that the great Yogī Padmasambhava, who arrived at the time of building up of bSam-yas monastery—the first in Tibet—compiled many treatises in this land of snow. Though the *Padma-thaṅ-yig* and *Thaṅ-yig-sde-lṅa* were also compiled during his period, it is doubtful if there are no interpolations in them. As regards the other works, for instance *Ma-ṇi-bka'-'bum*, *Bar-do-thos-grol* and texts included in the *gZuṅs-'dus—Nis-pa-kun-sel*, *rNa-sgra*, and *Nan-sṅags-phyir-zlog-'khor-lo*—already mentioned[171] and other similar numerous old books which are now used in Tibet, one can easily understand even from the very first words that they have not been compiled by those [authors, to whom they are attributed]. Any learned and sensible person who looks on them will easily understand that these old books later attributed to Padma from Udyāna, and other books known as "sealed" and "treasured" were compiled by a personal survey by various foolish persons by adding some terms accepted in the Buddhist texts". In his earlier work on the history of Buddhism in India, China (including Tibet) and Mongolia, about which we have mentioned above, the same author gives a number of propositions illustrating canonical and partly historical unfoundedness of the *Padma-thaṅ-yig*, *bKa'-thaṅ-sde-lṅa* and *Ma-ṇi-bka'-'bum*. He also names many authors who had earlier commented on these obviously apocryphal works.[172]

These very works were the first to be known to European scholarship—and those too as historical works of Tibet. This is why an extremely pessimistic outlook developed on Tibetan literature in general and historical literature of Tibet in particular, which unfortunately was long enough known to a number of European scholars.[173]

Bar-do-thos-grol-shes-pa-daṅ Goṅ-smos-gzuṇs-'dus-na-yod- pa'i-ñis- pa-kun- sel rÑa-sgra Ñan-sṅags-phyir-zlog-'khor-lo-sogs-gaṅs-can-du-khyab-pa'i-deṅ-saṅ-gi-rñiṅ-chos-du-ma'ṅ-de-dag-gis-brtsams-pa-min-par-tshig-gi-zur-yan-chad-kyis-kyaṅ-śes-sla-la rÑiṅ-chos-de-dag-phyis-su-u-rgyan-padma'i-mtshan-'chaṅ-ba-daṅ-gshan-bka'-ma-gter-par-grags-pa-sñiṅ-kham-can-du-mas-rgyal-gsuṅ-gi-tshig-'ga'-re-bsres-nas-gaṅ-'dod-du-sbyar-bar-śes-rig-daṅ-ldan-pa-su-mthoṅ-yaṅ-śes-sla'o (*ibid.*, fol. 11ª 1-4).

171. *Ibid.*, fols. 6ª 6-7ª 3.
172. *dPag-bsam-ljon-bzaṅ*, fols. 249ᵇ 2-250ᵇ 3 (S. C. Das, *Pag Sam Jon Zang*, p. 394, 1.20—p. 396, 1.2).
173. Cf. C. F. Koeppen, *Die lamaische Hierarchie und Kirche*, Berlin 1859, SS. 278, 283; L. A. Waddell, *The Buddhism of Tibet*, pp. x, 157, 166-167; L. A. Waddell, *Ancient Historical Edicts at Lhasa*,—JRAS, 1909, pp. 923-924 etc.

Chapter Three

MAIN TYPES OF TIBETAN HISTORICAL LITERATURE

1. General Remarks

Tibetan historical literature of the past is marked by all the characteristics and shortcomings inherent in feudal historiography. Its first and foremost defect is its sharply expressed religious and clerical character. Tibetan historical literature is not only the literature of the dominant feudal class ; it is the literature created by Tibetan Lamas, the eminent representatives of Tibetan Buddhism.

In the process of historical development of feudalism in Tibet, the ecclesiastical feudals (the Lamas), aided by the Mongolian and particularly Manchurian dynasties of China, which found it expedient to weaken the secular hereditary rulers of Tibet, have long had an upper hand in their century-old struggle against the secular feudals. This is why the state structure of Tibet acquired distinctive theocratic features. The supreme power and the main riches of the Tibetan lands were concentrated in the hands of Lamas and Buddhist monasteries. Everything—education, science, philosophy and art — was in their hands. It is therefore quite natural that the Tibetan historical works, written largely by the members of Buddhist Order who had a monopoly of literacy and education, are ecclesiastical in character.

The Tibetan historiographers are interested not so much in the political history of Tibet as in the history of Buddhist Order. The history of Tibet and other countries was regarded by them primarily as that of the spread of Buddhism in these countries ; the latter therefore usually dominates the accounts of the general political history in Tibetan historical literature. Thus the historical works themselves are often written with the obvious intention of assisting the Buddhist religion to become more glorious and widespread. In no other historiography whatever, do we find so sharp and outspoken clerical tendencies in spite of the fact that the religious stamp generally is a fairly normal phenomenon in feudal literature, including the feudal historiography of various peoples. And this doubtless is the biggest defect of Tibetan historical literature.

In describing the past, especially far remote periods, Tibetan historians cannot always distinguish facts from myths—what is historical from what is legendary—and often mix one with the other. This is mainly observed in the works of Tibetan writers on ancient India, on the initial period of history of Tibet and on the life and exploits of more ancient and honoured teaehers of Buddhism.

Despite the fact that in drawing their conclusions about the historical past, Tibetan authors of the later historical works, as a rule, lean upon a careful study and comparison of earlier sources, the references to these sources are generally not given. Tibetan authors freely use the works of their predecessors and often literally reproduce whole extracts from them. But in such cases, they either do not usually indicate the sources of their information or give a most general list of the sources—which is far from exhaustive—in the introductions or conclusions of their works. Such works of the predecessors, with which an author does not agree, are mentioned somewhat more frequently. But in these cases also, the names of the authors with whom they are not in agreement or those of the titles of their works are not given even in short ; they are instead frequently substituted by the vague expression "some" (*kha-cig*).

There also exist many other lesser and more general defects of Tibetan historical works.

All this, however, does not deprive Tibetan historiography of its scientific value, though its marked weakness for the history of Buddhism and often inadequate attention to "civil" history make it inferior to Arabic and Chinese historiography, for instance. This nonetheless does not prevent it from being a very important and authoritative source in its field. Tibetan historical literature is a basic and most important source for the history of Tibet, for we have no real historical acts—inscriptions and archival documents—at our disposal.[174] Besides, Tibetan historical works are, as a rule, formulated on the basis of a fairly conscious study of earlier written monuments, reliable oral traditions and personal observations of authors and their contemporaries. Thus,

174. The inscriptions available in Ladakh in Western Tibet are comparatively well studied. A. Francke who undoubtedly has rendered a great service to the study of history of Western Tibet (see his works mentioned *supra*, note 4) was able to collect and publish a fairly large number of inscriptions available in this country. Of the inscriptions available in Tibet itself, only a few ancient inscriptions available in Lhasa are so far known to us. See S. W. Bushell, *The Early History of Tibet. From Chinese Sources. Appendix I* (with facsimiles and restoration),—JRAS, 1880, pp. 535-538 ; L. A. Waddell, *Ancient Historical Edicts at Lhasa*,—JRAS, 1909, pp. 923-952 ; JRAS, 1910, pp. 1247-1282 ; JRAS, 1911, pp. 389-435 ; A. H. Francke, *Tibetan Inscription on the Stone Monument in front of the Tao-chao-ssu Temple in Lhasa*, 822 A.D.—"Epigraphia Indica", vol. x, 1909, 1910, pt. iv, pp. 89-93; A. H. Francke, *List of Ministers' Names Found in the Tibetan Inscription in front of the Tao-chao-ssu Temple* (*Jo-khang*) *in Lhasa*, 822 A.D.—"Epigraphia Indica", vol. xi, 1912, pt. vi, pp. 272-276. In the field of study of Tibetan documents, a great service has been rendered by Professor F. Thomas who published a number of ancient Tibetan documents found in Sinkiang (see *supra*, note 7).

Tibetan historical literature alone can give an idea of the general course of events of the history of Tibet. As our experience tells us, the works of Tibetan authors are also an important and authoritative source for the history of other countries, particularly for the history of spread of Buddhism in them.

Coming to a survey of various types of Tibetan historical works, we must state beforehand that it is fairly difficult to draw a clear line of demarcation between them. These different types of Tibetan historical texts are so contiguous to each other that sometimes it becomes almost impossible to decide as to under which division a particular work should be classed.

Nevertheless, it is possible to have a classification of Tibetan historical literature. And this has to be done to facilitate a survey and study of exceptionally large number of really diverse texts.

Tibetan writers themselves have no complete, finished and elaborate classification of historical works. However, they realize the difference between their various types perfectly well, and use special more or less firmly established terms for denoting these types. This makes it possible for us not only to have a natural classification established by practice itself but also to use the terminology introduced in practice.

The main types of Tibetan historical works are: chronicles (*lo-rgyus*-s); various types of genealogical works (the so-called *rgyal-rabs*-s, *jo-rabs*-s, and *gduṅ-rabs*-s) and allied histories of the Heads (*gdan-rabs*-s) and Incarnations (*'khruṅs-rabs*-s); chronological treatises (*bstan-rtsis*-s); and finally works of combined nature devoted to an exposition of history of religion, philosophy and partly scholastic science (*chos-'byuṅ*-s). Besides, various other types of works are also classed under historical literature: the vast biographical literature and memoirs (*rnam-thar*-s, *thob-yig*-s, *them-yig*-s, etc.), historico-bibliographical and historico-geographical accounts (*dkar-chag*-s, *gnas-bśad*-s, etc.) and various historical narrations (*lo-rgyus*-s) and legends (*gtam-rgyud*-s) about individual events and persons.

We shall now give a brief description of these types, though it may be remarked that our object here is not to compile an exhaustive list of Tibetan historical texts.

2. *Chronicles* (*Lo-rgyus*-s)

The earliest form of a historical work in Tibet, as in many other countries, was probably a "chronicle" (*lo-rgyus*), i.e. an year-wise exposition of events. The extracts from the earliest Tibetan chronicles—discovered by A. Stein and Professor P. Pelliot in Tun-Huang[175]—published by Professor F. Thomas are exactly of the nature of such

175. F. W. Thomas, *Tibetan Documents Concerning Chinese Turkestan*,—JRAS, 1927, pp. 51-66.

annual record. However, this form did not apparently become widely popular in Tibet. The very name *lo-rgyus*—though it can be translated literally as "chronicle"—has long been certainly dissociated from the year-wise exposition of events, and is used instead for denoting any historical work and, more broadly, any narration in general. It is, of course, possible that somewhere in Tibet, there exist chronicles in their real form too. But these have not come down to us ; and nothing is mentioned of them in the Tibetan historical literature known to us.

Such works giving an year-wise account of historical events appeared again in the 18th century, but these works are distinguished by their special tabular form. They have their own special history and are designated quite differently. But more of these works (they are called *bstan-rtsis*-s i.e. "chronologies of the doctrine") later.[176]

3. *Genealogical Historical Works—Dynastic and Family Chronicles* (*rGyal-rabs*-s, *Jo-rabs*-s, *gDuṅ-rabs*-s)

One of the earliest and most "secular" forms of Tibetan historical works is the so-called "Royal genealogies"—*rgyal-rabs*-s.

In more ancient and primitive form preserved right up to the recent times, these works are simple genealogical lists of kings, sometimes supplemented with historical dates. These apart, there exists another and more developed form of such works, namely, brief dynastic chronicle which narrates—with or without the exact historical date—various events celebrating the reign of some king or the other. An example of such dynastic chronicle is *Ladakh Chronicle* (*La-dwags-rgyal-rabs*), which was first published by E. Schlagintweit.[177] Some parts of it concerning the history of Ladakh proper were re-published, with considerable additions and corrections, by Marx[178] on the basis of other three manuscripts. Again, recently, it has been brought out in full by A. Francke, who has published the text very accurately by collating five different manuscripts.[179] The main part of this chronicle apparently appeared in the first half

176. See *infra*.

177. E. Schlagintweit, *Die Konige von Tibet...*, SS. 797-879 (the Tibetan text is given separately in the form of an appendix in 19 pages).

178. K. Marx, *Three Documents Relating to the History of Ladakh*,—JASB, vol. lx, 1891, pt. i, N 3, pp. 97-135 ; JASB, vol. lxiii, 1894, pt. i, N 2, pp. 94-107 ; JASB, vol. lxxi, 1902, pt. i, N 1, pp. 21-34. The author of the latter part of the translation is Theodora A. Francke.

179. A. H. Francke, *Antiquities of Indian Tibet.* Part ii : *The Chronicles of Ladakh and Minor Chronicles. Texts and Translations With Notes and Maps*, Calcutta, 1926 (*Archaeological Survey of India, New Imperial Series*, Vol. L).

of the 17th century. It was then continued at different times and completed by the end of the 19th century.[180]

As rightly remarked by A. Francke, the *Ladakh Chronicle* published by him has a fairly large number of features, which are similar to Indian genealogies—the so-called *Vaṃśāvalī*-s. This fact even made him suggest that the Indian *Vaṃśāvalī* had served as a model for early historians of Tibet.[181] This suggestion, however, has to be checked again. Tibetan *rgyal-rabs*-s—and particularly the *Ladakh Chronicles*—are known to us in the form of works of comparatively later period ; their similarities with Indian genealogies, therefore, cannot always testify to the presence of such similarities in the earliest texts too, which have not reached us in original. Besides, the genealogies of various peoples generally are so closely similar outwardly that any conclusion about imitations and adoptions should be regarded with utmost caution. Of course, Tibetan historiography did not develop in isolation. Like the entire Tibetan culture, it was formed under the most powerful influence of two great cultures—the Indian and Chinese.

---

180. As remarked by A. Francke (*ibid.*, pp. 3-6, 10-11), the three main copies of the *Ladakh Chronicle*—namely, the copy of E. Schlagintweit (S Ms.), which is a copy of the manuscript belonging to the previous king of Ladakh, 'Jigs-med-rnam-rgyal, the copy of Marx (A Ms.) and the copy of the British Museum (L Ms.)—basically agree with each other and give an exposition of the events up to the reign of Seṅ-ge-rnam-rgyal (inclusive), i.e. up to the twenties of the 17th century. The lists of the subsequent rulers of Ladakh available in the end of copy of E. Schlagintweit and in that of the British Museum appear to be later additions. The fourth copy (B Ms.) expounds the history of the whole of the second dynasty of Ladakh—the rNam-rgyal dynasty. The first part of this copy (which expounds the history upto Seṅ-ge-rnam-rgyal), according to Marx (JASB, vol. lx, 1891, p. 100), almost entirely agrees with the corresponding part of the copy of Marx (A Ms.) mentioned above. Lastly, the fifth copy (C Ms.) contains, in its first part, an exposition of the whole *Ladakh Chronicle* from the most ancient times to war with Sikhs and the fall of the second Ladakh dynasty, as compiled by Munshi (Mun-śi) dPal-rgyas in the end of the 19th century. The second part of this copy gives an account of the history of war with Sikhs and was written by him at the instance of Marx himself. Mun-śi dPal-rgyas has also given an exposition of the later history of Ladakh upto A.D. 1886 and the chronological and tax tables (compiled by him in 1910)—see A. H. Francke, *Antiquities of Indian Tibet*, pt. ii, pp. 11, 53-59, 137-148.

181. A. H. Francke, *Antiquities of Indian Tibet*, pt. ii, p. 7.

However, the great influence that the Indian and partly Chinese ideas had on Tibetan historical literature does not eliminate the possibility of independent appearance of such primitive historical works as the genealogies. The origin of Tibetan *rgyal-rabs*-s is lost in the remote past of Tibetan history. At present, we are not in a position to assign their initial appearance to some specific date. We can only assume that such works were already there during the time of the king Khri-sroṅ-lde'u-btsan (8th century) and his nearest successors. This is obvious from the very title of *rGyal-rabs sBa-bshed*, one of the earliest Tibetan historical texts, about which we have said above.[182] As already mentioned, this text has not come down to us. However, from the writings of the later Tibetan historians, we can conclude that it was a complex work in which the genealogy of Tibetan kings (i.e. *rgyal-rabs* in proper sense of this word) was combined with a description and history of the building up of bSam-yas monastery and an account of the career of Padmasambhava[183] etc. Chronological dates of individual persons and events[184] were also given there.

The earliest "Royal genealogy" of Tibet (*rgyal-rabs*), of which I could have first-hand-knowledge has a simple title—"Genealogy of the Kings of Tibet" (*Bod-kyi-rgyal-rabs*) and belongs to Grags-pa-rgyal-mtshan (1147-1216), the third great scholar from the remarkable family of 'Khon dKon-mchog-rgyal mtshan (1034-1102), the founder and chief of Sa-skya monastery (founded in 1073).[185] This text is available among other works of the same author in "Complete Works of Five Scholars from Sa-skya" (*Sa-skya-bka'-'bum*) published in sDe-dge[186] and covers a little more than three hundred

---

182. See *supra*, Chapter 1.
183. See *dPag-bsam-ljon-bzaṅ*, fols. 101ᵃ 5-6, 242ᵃ 6ff. (S. C. Das, *Pag Sam Jon Zang*, pp. 155-156, 383).
184. See *supra*.
185. The dates given in the text are taken from the "Chronological Tables". S. C. Das has wrongly advanced all these dates by one year (see S. C. Das, *Life of Sumpa Khanpo*,—JASB, vol. lviii, 1889, pt. i, p. 40ff).
186. "The full collection of works of scholars from Sa-skya" (*Sa-skya-bka'-'bum*) consists of 15 volumes of usual Tibetan long format. The first two volumes (*ka*—428 folios ; *kha*—419 folios) contain the works of Sa-chen Kun dga'-sñiṅ-po (1092-1158). The next three volumes (*ga*—377 folios ; *ṅa*—326 folios ; and *ca*—335 folios) contain works of his son bSod-nams-rtse-mo (1142-1182). The four volumes thereafter (*cha*—350 folios ; *ja*—376 folios ; *ña*—400 folios ; and *ta*—401 folios) contain works of another son of his, Grags-pa-rgyal-mtshan (1147-1216). The following three volumes (*tha*—312 folios ; *da*—286 folios ; and *na*—308 folios) are occupied by the works of the well-known Sa-skya-paṇḍita Kun-dga'-rgyal-mtshan (1182-1251)—a nephew to the previous two scholars. Finally, the last three volumes (*pa*—401 folios ; *pha*—430 folios

folios of the usual Tibetan long format.[187] Eight lines in verse (*śad*) in the beginning of the text give the list of Tibetan kings according to their dynasties. Then follows a genealogical list of Tibetan kings—partly in verse and partly in prose—beginning with their mythological ancestor gÑa'-khri-btsan-po and ending with Ral-pa-can. Thereafter, Grags-pa-rgyal-mtshan passes over, as he himself says, to an exposition of the dates of birth, of accession to the throne and of death of Tibetan kings in the usual Tibetan calendar, indicating the total number of years of their life and those of their reign. This exposition, written largely in verses, includes Tibetan kings from Sroṅ-btsan-sgam-po (7th cent.) to dPal-'khor-btsan (10th cent.)—both inclusive—and also gives the places of birth and death of these kings in addition to the dates. This is followed by a brief reference to the religious history of Tibet which covers about three lines. The text ends with a list of the nearest descendants of dPal-'khor-btsan along with their appanages.

The same author has, by the way, written the genealogy of the Śākya-s—*Śā-kya-rnams-kyi-rgyal-rabs*[188]—which tells about the ancestors of Buddha Śākyamuni.

The next genealogy in order of chronology is the "Genealogy of the Kings of Tibet" (*Bod-kyi-rgyal-rabs*), compiled in 1275 by the famous associate of Emperor

---

and *ba*—409 folios) cover the works of another no less known scholar 'Phags-pa-bla-ma bLo-gros-rgyal-mtshan (1235-1280), the nephew of Sa-skya-paṇḍita Kun-dga'-rgyal-mtshan. Each work in this collection has its own separate pagination in addition to the continuous paging of the volume. For this, small works are united into collections which, on their title page, bear the title of the first of the works included.

The five authors enumerated here are held in high esteem in Tibet. They together form the so-called "first five" or "supreme" (*goṅ-ma-rnam-lṅa*) teachers of the Sa-skya-pa dynasty. Besides, the first three of these, who did not take the highest spiritual vows, are called the "three white ones from Sa-skya" (*Sa-skya'i-dkar-po-rnam-gsum*). The last two, as *bhikṣu*, are known as the "two red ones from Sa-skya" (*Sa-skya'i-dmar-po-rnam-gñis*). Cf. *Grub-mtha'-śel-gyi-me-loṅ*, book 6 (*cha*), fol. 7ª 4-5. Cf. also G. Huth, *Geschichte des Buddhismus in der Mongolei*, t. i, S. 102, Zz. 15-18 ; t. ii, S. 160. Sometimes, to the last two is also added the name of bLa-ma-dam-pa bSod-nams-rgyal-mtshan (see *bsTan-'dsin-gyi-skyes-bu-rgya-bod-du-byon-pa'i-miṅ-gi-graṅs*, fol. 31ª 6 ff ; for a detailed account of this work, see note 317 *infra*). The dates of all these authors are given in the "Chronological Tables".

187. *Sa-skya-bka'-'bum*, vol. ix (*ta*), fols. 196ᵇ 6-200ª 2.

188. *Ibid.*, fols. 193-196ᵇ 5. This work is a collection of small works of the author. These include the "Genealogy of the Kings of Tibet" (described by us) and an extremely interesting work on the division of Indian and Tibetan Buddhist schools—*rGya-bod-kyi-sde-pa'i-gyes-mdo* (fols. 200ª 2-203ᵇ 3).

Kublai—the great Lama 'Phags-pa-bla-ma bLo-gros-rgyal-mtshan (1235-1280),[189] the fifth and the last representative of the above-mentioned galaxy of scholars from Sa-skya monastery. This text covers only one folio of the usual Tibetan long format (i.e. 12 lines) and is included in the above-mentioned ' Complete Works of the Five Scholars from Sa-skya" among other works of this author and his messages to Kublai and others.[190] This text is a bare list of names of Tibetan kings from Sroṅ-btsan-sgam-po to dPal-'khor-btsan and his grandsons and great grandsons, with dates of birth, accession to throne and death of every king in the usual Tibetan calendar. Besides, the age of a king at the time of his accession to throne and at the time of death and the duration of his reign are also mentioned. This work of 'Phags-pa-bla-ma does not differ substantially from that of his relation and predecessor Grags-pa-rgyal-mtshan ; it is however more concise and better expressed.

Sum-pa-mkhan-po Ye-śes-dpal-'byor[191] retells this work briefly in his historical work. He even bases his own chronology on it assuming, as he himself says, that 'Phags-pa-bla-ma, who had a very close contact with the Mongolian-Chinese court, had undoubtedly compiled his work in accordance with the ancient Chinese and Tibetan sources.[192]

Of course, there existed even earlier *rgyal-rabs*-s than these two. The above-mentioned Grags-pa-rgyal-mtshan, in the end of his text, directly states that he has seen

---

189. For biographical data on 'Phags-pa-bla-ma, see : G. Huth, *Geschichte des Buddhism in der Mongolei*, vol. ii, S. 86, Z. 16-S. 102, Z. 18 ; vol. ii, SS.138-160 ; I. J. Schmidt, *Geschichte der Ost-Mongolen und ihres Fürstenhauses verfasst von Ssanang Ssetsen Chungtaidschi der Ordus*, St. Petersburg, 1829, SS. 114-119 (Mongolian text and translation). See also the historical work of the Fifth Dalai Lama : *Gaṅs-can-yul-gyi-sa-la-spyod-pa'i-mtho-ris-kyi-rgyal-blon-gtso-bor-brjod-pa'i-deb-ther* (*rGyal-ba-lṅa-pa'i-deb-ther*), fols. 56ª 4-57ᵇ 4. Here, it should be kept in mind that G. Huth—as already shown by Professor P. Pelliot (see P. Pelliot, *Le cycle sexagénaire*.. ,—"Journal Asiatique", vol. i, 1913, pp. 655-657)—has wrongly advanced all Tibetan dates by one year by following wrong principle of conversion of Tibetan dates into our calendar.
190. *Sa-skya-bka'-'bum*, vol. xv (*ba*), fols. 360ᵇ 4-361ᵇ 4. The date of compilation of this genealogy—Wood-Pig year corresponding to A.D. 1275—is mentioned in the concluding remarks. The date given here is correct but the name of the month is omitted. In the collection, the text of the genealogy is preceded by a verse in praise of the Tibetan royal dynasty—*Bod-kyi-rgyal-rabs-la-bsṅags-pa'i-tshigs-bcad*—compiled by the same author. It occupies folios 360ª 1-360ᵇ 4.
191. *dPag-bsam-ljon-bzaṅ*, fols. 99ᵇ 7-100ª 3 (S. C. Das, *Pag Sam Jon Zang*, pp. 153-154).
192. *dPag-bsam-ljon-bzaṅ*, fol. 101ᵇ 3 (S. C. Das, *Pag Sam Jon Zang*, p. 156).

many inaccurate and a few accurate genealogies.[193] But these have not come down to us just like other genealogies contemporary to the two mentioned above or chronologically immediately following them.

However, the "genealogies of kings" (*rgyal-rabs*-s) are included in many works on the history of Buddhism in Tibet (*chos-'byuṅ*-s), though they often retain their complete independence. The genealogies of Tibetan kings can be found in the historico-bibliographical work of Bu-ston Rin-chen-grub where they are closely interwoven with the history of Buddhism,[194] in *Deb-ther-sṅon-po* where even the genealogies of the Mongolian Khans and Chinese emperors are added to it,[195] in the above-mentioned historical work of Sum-pa-mkhan-po Yes-śes-dpal-'byor[196] where the views of other authors are quoted in addition to the account of "genealogy of Tibetan kings" proper (brief genealogical lists of the Chinese[197] and Mongolian[198] dynasties are also given) and in other similar texts.

In spite of all this, they sometimes occupy so important a place in such general synthetic texts and mix so much of varied "secular" material with religious history that they pass on even their name—*rgyal-rabs*-s—to these texts. One can point out a number of such works which, like any general composite work of Tibetan historiography, are mainly histories of religion but still contain a great deal of "secular" material and are, in addition to being known as "histories of religion" (*chos-'byuṅ*-s), also called "Royal genealogies" (*rgyal-rabs*-s).

To this category belong primarily *rGyal-rabs-gsal-ba'i-me-loṅ* ("Royal Genealogy —a Clear Mirror"), which is also sometimes called *rGyal-rabs-rnams-kyi-byuṅ-tshul-gsal-ba'i-me-loṅ-chos-'byuṅ*[199] and "A Clear Mirror of Royal Genealogy and History of Religion" (*rGyal-rabs-chos-'byuṅ-gsal-ba'i-me-loṅ*).[200] This work, as is obvious from the title itself, is simultaneously a history of Buddhist faith and a genealogy of Tibetan kings. The Institute of Peoples of Asia (Academy of Sciences, U. S. S. R.) has two different editions of this text: an old and highly incomplete Lhasa edition[201] and an

193. *Sa-skya-bka'-'bum*, vol. ix (*ta*), fol. 199^b 6 ff.
194. Bu-ston, *Chos-'byuṅ*, fols. 127^a 4-147^a 1; E. Obermiller, *History of Buddhism*, vol. ii, pp. 181-202.
195. *Deb-ther-sṅon-po*, vol. i, fols. 20^a 4-31^a 4.
196. *dPag-bsam-ljon-bzaṅ*, fols. 95^a 6-108^a 7 (S. C. Das, *Pag Sam Jon Zang*, pp. 147-166).
197. *dPag-bsam-ljon-bzaṅ*, fols. 288^a 1-292^b 6.
198. *Ibid.*, fols. 300^b 2-312^b 2.
199. This title is there on the title page of the sDe-dge edition of this text.
200. See C. Bell, *The Religion of Tibet*, p. 207.
201. *Old Collection*, No. 438^a. See A. Schiefner, *Bericht über die neueste Büchersendung aus Peking*,—"Bulletin historico-philologique de l'Académie des Sciences de St. Pétersbourg", t. vii, N 1, 2.

excellent sDe-dge edition (in Baradiin's collection). The work consists of 18 chapters and covers (in sDe-dge edition) 104 folios of the usual Tibetan long format. The first seven chapters (23 folios of the text) are like an introductory part. They deal with the appearance and spread of Buddhism, origin of images of Buddha, history of the neighbouring peoples,—the Chinese, Tanguts and Mongols,—the sacred formula *Oṃ maṇi padme huṃ*, etc.... Chapter 8 gives (in four folios) the genealogy of Tibetan kings up to Sroṅ-btsan-sgam-po. The next nine chapters—from ninth to seventeenth (53 folios) —give an account of the king Sroṅ-btsan-sgam-po and his period. Finally, the last, viz, eighteenth chapter (in 23 folios) gives a brief history of the reign of kings from Sroṅ-btsan-sgam-po to dPal-'khor-btsan and gives the genealogical lists of the descendants of the latter—various individual princes—right up to those who lived in the 13th-14th centuries.[202]

---

202. I do not consider it superfluous to give here a full list of chapters of this extremely interesting text. I am giving the folio and line numbers as per sDe-dge edition.

Chapter I : Daṅ-po-bkal-pa-ji-ltar-chags-pa-nas rgya-gar-gyi-chos-rgyal-rim-par-byon-pa-daṅ ston-pa-śākya-thub-pa-'jig-rten-du-byon-nas-dam-pa'i-chos-dar-pa'i-le'u (How the universe was formed, what kings ruled in India and how, with the appearance of Buddha Śākyamuni, the Buddhist creed was spread), fols. 1-6ª 5.

Chapter II : Saṅs-rgyas-śākya-thub-pa'i-sku-gsum-bsheṅs-pa-daṅ-rab-tu-gnas-par-mdsad-pa'i-le'u (How the three images of Buddha Śākyamuni were raised and how they were consecrated), fols. 6ª 5-10ª 2.

Chapter III : rGya-hor-gyi-yul-du-dam-pa'i-chos-dar-ba-daṅ rGyal-pa'i-rnam-grans-ji-ltar-byon-pa-bstan-pa'i-le'u (How the Buddhist creed was spread in China and Mongolia and what sort of kings were there in these countries), fols. 10ª 2-12ᵇ 5.

Chapter IV : 'Phags-pa-padma-la-'khruṅs-pa-las Ye-ge-drug-pa'i-phan-yon-bstan-pa'i-le'u (How Bodhisattva Avalokiteśvara was born in a lotus and the use of six-syllabic formula *Oṃ maṇi-padme-huṃ*), fols. 12ᵇ 5-17ª 3.

Chapter V : 'Phags-pa-spyan-ras-gzigs-dbaṅ-phyug-gis Kha-pa-can-pa'i-sems-can-rnams-smen-grol-la-'khod-pa-daṅ-po'i-le'u (How the Boddhisattva Avalokiteśvara first called the inhabitants of Tibet to the path of salvation), fols. 17ª 3-19ª 1.

Chapter VI : rTa'i-rgyal-por-sprul-nas-sems-can-gyi-don-mdsad-pa'i-le'u (How he, incarnating himself as the king of horses, helped the living beings), fols. 19ª 2-22ª 3.

Chapter VII : Bod-kyi-mi-brgyad-spre'u-daṅ-brag-srin-mo-nas-chad-pa'i-le'u (About the origin of the Tibetans from the monkey and the fiendess of a rock), fols. 22ª 3-24ª 3.

In its structure, "Clear Mirror" (*rGyal-rabs-gsal-ba'i-me-loṅ*) is very closely

---

Chapter VIII : Bod-rgyal-po'i-gduṅ-rabs-daṅ-pa-ji-ltar-byon-ba-bstan-pa'i-le'u (How the earliest Tibetan kings appeared), fols. 24ᵃ 3-28ᵃ 3.

Chapter IX : 'Phags-pa-spyan-ras-gzigs-kyi-sku-la-'od-zer-bshi-'phros-pa-las Chos-rgyal-'khruṅs-pa'i-le'u (How four rays emanated from the body of Bodhisattva Avalokiteśvara, and how from one of these was born the king Sroṅ-btsan-sgam-po and from the other two his wives—the Nepali and Chinese princesses), fols. 28ᵃ 3-29ᵇ 6.

Chapter X : bLon-po-thon-mis-rgya-gar-nas-ye-ge-bsgyur-pa-las rGyal-pos-dge-ba-bcu'i-khrims-bcas-pa'i-le'u (How the minister of Thon-mi-sa-mbho-ṭa borrowed the alphabet from India, and about the noble precepts of the king), fols. 29ᵇ 6-34ᵃ 4.

Chapter XI : rGyal-po'i-thugs-dam-gyi-lha-rgya-gar-daṅ Bal-po'i-yul-nas-spyan-draṅs-pa'i-le'u (How the holy images were brought from India and Nepal), fols. 34ᵃ 4-37ᵇ 2.

Chapter XII : Bal-mo-bza'-khri-btsun-gdan-draṅs-pa'i-le'u (About the invitation to the Nepali princess), fols. 37ᵇ 2-43ᵃ 2.

Chapter XIII : rGyal-mo-bza'-koṅ-jo-gdan-draṅs-pa'i-le'u (About the invitation to the Chinese princess), fols. 43ᵃ 2-57ᵇ 2.

Chapter XIV : mTha'-'dul-yaṅ-'dul-gyi-lha-khaṅ-daṅ 'Phrul-snaṅ-ra-mo-che-rnams-legs-par-bsheṅs-pa'i-le'u (How the two temples of Lhasa—'Phrul-snaṅ and Ra-mo-che—and other temples of Tibet were erected), fols. 57ᵇ 2-65ᵃ 1.

Chapter XV : Lha-sa-rnam-gñis-daṅ mTha'-'dul-daṅ-yaṅ-'dul-gyi-gtsug-lag-khaṅ-la-sogs-pa-legs-par-tshar-nas-rab-tu-gnas-pa-mdsad-pa'i-le'u (How these temples were consecrated), fols. 65ᵃ 1-68ᵇ 4.

Chapter XVI : Phan-pa-daṅ-bde-ba-thams-cad-'byuṅ-bar-bya-ba'i-phyir gTer-spas-pa-daṅ-bod-'baṅs-thams-cad-chos-la-bkod-par-mdsad-pa'i-le'u (About the buried treasures and about the conversion of all Tibetan subjects to Buddhism), fols. 68ᵇ 4-73ᵃ 2.

Chapter XVII : rGyal-po-yab-yum-gyi-mdsad-pa-yoṅs-su-rjogs-te Raṅ-byon-bcu-gcig-shal-gyi-thugs-kar-thim-pa'i-le'u (How the king and his wives, after completing their work, returned to the heart of Bodhisattva Avalokiteś-vara), fols. 73ᵃ 3-81ᵃ 3.

Chapter XVIII : Tibetan dynastic history from Sroṅ-btsan-sgam-po to his distant descendants who ruled in the various parts of Tibet in the 13th-14th centuries, fols. 81ᵃ -103ᵇ 5. This concluding chapter has no Tibetan title.

allied to the apocryphal works described above,[203] viz. "Legend of Kings" (*rGyal-po-bka'i-thaṅ yig*), the biographies of Sroṅ-btsan-sgam-po included in *Ma-ṇi-bka'-'bum*, and especially the "Will hidden near the column" (*bKa'-chems-ka-khol-ma*)[204] which incidentally were some of the main sources of this work.[205] Like these apocrypha, *rGyal-rabs-gsal-ba'i-me-loṅ*, for most of its part, is full of legends from the life of the king Sroṅ-btsan-sgam-po. However, it is different from the apocrypha in the sense that in addition to the biography of Sroṅ-btsan-sgam-po, it gives much accurate historical information taken from various authoritative sources, and has thus a place between an apocryphal work and the historical work proper.

The Kalmuck edition of this work was known to I. Schmidt who, in the notes to his history of the Mongols—*Sagan Setsen*—translated a number of interesting and important incidents of Tibetan history from it.[206] Thanks to the work of I. Schmidt,

---

Immediately after this chapter are the colophons : author's (fols. 103b 6-104a 5) and publisher's (fol. 104a 5-6).

As is seen from the above table of contents, the chapters of historical interest are the third and the eleven last chapters from eighth to eighteenth. Other chapters are only of literary and folkloristic interest. Again, in almost all the nine chapters (from ninth to seventeenth), which describe the period of Sroṅ-btsan-sgam-po, the folkloristic material dominates the historical one.

203. See Chapter 2.

204. Compare the table of contents (quoted *supra*, footnote 70) of another manuscript of *bKa'-chems-ka-khol-ma* available in the Institute of Peoples of Asia with that of *rGyal-rabs-gsal-ba'i-me-loṅ* reproduced in note 202.

205 The author himself names these apocrypha among his sources. See *rGyal-rabs-gsal-ba'i-me-loṅ*, sDe-dge edition, fols. 24a 4, 28a 2, 72a 3, 78a 3, 103b 2.

206. I. J. Schmidt, *Geschichte der Ost Mongolen* , *Anmerkungen und Erlauterungen*, SS. 316-371. I. Schmidt himself does not correctly indicate what parts of the text he is translating. But this is not difficult to find because the Kalmuck text which he used was, in all probability, an absolutely literal translation of the Tibetan original. It is, however, possible that various small annotations of explanatory and reference character—which are there in the text of the Tibetan original (in Lhasa edition—in italics ; in sDe-dge edition—in brevier)—were wanting in the Kalmuck text, for these are not found in Schmidt's translation. The rest of Schmidt's translation clearly agrees with the Tibetan text if, of course, the passages omitted by Schmidt himself are not taken into account. In notes 4-9 and 11 to the second section (SS. 316-320) and in note 2 to the third section (SS. 321-322), I. J. Schmidt consistently gives, with minor omissions, the translation of the whole of eighth chapter of the text. In note 3 to the third section (S. 323), he gives a translation of the account (in verse)

the *rGyal-rabs-gsal-ba'i-me-loṅ* became widely known (under the title *Bodhimor*)[207] in

---

of Sukhāvatī paradise, which he borrowed from the 4th chapter. In the sDe-dge edition of the Tibetan text, this occupies fol. 13ᵇ 2-5. In note 4 to the same 3rd section (SS. 323-325), I. Schmidt gives a translation of the 4th chapter. In notes 6 and 7 (SS. 327-330), he gives translation of the 10th chapter (with many omissions). Note 10 (SS. 330-333) contains translation of the first and the larger part of the 11th chapter. In note 13 (SS. 333-343), he gives a translation of a number of passages from the 12th and 13th chapters and expounds, in brief, the contents of the 14th and 15th chapters. In note 16 (SS. 344-347), he gives the translation of the concluding words of the 16th chapter and of the whole of 17th chapter (with omissions). Finally, in notes 18-22, 29, 37, 38, 42, 46, 47, 49 and 53 (SS. 347-352, 354-371) to the same third section, I. Schmidt consecutively gives the translation of the 18th chapter. Unfortunately, the translation of this chapter—the most interesting in historical sense—is also full of various types of omissions.

See also I. J. Schmidt, *Forschungen in Gebiete der alteren religiosen, politischen und literarischen Bildungsgeschichte der Volker Mittel-Asiens, vorzüglich der Mongolean und Tibeter*, St. Petersburg, 1824, SS. 193-206, where the whole of 4th chapter of the text (SS. 193-201) and the entire 5th chapter (SS. 202-206) have been translated, though with minor omissions. The Mongolian text of the first—the largest—part of the 4th chapter (this part, with omissions, corresponds to fols. 12ᵇ 6-15ᵃ 4 of the sDe-dge edition of the Tibetan text) was published by O. Kovalevsky (see O. Kovalevsky, *A Mongolian Chrestomathy*, Kazan, 1837, pp. 32-37).

While giving its due to the high skill with which I. Schmidt—more than hundred years back, at the dawn of scientific study of the Mongolian language and literature—completed his translation, one has, nevertheless, to wish greatly for a new complete translation of this monument (so important in many respects) direct from the Tibetan original. In this, of course, even the Tibetan text ought to be published.

207. Personally, it appears to me that I. Schmidt has used the name *Bodhimor* for denoting the Kalmuck translation of the *rGyal-rabs-gsal-ba'i-me-loṅ* because of some sad misunderstanding. The expression *Bodhimor* is an exact translation of the Tibetan title "Stages of the Path of Glory" (*Byaṅ-chub-lam-rim*). This is how the celebrated work of Tsoṅ-kha-pa bLo-bzaṅ-grags-pa (1357-1419), the founder of the dominant dGe-lugs-pa sect in Tibet, is called. This work discusses, as its title itself indicates, the gradual path of *Bodhi* and is one of the

European scientific literature. It was used by E. Schlagintweit,[208] Koeppen[209], W. W. Rockhill,[210] B. Laufer,[211] A. Francke[212] and many other scholars working on the history of Tibet. So far as I know, G. Huth was the first to give the name of the author and the year of compilation of this work. In his opinion based exclusively on the colophon of this work, it was completed in A. D. 1327 and was compiled by bSod-nams-rgyal-mtshan, a Lama from Sa-skya monastery.[213] This opinion was also subscribed to by B. Laufer who, however, says that bSod-nams-rgyal-mtshan was from bSam-yas monastery. He also corrected the date given by G. Huth by one year,

---

most honoured works of the Buddhists of Tibet and Mongolia. The first part of this work, in Mongolian and Russian translations, was published by G. Tsybikov in his work *Lam-rim-chen-po* ("Stages of the Path to Bliss"), vol. 1, nos. 1 & 2, Vladivostok, 1910-1913. The use of this title—which is closely associated with the work of Tsoṅ-kha-pa—for denoting *rGyal-rabs-gsal-ba'i-me-loṅ* appears very odd to me, more so because even the meaning of this term is far from being close to the latter text. In the words of I. Schmidt himself (see I. J. Schmidt, *Geschichte der Ost-Mongolen*, S. 316), the monument used by him was called *Nom gharchoi todorchoi Tolli*. One may even surmise that this name, being a literal translation of the Tibetan *Chos-'byuṅ-gsal-ba'i-me-loṅ*, is the actual title of the text used by I. Schmidt.

208. E. Schlagintweit, *Die Konige von Tibet*, SS. 807, 811, 803-855 (notes) and Table 1.

209. C. F. Koeppen, *Die lamaische Hierarchie und Kirche*, S. 48 ff.

210. W. W. Rockhill, *The Life of the Buddha*, p. 211 ff.

211. B. Laufer, *Skizze der mongolischen Literatur*,—"Keleti Szemle—Revue Orientale", viii, 1907, pp. 213-214 (see also : B. Laufer, *Ocherk mongol'skoi literatury* [An Outline of Mongolian Literature], tr. by V. A. Kazakevich, ed. with a preface by B. Ya. Vladimirtsov, Leningrad, 1927, p. 48-49) ; B. Laufer, *Die Bru-za Sprache*,—"T'oung pao", vol. ix, 1908, p. 18 ff, 38-46 (on p. 39-46, B. Laufer gives a translation of the description, in verse, of the consecration of bSam-yas monastery ; this description is available in *rGyal-rabs-gsal-ba'i-me-loṅ* (fols. 90^a 3-91^b 4) as a quotation from the work *bKa'i-thaṅ-yig-chen-mo* which is no longer extant). Besides, see B. Laufer, *Der Roman einer tibetischen Konigin*, SS. 5 ff. and B. Laufer, *The Application of the Tibetan Sexagenary Cycle*,—"T'oung pao", vol. xiv, 1913, p. 588.

212. A. H. Francke, *Antiquities of Indian Tibet*, pt. ii, p. 80 ff.

213. G. Huth, *Nachtragliche Ergebnisse bezügl. der chronologischen Ansetzung der Werke im tibetischen Tanjur, Abtheilung mDo* (Sûtra), Bd 117-124,—ZDMG, Bd xlix, 1895, S. 279.

dating this work as 1328[214] instead of 1327 in accordance with the principles of conversion of Tibetan dates into European calendar as accurately determined by Professor P. Pelliot.[215] F. Thomas[216] and Professor G. Tucci[217] also give 1328 as the date of compilation of this text ; this is however totally incorrect. There is no doubt that the colophon states that the author of this work was Sa-skya-pa bSod-nams-rgyal-mtshan and also gives the date of compilation of the text as Earth-Dragon year (*Sa-pho-'brug*).[218] But this is no more than a forgery. We know from the history of Tibet that Sa-skya-pa bSod-nams-rgyal-mtshan was born in 1312 and that he died in 1375.[219] During this span of time, there is only one Earth-Dragon year, i. e. the second year of Tibetan sexagenary cycle, which corresponds to A. D. 1328. But on this date, the person supposed to be the author of this text— a text based on a study of vast historical literature which has been indicated and cited in it —was only 16 years of age. This fact alone makes the statement of the colophon doubtful. An examination of the text itself finally strips this statement of the colophon of all its authenticity, for this text could, in no way, have appeared earlier than the first half of the 15th century. The exposition of the genealogy of the Mongolian Khans ends with the last emperor of Yüan dynasty, Togon Timur (Shun-ti), who is known to have reigned from 1333 to 1368, and gives besides the total number of years of his reign[220] (though there is a mistake of 12 years). The gloss given here also states that after Togon Timur, the

214. B. Laufer, *Skizze der mongolischen Literatur*,—"Keleti Szemle-Revue Orientale", p. 213 (see also : B. Laufer, *Ocherk mongol'skoi literatury* [An Outline of Mongolian Literature], p. 49 ; B. Laufer, *Die Bru-za Sprache...*,—"T'oung pao", vol. ix, 1908, p. 38 ; B. Laufer, *Der Roman einer tibetischen Konigin*, S. 5 ; B. Laufer, *The Application of the Tibetan Sexagenary Cycle*,—"T'oung pao", vol, xiv, 1913, p. 588. In the first three works, the date of the Tibetan cycle (Earth-Dragon year) mentioned in the colophon was wrongly converted by B. Laufer to A. D. 1327 (instead of A. D. 1328). In the last article, however, this mistake was corrected by him.

215. P. Pelliot, *Le cycle sexagénaire dans la chronologie tibétaine*,—JA, 1913, t. I, pp. 633-667.

216. F. W. Thomas, *Tibetan Literary Texts..*, pt. i, p. 292.

217. G. Tucci, *Indo-Tibetica. Rin c'en bzan po e la rinascita del Buddhismo nel Tibet intorno al mille*, Rome, 1933 (*Reale Academia d'Italia. Studie documenti*, i), p. 93. On pp. 88-90 of this work, G. Tucci has published a small passage of the Tibetan text of *rGyal-rabs-gsal-ba'i-me-loṅ* containing a list of descendants of the Tibetan king dPal-'khor-btsan.

218. *rGyal-rabs-gsal-ba'i-me-loṅ*, fol. 104a 5.

219. See "Chronological Tables".

220. *rGyal-rabs-gsal-ba'i-me-loṅ*, fol. 12b 3.

throne passed on to the Chinese Ming dynasty. Moreover, the genealogy of the king who reigned in Ku-ke covers the period up to about early 15th century, including the Ya-tse dynasty founded by bTsan-phyug-lde, son of Na-ga-lde, and under the reign of whose first cousin Lha-bla-ma-byaṅ-chub-'od in the first half of the 11th century, Atiśa (982-1054)[221] was invited to Tibet. In addition to 11 generations of Ya-tse dynasty, *rGyal-rabs-gsal-ba'i-me-loṅ* mentions two more generations of another new dynasty of Ku-ke rulers.[222]

All this leads us to reject the idea of regarding *rGyal-rabs-gsal-ba'i-me-loṅ* as the work of Sa-skya-pa bSod-nams-rgyal-mtshan—more so because the Tibetan sources themselves name another person as the author. In his description of the main temple of Lhasa, the Fifth Dalai Lama states incidentally that in this temple, there is an urn of some dKon-gñer-dpon Legs-pa'i-śes-rab, the author (*rtsom-pa-po*) of a work entitled *rGyal-rabs-gsal-ba'i-me-loṅ*.[223] Enumerating various historical works in the "Catalogue of Collected Works of the Teachers of bKá'-gdams-pa and dGe-lugs-pa Sects", kLoṅ-rdol-bla-ma Ṅag-dbaṅ-blo-bzaṅ also states that the author of this work was bShu-khaṅ-pa Legs-pa'i-śes-rab.[224] The same name is also mentioned by a much later author of a list of historical works, the aforementioned Brag-dgon-shabs-druṅ dKon-mchog-bstan-pa-rab-rgyas, who contends that the *rGyal-rabs-gsal-ba'i-me-loṅ* was carved out for the press by dKon-gñer-dpon Legs-pa'i-śes-rab of Lhasa. He also states that this work, according to its colophon, is supposed to have been composed by Sa-skya-pa bSod-nams-rgyal-mtshan.[225]

---

221. *Ibid.*, fols. 101ᵇ 2-102ᵃ 2. Atiśa arrived in Tibet in the end of the 30's or in the beginning of the 40's of the 11th century. The views of the Tibetan sources differ on the exact date of his arrival. See the information in "Chronological Tables" in this regard.
222. *rGyal-rabs-gsal-ba'i-me-loṅ*, fol. 102ᵃ 3-6. Cf. E. Schlagintweit, *Die Konige von Tibet*, Table 1, where this genealogy is given.
223. *Lha-ldan-sprul-pa'i-gtsug-lag-khaṅ-gi-dkar-chag-śel-dkar-me-loṅ*, fol. 6ᵇ 5. This states : *dKon-gñer-dpon-rgyal-rabs-gsal-ba'i-me-loṅ-rtsom-pa-po-legs-pa'i-śes-rab-kyi-gduṅ-rten.* See also translations of this text : L. A. Waddell, *Description of Lhasa Cathedral*, translated from Tibetan,—JASB, vol. lxiv, 1895, pt. i, Nr. 3, p. 268 and A. Grünwedel, *Die Temple von Lhasa*,—"Sitzungsberichte der Heidelberger Akademie der Wissenschaften", Philosophisch-historische Klasse, Heidelberg, 1919, 14 Adhandlung, S. 27.
224. *bKa'-gdams-pa-daṅ- dge-lugs- pa-bla-ma-rags- rim-gyi-gsuṅ -'bum-mtshan-tho*, fol. 62ᵃ 4-5.
225. *Deb-ther-rgya-mtsho*, vol. 1, fol. 8ᵃ 2-3, which states : *rGyal-rabs-gsal-ba'i-me-loṅ 'Di-lha-sa'i-dkon-gñer-dpon-legs-pa'i-śes-rab-kyis-par-du-brkos-śiṅ brTsams-byaṅ-las-sa-skya-pa-bsod-nams-rgyal-mtshan-zer-ba-yod.*

The publisher's colophon (*par-byan*) of the first Lhasa edition of the *rGyal-rabs-gsal-ba'i-me-lon* actually states that this edition was brought out by Legs-pa'i-śes-rab, the keeper of Lhasa temple (Jo-po'i-dkon-gñer); the date viz. Earth-Dog year[226] is also mentioned. A scrutiny of this colophon reveals that the author—the above-mentioned Legs-pa'i-śes-rab—was a contemporary of the Tibetan ruling prince dPal-'byor-rgyal-po, for the colophon contains good wishes for the health and prosperity of this prince and his family.[227] This fact enables us to ascertain the date of publication of the text and besides, the date of its compilation, for the ruling prince, dPal-'byor-rgyal-po, from sNel-ba dynasty, which alone could have been kept in view in the colophon, lived in about the middle of the 15th century. His younger sons, Nag-dbaṅ bSod-nams-lhun-po and Ṅag-dbaṅ bSod-nams-rgyal, lost their power after the capture of Ui province in 1481 by the Tsang prince Riṅ-spuṅs-pa Don-yod-rdo-rje.[228] Under these circumstances, the date mentioned in the colophon can correspond only to A.D. 1478.[229] The text was obviously compiled somewhat earlier—most probably in the middle of the 15th century. An analysis of the text fully corroborates this hypothesis because the exposition of all genealogies in this work ends up at the end of the 14th century or at the beginning of the 15th century. Besides, while mentioning various sources written in the 14th century or earlier, the author does not name even one of the numerous historical texts compiled later.

---

226. *rGyal-rabs-gsal-ba'i-me-loṅ*, Lhasa edition, fols. 100b 5-101a 7. This colophon is not repeated in the sDe-dge edition.
227. *Ibid.*, fols. 100b 6-101a 1.
228. See *rGyal-ba-lṅa-pa'i-deb-ther*, fols. 98b 1-99b 6, which gives an account of the ruling dynasty of gShis-ka sNel-pa. Information on dPal-'byor-rgyal-po and his sons is given towards the end of this account (fol. 99b 3-6). This ruler is portrayed as an extremely powerful feudal and as a patron of religion in general and of dGe-lugs-pa sect in particular. The Tibetan ruling dynasty of sKyid-śod-pa was dependant upon him (*ibid.*, fols. 103b 6-104a 1).

    For date of capture of Ui province by the prince Riṅ-spuṅs-pa Don-yod-rdo-rje, see *dPag-bsam-ljon-bzaṅ*, fol. 105a 3ff (S. C. Das, *Pag Sam Jon Zang*, p. 162).
229. The cyclic date, Earth-Dog year, should not be considered to date from a later period, because already in the 80's of the 15th century, the rulers were the sons of dPal-'byor-rgyal-po, who lost their power about the same time. This year (the Earth-Dog year) also cannot date from an earlier period (i.e. from A. D. 1418), because in the second decade of the 15th century, the step-brother of the grandfather of dPal-'byor-rgyal-po—prince Nam-mkha'-bzaṅ-po, whose main spiritual teacher (*rtsa-ba'i-bla-ma*) was Tsoṅ-kha-pa (1357-1419) and who subsidized the construction of the 'Bras-spuṅs monastery (founded in 1416)—was still ruling (see *rGyal-ba-lṅa-pa'i-deb-ther*, fol. 99a 4 ff.)

C. Bell opines that the *rGyal-rabs-gsal-ba'i-me-loṅ* appeared later than the *Deb-ther-sṅon-po* (1476-1478),[230] for it contains a reference to a *deb-ther* which, according to him, should be taken to mean the *Deb-ther-sṅon-po.*[231] This opinion is based on a clear misunderstanding. The same place in the text, to which C. Bell refers, states quite clearly as to which text was there in view. The *deb-ther* in question is the one compiled by Si-tu dGe-ba'i-blo-gros, a Lama from Tshal-ba monastery.[232] This author whose real [secular] name was Kun-dga'-rdo-rje[233] was a contemporary of Bu-ston Rin-chen-grub (1290-1364),[234] whose historical work is also mentioned in the *rGyal-rabs-gsal-ba'i-me-loṅ.*[235] The work of Lama Si-tu dGe-ba'i-blo-gros was

230. For more details on the date of compilation of *Deb-ther-sṅon-po*, see *infra* note 240.

231. C. Bell, *The Religion of Tibet*, p. 207.

232. This is directly stated in the place referred to by C. Bell (see *rGyal-rabs-gsal-ba'i-me-loṅ*, sDe-dge edition, fol. 12^{b} 4—Lhasa edition, fol. 12^{a} 5). C. Bell has erred in that he has paid attention only to the second half of the phrase. The text reads : *Tshal-pa-thams-cad-mkhyen-pa-si-tu-dge-ba'i-blo-gros-kyis-deb-ther-du-bsgrigs-pa-las-zur-tsam-bsdus-pa-yin-gyis rgya-hor-yig-tsaṅ-rgyas-par-śes-'dod-na deb-ther-de-ñid-la-gzigs-śig*. C. Bell translates as : "If you wish to know the full details of China and Hor, look in Tep-ter", and assumes that "Tep-ter" is *Deb-ther-sṅon-po*. However, a full translation of the entire phrase will read : "Since (the present work) is a simple abridgement of what has been expounded by the omniscent Tshal-ba Si-tu dGe-ba'i-blo-gros in *Deb-ther*, any one wishing to know the history of China and of the Mongols in details may see in this *Deb-ther*" [lit. : if any one wishes to know, in details, the history of China and of the Mongols, let him look up in this *Deb-ther*].

233. See *rGyal-ba-lṅa-pa'i-deb-ther*, fol. 63^{a} 2-4 ; *dPag-bsam-ljon-bzaṅ*, fol. 103^{b} 1-2. In the edition of S. C. Das (S. C. Das, *Pag Sam Jon Zang*, p. 159), Si-tu-dge-blo (abridgement of Si-tu dGe-ba'i-blo-gros) is misprinted as Si-tu-dge-sloṅ.

The view of the Tibetan writer bSod-nams-grags-pa (1478-1554) that Druṅ-chen Kun-dga'-rdo-rje and Si-tu dGe-ba'i-blo-gros are different persons is totally unfounded and is considered an annoying conjecture of the author ('Ol-tshod-kyi-gtam) by the Tibetan historians. See *rGyal-ba-lṅa-pa'i-deb-ther*, fol. 63^{a} 5-6.

234. See *rGyal-ba-lṅa-pa'i-deb-ther*, fol. 63^{a} 4-5 and *gSuṅ-rabs-rnam-dag-chu'i-dri-ma-sel-byed-nor-bu-ke-ta-ka*, fol. 3^{b} 2. See also the Tibetan catalogue to the sNar-thaṅ edition of *bKa'-'gyur* (*bKa'-'gyur-rin-po-che'i-gsuṅ par-srid-gsum-rgyan-gcig-rdsu-'phrul-śiṅ-rta'i-dkar-chag-ṅo-mtshar-bkod-pa-rgya-mtsho'i-lde-mig*, fol. 26^{a} 4).

235. *rGyal-rabs-gsal-ba'i-me-loṅ*, fols. 6^{a} 3, 24^{a} 6.

called *Deb-ther-dmar-po* ("Red Annals") and was extremely famous in Tibet. This work is mentioned, among others, in the *Deb-ther-snon-po* ("Blue Annals") under the secular name of its author.[236]

Unfortunately, C. Bell is not alone in his efforts to find, in the *rGyal-rabs-gsal-ba'i-me-loṅ*, a reference to *Deb-ther-sṅon-po*. A similar opinion was also expressed by Professor F. W. Thomas,[237] but this is based on a still sadder misunderstanding. Agreeing with B. Laufer that the *rGyal-rabs-gsal-ba'i-me-loṅ* was written in 1328, Professor F. Thomas contradicts his ownself by saying that this work appeared after the *Deb-ther-sṅon-po* but earlier than Tsoṅ-kha-pa.[238] Tsoṅ-kha-pa, as is known, was born in 1357 and died in 1419 whereas the *Deb-ther-sṅon-po*—as positively and repeatedly mentioned in the text itself—was begun in 1476.[239] In European literature, C. Bell has already examined this date of compilation of the *Deb-ther-sṅon-po*.[240] This

236. *Deb-ther-sṅon-po*, vol. 1, fols. 26ª 4, 27ª 2, 30ª 3. See also *rGyal-ba-lṅa-pa'i-deb-ther*, fols. 52ª 6-52ᵇ 1. Besides, references to *Deb-ther-dmar-po* are also met with in *Vaidūrya-gya'-sel*, fol. 13ª 3 and *dPag-bsam-ljon-bzaṅ*, fol. 101ª 4 (S. C. Das, *Pag Sam Jon Zang*, p. 155).

237. F. W. Thomas, *Tibetan Literary Texts*..., pt. i, pp. 292-293.

238. *Ibid*., p. 293.

239. *Deb-ther-sṅon-po*, vol. i, fols. 34ᵇ 4-5, 214ª 4 ; vol. ii, fols. 16ª 1, 255ᵇ 1, 265ᵇ 5. In giving the cyclic date on which he began his work—Fire-Monkey year—the author, in all these cases, mentions the number of years that have passed from the time of particular events of Tibetan history. Besides, the date of compilation of *Deb-ther-sṅon-po* is also available in the "Chronological Tables".

240. C. Bell, *The Religion of Tibet*, pp. 202-203. However, C. Bell errs in saying that this work was completed in A. D. 1476 (*ibid*., pp. 203-204). In 1476, as stated in the "Chronological Tables", this work was only begun (*mgo-brtsams*). As quite specifically mentioned in its colophon (see *Deb-ther-sṅon-po*, vol. ii, fols. 270ª 6-270ᵇ 1), *Deb-ther-sṅon-po* was completed in 1478. The colophon states that this work was compiled in the year 850 from the traditional date of birth of the king Sroṅ-btsan-sgam-po (629)—the year, bearing the cyclic symbol "Earth-Dog". This corresponds to A.D. 1478. Thus, though *Deb-ther-sṅon-po* was completed in 1478, the author, in calculating the number of years that had passed from the time of a particular event, has—following the general rule—reckoned the number of years up to the year of beginning (1476) and not up to the date of completion. Unfortunately, this habit of the Tibetan authors was apparently unknown to C. Bell. B. Baradiin (see *Statue of Maitreya in the Golden Temple in bLa-braṅ*, p. 04) mentions 1478 as the date of compilation of *Deb-ther-sṅon-po* obviously on the basis of the colophon.

discrepancy, unfortunately, is not the only error of Professor F. Thomas. His major error lies in that he regards an entirely different work as *rGyal-rabs-gsal-ba'i-me-loṅ*. Speaking all along of the *rGyal-rabs-gsal-ba'i-me-loṅ*, Professor F. Thomas actually has in view the historical work of the Fifth Dalai Lama—*Gaṅs-can-yul-gyi-sa-la-spyod-pa'i-mtho-ris-kyi-rgyal-blon-gtso-bor-brjod pa'i-deb-ther* or briefly, *rGyal-ba-lṅa-pa'i-deb-ther*—compiled in 1643,[241] which we shall discuss later in greater detail. All the passages from this work quoted and translated by Professor Thomas have been taken from 'Bras-spuṅs xylograph edition of this work of the Fifth Dalai Lama which bears, in margins, its conventional title *rgyal-rabs*. It is probably this latter circumstance that put Professor Thomas in confusion, thus making him mix two different works. The historical work of the Fifth Dalai Lama actually contains—at the places referred to by Professor F. Thomas[242] and at other places[243]—references to the *Deb-ther-sṅon-po*. The *rGyal-rabs-gsal-ba'i-me-loṅ* has no such references ; it also does not contain the passages quoted by Professor F. Thomas.

The fact that the *rGyal-rabs-gsal-ba'i-me-loṅ* is, in its colophon, attributed to a person who could not have been its author does not deprive this work of its value. It undoubtedly deserves to be carefully studied and translated, for much information recorded in it is wanting in other sources.

Another large work which also is often regarded as a *rgyal-rabs* is that of the Fifth Dalai Lama Ṅag-dbaṅ bLo-bzaṅ-rgya-mtsho (1617-1682).[244] Its full title is *Gaṅs-can-yul-gyi-sa-la-spyod-pa'i mtho-ris-kyi-rgyal-blon-gtso-bor-brjod-pa'i-deb-ther rdsogs-ldan-gshon-nu'i-dga'-ston-dpyid-kyi-rgyal-mo'i-glu-dbyaṅs*, but it is better known by its short titles : *Bod-kyi-rgyal-rabs-deb-ther-rdsogs-ldan-gshon-nu-ma*, *rGyal-ba-lṅa-pa'i-deb-ther* etc. This work (in 113 folios) is included in the Complete Works (*gsuṅ-'bum*) of the Fifth Dalai Lama.[245] It was written, as just stated, in A.D. 1643. The chapters in this work are not numbered. Even the usual division of material (*sa-bcad*) inside the text itself—

---

241. This date is indicated in the colophon (see *rGyal-ba-lṅa-pa'i-deb-ther*, fol. 113ᵃ 3-5) and in the "chronological table" of 'Jam-dbyaṅs-bshad-pa Ṅag-dbaṅ-brtson-'grus.
242. *rGyal-ba-lṅa-pa'i-deb-ther*, fol. 33ᵃ 5 ; F. W. Thomas, *Tibetan Literary Texts...*, pt. i, p. 293.
243. *rGyal-ba-lṅa-pa'i-deb-ther*, fols. 7ᵃ 5-6, 11ᵃ 6, 36ᵇ 4, 52ᵇ 1.
244. The dates of birth and death of this most famous leader of Tibetan history are given in the "Chronological Tables". These have been frequently quoted in European scientific literature. But unfortunately, the false dates have also been mentioned together with the correct dates—sometimes in the same works (see, for instance, C. F. Koeppen, *Die lamaische Hierarchie und Kirche*, SS. 148, 173 ; L. A. Waddell, *The Buddhism of Tibet*, pp. 233, 577, etc.).
245. See the *Collected Works* of the Fifth Dalai Lama, vol. xix (*dsa*).

the division which, to a certain extent, replaces our table of contents—is not there. The whole work constitutes a single account interrupted at times by dividing verses (*bar-skabs-kyi-tshigs-su-bcad-pa*). Being extremely refined conclusions to various topics in the exposition of historical events, these verses divide the entire work of the Fifth Dalai Lama into 21 parts or subjects (not taking into account the introduction and the general conclusion to the whole work.)[246]

---

246. The work begins with a prefatory note in verse (fols. 1-6^a 6). This is followed by the main text in prose, which gives an account of:

1) the life of Buddha and of spread of Buddhist doctrine, the origin of the Tibetans and the first Tibetan kings, fols. 6^a 6-12^b 4 ;
2) the king Lha-tho-tho-ri and his successors, fols. 12^b 4-14^a 1 ;
3) the king Sroṅ-btsan-sgam-po, invention of Tibetan script and the laws of this king, fols. 14^a 1-16^b 3 ;
4) the marriage of the king Sroṅ-btsan-sgam-po to Nepalese and Chinese princesses, fols. 16^b 3-23^b 3 ;
5) the construction of Lhasa temples etc. by these princesses, fols. 23^b 3-27^b 6 ;
6) the successors of Sroṅ-btsan-sgam-po, fols. 27^b 6-31^b 2 ;
7) the king Khri-sroṅ-lde'u-btsan, fols. 31^b 2-37^b 2 ;
8) the construction of bSam-yas monastery etc., fols. 37^b 2-39^b 2 ;
9) the successors of the king Khri-sroṅ-lde'u-btsan, fols. 39^b 3-41^b 3 ;
10) the king Ral-pa-can, fols. 41^b 3-44^a 6 ;
11) the king gLaṅ-dar-ma and his successors upto Byaṅ-chub-'od, fols. 44^a 6-48^b 5 ;
12) the invitation to Atīśa for coming to Tibet and the later kings of the first great Tibetan dynasty, fols. 48^b 5-52^a 2 ;
13) the subjugation of China and Tibet by the Mongols and the dynasty of Sa-skya-pa which, under Kublai, held sway over the whole of Tibet, fols. 52^a 2-61^a 6 ;
14) the dynasties of Tshal-ba, 'Bri-guṅ-pa, Yar-'brog-khri-dpon and Byaṅ-pa-bdag-po, fols. 61^a 6-67^b 5 ;
15) the ancestors of the founder of the Phag-mo-gru-pa dynasty, fols. 67^b5-71^b5 ;
16) the founder of this dynasty, the famous Si-tu Byaṅ-chub-rgyal-mtshan, fols. 71^b5-81^a 4 ;
17) his successors up to Grags-pa-rgyal-mtshan, fols. 81^a 4-85^a 3 ;
18) subsequent representatives of the Phag-mo-gru-pa dynasty up to Mi-pham bSod-nams-dbaṅ-phyug-grags-pa-rnam-rgyal, the contemporary of the Fifth Dalai Lama, fols. 85^a 3-90^a 5 ;
19) the largest feudal dynasties of Tibet: Riṅ-spuṅs-pa, fols. 90^a 6-92^b 6, Hor

In spite of its comparatively small size, this work doubtless is one of the most important and interesting works of Tibetan historiography. Unlike a great majority of other Tibetan historical works, the *rGyal-ba-lṅa-pa'i-deb-ther* pays a fairly good attention to the civil and political history of the country and briefly expounds the dynastic chronicles of the Tibetan feudals that have not come down to us. It is therefore particularly important that this text should be carefully studied, published and translated. It is true that S. C. Das gave a brief exposition of this text,—without specifically mentioning his source,—in the third section of his article *Contributions on....*[247] But this exposition, besides being far from complete, is so slip-shod that it can only lead to all sorts of further discrepancies.

One could enumerate more of such general synthetic works of Tibetan historical literature, in which the secular chronicles occupy an equally—and sometimes even a more—important place. But then we shall have to quote almost a whole list of such works, for none of their authors—though primarily interested in the exposition of the history of Buddhism—can do without the secular political canvas of this history. However, since these works form a special class of Tibetan historical literature, namely that of the so-called "histories of religion" (*chos-'byuṅ*-s), we shall say more of these later.

As we have referred to these works, we shall mention here at least one of them—the *Deb-ther-dmar-po*—which apparently provides most copious information, particularly on general political history of Tibet. Unfortunately, I could not obtain this work ; and generally speaking, it is very difficult to procure it, for it now appears on the list of bibliographical rarities.[248] But some information from this work has been briefly set forth in the *rGyal-rabs-gsal-ba'i-me-loṅ*,[249] in the *Deb-ther-sṅon-po*[250] and again from the latter by the Fifth Dalai Lama.[251] From these expositions and their accompanying annotations, we learn that the *Deb-ther-dmar-po* was based on a study of not only the

---

gShon-nu-bzaṅ-po, fols. 92ᵇ 6-97ᵇ 2 ; Druṅ-chen Grags-pa-bzaṅ-po, fols. 97b2-98b1 ; gShis-ka sNel-pa, fols. 98b1-99b6, rGyal-mkhar-rtse-ba, fols. 99b6-101ᵃ 2 ; sDe-pa 'Ol-kha-pa, fols. 101ᵃ 2-101b2 ; Yar-rgyab-pa, fols. 101b2-102ᵃ 3, Bya-ba Khri-dpon, fols. 102ᵃ 3-103b5 and dGa'-ldan-pa dMag-dpon bSod-nams-rgyal-po, fols. 103b5-105b2 ;

20) the prince Sa-skyoṅ Lha-rgya-ri-pa, fols. 105b2-106b4 ;

21) Gu-shi Khan, the conqueror of Tibet, fols. 106b4-110ᵃ 5. The text ends with a conclusion in verse and a colophon in prose, fols. 110ᵃ 5-113ᵃ 5.

247. JASB, vol. L, 1881, pt. i, N 3-4, pp. 213-251.

248. *dPe-rgyun-dkon-pa-'ga'-shig-gi-tho-yig*, fol. 3ᵃ 4.

249. *rGyal-rabs-gsal-ba'i-me-loṅ*, chapter iii, fols. 10ᵃ 2-12ᵇ 5.

250. *Deb-ther-sṅon-po*, vol. i, fols. 26ᵃ 3-30ᵃ 4.

251. *rGyal-ba-lṅa-pa'i-deb-ther*, fol. 52b1 ff.

Tibetan but also Chinese sources which, it is found, were repeatedly translated into Tibetan. A comparison of the account of the T'ang dynasty and of its connections with Tibet as briefly quoted from this work in the *Deb-ther-sňon-po*[252] with the Chinese history of the T'ang (*T'ang-shu*) reveals a striking similarity between the two—so much so that the names of some Tibetan kings are given not only in Tibetan but also in Tibetan transcription of their distorted Chinese pronunciation.[253]

As stated in the *Deb-ther-sňon-po*, the author of the *Deb-ther-dmar-po*, the aforementioned Kun-dga'-rdo-rje (monastic name—Si-tu dGe-ba'i-blo-gros) from Tshal-ba monastery himself establishes the date of composition of his work by stating that 700 years had passed from the time of departure to Tibet in Iron-Ox year (641) of the Chinese princess Khun-śiň-koň-jo married to the Tibetan king Sroň-btsan-sgam-po to the Fire Dog year in which this work was written.[254] Of course, there is a mistake in the calculations of the author. Actually, the number of years to this date comes to 705 and not 700, for the Fire-Dog year corresponds to A.D. 1346 and not to 1341. This inaccuracy is also noted by the *Deb-ther-sňon-po* which states quite justly that the period of seven hundred years ended five years earlier, namely in the Iron-Snake year which corresponds to A.D. 1341.[255] This minor inaccuracy, however, is not significant because it stands easily corrected from the names of the years. This information of Si-tu dGe-ba'i-blo-gros that his work dates to A.D. 1346 fully tallies with the testimony of other sources which state that the author was the contemporary of Bu-ston Rin-chen-grub (1290-1364).[256]

According to the *Deb-ther-sňon-po*, the author of the *Deb-ther-dmar-po* used, for the exposition of Tibetan-Chinese relations, a translation made by some Lama Rin-chen-grags-pa.[257] The author of the *rGyal-rabs-gsal-ba'i-me-loň*, on the other hand, states that Si-tu dGe-ba'i-blo-gros used a translation made by some scholar of Chinese and Mongolian historical texts, Tsen-tshe sLob-dpon Śes-rab-ye-śes.[258] We cannot at present judge as to which of these informations is correct. It is possible that both of these are correct. Elsewhere, the *rGyal-rabs-gsal-ba'i-me-loň* also refers to the translation mentioned in the *Deb-ther-sňon-po* and states that bLa-ma-gu-śrī Rin-chen-grags-pa published this translation in the Wood-Hen year [259] which, in the present case, can correspond either to A. D. 1285 or—as is most probable—to A. D. 1345.

252. *Deb-ther-sňon-po*, vol. i, fols. 26ª 3-29b2.
253. For example, Tha-mu together with Tibetan gLaň-dar-ma (*Deb-ther-sňon-po*, vol. i, fol. 28b2), or Ju-tsa-btsan-po (*ibid.*, fol. 28ª 4).
254. *Deb-ther-sňon-po*, fol. 27ª 1-2.
255. *Ibid.*, fol. 27ª 2.
256. See *supra* note 234.
257. *Deb-ther-sňon-po*, vol. i, fol. 26ª 3-4.
258. *rGyal-rabs-gsal-ba'i-me-loň*, fol. 12b3-4.
259. *Ibid.*, fol. 96b5-6.

Apparently, apart from the *Deb-ther-dmar-po*, there also were other attempts to expound the history of Tibet on the basis of not only the Tibetan but also Chinese materials, for we find references to Chinese-Tibetan histories—*rGya-bod-yig-tshaṅ*[260] — in the Tibetan historical literature. But, at present, we know almost nothing of these texts. One such text was in the hands of S. C. Das who mentions the *rGya-bod-yig-tshaṅ* in the list of literature given by him in his Tibetan dictionary.[261] It is possible that this very text may have been used by S. C. Das in his article *Tibet under the Tartar Emperors of China in the 13th Century A.D.*[262] But whether this is actually so—and if so, how faithfully he has used this text—is impossible to say, because S.C. Das had the habit of not mentioning the sources from which he borrowed the contents of his articles. In the present case, this is particularly distressing, because the article of S. C. Das is full of most interesting information on the economy of Tibet in the 13th century. A complete and correct scientific publication and translation of the monuments from which these data are taken would have been utterly desirable.

The inclusion of parts of old chronicles in the Tibetan historical texts of general synthetic character cannot, of course, compensate for the actual absence of these chronicles. The authors of such composite texts, in their tendency to cover the most diverse aspects of political and particularly ecclesiastical history of Tibet and sometimes even of the neighbouring countries, had to abridge considerably the information of their sources and sometimes to convert into a dry exposition what in these sources was lively and most valuable historical evidence. In a number of cases, what in the text of the later works appears in the form of a simple list of rulers is actually a mere abridgement of some ancient chronicle—which contained an account of the life and work of many (if not all) persons enumerated in the list. Thus, for example, before concluding his exposition of the genealogies of Yar-luṅs princes (Yar-luṅs-kyi-jo-bo), the author of the *rGyal-rabs-gsal-ba'i-me-loṅ* directly states that "this is only a summary" and that "anyone wishing to know about the work of the successive princes of Yar-luṅs may read the genealogy compiled by Lha-btsun Tshul-khrims-bzaṅ-po".[263] The latter was the son of the Yar-luṅs prince, mÑa'-bdag Grags-pa-rin-chen, who was a contemporary of 'Phags-pa-bla-ma and his associate in travels to the Chinese court.[264] For us, his chronicle would have been of no small importance.

The author of the *rGyal-rabs-gsal-ba'i-me-loṅ* makes the same observation in

---

260. See *dPag-bsam-ljon-bzaṅ*, fol. 101b3 (S. C. Das, *Pag Sam Jon Zang*, p. 156).
261. S. C. Das, *A Tibetan-English Dictionary*, Calcutta 1902, p. xxxii.
262. JASB, vol. lxxiii, 1904, pt. i, extra N, pp. 94-102.
263. *rGyal-rabs-gsal-ba'i-me-loṅ*, fol. 103b1. Text reads : *Yar-luṅ-jo-bo-rim-par-byon-pa-rnams-kyi-mdsad-pa-'phriṅ-las-rgyas-par-'dod-na lha-btsun- tshul- khrims- bzaṅ-pos-bsgrigs-pa'i-rgyal-rabs-la-gzigs-śig*. Cf. I. J. Schmidt, *Geschichte der Ost-Mongolen.*, S. 371.
264. *Ibid.*, fol. 93a 4 ff.

respect of the historical work (*yig-tshaṅ*) of some gSer-thog-pa Rin-chen-rdo-rje, from which he borrows the list of names of the descendants of the king dPal-'khor-btsan who ruled in Ya-tse and in other principalities and to which he refers for all information on their life and work.[265] The same is also repeated in respect of the *Deb-ther-dmar-po*[266] and Chinese sources.[267]

Similar phenomenon is also observed in other historical texts—in the *Deb-ther-sṅon-po*, in the historical treatise of Sum-pa-mkhan-po, in the work of the Fifth Dalai Lama etc. (not to speak of the less important works). But since in a majority of cases, the chronicles expounded in these texts have not come down to us, we have to be satisfied only with such expositions that nevertheless do give us a general idea of the course of events of Tibetan history.

All the Tibetan chronicles and genealogies mentioned by us bear a more or less distinct Buddhist stamp. But these apart, there also exist chronicles written in the spirit of the ideas of ancient Tibetan religion of Bon. One such Bon chronicle—*rGyal-rabs-bon-gyi-'byuṅ gnas*—was published in Darjeeling by Sarat Chandra Das. A small portion from it was translated by B. Laufer.[268] This work was compiled not later than the 14th-early 15th century, because the genealogy of the successors of Genghis [Chinghiz] as included here ends with the last emperor of the Yüan dynasty, Togon Timur (1333-1368), and his son.[269] This work, in its character, is similar to the works of the Buddhist authors and deals primarily with the exposition of the history of Bon religion.

Besides the genealogies of kings (*rgyal-rabs*-s or *rgyal-po'i-gduṅ-rabs*-s), there also exist in Tibet the genealogies of various specific princes and rulers—the so-called *jo-rabs*-s. The latter do not substantially differ from the former, and are considerably fewer in number. Normally, these are pure genealogical lists without the dates and without any account of life and work of the persons enumerated. Such genealogical lists of petty rulers and their genealogical tables were published by A. Francke.[270] All these are of modern origin. But one may, no doubt, find in Tibet even more ancient works.

---

265. *rGyal-rabs-gsal-ba'i-me-loṅ*, fol. 102ᵃ 5-6, which states: *'Di-rnams gser-thog-pa-rin-rdor-gyis-yig-tshaṅ-las-zur-tsam-bris-pa-yin-gyis-rgyal.po-re-re-bshin-gyi-mdsad-pa-'phrin-las-rnams-shib-par-śes-'dod-pa-de-ñid-kyi-yig-tshaṅ-la-gzigs-śig.*
266. *Ibid.*, fol. 12ᵇ 3-4.
267. *Ibid.*, fol. 96ᵇ 4-6. A brief exposition of these sources is given on fols. 95ᵃ 3-96ᵇ 4.
268. B. Laufer, *Uber ein tibetisches Geschichtswerk der Bon-po*,—"T'oung Pao", série 2, vol. ii, 1901, pp. 24-44. Of the twenty-six chapters of the Tibetan text, Chapters 21, 22 and 23 have been translated.
269. *Ibid*, pp. 33-35.
270. A. H. Francke, *Antiquities of Indian Tibet*, pt. ii, pp. 172-182.

Lastly, there also exist pure family genealogies, the so-called *gduṅ-rabs*-s or "genealogies" in general. Compared with these, the afore-mentioned *rgyal-rabs*-s and *jo-rabs*-s may be and ought to be regarded as individual specialized forms. Strictly speaking, the term *gduṅ-rabs* denotes any genealogy (royal or of any ordinary family) but in actual practice, this usually stands for genealogies which are not those of "kings" (*rgyal-rabs*-s or *rgyal-po'i-gduṅ-rabs*-s), "princes" (*jo-rabs*-s) etc. Such family genealogies are of very ancient origin. For an example, I can refer to a brief chronology of the afore-mentioned family of the founder and chief of the Sa-skya monastery. This genealogy was compiled by a member of this family, Grags-pa-rgyal-mtshan (1147-1216),[271] in the sixtieth year of his life (i.e. in 1206) and is available in his letter to the king of Ga-riṅ. This letter is included in the Complete Works of Grags-pa-rgyal-mtshan under the title *Ga-riṅ-rgyal-po-la-rtsis-bsdur-du-btaṅ-ba'i-yi-ge* and covers 1½ folio of the usual Tibetan long format.[272] The genealogy contained in it is a simple list of names which begins with the famous 'Khon kLu'i-dbaṅ-po (a contemporary of the king Khri-sroṅ-lde'u-btsan) and his younger brother rDo-rje-rin-chen, the fore-father of Sa-skya-pa family and ends with the nephews of the author. The dates of birth and death are given only from 'Khon dKon-mchog-rgyal-po (grandfather to the author) onwards. The history of this famous family has repeatedly attracted the attention of the Tibetan authors, and can be found in the *Deb-ther-sṅon-po*,[273] in the historical work of the Fifth Dalai Lama,[274] in the *Grub-mtha'-śel-gyi-me-loṅ*,[275] in the *Hor-chos-'byuṅ*[276] etc. In the special works which are now a bibliographical rarity, the history of the "line of Sa-skya" (*Sa-skya'i-gduṅ-rabs*) was expounded by the well-known sTag-tshaṅ Lo-tsā-ba

271. See *infra*.
272. *Sa-skya-bka'-'bum*, vol. viii (*ña*), fols. 209b 6-211a 5.
The date of the letter has been established on the basis of the information given by the author himself on his date of birth and on the age attained by him at the time of writing the letter (see fol. 210a 5-6). The purpose of the letter —as the very title shows—is to make a request for "finding out" the future on the basis of the data given. This request is contained in the second part of the letter (fols. 210b 3-211a 4). The first part, fols. 210a 1-210b 3, is fully occupied by the genealogy.
273. *Deb-ther-sṅon-po*, vol. i, fols. 109a 5-113a 1.
274. *rGyal-ba-lṅa-pa'i-deb-ther*, fols. 53b 3-61a 4.
275. *Grub-mtha'-śel-gyi-me-loṅ*, dGon-luṅ edition, book 6 (*cha*), fols. 1a 4-8b 3. For more details on this work, see *infra*.
276. G. Huth, *Geschichte des Buddhismus in der Mongolei*, t. 1, SS. 67-85, 86-102; t. ii, SS. 106-136. About the dates given in this translation, see *supra* (note 189).

Śes-rab-rin-chen (b. 1405), by the historian Ňor-pa dKon-mchog-lhun-grub (17th cent.) and by other authors.[277]

Apart from the history of the line of Sa-skya-pa, there also are, in Tibetan literature, histories of other families. In our collections which as yet are not fully catalogued, I could not locate such works so far. But in Tibetan historical literature, one can find a number of references to the chronicles of large feudal families of Tibet. From these references we know that some bLa-mchog-rdo-rje is the author of the chronicle of the ancient feudal family of rLaṅs in the same line to which Tā'i Si-tuByaṅ-chub-rgyal-mtshan (b. 1302)[278] belonged. Tā'i Si-tu Byaṅ-chub-rgyal-mtshan was the ruler (*khri-dpon*) of the principality of Phag-mo-gru. From 1349, he became the ruler of the entire Ui province and from 1354, also of the Tsang province and established the supremacy of Phag-mo-gru-pa dynasty in Tibet.[279] The chronicle of his line mentioned

277. See the list of works on the history of Sa-skya-pa dynasty in the *Deb-ther-rgya-mtsho* (vol. 1, fol. 8ᵃ 4-6) and in the *dPe-rgyun-dkon-pa-'ga'-shig-gi-tho-yig* (fol. 5ᵇ 4-6). The genealogy of the Sa-skya-pa house, compiled by Chos-rje (or Ňor-pa) dKon-mchog-lhun-grub is given by the Fifth Dalai Lama (see *rGyal-ba-lṅa-pa'i-deb-ther*, fols. 53ᵇ 6, 61ᵃ 3-4).

278. The date of birth of Si-tu Byaṅ-chub-rgyal-mtshan (the Water-Tiger year of the v cycle, corresponding to A.D. 1302) is given in the "Chronological Tables". The date of his death is mentioned in the *Deb-ther-sṅon-po* which states that he died in the Water-Cow year (1373)—in the twenty-fifth year from the time of the capture of power (Earth-Cow year ; A.D. 1349) by him (see the *Deb-ther-sṅon-po*, vol. i, fol. 113ᵃ 2-3).

However, in the translation, as published by S. C. Das, of a passage from some historical monument—not mentioned by him—dating from A.D. 1434 (Wood-Tiger year, wrongly converted by S. C. Das into A.D. 1432), the birth of Si-tu Byaṅ-chub-rgyal-mtshan has been ascribed to the Wood-Tiger year, i.e. A.D. 1314 (wrongly equated by S. C. Das to 1302). His death, it is stated, occurred in the 63rd year from his birth—viz. in the Fire-Dragon year which corresponds to A.D. 1376 (see S. C. Das, *A Short History of the House of Phagdu, which ruled over Tibet on the Decline of Sakya till 1432 A.D.*—JASB, New Series, vol. i, 1905, p. 204).

279. The biography of Tā'i Si-tu Byaṅ-chub-rgyal-mtshan is given by the Fifth Dalai Lama (see *rGyal-ba-lṅa-pa'i-deb-ther*, fols. 73ᵇ 1-80ᵇ 6). At the same place is given a list of his ancestors (fols. 67ᵇ 5-73ᵇ 1) and his successors (fols. 81ᵃ 4-90ᵃ 5). The history of his dynasty is set forth in brief by S. C. Das (see S. C. Das, *Contributions on...*,—JASB, vol. L, 1881, pt. i, no. 3-4, pp. 242-245 ;

here is included in bibliographical rarities.[280] Again, one mKhas-pa dKar-śag-pa compiled the chronicle of the ancient feudal family of Riṅ-spuṅs-pa[281]—which separated from Phag-mo-gru-pa and, in 1435, captured all power over the Tsang province.[282] Besides, there also exist family chronicles of other large vassals of Phag-mo-gru-pa dynasty as for instance, the chronicle of the line of Yar-rgyab-pa, compiled by Pan-chen Byams-pa-gliṅ-pa bSod-nams-rnam-par-rgyal-ba (b. 1400),[283] the chronicle of the lines

---

see also S. C. Das, *A Short History of the House of Phagdu*,—JASB, New Series, vol. 1, 1905, pp. 202-207).

Besides, some information on him may be found in the *dPag-bsam-ljon-bzaṅ* (fols. 104ᵃ 2 ff. ; S. C. Das, *Pag Sam Jon Zang*, pp. 160-161), which also mentions the dates (quoted by us) of the capture of power by him over the Ui and Tsang provinces. These dates are also available in the 'chronological table' included in this work (fol. 278). The 'chronological table' of the first 'Jam-dbyaṅs-bshad-pa assigns the date of accession of power by Si-tu Byaṅ-chub-rgyal-mtshan over both the provinces to 1349. The *Vai-dū-rya-dkar-po* (fol. 20ᵇ 4) also states that in 1349, Si-tu Byaṅ-chub-rgyal-mtshan became the sovereign of the whole of Tibet (cf. A. Csoma de Koros, *A Grammar of the Tibetan Language*, p. 186).

280. This chronicle is mentioned in the bibliographical list included in the *Deb-ther-rgya-mtsho* (vol. i, fol. 8ᵇ 1-2) and in the list of rare books *dPe-rgyun-dkon-pa-'ga'-shig-gi-tho-yig* (fol. 5ᵇ 6). Along with this chronicle, both the lists mention *rLaṅs-kyi-bo-ti-bse-ru* which obviously is another chronicle of the same rLaṅs [Lan] dynasty. Extracts from this work are quoted by the Fifth Dalai Lama (see *rGyal-ba-lṅa-pa'i-deb-ther*, fols. 68ᵃ 4-5, 68ᵇ 1-2) and Sum-pa-mkhan-po (see *dPag-bsam-ljon-bzaṅ*, fol. 96ᵃ 6-7 ; S. C. Das, *Pag Sam Jon Zang*, p. 148).

281. See *Deb-ther-rgya-mtsho*, vol. i, fol. 8ᵇ 2 ; *dPe-rgyun-dkon-pa-'ga'-shig-gi-tho-yig*, fol. 5ᵇ 6.

282. About the line of Riṅ-spuṅs-pa, see *rGyal-ba-lṅa-pa'i-deb ther*, fols. 80ᵃ 6-92ᵇ 6. A brief and extremely careless exposition of this account is given by S. C. Das (see S. C. Das, *Contributions on...*,—JASB, vol. L, 1881, pp. 245-246). Besides, an account of the line of Riṅ-spuṅs-pa and of the wars which his representatives fought is given in the *dPag-bsam-ljon-bzaṅ* (fol. 105ᵃ 1 ff ; S. C. Das, *Pag Sam Jon Zang*, p. 161 ff). The date when this dynasty captured all power over the Tsang province has been taken by me from this latter source. This date is also quoted in the very text of this work (*dPag-bsam-ljon-bzaṅ*, fol. 105ᵃ 2-3 ; S. C. Das, *Pag Sam Jon Zang*, p. 161) and in the "Chronological Tables".

283. See *rGyal-ba-lṅa-pa'i-deb-ther*, fol. 91ᵃ 4 ; *Deb-ther-rgya-mtsho*, vol. i, fol. 8ᵇ 2 ;

of Lha-bya-ri-pa,[284] sKyid-śod-pa[285] and others.[286] Many of these chronicles are briefly expounded in the afore-mentioned historical work of the Fifth Dalai Lama.[287] There also exists a special work devoted to an account, in verses, of the most important family chronicles. This work belongs to Ā-kya-sku-skye bLo-bzaṅ bsTan-pa'i-rgyal-mtshan and bears the title *sTobs-kyi-'khor-los-sgyur-pa-sde-srid-phag-mo-gru-pa-sogs-bod-kyi-rgyal-blon-maṅ-po'i-gduṅ-rabs-mdo-tsam-brjod-pa'i-rab-tu-byed-pa-ya-rabs-mgul-rgyan.* It comprises 12 folios in all, of the usual Tibetan format, and is included in the Complete Works of the author published in Peking.[288] The works enumerated here do not, in any way, exhaust the list of Tibetan genealogical chronicles (*gduṅ-rabs*-s). In Tibetan

---

dPe-rgyun-dkon-pa-'ga'-shig-gi-tho-yig, fol. 5ᵇ 6. The date of birth of the author of this chronicle as given in the 'chronological table' of the first 'Jam-dbyaṅs-bshad-pa is 1400 and in the 'chronological table' of Sum-pa-mkhan-po—A.D. 1401.

284. See *Deb-ther-rgya-mtsho*, vol. i, fol. 8^b 4.
285. *Ibid.*, fol. 8^b 3-4.
286. See the list of family chronicles given in the *Deb-ther-rgya-mtsho* (vol. i, fol. 8^a 4-8^b 6).
287. See *supra*. As is clear from the title of this work quoted by me in note 246, the second half of it is largely an exposition of a number of chronicles of the largest Tibetan feudal dynasties. Unfortunately, this work seldom gives the dates.
288. A copy of this Collection of Works is available in the Institute of Peoples of Asia (*Old Collection*, No. 462^b). The text mentioned comprises the second book (*kha*) in this collection.

    This text contains, in verses, the chronicles of the dynasties of: Phag-mo-gru-pa (fols. 1^b 1-3^b 6), Tshal-ba (fols. 3^b 6-4^b 2), 'Bri-guṅ-pa (fols. 4^b 2-5^a 2), Yar-'brog-khri-dpon (fol. 5^a 4-4), Byaṅ-pa-bdag-po (fols. 5^a 4-6^a 2), Riṅ-spuṅs-pa (fols. 6^a 2-6^b 6), sKyid-śod-pa i.e. the dynasty to which dGa'-ldan-pa dMag-dpon bSod-nams-rgyal-po belonged (fols. 6^b 6-7^b 5), 'Ol-kha-pa (fols. 7^b 5-8^a 3), Yar-rgyab-pa (fol. 8^a 3-6), Thag-dkar-pa i.e. the dynasty to which Druṅ-chan Grags-pa-bzaṅ-po (fols. 8^a 6-8^b 5), Bya-ba-khri-dpon (fols. 8^b 5-9^b 3), Lha-rgya-ri-pa (fols. 9^b 3-10^a 5), 'Phyoṅ-rgyas Hor-rigs-pa i.e. the dynasty to which Hor gShon-nu-bzaṅ-po belonged (fols. 10^a 5-12^a 3). As is seen from a comparison of this text with the work of the Fifth Dalai Lama described above (note 246) —to which the former repeatedly refers—this text is an abridged account of the latter.

sources, we also find references to the chronicles of such feudal families as sTag-luṅ-pa, rDo-riṅ, sDe-dge etc.[289] But we shall not take these up here.

4. *Monastery Chronicles* (*gDan-rabs*-s)

Along with the "family chronicles" in which the axis (and sometimes even the entire subject-matter) of the historical account is the change in generations of one family (*gduṅ-rabs*-s), there also exist, in Tibetan historical literature, "monastery chronicles" in which the exposition is based on the successive change of Heads—*gdan-rabs*-s. Such works have not at all been studied in European scientific literature, though they are extremely important as historical monuments and tell us not only about the events of internal life in the monastery but also about the events and persons of Tibetan history in general—insomuch as the monasteries and their Heads played an important and sometimes even a dominant role amidst the ruling class of Tibetan society.

In their shortest form, these monastery chronicles are simple lists of names of successively changing Heads. But whatever chronicles I could come across in this form formed a part of general composite historical works and were often accompanied by all sorts of additional information. As separate independent works, the monastery chronicles normally consist in a more or less detailed exposition of the history of the origin of the monasteries and special schools or faculties and of an account of the life and work of successively chaging Heads (often along with brief biographies or with a simple list of previous and subsequent "incarnations" of these Heads. Sometimes, these chronicles also include accounts (*dkar-chag*-s) of main sanctities of the monasteries.

A brilliant specimen of a chronicle of this type is the chronicle of the bLa-braṅ monastery in Amdo—*mDo-smad-bstan-pa'i-'byuṅ-gnas-dpal-ldan-bkra-śis-'khyil-gyi-gdan-rabs-raṅ-bshin-dbyaṅs-su-brjod-pa'i-lha'i-rṅa-bo-che*—compiled by the twenty-fourth Head of this monastery, dPal-maṅ dKon-mchog-rgyal-mtshan (1764-1853).[290] This work covers

289. See *Deb-ther-rgya-mtsho*, vol. i, fols. 8ᵃ 4-8ᵇ 6.

290. A detailed biography of dPal-man dKon-mchog-rgyal-mtshan, bearing the title *Yoṅs-rdsogs-bstan-pa'i-mṅa'-bdag-rje-btsun-bla-ma-rdo-rje-'chan-dkon-mchog-rgyal-mtshan-dpal-bzaṅ-po'i-shal-sṅa-nas-kyi-rnam-thad-'dod-'jug-ṅogs*, is compiled in 1864 by his pupil, Brag-dgon-shabs-druṅ dKon-mchog-bstan-pa-rab-rgyas. This biography is included in the tenth volume of the Collected Works of dPal-man dKon-mchog-rgyal-mtshan published in 11 volumes in the A-mchog-dkon-pa monastery in Amdo, and covers 282 folios (a copy of this work is available in the Institute of Peoples of Asia ; *Baradiin Collection*, No. 6). Besides, brief biographical data on dPal-man dKon-mchog-rgyal-mtshan are given in the

307 folios of the usual Tibetan format and is included in the Complete Works of the author.[291] The entire second volume of the aforementioned[292] history of Buddhism in Amdo—the *Deb-ther-rgya-mtsho*—belonging to the forty-ninth Head of the same

---

historical work of the same author—the *Deb-ther-rgya-mtsho* (vol. ii, fols. 50b 2-56b 4). The dates of his birth and death are taken from these sources.

291. See the Collected Works of dPal-man dKon-mchog-rgyal-mtshan (vol. i) mentioned in the previous note. According to the information of the colophon (fols 306b 4-307a 4), this chronicle was compiled in 1800 (Iron-Monkey year of the xiii cycle). Its xylograph edition was brought out in the A-mchog-dkon-pa monastery in 1821 (Iron-Snake year of the xiv cycle ; see *ibid*, (fol. 307a 4-5).

The contents of this chronicle of the bLa-bran monastery are :

1) an introduction in verse, fols. 1-3a 6 ;

2) a biography of the founder of bLa-bran—the first 'Jam-dbyaṅs-bshad-pa Ṅag-dbaṅ-brtson-'grus (1648-1722), fols. 3a 6-27a 3 ;

3) a biographyy of the second 'Jam-dbyaṅs-bshad-pa dKon-mchog-'jigs-med-dbaṅ-po (1728-1791), the chief builder of bLa-braṅ, fols. 27a 3-30b 6, and apotheosis of his works, fols. 30b 6-67a 2 ;

4) an apotheosis of the merits of the third 'Jam-dbyaṅs-bshad-pa bLo-bzaṅ-thub-bstan-'jigs-med-rgya-mtsho (b. 1792) who, at the time of composition of this work, was in the ninth year of his age, fols. 67a 2-77a 2 ;

5) a history of the rise of the bLa-braṅ (founded in 1710), fols. 77a 2-92a 6 ;

6) brief historical information on the teaching arrangement in the main philosophical faculty (*mtshan-ñid-grwa-tshaṅ*) of bLa-braṅ and on the five disciplines studied there, fols. 92a 6-111a 6 (i. e. Vinaya, fols. 97b 3-99b 3 ; Abhidharmakoṣa, fols. 99b 4-101b 3 ; Pramāṇavārtika, fols. 101b 3-105a 4, Mādhyamika, fols. 105a 4-107b 4 and Paramitā, fols. 107b 4-111a 1).

7) brief historical information on the *tantra*-s studied at the faculty of occult sciences (*rgyud-pa-grwa-tshaṅ*), fols. 111a 6-119b 4 ;

8) brief historical information on *tantra*-s studied at the astrological faculty (*dus-'khor-grwa-tshaṅ*), fols. 119b 4-136a 3 ;

9) brief information on the history of medicine, fols. 136a 3-151a 5 ;

10) information on the arrangement of prayer and worship meetings, fols. 151a 5-158a 4 ;

11) biographies of first 22 Heads of bLa-braṅ, fols. 158a 5-264a 6 ;

12) brief biographical data on 21 Deans of the faculty of occult sciences, fols. 264a 6-281a 3 ;

monastery, Brag-dgon-shabs-druṅ dKon-mchog-bstan-pa-rab-rgyas (b. 1801), is also essentially a work of this type. This volume too is devoted to the history of bLa-braṅ monastery and bears the sub-title *Chos-sde-chen-po-bkra-śis-'khyil-gyi-dkar-chag-gdan-rabs-kha-sgoṅ-daṅ-bcas-pa.* The work runs to 216 folios.[293]

Considerably shorter is the chronicle of the sKu-'bum monastery—the second famous monastery of the Amdo province. This chronicle is entitled *gDan-sa-chen-po-sku-'bum-byams-pa-gliṅ-gi-gdan-rabs-mu-tig-phreṅ-ba.* Its author was the second 'Jam-dbyaṅs-bshad-pa named dKon-mchog-'jigs-med-dbaṅ-po (1728-1791).[294] The chronicle is included in his Complete Works and occupies 42 folios.[295] This chronicle of the

---

13) brief biographical data on 10 Deans of the astrological faculty, fols. 281ᵃ 3-289ᵃ 4 ;

14) brief biographical data on the first three Deans of the faculty of medicine, fols. 289ᵃ 4-291ᵃ 3 ;

15) an account of various sanctities of bLa-braṅ, fols. 291ᵃ 3-304ᵇ 3 ; Conclusion, fols. 304ᵇ 3-306ᵇ 4 ; and Colophon, fols. 306ᵇ 4-307ᵃ 5.

292. See *infra* (Section 7 of this Chapter).

293. For the contents of this volume, see *infra* (note 498).

294. A detailed biography of dKon-mchog-'jigs-med-dbaṅ-po is available in the first volume of the collection of his works. This biography (in 278 folios) was compiled by his pupil Guṅ-thaṅ dKon-mchog-bstan-pa'i-sgron-me (1762-1823) in the 38th year of his life (i.e. in 1799), and bears the title *Dus-gsum-rgyal-bai'i-spyi-gzugs-rje-btsun- dkon-mchog-'jigs-med- dbaṅ-po'i-shal-sṅa-nas- kyi-rnam-par-thar-pa-rgyal-sras-rgya-mtsho'i-'jug-ṅogs.* A "secret biography" of dKon-mchog-'jigs-med-dbaṅ-po—*rJe-btsun-dkon-mchogs-med-dbaṅ-po'i-rnam-thar* (5 folios)—compiled by the same author is also available at the same place. Besides, a short biography of dKon-mchog-'jigs-med-dbaṅ-po is included in the chronicle of bLa-braṅ monastery (fols. , 27ᵃ 3-30ᵇ 6 etc.)—referred to by us in note 291—and in the *Deb-ther-rgya-mtsho* (vol. ii, fols. 10ᵃ 4-16ᵇ 4).

295. The Collected Works of dKon-mchog-'jigs-med-dbaṅ-po are published in 12 volumes in the monastery of bLa-braṅ in Amdo. A copy of this publication is available in the Institute of Peoples of Asia (*Baradiin Collection*, No. 1). The chronicle mentioned here is available in the second voulume of this Collected Works and is dated as 1781 (Iron-Cow year of the xiii cycle)—see colophon, fol. 22ᵃ 4-5.

This chronicle of sKu-'bum monastery contains an introduction in verse (fols. 1-3ᵇ 2), a short biography of Tsoṅ-kha-pa (fols. 3ᵇ 2-6ᵇ 6), a short history of the rise of sKu-'bum and a discussion on the date of its inauguration (fols. 6ᵇ 6-12ᵇ 1), some biographical information on the first 33 Heads of this monastery (fols. 12ᵇ 2-33ᵇ 4), brief information on its faculties of occult sciences

sKu-'bum monastery is set forth in greater detail in a work entitled *Chos-sde-chen-po-sku-'bum-byams-pa-gliṅ-gi- gdan-rabs-rten-daṅ-brten- par-bcas- pa'i-dkar-chag-ched-du-brjod-pa-don-ldan-tshaṅs-pa'i-dbyaṅs-sñan*, written in 1903[296] by the sixty-third Head of this monastery, named gSer-tog-ho-thog-thu bLo-bzaṅ-tshul-khrims-rgya-mtsho (b. 1845).[297] The chronicle is included in the Collected Works of the author and covers 275 folios.[298]

(fols. 33b4-34a 6) and medicine (fols. 34a 6-35a 2), a description of its various sanctities (fols. 35a 6-41a 3), the conclusion and colophon (fols. 41a 3-42a 6).

This work continues in form of the description of sKu-'bum (mentioned *infra* which, in its turn, continues as the chronicle compiled by gSer-tog-ho-thog-thu bLo-bzaṅ-tshul-khrims-rgya-mtsho (see *infra*, note 298).

296. The date of composition of this work—Water-Hare year of the xv cycle corresponding to A. D. 1903—is correctly mentioned in the colophon (fol. 275a 3-4). Besides the cycle date (which the author quotes in four languages—Sanskrit, Chinese, Mongolian and Tibetan), the author also indicates in the colophon the number of years that had passed from the *nirvāṇa* of Buddha and other events (see fols. 274a 3-275a 6).

297. The author himself gives his biographical data in brief (*op. cit.*, fols. 101b 6-114b 2).

298. The Collected Works of gSer-tog-ho-thog-thu bLo-bzaṅ-tshul-khrims-rgya-mtsho are published in sKu-'bum. A copy (incomplete) of this publication is available in the Institute of Peoples of Asia (*Baradiin Collection*, No. 18). The chronicle mentioned is included in the sixth volume (*cha*).

The chronicle contains an introduction in verse (fols. 1-4b3), a biography of Tsoṅ-kha-pa and various prophecies about him (fols. 4b6-18b3), a description of the place where he was born and an account of as to how the monastery of sKu-'bum was raised at this place (fols. 19a 1-35a 3). Then follow the reports on the life and work of 78 successively changing Heads of this monastery (fols. 35a 3-161a 3), on the establisment in 1612 of a faculty of philosophy, on the teaching programmes in it (fols. 161a 3-168b5), on the establishment in 1649 of the faculty of occult sciences, on 75 successively changing Deans of this faculty, on its teaching and theological programmes (168b5-208b 1), on the inauguration in 1757 of the faculty of medicine, on its 64 successively changing Heads, on its teaching programmes and prayer meetings (fols. 208b 1-236b4), on the inauguration in 1820 of an astrological faculty, and on its 40 Heads and teaching programmes (fols. 236b 4-249b 1). The text ends with an account of various temples of sKu-'bum monastery (fols. 249b 1-1-273a). In the end are the concluding note in verse (fols. 273a 1-274a 3) and the colophon (fols. 274a 3-275a 6).

There exist such chronicles of a number of other monasteries too—particularly the chronicle of 'Bri-guṅ monastery (a rival of Sa-skya), the chronicle of gSaṅ-phu monastery and of many others.[299] Such works are found dealt with in almost every work on the history of religion (*chos-'byuṅ*) as, for instance, in the *Deb-ther-sṅon-po*,[300] in the historical work of Sum-pa-mkhan-po[301] etc.

5. *Histories of Incarnations* (*'Khruṅs-rabs*-s)

The belief in re-birth, characteristic of all the religions of ancient India including Buddhism, assumed particularly extreme and crude forms in Tibetan Buddhism. The followers of the Tibetan Buddhism were not satisfied with a mere general theoretical statement that consciousness (*sems* or *rnam-ses*) continues to exist even after the death of a living being and that, on leaving a body, it has to acquire a new body conforming to its previous activity (*las*). The Tibetan Buddhism brought this notion to its logical end by giving it an absolutely concrete and practical shape. Regarding every person as a link in the chain of countless manifestations of consciousness, the Tibetan Lamas thought themselves capable of discovering, in historical and mythical figures of the past, previous manifestations of this consciousness and of ascertaining beforehand where and in what form this consciousness will be born again. Such investigations into the previous and future incarnations of a person, made at his own request or at the request of his relatives, teachers and admirers—and sometimes even at the instance of the leaders of Tibetan Buddhism themselves—were a regular function of the Buddhist hierarchs of Tibet and constituted for them an equally important source of income. Besides, this view served as a base for the formation of a large number of peculiar "dynasties" of the [Buddhist] Order based not on the succession of blood relations in the line (*gduṅ-rabs*)—which the celibate members of the Order of the dominant dGe-lugs-pa sect in Tibet could not have—but on the succession of Heads in the monasteries (*gdan-rabs*) and of "incarnations" (*skyes-rabs* or *'khruṅs-rabs*) who are looked for in the established order after the death of individual representatives of such a "dynasty".

This fact could not but have its effect also on the Tibetan literature. Every somewhat noted figure of Tibetan history—particularly from among the members of the Order—began to be regarded not only as the descendant of a specific dynasty of a person but also as a new embodiment of the person born again and again. In the biographies

---

299. See *Deb-ther-rgya-mtsho*, vol. i, fols. 8ᵇ 6-9ᵃ 6 where many such chronicles are enumerated. See also *dPe-rgyun-dkon-pa-'ga'-shig-gi-tho-yig*, fols. 7ᵃ 5-7ᵇ 2.

300. *Deb-ther-sṅon-po*, vol. i, fols. 269ᵇ 4-270ᵇ 2 ; vol. ii, fols. 1-16ᵃ 1 ; 249ᵇ 6-254ᵇ 5 ; 260ᵇ 2-265ᵇ 5 etc.

301. See *dPag-bsam-ljon-bzaṅ*, fols. 175ᵃ 6-228ᵃ 5 (S. C. Das, *Pag Sam Jon Zang*, pp. 271-359).

of various Tibetan leaders, therefore, one may often come across, along with the data on their ancestors, similar accounts of their previous incarnations. Besides, there also exist special works, the so-called "histories of incarnations"—*skyes-rabs*-s or, more respectfully, *'khruṅs-rabs*-s—which give a consecutive account of such incarnations of a particular person.

A proto-type of such works may, of course, be found in the Buddhist *jātaka*-s—the legends on the feats of Buddha in his previous incarnations, from which they have derived their name. In Tibet, there exists a sufficient number of works, which are nothing but expositions of the Indian *jātaka*-s (particularly, of the famous collection of 34 *jātaka*-s entitled *Jātakamālā*, belonging to the well-known poet Āryaśūra[302]) or their

---

302. The Tibetan translation of the *Jātakamālā* (*sKyes-rabs-kyi-rgyud*) is available in the *bsTan-'gyur* [see *bsTan-'gyur*, mDo-'grel, vol. xci (*ke*), fols. 1-152^b 1]. A translation of a commentary on this work is also included here (fols. 152^b 2-394^a 8).

Original Tibetan commentaries on the *Jātakamālā* are, as a rule, its expositions—sometimes abridged and sometimes, on the other hand, extremely extensive. The most remarkable of such commentaries-expositions is the work entitled *sKyes-rabs-so-bshi-pa'i-don-rnam-par-bśad-pa-theg-chen-gsal-ba'i-sgron-me* written in 1781 by the well-known Tibetan writer, Yoṅs-'dsin Ye-śes-rgyal-mtshan, the teacher of the eighth Dalai Lama. This work occupies the first three volumes (vol. 1—388 fols., vol. ii—370 fols., and vol. iii—271 fols.) in the Complete Works of the author. Besides, the first volume contains a brief exposition in verse of the essence of the collection of 34 *jātaka*-s—entitled *sTon-pa-thugs-rje-can-gyi-'khruṅs-rabs-so-bshi-pa'i-sñiṅ-po-bsdus-pa'i-tshigs-su-bcad-pa-theg-chen-chos-kyi-sgra-dbyaṅs* (4 fols.). The third volume contains a short survey of the works of the author, bearing the title *bDag-ñid-chen-po-mkhas-mchog-dpa'-pos-mdsad-pa'i-skyes- rabs-so-bshi'i-dod-rnam- par-bśad-pa-theg-chen-gsal-ba'i-sgron-me'i-bsdus-don* (66 fols.). A copy of the Collected Works of Yoṅs-'dsin Ye-śes-rgyal-mtshan is available in the Institute of Peoples of Asia (*Tsybikov Collection*, No. 17). Besides, one may mention a much later work entitled *sLob-dpon-dpa'-pos-mdsad-pa'i-skyes-rabs-so-bshi-pa'i-'grel-bśad-dad-pa'i-rin-chen-'dren-pa'i-śiṅ-rta* (269 fols.). This work, which is considerably smaller in volume, was written by Ku-ke-yoṅs-'dsin bLo-bzaṅ-bstan-'dsin and published in Aginsky *datsan* (*bde-chen-lhun-grub-gliṅ*) in Buryatia. A copy of this publication is also available in the Institute of Peoples of Asia (*Nova Collection*).

imitations.[303] Such purely narrative works apart, there also exist, in Tibet, under the same name, the *skyes-rabs*-s or *'khruṅs-rabs*-s and works of historical nature which are either simple enumerations or more or less detailed biographies of a number of really historical persons. It is true that such works also contain, on the few pages in the beginning, certain biographies of purely mythical personages, but this does not prevent the remaining biographies of genuine persons—purely mechanically connected with each other—from being truly authoritative historical sources.

---

303. Such imitations include the above-mentioned *jātaka*-s of the king Sroṅ-btsan-sgam-po included in the *Ma-ṇi-bka'-'bum*. Like the Indian *jātaka*-s, these stories of the previous re-births of the king Sroṅ-btsan-sgam-po are also not historical works but simply short stories—more didactic in spirit than their Indian prototypes.

Of similar nature are the Tibetan stories of the previous incarnations of the famous 'Brom-ston-pa rGyal-ba'i-'byuṅ-gnas, the pupil and the associate of Atīśa. These stories are cumulated into a work known under its short title *Bu-chos* (i.e. "Book of the Son"). The full title of this work is *'Brom-ston-pa-rgyal-ba'i-'byuṅ-gnas-kyi-skyes-rabs-bka'-gdams-bu-chos-le'u-ñi-śa-pa*. Along with another treatise of didactic nature, entitled *Pha-chos* (i.e. "Book of the Father"), with which it is textually connected, this work is included in a cumulative work entitled *bKa'-gdams-rin-po-che'i-glegs-bam* (i.e. "Book of Precious Precepts") which includes, besides, a biography of Atīśa and various other works of the bKa'-gdams-pa sect. This work was published in two volumes in the dGa'-ldan-phun-tshogs-gliṅ monastery in Tibet. It was also published in the bKra-śis-lhun-po monastery in Tibet—again in two volumes, but some of the texts included were, in this case, separately paginated (a copy of this edition, though incomplete, is available in the Institute of Peoples of Asia ; *Nova*, B 2773-2777). Again, this work was published from mDsod-dge (mDsod-dge-dgon-gsar-dga'-ldan-rab-rgyas-gliṅ) in Amdo (a copy of this edition is also available in the Institute of Peoples of Asia ; *Baradiin Collection*, No. 44). The *Bu-chos* contains 20 stories expounded by Atīśa himself who narrated them at the request of his pupil rÑog Legs-pa'i-śes-rab. After the name of the latter, these stories are sometimes called *rNog-chos*. Besides, the *bKa'-gdams-rin-po-che'i-glegs-bam* contains two more such stories narrated at the request of another pupil of Atīśa, Khu-ston brTson-'grus-gyuṅ-druṅ, and hence named *Khu-chos*. In the edition of the dGa'-ldan-phun-tshogs-gliṅ monastery, the text of *Bu-chos* covers fols. 1-308 of the second volume and that of *Khu-chos* fols. 343^b 1-398^b 3. The stories in both the texts are narrated to explain the didactic sentences given in verse in the aforementioned treatise *Pha-chos*. The latter occupies fols. 383-562^a 4 of the first volume of the edition mentioned. As

A most extensive work of this type is that containing the biographies of previous incarnations of the sixty-first Head of dGa'-ldan monastery, Ṅag-dbaṅ-tshul-khrims (1721-1791),[304] the famous regent of the eighth Dalai Lama. This biographical work is

---

in the Indian *jātaka*-s, one can, in these stories, distinguish five main parts: (1) a story about present (*paccupannavatthu*), the outer frame of the *jātaka*; (2) a story about the past (*atitavatthu*) comprising the very subject matter of the work; (3) a maxim in verse (*gāthā*) which, so to say, is the moral of the *jātaka* and a formal end of its exposition; (4) identification (*samodhāna*) of the characters in the *jātaka*-s with the persons figuring in the story about the past, i.e. with Atīśa himself and his pupils. The locale of the story, in most of the cases, is India. Only one re-birth of 'Brom-ston-pa rGyal-ba'i-'byuṅ-gnas is shown in China (see *Bu-chos*, eighth *jātaka*, fols. 190ª 3-202ᵇ 1).

In European literature, S. C. Das was the first to pay attention to the *bKa'-gdams-rin-po-che'i-glegs-bam*. The biography of Atīśa published by him (see S. C. Das, *Indian Pandits in Tibet*,—JBTS, 1893, vol. i, pt. i, pp. 7-31) and reprinted by him, without any annotations, in his *Indian Pandits in the Land of Snow* (Calcutta, 1893, pp. 50-76) is based almost exclusively on materials taken by him from the biography of Atīśa available in this compilation (fols. 28-144ᵇ 5)—attributed to mChims-thams-cad-mkhyen-pa. S. C. Das also paid attention to the collection of *jātaka*-s, *Bu-chos*, mentioned above. Without specifying his source, S. C. Das, in his article *The Lamaic Hierarchy of Tibet* (JBTS, 1893, vol. i, pt. i, pp. 31-38—also in his *Indian Pandits in the Land of Snow*, pp. 82-92—and pt. ii, pp. 44-57) gave a translation of the introduction to the first *jātaka* (JBTS, vol. i, pt. i, p. 32, 1.27 ff), an abridged translation (partly, a re-rendering) of the first *jātaka* (*ibid.*, pp. 33-38), a translation of the introduction to the second *jātaka* (JBTS, vol. i, pt. ii, pp. 44-45), and then suddenly (without giving any excuse) an exposition of the sixth *jātaka* without its introductory and concluding notes (*ibid.*, p. 45, 1.4 ff.) and finally, a half-translation and half-exposition of the second *jātaka* (*ibid.*, pp. 51-57).

304. The date of birth of Ṅag-dbaṅ-tshul-khrims—Iron-Cow year of the xii cycle—is mentioned in his biography surveyed here (pt. 14, *pha*, fol. 9ᵇ 2). The date of his death, which occurred in the 71st year of his life—i.e. in Iron-Pig year—is also mentioned at the same place (pt. 15, *ba*, fols. 374ª 5 ff.). He took over the office of the regent (*rgyal-tshab*) in 1777 (Fire-Hen year of the xiii cycle) after the death of his predecessor De-mo-no-mun-han Ṅag-dbaṅ-'jam-dpal-bde-legs-rgya-mtsho who had ruled from 1757 to 1777 (*ibid.*, pt. 15, *ba*, fol. 12ª 6-12ᵇ 3 and fols. 19ª 2 ff.). Cf. also *infra*—the work of kLoṅ-rdol-bla-ma

compiled by bLo-bzaṅ-thugs-rje,—otherwise known as Dad pa-mkhan-po,[305]—the Head [*upādhyāya*] of the "lower" (*smad*) *datsan* in Se-ra monastery. The work is entitled *sKyes-rabs-rnam-thar-dad-pa'i-sgo-'byed* and covers two large Tibetan volumes (751 folios).[306] It is composed of 15 parts, each of which has its separate pagination. The first part contains a general introduction to the incarnations of Ṅag-dbaṅ-tshul-khrims. The next twelve parts expound the biographies of persons who are regarded as his previous incarnations.[307] The last two parts contain a biography of Nag-dbaṅ-tshul-khrims himself, and together cover 548 folios, i.e. almost three-fourths of the entire text.

---

entitled bsTan-pa'i-spyin-bdag-byuṅ-tshul-gyi-miṅ-gi-graṅs (published from Kun-bde-gliṅ monastery in Lhasa, fols. 18ᵇ 2-19ᵃ 1).

The eighth Dalai Lama, 'Jam-dpal-rgya-mtsho [bLo-bzaṅ-bstan-pa'i-dbaṅ-phyug-'jam-dpal-rgya-mtsho] was born in 1758 (Earth-Tiger year) and he died in 1804 (see G. Ts. Tsybikov, *Buddist-palomnik u svyatyn' Tibeta* [A Buddhist Pilgrim in the Holy Places of Tibet], Petrograd, 1919, pp. 265-268. Both his regents are also mentioned here).

305. See the author's colophon (*mdsad-byaṅ*) of this work (pt. 15, *ba*, fols. 397ᵃ 5-399ᵃ 3). See also the publisher's colophon (*par-byaṅ*) written by the eighth Dalai Lama (*ibid.*, fol. 400ᵃ 3). According to the author's colophon, this work was begun in 1796 (Fire-Dragon year) and completed in 1798 (Earth-Horse year).

306. The biography is published in Se-ra monastery. A copy of this publication is available in the Institute of Peoples of Asia (*Tsybikov Collection*, No. 67). The references made by us are to this edition.

307. The second part (*kha*, 29 fols.) gives an account of the Buddha Krakucchanda; the third part (*ga*, 13 fols.)—of Svastika, the son of a grass merchant mentioned in the end of the 19th chapter of the *Lalitavistara* [see *Lalitavistara*, herausgegeben von Dr. S. Lefmann. Erster Theil: Text. Halle a. S. 1902, SS. 285-287 and Rgya tch'er rol pa ou Développment de jeux du contenant l'histoire du Buddha Śakya-mouni, traduit dur la version tibetaine du Bka'-'gyur et revu sur l'original sanscrit (*Lalitavistara*) par Ph. Ed. Foucaux. Premiere partie: Texte tibétain, Paris, 1847, pp. 249-252]. The fourth part (*ṅa*) contains an account of the *sthavira* Vakula; the fifth part (*ca*; 11 fols.)—of the Indian grammar of Vararuci; the sixth part (*cha*, 15 fols.)—of the *mahāsiddha* Kambala; and the seventh part (*ja*, 31 fols.)—of the *mahāsiddha* Tailopa. The remaining six parts deal with Tibetan historical leaders: the eighth part (*ña*, 17 fols.) expounds the biography of Phag-mo-grub-pa rDo-rje-rgyal-po (1110-1170), the well-known leader of bKa'-rgyud-pa sect; the ninth part (*ta*, 9 fols.) gives a short account of Ri-phug-pa; the tenth part (*tha*, 19 fols.) expounds the biography of rDo-riṅ-pa Kun-bzaṅ-chos-kyi-ñi-ma (1449-1524); the eleventh part

Then, one may mention the history of incarnations of the Peking khutukhta lCaṅ-skya Rol-pa'i-rdo-rje (1717-1786),[308]—compiled by the aforementioned second

(*da*, 13 fols.) contains a biography of the founder and first Head of Chab-mdo (Chab-mdo-chos-'khor-gliṅ) monastery (founded in 1444), Byaṅ-sems Śes-rab-bzaṅ-po (1395-1457), the pupil of Tsoṅ-kha-pa; the twelfth part (*na*; 7 fols.) describes the ninth Head of bKra-śis-lhun-po monastery (founded in 1447), Śaṅs-ston bLo-gros-legs-bzaṅ (b. 1491); and the thirteenth part (*pa*, 13 fols.) gives an account of the closest pupil of the Fifth Dalai Lama, 'Jam-dbyaṅs-grags-pa.

As is seen from these chapter headings, the account of "incarnations" as given in this work does not follow a strict chronological sequence. Besides, some "incarnations" described are partly contemporaries. Such peculiarities are also observed in other works of this type (see, for instance, *infra*, note 311). These are explained by the fact that the "histories of incarnations" (*'khruṅs-rabs*-s) are, as already stated, based on small texts of cultic nature—the so-called *'khruṅs-rabs-gsol-'debs*-s, i.e. "prayers to incarnations", which usually have been compiled by persons who, though occupying high positions in the Buddhist hierarchy, have most superfluous ideas of history. As a rule, these very texts serve as official acts specifiying the previous incarnations of a person. The Tibetans do not pay much attention to the lack of chronological sequence in the listing of incarnations. The fact that these texts ascribe, to the same person, two or more simultaneous re-births in the past is also taken by the Tibetan very lightly. This person is normally regarded by these texts as an embodiment of the Buddha or Bodhisattva and, according to the Buddhist ideas, the Buddhas and the Bodhisattvas can be embodied simultaneously in various places and in various persons.

308. Another name of his is lCaṅ-skya Ye-śes-bstan-pa'i-sgron-me. A most detailed biography of his is compiled by his pupil, Thu'u-bkwan bLo-bzaṅ-chos-kyi-ñi-ma (1737-1802). It bears the title *Khyab-bdag-rdo-rje-sems-dpa'i-ṅo-bo-dpal-ldan-bla-ma-dam-pa-ye-śes- bstan-pa'i-sgron-me- dpal-bzaṅ-po'i-rnam-par- thar-pa-mdo-tsam-brjod-pa-dge-ldan-bstan-pa'i-mdses-rgyan* and is included in the first (241 fols.) and second (245 fols.) volumes of the Complete Works of Thu'u-bkwan bLo-bzaṅ-chos-kyi-ñi-ma. A copy of this Complete Works published in dKon-luṅ monastery in Amdo is available in the library of Leningrad State University (Xy I. Q 344). Another detailed biography of lCaṅ-skya Rol-pa'i-rdo-rje is by Chu-bzaṅ-pa Ṅag-dbaṅ-thub-bstan-dbaṅ-phyug (b. 1736) who twice held the post of the Head of sKu-'bum monastery (28th and 32nd)—see the aforementioned chronicle of this monastery, written by gSer-tog-ho-thog-thu bLo-bzaṅ-tshul-khrims-rgya-mtsho—fols. 47ᵃ 3-47ᵇ 1 and 48ᵃ 5-49ᵃ 3. This

'Jam-dbyaṅs-bshad-pa dKon-mchog-'jigs-med-dbaṅ-po in 1776.[309] This work entitled *rJe-btsun-bla-ma-thams-cad-mkhyen-pa-lcaṅ-skya- rol-pa'i-rdo-rje'i- 'khruṅs-rabs- kyi- phreṅ-ba-gtam-du-brjod-pa-ṅo-mtshar-dad-pa'i-ljon-śiṅ* is included in the Complete Works of dKon-mchog-'jigs-med-dbaṅ-po and covers 121 folios.[310] It contains biographies of 14 persons regarded as the previous incarnations of lCaṅ-skya Rol-pa'i-rdo-rje.[311]

Another similar work is that entitled *Thams-cad-mkhyen-pa-chen-po-'jam-dbyaṅs-bshad-pa'i-rdo-rje'i-yaṅ-sprul-mthoṅ-ba-don-ldan-blo-bzaṅ-thub-bstan-'jigs-med-rgya-mtsho'i-'khruṅs-rabs-rnam-par-thar-pa-rin-po-che'i-ljon-śiṅ*—or briefly, *'Jam-dbyaṅs-bshad-pa'i-'khruṅs-rabs*—which contains the history of the incarnations of the third 'Jam-dbyaṅs-bshad-pa named bLo-bzaṅ-thub-bstan-'jigs-med-rgya-mtsho (b. 1792).[312] It was written

---

biography is entitled *rDo-rje-'chaṅ-lcaṅ-skya-rol-pa'i-rdo-rje-ye-śel-bstan-pa'i-sgron-me-dpal-bzaṅ-po'i-rnam-par-thar-pa-dad-pa'i-padma- rnam-par-'byed-pa-ñi-ma'i-'od-zer* (151 fols.). It was written in 1787 (Fire-Sheep year of the xiii cycle) and published in Peking. A copy of this publication is available in the Institute of Peoples of Asia (*Old Collection*, No. 436). Brief biographical data on lCaṅ-skya Rol-pa'i-rdo-rje are, besides, available in the *Deb-ther-rgya-mtsho* (vol. i, fols. 78ᵃ 6-79ᵃ 5) and in the 'chronological table' of Sum-pa-mkhan-po.

309. See the colophon of this text, fol. 121ᵃ 4-6.

310. See the Complete Works of dKon-mchog-'jigs-med-dbaṅ-po (vol. ii, *kha*) mentioned *supra* (note 295).

311. After a short introduction, which shows that lCaṅ-skya Rol.pa'i-rdo-rje is the embodiment of Buddha, this work gives an account of: 1) *arhat* Cunda, fols. 4ᵇ 6-5ᵃ 6; 2) *ācārya* Śākyamitra, fols. 5ᵃ 6-5ᵇ 6; 3) *mahāsiddha* Darpaṇa-ācārya, fols. 5ᵇ 6-6ᵇ 1; 4) the translator Ka-ba dPal-brtsegs, fols. 6ᵇ 1-6; 5) Lha-rje sGro-phug-pa (b. 1074), fols. 6ᵇ 6-8ᵇ 3; 6) one Si-si-ri-pa, fols. 8ᵇ 3-9ᵃ 3; 7) gLaṅ-ri-thaṅ-pa (1054-1123), fols. 9ᵃ 3-11ᵃ 3; 8) 'Phags-pa-bla-ma bLo-gros-rgyal-mtshan (1235-1280), fols. 11ᵃ 3-22ᵇ 3; 9) bLa-ma-dam-pa bSod-nams-rgyal-mtshan (1312-1375), fols. 22ᵇ 3-35ᵃ 3; 10) the well-known Byams-chen-chos-rje Śākya-ye-śes (1354-1435), the pupil of Tsoṅ-kha-pa and the founder of Se-ra monastery, fols. 35ᵃ 3-40ᵇ 1; 11) Se-ra-rje-btsun Chos-kyi-rgyal-mtshan (1469-1546), fols. 40ᵇ 1-60ᵃ 6; 12) 'Khon-ston dPal-'byor-lhun-grub (1561-1637), fols. 60ᵃ 6-85ᵇ 4; 13) Chos-rje Grags-pa-'od-zer, fols. 85ᵇ 4-87ᵃ 6; and 14) lCaṅ-skya Ṅag-dbaṅ bLo-bzaṅ-chos-ldan (1642-1714), fols. 87ᵃ 6-121ᵃ 8. All these persons are regarded as the previous incarnations of lCaṅ-skya Rol-pa'i-rdo-rje but the present dynasty of the incarnations of lCaṅ-skya-khutukhtas begins only from this lCaṅ-skya Ṅag-dbaṅ bLo-bzaṅ-chos-ldan.

312. The date of birth of bLo-bzaṅ-thub-bstan-'jigs-med-rgya-mtsho as given in this work is not correct. It mentions Iron-Mouse year, i.e. A.D. 1780 (see fol. 70ᵇ 6) in place of Water-Mouse year which corresponds to A.D. 1792. This

in 1837 by bLo-bzaṅ-'jigs-med,—otherwise known as Rigs-pa'i-ral-gri (b. 1764,[313]—the former Dean of the astrological faculty (*dus-'khor-grwa-tshaṅ-e-phe-chos-'khor-gliṅ* of bLa-braṅ monastery. This work in 82 folios,[314] published in A-mchog dGa'-ldan-chos-'khor-gliṅ monastery in Amdo, contains biographies of 17 persons regarded as previous incarnations of the third 'Jam-dbyaṅs-bshad-pa and a biography of the latter up to the twentysixth year of his age.[315]

---

error was noticed by gSer-tog-ho-thog-thu bLo-bzaṅ-tshul-khrims who, in his chronicle of sKu-'bum monastery, gives some information on the third 'Jam-dbyaṅs-bshad-pa, for the latter was the 55th Head of this monastery (see this chronicle, fols. 61ᵇ 4-66ᵃ 1). gSer-tog-ho-thog-thu bLo-bzaṅ-tshul-khrims rightly remarks in this chronicle (fols. 61ᵇ 6-62ᵃ 4) that the author himself assigns the birth of this person to Water-Mouse year (1792) by stating that he was in his seventh year in the Earth-Horse year (A.D. 1798)—cf. *'Jam-dbyaṅs-bshad-pa'i-'khruṅs-rabs*, fol. 71ᵇ 3—in his twenty-fifth year in the Fire-Mouse (A.D. 1816) year (*ibid.*, fol. 80ᵃ 1), and in his twenty-sixth year in the Fire-Cow (1817) year (*ibid.*, fol. 80ᵃ 3). At another place, however, the author again errs in saying that in Wood-Dragon year (A.D. 1784), the third 'Jam-dbyaṅs-bshad-pa was in his seventeenth year (*ibid.*, fol. 74ᵃ 3) whereas this year actually was the Earth-Dragon year (1808). In this case—as while giving the date of birth—the author correctly names the animal of the sexagenary cycle but errs in giving the name of the element of the cycle.

The correct date of birth of the third 'Jam-dbyaṅs-bshad-pa is also given by Brag-dgon-shabs-druṅ dKon-mchog-bstan-pa-rab-rgyas who expounds a short biography of his in the *Deb-ther-rgya-mtsho* (vol. ii, fols. 78ᵃ 4-101ᵃ 6). The incarnation of the founder of bLa-braṅ monastery, the third 'Jam-dbyaṅs-bshad-pa, was the 27th Head of this monastery.

313. See the colophon of this work, fols. 81ᵇ 1-82ᵃ 4.
314. A copy of this work is available in the Institute of Peoples of Asia (*Baradiin Collection*, No. 21, 3).
315. It narrates first about five mythical personages, then about the four famous Indian teachers: Buddhapālita, fols. 19ᵇ 1-20ᵇ 3; Dignāga, fols. 20ᵇ 3-24ᵃ 5; Candrakīrti, fols. 24ᵃ 5-29ᵇ 6 and Jetāri, fols. 29ᵇ 6-31ᵇ 6. The remaining nine chapters are about various Tibetan leaders, namely: Po-to-pa Rin-chen-gsal (1027-1105) fols. 31ᵇ 6-35ᵇ 1; sTo-sde Ṅag-gi-dbaṅ-phyug, the pupil of Ma-gcig Lab-kyi-sgron-me, fols. 35ᵇ 1-37ᵃ 5; bLa-ma dBu-ma-pa dPa'-po-rdo-rje, fols. 37ᵃ 5-40ᵃ 3; Shwa-lu-pa Legs-pa-rgyal-mtshan (1375-1450), fols. 40ᵃ 4-42ᵇ 5; rGyud-chen brTson-'grus-'phags, fols. 42ᵇ 5-44ᵃ 3; rGyud-chen dKon-mchog-rgya-mtsho (1559-1628), fols: 44ᵃ 3-50ᵃ 1; the famous 'Jam-dbyaṅs-bshad-pa'i-rdo-rje Ṅag-bdaṅ-brtson-'grus (1648-1722), the founder of the

From the writings of Tibetan authors, we know that the well-known regent of Tibet, sDe-srid Saṅs-rgyas-rgya-mtsho (1653-1705), wrote the "History of Embodiments" (entitled *rGyal-ba-lṅa-pa'i-'khruṅs-rabs-rmad-byuṅ-bskal-pa-ma,* in 13 folios) of the Fifth Dalai Lama along with his commentary *Mu-tig-chun-po* (in 79 folios), and also compiled in four folios a "history of his own embodiments" (known under the title *Saṅs-rgyas-rgya-mtsho-raṅ-gi-'khruṅs-rabs-thogs-med-bskal-pa-ma*).[316] Then, sTag-phu bLo-bzaṅ-bstan-pa'i-rgyal-mtshan compiled the "History of Embodiments" of kLoṅ-rdol-bla-ma Ṅag-dbaṅ-blo-bzaṅ (b. 1719) and a history of his own embodiments, which is mentioned under the title *sTag-phu bLo-bzaṅ-bstan-pa'i-rgyal-mtshan-gyi-raṅ-gi-skyes-rabs-phan-bde'i-ljon-pa-bskyed-pa'i-sa-pon.*[317] However, I could not see these works.

One such work, namely the "History of Embodiments of Dalai Lamas" (*rGyal-ba'i-'khruṅs-rabs*) was composed by Lama Guṅ-thaṅ-pa, the minister of the thirteenth Dalai Lama at the instance of S. C. Das who published it as an *appendix* to his *Introduction to the Grammar of Tibetan Language.*[318]

Besides, brief expositions of such works may be found in general works on the history of Buddhism.•

The histories of incarnations—*skyes-rabs*-s or *'khruṅs-rabs*-s—ought to be distinguished from the so-called *'khruṅs-rabs-gsol-'debs* i.e. "Prayers to successive incarnations". The latter are special works of a small size, which are usually written by the leading hierarchs of Tibetan Buddhism at the request of the relations or admirers of

---

dynasty of the incarnations of various 'Jam-dbyaṅs-bshad-pa-s, the supreme sovereigns of bLa-braṅ monastery, fols. 50ᵃ 1-61ᵇ 5 ; the second 'Jam-dbyaṅs-bshad-pa, the well-known dKon-mchog-'jigs-med-dbaṅ-po (1728-1791), fols. 61ᵇ 5-70ᵇ 1 and finally, the third 'Jam-dbyaṅs-bshad-pa (b. 1792), fols. 70ᵇ 1-80ᵇ 4.

316. See *bKa'-gdams-pa-daṅ-dge-lugs-pa-bla-ma-rags-rim-gyi-gsuṅ-'bum-mtshan-tho,* fol. 59ᵃ 5-6.

317. See *Deb-ther-rgya-mtsho,* vol. i, fol. 17ᵇ 2-3. The author of the history of incarnations of kLoṅ-rdol-bla-ma is called, in the text, by a short name "sTag-phu". But obviously, the reference here is to sTag-phu bLo-bzaṅ-bstan-pa'i-rgyal-mtshan (mentioned in the text in an earlier line) in spite of the fact that he died during the life-time of kLoṅ-rdol-bla-ma who, in his work *bsTan-'dsin-gyi-skyes-bu-rgya-bod-du-byon-pa'i-miṅ-gi-graṅs* (fol. 21ᵇ 4), names an incarnation of sTag-phu bLo-bzaṅ-bstan-pa'i-rgyal-mtshan. The histories of incarnations were quite often compiled during the life-time of a person by his senior contemporaries.

318. S. C. Das, *An Introduction to the Grammar of the Tibetan Language with the Texts of Situhi Sum-rtags, Dag-je Sal-wai Me long and Situhi Shal-luṅ,* Darjeeling, 1915, *Appendix* VII, pp. 18-23.

some person with a view to glorify this person in his previous famous incarnations. These works, of course, have no historical value by themselves, but they are sometimes used by the Tibetan historians as a canvas on which the biographies of all sorts of persons are mechanically combined into a history of successive incarnations of the same person.[319] In spite of the fact that there are plenty of such works in Tibetan literature and that some of these are widely popular and authoritative, even the Tibetans themselves do not take the risk of assigning them to the class of historical texts. We shall not therefore take these up here.

6. *Chronological Treatises* (*bsTan-rtsis*-s)

The so-called *bstan-rtsis*-s (the term *bstan-rtsis*, literally translated, means "chronology of doctrine"),—the special chronological works—have a special place in Tibetan historical literature.

These works originated in connection with the repeated attempts, in Tibet, at ascertaining the date of the *nirvāṇa* of Buddha for finding out the number of years that had passed from the time of the *nirvāṇa* inasmuch as each of the sources at the disposal of the Tibetan writers calculated this date in its own way. These calculations were specially developed in connection with the eschatological notions of the Buddhists and the prophecies about the period of existence of the Buddhist religion on earth. The famous bSod-nams-rtse-mo (1142-1182), the second of the "five great (scholars) of Sa-skya-pa"[320] and, after him, other Tibetan authors give us a number of such calcu-

---

319. Thus, for instance, the "history of incarnations" of the regent of Tibet, Ṅag-dbaṅ-tshul-khrims is based on two "prayers to incarnations" (*'khruṅs-rabs-gsol-'debs*-s). One of these was written during his life time by the third Paṇ-chen-bla-ma dPal-ldan-ye-śes (1740-1780) and the other by the eighth Dalai Lama 'Jyams-dpal-rgya-mtsho (1758-1804)—see the "history of incarnations" of Ṅag-dbaṅ-tshul-khrims, pt. i, fol. 6ᵃ 5 ff. and 6ᵇ 4 ff. Similarly, the "history of incarnations" of Saṅs-rgyas Rol-pa'i-rdo-rje is based on the "prayers to his incarnations", written by the same third Pan-chen-bla-ma dPal-ldan-ye-śes (*op. cit.*, fol. 4ᵇ 3 ff.).

320. The dates of birth and death of bSod-nams-rtse-mo are indicated in the above-mentioned letter of his younger brother Grags-pa-rgyal-mtshan (1147-1216)—entitled *Ga-riṅ-rgyal-po-la-rtsis-bsdur-du-btaṅ-ba'i-yi-ge* (fol. 210ᵃ 4)—and in the "Chronological Tables". Besides, brief biographical data on him are given in the *Hor-chos-'byuṅ* (see G. Huth, *Geschichte des Buddhismus in der Mongolei*,

lations (*rtsis*). The earliest calculation of the date of the *nirvāṇa* was made during the reign of Khri-gtsug-lde'u-btsan (Ral-pa-can) in 822, when the peace treaty between Tibet and China was concluded. In 836, in the cloister of Śib-pe-cog-la Tshal of Bru-sha country, one Bande Chos-kyi-blo-gros along with some other persons calculated the number of years that had passed from the time of the *nirvāṇa*. Again, such calculation was made in 905 when the Tibetan king dPal-'khor-btsan was mourning the death of his father.[321]

Obviously, one must see, in these calculations made from time to time, the nucleus of the special chronological literature of Tibet (*bstan-rtsis*). As it was, these calculations could hardly have aimed at a somewhat detailed chronological investigation. Their object was merely to ascertain the date of the *nirvāṇa*. However, since these were based on a comparison of the data on various events and corresponding similar calculations made earlier, their purpose was not only and not so much the ascertaining of the date of the *nirvāṇa* (a controversial question as it was) as the establishment of the exact date of the current events. It is a pity that the earliest chronological calculations of the Tibetans have not reached us in the original ; we can only form some idea of these on the basis of the works composed later than the 12th century.

Of the Tibetan texts known to me, the earliest to contain a special chronological study of the initial and last dates of the existence of the Buddhist doctrine—i.e. *bstan-rtsis* in the real sense of the word—is the one entitled *Chos-la-'jug-pa'i-sgo* [The Door Leading to the (Buddhist) Faith] written in 1167[322] by the aforementioned bSod-nams-rtse-mo. It is included in the Complete Works of this author and covers 55 folios.[323] As is clear from the title itself, this work essentially is a general introduction to the Buddhist philosophy. The chronological investigation is included in it only casually (*shar-las-'oṅs-pa*) and covers merely two folios in the end of the book.[324] Here, the author lists the ten periods of Buddhist era, points out the difference between the Tibetan and the Indian and Chinese ways of reckoning time, cites data from the Indian chronology up to and after Buddha, gives principal dates from the life of Buddha himself and then enumerates the cases in which the calculations, made in Tibet, of the number of years

---

T. I., S. 70, Z. 13 ; S. 71, Z. 16), which, however, wrongly states that bSod-nams-rtse-mo died in the 44th year from his birth. Actually, he died in the 41st year of his life as clearly mentioned in the letter of his brother.

321. See the work of bSod-nams-rtse-mo, entitled *Chos-la-'jug-pa'i-sgo* (fol. 316ᵃ 2-5), included in the fourth volume (*ṅa*) of the *Sa-skya-bka'-'bum*.

322. The date of composition (Fire-Pig year) when, according to bSod-nams-rtse-mo, 3300 years had passed from the *nirvāṇa*—and which corresponds to A.D. 1167—is mentioned in the text itself (fol. 316ᵇ 4-5).

323. See *Sa-skya-bka'-'bum*, vol. iv (*ṅa*), fols. 263-317.

324. *Ibid.*, fols. 314ᵇ 6-316ᵇ 6.

that had passed from the time of the *nirvāṇa* were in conformity with the tradition to which the author belonged.

This brief chronological excursus is reproduced in full, with minor additions, by the nephew of the author, the well-known Sa-skya-paṇḍita Kun-dga'-rgyal-mtshan (1182-1251),[325] in the biography of Grags-pa-rgyal-mtshan compiled in 1216[326] (viz. in

325. A short biography of Sa-skya-paṇḍita Kun-dga'-rgyal-mtshan is available in his Collected Works [see *Sa-skya-bka'-'bum*, vol. xii (*na*), fols. 279-290] under the title *dPal-ldan-sa-skya-paṇḍita-chen-po'i-rnam-par-thar-pa*.

The author of this biography is some Shaṅ rGyal-ba-dpal, a monk from the monastery of Guṅ-thaṅ. It treats exclusively of the academic and scholarly activity of Sa-skya-paṇḍita and mentions no dates. Another biography of Sa-skya-paṇḍita, entitled *Chos-kyi-rje-sa-skya-paṇḍita-kun-dga'-rgyal-mtshan-gyi-rtogs-pa-brjod-pa-dri-za'i-glu-dbyaṅs* (7 fols.), is by the first Panchen Lama [Paṇ-chen-bla-ma] bLo-bzaṅ-chos-kyi-rgyal-mtshan (1570-1662) and is included in the complete works of this author (vol. i ; *ka*). A copy of the collected works of the first Panchen Lama is available in the Institute of Peoples of Asia (*Tsybikov Collection*, No. 10). The list of historical literature given in the *Deb-ther-rgya-mtsho* (vol. i, fol. 12ᵇ 5-6) mentions five different biographies of Sa-skya-paṇḍita. Four of these are also mentioned in the list of rare books (see *dPe-rgyun-dkon-pa-'ga'-shig-gi-tho-yig*, fol. 4ᵇ 5-6). Besides, a short biography of this famous Tibetan scholar is given in the *Hor-chos-'byuṅ* (see G. Huth, *Geschichte des Buddhismus in der Mongolei*, vol. i, S. 73, Z. 14 ; S. 87, Z. 17 ; vol. ii, SS. 118-136). Stray pieces of information on him and the dates of his birth and death are found recorded in numerous historical texts including the "Chronological Tables".

326. This work bears the title *bLa-ma-rje-btsun-pa-chen-po'i-rnam-thar* and is included in the *Sa-skya-bka'-'bum* (vol. x, *tha*) fols. 288ᵇ 1-299ᵇ 4. The date of composition of the work—Fire-Mouse year, in which Grags-pa-rgyal-mtshan passed away and in which, according to the views of Sa-skya-pa school, 3349 years had passed from the date of the *nirvāṇa*—is mentioned in the text itself on folios 298ᵃ 5-298ᵇ 2. (There is, however, a misprint in the xylograph, which wrongly mentions 3350 years. But this error is clearly eliminated on the basis of the quotations and references available in other works which mention 3349 years: Bu-ston, *Chos-'byuṅ*, fol. 103ᵇ 4 ; *Dus-'khor-ṭīk-chen*, pt. i, fol. 23ᵃ 1-2, and *dPag-bsam-ljon-bzaṅ*, fols. 79ᵇ 7-80ᵃ 1 ; S. C. Das, *Pag Sam Jon Zang*, p. 124). See also the statement of the 'chronological table' of the first 'Jam-dbyaṅs-bshad-pa. The chronological excursus covers fols. 296ᵃ 6-299ᵃ 5 in this work of Sa-skya-paṇḍita.

the year in which the latter died). Among the other things that Sa-skya-paṇḍita has added are some works of Sa-skya-pa-chos-rje[327] which obviously should be taken to mean Grags-pa-rgyal-mtshan, for only a few lines earlier, the author uses this respectful title for the latter.[328] However, during all my travels, I could not trace the text from which these words are taken. Probably, Sa-skya-paṇḍita has referred not to a written source but simply to something that he might have personally heard from his uncle, Grags-pa-rgyal-mtshan.

The chronological calculations of the Sa-skya-pa scholars have been frequently quoted in the later works as one of the main opinions on the dates of birth and death of Buddha. In particular, these have been quoted, in fairly good details, by Bu-ston Rin-chen-grub,[329] Yid-bzaṅ-rtse-ba ('Gos-lo-tsā-ba gShon-nu-dpal) and, from him, by Lha-dbaṅ-blo-gros,[330] Sum-pa-mkhan-po Ye-śes-dpal-'byor[331] and others.

---

327. *Sa-skya-bka'-'bum*, vol. x (*tha*), fol. 298ᵇ 6 ff.
328. *Ibid.*, fol. 298ᵃ 5.
329. Bu-ston, *Chos-'byuṅ*, fols. 103ᵃ 5-104ᵃ 6 (E. Obermiller, *History of Buddhism*, pt. ii, pp. 106-108. This translation, however, is full of errors).
330. See E. Schlagintweit, *Die Berechnung der Lehre*, München, 1897, S. 662, Z. 13-S. 663, Z. 16 (Tibetan text). Since there are numerous errors and discrepancies in the translation mady by E. Schlagintweit and particularly in his annotations to this translation, we have to refer only to the Tibetan text (bearing the title *bsTan-rtsis-'dod-spyin-gter-'bum*) published by him as an *appendix* to his work.

    A survey of the chronological exposition of the Sa-skya-pa scholars as included in this text reveals that, as compared with the chronology in the works of Sa-skya-pa scholars themselves, the numbers of years that have passed from the *nirvāṇa* to some particular events are throughout found increased by one year. Thus, for example, the number of years from the *nirvāṇa* to A.D. 822 is reckoned not as 2955 (as in the original texts) but as 2956 etc. In other words, in all these cases, the current year of the happening of a particular event is also included in the number of years reckoned to have passed from the date of the *nirvāṇa*. The only exception is the figure for the number of years that have passed from the *nirvāṇa* to the year of composition of the text of *Chos-la-'jug-pa'i-sgo*—which somehow has been left unchanged. In the same way, the dates of composition of *'Khrul-sel* (A.D. 1442) and *bsTan-rtsis- dod-spyin-gter-'bum* (A.D. 1592) as reckoned from the date of *nirvāṇa* do not include the year of the event itself.
331. *dPag-bsam-ljon-bzaṅ*, fols. 79ᵇ 2-80ᵃ 2; S. C. Das, *Pag Sam Jon Zang*, pp. 123-124.

Besides the chronological calculations of the Sa-skya-pa scholars,[332]—which represent one of the best known trends in the Tibetan chronology of Buddhism,—there have also been other attempts to calculate the date of the *nirvāṇa*. These also include such trends which, like the Sa-skya-pa school, assign the date of the *nirvāṇa* to a much remote period (25th-20th century B.C.). One such trend is represented in the apocryphal *bKa'-chems* [Will] of the king Sroṅ-btsan-sgam-po,[333] another—by Nel-pa-

---

332. As already stated in note 96, according to the Sa-skya-pa scholars, Buddha was born in the Earth-Dragon year and he attained *nirvāṇa* on the boundary of the Fire-Pig and Earth-Mouse years. See *Chos-la-'jug-pa'i-sgo*, fol. 315ᵇ 5-6 ; *bLa-ma-rje-btsun-pa-chen-pa'i-rnam-thar*, fol. 297ᵃ 3-4. The Sa-skya-pa scholars opine that from the date of the *nirvāṇa* up to A.D. 822 (inclusive) in which the peace treaty between Tibet and China was concluded, there is a span of 2955 years ; up to A.D. 1167 in which the work entitled *Chos-la-'jug-pa'i-sgo* was written, there is a space of 3300 years, and up to A.D. 1216 when Grags-pa-rgyal-mtshan passed away—that of 3349 years etc. Thus, as already remarked (see note 96), the Sa-skya-pa scholars assign the date of the *nirvāṇa* of Buddha to the end of the year 2134 B.C. (Fire-Pig year) and regard the year 2133 B.C. (Earth-Mouse year) as the first year after the *nirvāṇa*. They date the birth of Buddha to 2213 B.C. (Earth-Dragon year). For the conversion of dates according to Tibetan sexagenary cycle into European calendar and vice-versa, see : P. Pelliot, *Le cycle sexagénaire*..., JA, 1913, t. 1, pp. 664-665 (*Tableau des dates cycliques anterieurs a l'ére chrétienne*).
333. As mentioned in the *bsTan-rtsis-'dod-spyin-gter-'bum* published by E. Schlagintweit (see E. Schlagintweit, *Die Berechnung der Lehre*, S. 662, Z. 8-11), there passed 3862 years (if the calculations of the "Will" of the king Sroṅ-btsan-sgam-po be accepted) from the date of the *nirvāṇa* to A.D. 1442 (inclusive) in which the work '*Khrul-sel* was written, and 4012 years up to A.D. 1592 when the work *bsTan-rtsis-'dod-spyin-gter-'bum* itself was written. In the usual case, the *nirvāṇa* of Buddha, according to this calculation, should be assigned to 2421 B.C., for, in order to obtain the ordinal number of the year before our era, it is necessary to add one unit to the absolute value of the mathematical difference of the given numbers 1442 and 3862 (or 1592 and 4012). [For this rule, see W. Wislicenus, *Astronomische Chronologie*, Leipzig, 1895, S. 46 ; F. K. Ginzel, *Handbuch der mathematischen und technischen Chronologie*, Bd i, S. 99 ; Bd III, S. 182]. It should, however, be noted that the Tibetans include, in this number, not only the current year (i.e. the year to which the calculations are made) but also the year of completion of a particular event as whole units. For instance, A.D. 1282 (Water-Horse year) is regarded as the third year from the time of death of

paṇḍita.[334] Then there are three closely allied trends which do, to some extent, approach the date of the *nirvāṇa* (assigning it to the 14th-9th centuries B.C.). These

---

'Phags-pa-bla-ma, which occurred in A.D. 1280. The number of years as reckoned from A.D. 1282 to A.D. 1442 comes to 161. Cf. *bsTan-rtsis-'dod-spyin-gter-'bum*, E. Schlagintweit, *Die Berechnung der Lehre*, S. 664, Zz. 9-10. (This is like our expression "the third day", which means "two days back"). This manner of calculation is followed by a majority of Tibetan writers particularly by Yid-bzaṅ rtse-ba who applies it in his *'Khrul-sel* and in the *Deb-ther-sṅon-po*. Therefore, the number of years from the *nirvāṇa* to A.D. 1442 (inclusive), viz. 3862 years, as mentioned by Yid-bzaṅ-rtse-ba—exactly as the number of years from the *nirvāṇa* to A.D. 1592, viz. 4012 years as mentioned by Lha-dbaṅ-blo-gros—should be increased by one year for finding out the date of this event. Taking into account all these facts, the *nirvāṇa* of Buddha should, from the viewpoint of the "Will" of the king Sroṅ-btsan-sgam-po, be assigned to A.D. 2420 (Iron-Cow year according to the Tibetan sexagenary cycle). This agrees with the testimony of Sum-pa-mkhan-po who says that the Buddha was born, according to this viewpoint, in the Iron-Dragon year and that 4247 years have passed from this event to A.D. 1747 (see *dPag-bsam-ljon-bzaṅ*, fol 287b 3). However, in the text of *bsTan-rtsis-'dod-spyin-gter-'bum*, the *nirvāṇa* is dated (obviously by mistake) to Water-Cow year which, in the present case, can correspond only to 2408 or 2468 B.C. This error was noticed and mentioned, in his annotations, by the anonymous scribe of the Tibetan text of this work (see *bsTan-rtsis-'dod-spyin-gter-'bum*, E. Schlagintweit, *Die Berechnung der Lehre*, S. 662, Z. 1, where the correct cyclic date—Earth-Cow year—is mentioned).

334. In accordance with *bsTan-rtsis-'dod-spyin-gter-'bum* (*Ibid.*, S. 662, Zz. 11-13), Nel-pa-paṇḍita dated the *nirvāṇa* to Wood-Pig year. If his calculations be accepted, there is a span of 3588 years from this date of the *nirvāṇa* to A.D. 1442 and that of 3738 years up to A. D. 1592. Considering that the Tibetan authors add, to this number, the year of completion of a particular event (see the previous note), it may be gathered that the date of the *nirvāṇa* as ascertained by Nel-pa-paṇḍita, on conversion to our calendar, comes to 2146 B.C. which actually is the Wood-Pig year in Tibetan sexagenary cycle. From this standpoint, the birth of Buddha—who, according to the generally prevalent tradition, passed away in the 80th (according to some other versions, in the 81st or 82nd) year of his life—can be dated to Fire-Dragon year corresponding to 2225 B.C. However, the text—probably by mistake—mentions Water-Mouse year (i.e.2229 B.C.). This error is also noted by the scribe of the Tibetan text (*ibid.*, S. 662, Anm. 2, 3).

include the views expressed in : (1) the *'Khrul-sel* by the well-known historian Yid-bzaṅ-rtse-ba who, as he himself says, has depended on the calculations of the Khotan chronicles translated into Tibetan ;[335] (2) the astronomical works of gYuṅ-ston rDo-rje-dpal[336] and other authors ; and (3) the works of the scholars of Jo-naṅ-pa school,

---

On the other hand, the Fifth Dalai Lama ascribes this last date to Nel-pa-paṇḍita (see his work entitled *rTsis-skar-nag-las-brtsams-pa'i-dris-lan-ñin-byed-dbaṅ-po'i-snaṅ-ba*, fol. 43ᵇ 6. This work in 56 folios was written in A.D. 1656 and is included in vol. xx (*pha*) of the Complete Works of the Fifth Dalai Lama). This is also mentioned by Sum-pa-mkhan-po (see *dPag-bsam-ljon-bzaṅ*, fol. 287ᵇ 3). The original work of Nel-pa-paṇḍita has not come down to us.

335. According to Yid-bzaṅ-rtse-ba, Buddha was born in Water-Cow year and he attained *nirvāṇa* in Water-Hen year (see *bsTan-rtsis-'dod-spyin-gter-'bum*, E. Schlagintweit, *Die Berechnung der Lehre*, S. 666, Z. 3—S. 667, Z. 10, which quotes the relevant passage from his work *'Khrul-sel*. The cyclic date of the *nirvāṇa*—Water-Hen year—is also mentioned in another work of his—the *Deb-ther-sṅon-po* (vol. i, fol. 13ᵃ 1-2). According to the calculations made by Yid-bzaṅ-rtse-ba, 2750 years had passed from the date of the *nirvāṇa* to A.D. 1442 (including the current year and the year of actual occurrence of the event). This means that he has dated the *nirvāṇa* to 1308 B.C. (on conversion to European calendar),—which, in Tibetan sexagenary cycle, actually corresponds to Water-Hen year,—and the birth of Buddha to 1388 B.C. (Water-Cow year).

336. Brief biographical data on gYuṅ-ston rDo-rje-dpal are given in the *Deb-ther-sṅon-po* (vol. i, fols. 76ᵇ 3-77ᵃ 5). According to this text, he was the pupil of Karma Raṅ-byuṅ-rdo-rje (1284-1339) and Bu-ston Rin-chen-grub (1290-1364), and was born in Wood-Monkey year which, in the present case, corresponds to A.D. 1284. He died in the 82nd year of his life, viz. in Wood-Snake year, which corresponds to A.D. 1365. In the 'chronological table' of Sum-pa-mkhan-po, the dates of birth and death of gYuṅ-ston rDo-rje-dpal are given as A.D. 1287 and 1368.

As stated in the *bsTan-rtsis-'dod-spyin-gter-'bum* (E. Schlagintweit, *Die Berechnung der Lehre*, S. 664, Zz. 24-30), gYuṅ-ston rDo-rje-dpal assigned the birth of Buddha to Wood-Mouse year. It is further stated that if this view-point of gYuṅ-ston rDo-rje-dpal is accepted, it will be found that 2320 years have passed from the *nirvāṇa* (which, according to him, was attained by Buddha in the 80th year after his birth) to A.D. 1442, and that 2470 years (including also the current year and the year of the occurrence of the event) have passed up to A.D. 1592 (*ibid.*, S. 664, Zz. 33-34 ; S. 670, Zz. 5-8 and the table). This means that gYuṅ-ston rDo-rje-dpal dated the *nirvāṇa* to 878 B.C. (on conversion to our calendar) and the birth of Buddha to 957 B.C. This is

etc.[337] Finally, there also are opinions, which assign the *nirvāṇa* to a much nearer period (8th-6th century B.C.). One of these is set forth in the *Tsan-dan-gyi-sku-rgya-nag-sa-na-bshugs-ba'i-byuṅ-tshul* [Acount of how the sandal-wood image (of Buddha) in the

---

also corroborated by Sum-pa-mkhan-po who thinks that, according to gYuṅ-ston, 2704 years had passed from the birth of Buddha to A.D. 1747 (see *dPag-bsam-ljon-bzaṅ*, fol. 287ᵇ 3).

According to the *bsTan-rtsis-'dod-spyin-gter-'bum* (*ibid.*, S. 664, Zz. 30-34 ; S. 670, table), even the famous Bu-ston Rin-chen-grub is a representative of this trend in the Tibetan chronology of Buddhism. According to other indications, however, the latter's opinion in this regard agrees with that expressed by the astronomers of the Jo-naṅ-pa school (see below, note 337). At the same time, the view of gYuṅ-ston was accepted by 'Brug-pa Padma-dkar-po (see *bsTan-rtsis-'dod-spyin-gter-'bum*, *ibid.*, S. 670, Zz. 5-8).

337. According to *bsTan-rtsis-'dod-spyin-gter-'bum* (*ibid.*, S. 664, Z. 34—S. 665, Z. 5. S. 670, Zz. 8-9), the three representatives of Jo-naṅ-pa heretic school—Phyogs-las-rnam-rgyal (1306-1386), the well-known astronomer (short biographical data on him are given in the *Deb-ther-sṅon-po*, vol. ii, fols. 112ᵃ 5-113ᵃ 1), from whom Tsoṅ-kha-pa heard the *Kālacakra* doctrine (see *Grub-mtha'-śel-gyi-me-loṅ*, book 7, fol. 4ᵃ 2), 'Jam-dbyaṅs-chos-kyi-mgon-po, and Byaṅ-bdag rNam-rgyal-grags-bzaṅ, the representative of the large feudal Byaṅ-bdag dynasty and celebrated for his astronomical knowledge (see *rGyal-ba-lṅa-pa'i-deb-ther*, fols. 66ᵇ 1-67ᵇ 1)—think that Buddha was born in Fire-Horse year and that he attained *nirvāṇa* in Fire-Hare year. This means that, from their point of view, 2276 years (as per Tibetan mode of calculation) had passed from the *nirvāṇa* to A.D. 1442, and 2426 years (wrongly put in the text as 2427) to A.D. 1592. Thus, according to the European calendar, they date the *nirvāṇa* to 834 B.C. which actually is the Fire-Hare year (in Tibetan sexagenary cycle) and the birth of Buddha to 915 B.C. (Fire-Horse year).

This view is fairly well-known in Tibetan literature. In particular, this view is accepted by Sum-pa-mkhan-po (see *dPag-bsam-ljon-bzaṅ*, fols. 272ᵃ 7, 316ᵇ 7). Again, it is the first of the two views accepted by Ñi-ma-thaṅ-pa Śes-rab-spyin-pa in his work entitled *Luṅ-daṅ-rigs-pa'i-gter-chen-po-legs-par-bśad-pa'i-dus-tshigs-gsal-bar-byed-pa'i-ñi-ma* (briefly, *Ni-thaṅ-dus-tshigs*), written in 1675. See the xylograph of this work published in Aginsky *datsan* in Buryatia (fols. 59ᵇ 5-69ᵃ 1). The second 'Jam-dbyaṅs-bshad-pa, dKon-mchog-'jigs-med-dbaṅ-po, in his catalogue of the Co-ne edition of *bsTan-'gyur*, regards Bu-ston and mKhas-grub dGe-legs-dpal-bzaṅ-po (1385-1438), the closest pupil of Tsoṅ-kha-pa as the followers of this view.

This is also stated by Sum-pa-mkhan-po (see *dPag-bsam-ljon-bzaṅ*, fols. 23ᵃ 7, 24ᵃ 6-7, 179ᵃ 3, 287ᵇ 3 ; S. C. Das, *Pag Sam Jon Zang*, pp. 36, 38, 277).

Chinese land arrived] dating from 1263.[338] Another work belongs to the associate of

According to him, Bu-ston, like other followers of this view, dates the birth of Buddha to 915 B.C. (Fire-Horse year) but the *nirvāṇa* not to 834 B.C. (Fire-Hare year) as is done by the astronomers of the Jo-naṅ-pa school but to Fire-Tiger year (a year earlier). How far this information on Bu-ston's views is correct is difficult to say, for his astronomical works are not at our disposal. Besides, as we have seen above (see note 336), absolutely different views are ascribed to this author. In his *Chos-'byuṅ*, Bu-ston states that from the point of view of the *Kālacakra* system, 2198 years should be reckoned to have passed from the time when Buddha preached the "Main text" (*Mūlatantra*) of this system to A.D. 1322 when the *Chos-'byuṅ* was written (see Bu-ston, *Chos-'byuṅ*, fol. 104b 2). This statement, however, is not adequate for our purpose. It does not clarify whether, as mentioned in the *bsTan-rtsis-'dod-spyin-gter-'bum* (E. Schlagintweit, *Die Berechnung der Lehre*, S- 664, Zz. 30-34), Bu-ston considered the "Main text" of the *Kālacakra* system as having been preached by Buddha a year before his *nirvāṇa* or whether, like the astronomers of the Jo-naṅ-pa school, he assumed that this sermon was delivered a year after the Śākyamuni became the Buddha. In the colophons to his historical work (Bu-ston, *Chos-'byuṅ*, fol. 244a 4-5) and in his commentary on *Abhisamayālaṃkāra* entitled *Luṅ-gi-sñe-ma* (or more fully, *Śes-rab-kyi-pha-rol-tu-phyin-pa'i-man-ṅag-gi-bstan-bcos-mṅon-par-rtogs-pa'i-rgyan-shes-bya-ba'i-'grel-ba'i-rgya-cher-bśad-pa-luṅ-gi-sñe-ma*),—published by Aginsky *datsan* in Buryatia, chapter viii, fol. 28b 1-2,—this author depends upon the year of the *nirvāṇa* as established by Sa-skya-pa school. As regards mKhas-grub dGe-legs-dpal-bzaṅ-po, he actually follows the point of view of the astronomers of Jo-naṅ-pa school. In his famous work entitled *dPal-dus-kyi-'khor-lo'i-'grel-chen-dri-ma-med-pa'i-'od-kyi-rgya-chen-cher-bsad-pa-de-kho-na-ñid-snaṅ-par-byed-pa*—which is an extensive commentary on *Vimalaprabhā*, the Indian commentary on *Kālacakratantra*—he clearly mentions that, in his opinion, the Śākyamuni became the Buddha in Water-Horse year. He further mentions that 1904 years had passed from this moment which, according to him, should be regarded as the beginning of the Buddhist era, to the end of the period of Me-mkha'-rgya-mtsho, i.e. up to A.D. 1026 (inclusive) and that 2312 years had passed up to A.D. 1434 when mKhas-grub dGe-legs-dpal-bzaṅ-po wrote his work [see the above-mentioned work of mKhas-grub dGe-legs-dpal-bzaṅ-po, pt. i (vol. ii of the Collected Works), fols. 30a 6-30b 2, 390b 4-5]. Thus, he has dated the event in question to 879 B.C. —the year to which the astronomers of the Jo-naṅ-pa school dated this event.

338. The "Account of how the sandal-wood image (of Buddha) in the Chinese land

Kublai, Lama Grub-chen U-rgyan-pa Rin-chen-dpal (1230-1309), who wrote his chronology in 1282.[339] A third work is by a scholar from Kashmir, Śākyaśrībhadra (1127-1225)[340] who calculated the date of the *nirvāṇa* many times—in 1204, 1207 and

---

arrived" is available in the *bsTan-'gyur* [rGyud, vol. lxxxv (*ru*), fols. 154ᵃ 1-155ᵃ 4].

339. A short biography of Grub-chen U-rgyan-pa Rin-chen-dpal is available in the *Deb-ther-sṅon-po* (vol. ii, fols. 68ᵇ 5-72ᵃ 1). The dates of his birth and death are also included in the "Chronological Tables". The 'chronological table' of the first 'Jam-dbyaṅs-bshad-pa mentions even the date of compilation of the chronology. This distinguished leader of the 'Brug-pa sect,—who was invited to the court of Kublai in 1292 (see A. Csoma de Koros, *A Grammar of the Tibetan Language*, pp. 200, 202, n. 7 ; E. Schlagintweit, *Berechnung der Lehre*, S. 627, Anm. 244, Ss. 629, 639, 641),—is often confused with Padmasambhava who, as is well known, has the title "Gu-ru U-rgyan-pa". The very text of *bsTan-rtsis-'dod-spyin-gter-'bum* clearly states that Grub-chen U-rgyan-pa Rin-chen-dpal calculated the date of the *nirvāṇa* in Water-Horse year which, according to the Tibetan calculation, was the third year after the death of 'Phags-pa-bla-ma (1235-1280)—viz. in 1282 and that 161 years had passed from this year to A.D. 1442 (*ibid.*, S. 664, Zz. 9-10).

According to the *bsTan-rtsis-'dod-spyin-gter-'bum* (*ibid.*, S. 663, Z. 27—S. 664, Z. 11) which contains the calculations of U-rgyan-pa Rin-chen-dpal, the latter thought that on the 5th day after the new moon of the 11th month of A.D. 1282, 1932 years 8 months and 5 days had passed from the time of the *nirvāṇa*. This means that he dated the *nirvāṇa* to 651 B.C. which, according to the Tibetan sexagenary cycle, is the Iron-Horse year. It is true that on the basis of the information of the same source, Yid-bzaṅ-rtse-ba thought that from the viewpoint of U-rgyan-pa Rin-chen-dpal, 2093 years (and not 2092, as would have been expected) had passed from the *nirvāṇa* to A. D. 1442. In accordance with this, even Lha-dbaṅ-blo-gros assumed that 2243 years had passed from the date of the *nirvāṇa* to A.D. 1592 when his work *bsTan-rtsis-'dod-spyin-gter-'bum* was written. But this discrepancy of one year cannot affect our calculation of the year to which U-rgyan-pa Rin-chen-dpal dates the *nirvāṇa*. This is explained by the fact that Yid-bzaṅ-rtse-ba, following the general habit of the Tibetan authors (cf. *supra*, note 333), reckoned 161 years from A.D. 1282 to 1442, added this figure to 1932 and thus got a total of 2093 years—a number which includes, as whole units, the current year viz. 1442 and the year of the *nirvāṇa*. And this is what he wanted.

340. A short biography of Śākyaśrībhadra is included in the *Deb-ther-sṅon-po* (vol. ii, fols. 255ᵃ 1-259ᵇ 5). The principal dates are also mentioned in the

1210.[341] His views[342] were cited, among others, by Sa-skya-paṇḍita[343]; the calculation

[Notes 342-3 : see *infra*]

"Chronological Tables". In Tibet, Śākyaśrībhadra spent ten years—from 1204 to 1213 (see *Deb-ther-sṅon-po*, vol. ii, fol. 256ᵃ 1-2).

341. As stated by Bu-ston Rin-chen-grub, Śākyaśrībhadra made one calculation in Khro-phu in A.D. 1204 (Wood-Mouse year), i.e. during the first year of his arrival in Tibet. Thereafter, he made two calculations in A.D. 1207 (Fire-Hare year). The first of these two calculations, made in Sol-nag-thaṅ-chen, is widely prevalent. According to this calculation, 1750 years 2 months and 20 days had passed from the time of the *nirvāṇa*,—which took place on the 8th day after the new moon in the month of Kārtika (*smin-drug*), the last month of the autumn—up to the date of calculation. From this, it may be inferred that this calculation itself was made on the 12th day after the full moon of Māgha (*mchu*), the last winter month. Śākyaśrībhadra, as testified by the Tibetan sources, reckoned the beginning of the year from the first day after the full moon of the month of Kārtika (*ston-zla-tha-chuṅ-smin-drug-zla-ba'i-mar-ṅo'i-tshes-gcig*). The same point of view was also accepted by Bu-ston and other authors (see *Ni-thaṅ-dus-tshigs*, fols. 13ᵇ 5-14ᵃ 1). Thus this calculation wasmade about two months earlier than the second one which, as Bu-ston tells us, was made on the 5th day of the middle spring month of the same year, viz. of A.D. 1207. Finally, the last calculation made by Śākyaśrībhadra was in Sa-skya in 1210 (Iron-Horse year). What Bu-ston actually states in this connection is : Kha-che-śākya-śrīs śiṅ-pho-byi-lo-la-khro-phur-brtsis-pa-daṅ me-yos-la-sol-nag-thaṅ-chen-du-brtsis-par smin-drug-zla-ba'i-dkar-phyogs-kyi tshes-brgyad-nam-guṅ-mñam-pa-la zla-ba-ri-po-la-nub-tshe de-rjes-lo-ni-stoṅ-phrag-gcig bdun-brgya-daṅ-ni-lṅa-bcu-daṅ zla-ba-gñis-daṅ-zla-ba-phyed de-bshin-ñi-ma-lṅa-rabs-'das lo-ni-stoṅ-phrag-gsum-daṅ-ni ñis-brgya-daṅ-ni-bshi-bcu-dgu zla-ba-dgu-daṅ-ñi-ma-bcu ma-'oṅs-bstan-pa'i-lhag-mar-gnas shes me-yos-dpyid-'briṅ-gi-tshes-lṅa-la-brtses-pa-daṅ lcags-pho-rta-la-sa-skyar-brtses-pa'i-lugs-kyis lo-stoṅ-brgyad-brgya-drug-cu-rtsa-lṅa-chu-pho-phya-lo-yan-chad-la-'das (see Bu-ston, *Chos-'byuṅ*, fols. 103ᵇ 6-104ᵃ 3).

The last portion of this passage has been so distorted by E. Obermiller in his translation that it makes no sense. Without understanding that the reference here was to the views expressed on the date of the *nirvāṇa* by one and the same person who had calculated this date four times, E. Obermiller converted the last two cases of calculation into independent theories. Thus he deprived the concluding words of the text of all sense—the words in which Bu-ston specifies the number of years that, according to the viewpoint of Śākyaśrībhadra, had passed from the *nirvāṇa* to the composition of his historical

made by him in 1207 is quoted by Bu-ston,[344] mKhas-grub dGe-legs-dpal-bzaṅ-po,[345] Yid-bzaṅ-rtse-ba,[346] Lha-dbaṅ-blo-gros[347] and others.

[Notes 344-7 : see *infra*]

work in 1322. E. Obermiller translates : "According to the point of view of those who count (the time of the Buddha's attainment of *nirvāṇa*) to have been the 5th of the middle-month of spring in the year of the fire-hare, and according to the tradition of the Sa-kya which counts from the male-iron-horse year,—1865 years have passed away up to the year of the male-water-dog" (see E. Obermiller, *History of Buddhism*, pt. ii, p. 107). Such a translation is all the more odd because the earlier portion of the passage has been translated correctly (except that it has been broken off from the later portion and that the numerical "five" has been erroneously substituted by "ten"). A correct translation of the whole passage would be : "In accordance with the calculation made by Śākyaśrībhadra of Kashmir in the year of the Wood-Mouse (1204) in Khro-phu and the calculation made (by him) in the year of the Fire-Hare (1207) in Sol-nag-thaṅ-chen,—which reads : "In the bright part of the month of Kārtika, on the 8th day, in the midnight, when the moon set behind the mountain, the sovereign of the hermits attained *nirvāṇa*, (and) 1750 years two-and-a-half months and five days have passed since then, (and that) the Doctrine (of the Buddha) is to exist (for) 3249 years 9 months and 10 days in future",—and according to the calculation made (by him) on the 5th day of the middle-month of spring in the year of the Fire-Hare (1207), and (again) according to the calculation made (by him) in Sa-skya in the year of the Iron-Horse (1210), 1865 years have passed to the year of the Water-Dog". The calculation made by Śākyaśrībhadra in 1210 is also referred to by Sa-skya-paṇḍita (see *bLa-ma-rje-btsun-pa-chen-po'i-rnam-thar*, fol. 298^b 4-5).

342. As already stated in the previous note, according to the calculation made in 1207 by Śākyaśrībhadra, 1750 years had passed from the date of the *nirvāṇa*. Again, calculating the date of the *nirvāṇa* in 1210, he—in full agreement with the previous calculation—reckoned that 1753 years had passed from the *nirvāṇa* (see *bLa-ma-rje-btsun-pa-chen-po'i-rnam-thar*, fol. 298^b 4-5). In accordance with this, Bu-ston Rin-chen-grub also, in ascertaining the number of years that had passed from the *nirvāṇa* of Buddha to 1322 when he wrote his historical work, assumed (as we have already seen) that 1865 years had passed from the point of view of Śākyaśrībhadra. This means that Śākyaśrībhadra placed the date of the *nirvāṇa* at the year 544 B.C. (as converted to our calendar). This is also corroborated by other Tibetan sources, though it must be kept in mind that most of them, following the usual convention in Tibet, also include the year then running and the year of completion of the event itself in the figure for the number of years that have passed from the date of the event. This has already

The nine trends enumerated here are expounded by the historian Yid-bzaṅ-rtse-ba—

---

been mentioned by us in the previous notes. Thus, for instance, Yid-bzaṅ-rtse-ba thinks that from the point of view of Śākyaśrībhadra, 1986 years had passed from the *nirvāṇa* to 1442 when his work *'Khrul-sel* was written (see the statement of *'Khrul-sel* quoted in the *bsTan-rtsis-'dod-spyin-gter-'bum* ; E. Schlagintweit, *Die Berechnung der Lehre*, S. 664, Zz. 22-23—the text erroneously mentions 1987 instead of 1986 probably because *ro*, the symbol for number "6" has been misprinted as *ri*, the symbol for number "7"). In the same way, Yid-bzaṅ-rtse-ba thinks that 2020 years had passed from the *nirvāṇa* to A.D. 1476 when he wrote his historical work *Deb-ther-sṅon-po* (see *Deb-ther-sṅon-po*, vol. ii, fols. 255ᵃ 4-255ᵇ 1). Accordingly, Lha-dbaṅ-blo-gros assumes that 2136 years had passed from the *nirvāṇa* to 1592, the year in which his work *bsTan-rtsis-'dod-spyin-gter-'bum* was written (*ibid.*, S. 670, Zz. 4-5). The Tibetan sources regard this date of the *nirvāṇa* calculated by Śākyaśrībhadra as corresponding to the year of the Fire-Serpent in Tibetan sexagenary cycle (see *Deb-ther-sṅon-po*, vol. ii, fol. 255ᵃ 6 ; *bsTan-rtsis-'dod-spyin-gter-'bum*, *ibid.*, S. 664, Zz. 22-23 ; *Legs-bśad-nor-bu'i baṅ-mdsod*, fol. 218ᵇ 1 etc.). And the year 544 B.C. actually bears the cyclic symbol of "Fire-Serpent". It is true that gTsug-lag-chos-kyi-snaṅ-ba, in his catalogue of the sDe-dge edition of the *bKa'-'gyur* (fol. 106ᵃ 6-7) —and, after him, dKon-mchog-'jigs-med-dbaṅ-po, in his catalogue of the Co-ne edition of the *bsTan-'gyur* (fol. 236ᵇ 3-4)—believes that from the point of view of Śākyaśrībhadra, the Fire-Serpent year is the year of the birth of Buddha and that his *nirvāṇa* dates from the year of the Fire-Mouse. But this is a clear discrepancy which is rectified by the statements of these authors themselves on the number of years that had passed from the date of the *nirvāṇa*. Sum-pa-mkhan-po rightly says that from the point of view of Śakyaśrībhadra, the birth of Buddha dates from Fire-Hen year, from which 2370 years had passed up to 1747 (see *dPag-bsam-ljon-bzaṅ*, fol. 287ᵇ 3).

Examining the views of Śākyaśrībhadra on the date of the *nirvāṇa*, one cannot help noticing the striking similarity of these views with the tradition of the southern Buddhism, which also dates the *nirvāṇa*, as is known, to 544-543 B.C. [see C. Lassen, *Indische Altertumskunde*, ii Band (2 Auflage). Leipzig, 1874, Ss. 53-67, which gives the various views expressed on the date of *nirvāṇa*].

343. *bLa-ma-rje-btsun-pa-chen-po'i-rnam-thar*, fol. 298ᵇ 4-5.

344. Bu-ston, *Chos-'byuṅ*, fols. 103ᵇ 6-104ᵃ 3.

345. *Dus-'khor-ṭīk-chen*, vol. i (second volume of the Complete Works of mKhas-grub dGe-legs-dpal-bzaṅ-po), fols. 23ᵃ 6-24ᵇ 1.

346. *Deb-ther-sṅon-po*, vol. ii, fols. 255ᵃ 4-255ᵇ 1.

347. *bsTan-rtsis-'dod-spyin-gter-'bum* (E. Schlagintweit, *Die Berechnung der Lehre*, S. 664, Zz. 11-18).

or, as he is otherwise called 'Gos-lo-tsā-ba gShon-nu-dpal (1392-1481)[348]—in his work *rTsi-kyi-bstan-bcos-'khrul-sel* [Elimination of Errors in Calculations] written during 1442-1443.[349] In the work *Pad-dkar-shal-luṅ* which appeared in 1447[350] and which is attributed to the famous Tibetan astronomers mKhas-grub Nor-bzaṅ-rgya-mtsho (1423-1513)[351] and Phug-pa Lhun-grub-rgya-mtsho,[352] the number of trends described is

---

348. According to the 'chronological table' of the first 'Jam-dbyaṅs-bshad-pa, the work *'Khrul-sel* was written in 1443 (Water-Pig year). But the author himself—as already frequently stated—mentions the year of composition of his work as 1442 (Water-Dog year).

    The date mentioned by the author himself does not, of course, raise any doubt. But this fact does not eliminate the possibility of the former date (viz. the date of the 'chronological table') being also correct. This is because the Tibetan writers often regard the date of beginning of a work as the date of its composition. It is therefore quite possible that the year 1442 is the date when the work was started and, besides, is also the date up to which the years that had passed from the time of particular events have been calculated, while the year 1443 is the date of the completion of the work.

349. Brief biographical data on this most celebrated Tibetan historian are given in the *bKa'-gdams-gsar-rñiṅ-gi-chos- byuṅ-yid-kyi-mdses-rgyan* (fols. 90ᵃ 4-90ᵇ 2) ; the principal dates of his life are also mentioned in the "Chronological Tables".

350. The date of composition of the *Pad-dkar-shal-luṅ* is given in the *Vaiḍūrya-dkar-po* (fol. 21ᵃ 6), *Vaiḍūrya-gser-po* (fol. 419ᵇ 3) and in the "Chronological Tables" of the first 'Jam-dbyaṅs-bshad-pa and Sum-pa-mkhan-po. See also the reference work, entitled *bZo-daṅ-gso-ba skar-rtsis-rnams-las-byuṅ-ba'i-miṅ-gi-graṅs* (fol. 17ᵃ 3)—by the aforementioned kLoṅ-rdol-bla-ma—comprising the 16th (*ma*) book of the Collected Works of kLoṅ-rdol-bla-ma published in the monastery of Kun-bde-gliṅ.

351. A short biography of Nor-bzaṅ-rgya-mtsho is given by Yoṅs-'dsin Ye-śes-rgyal-mtshan in the *Lam-rim-bla-ma-brgyud-pa'i-rnam-thar* (pt. ii, the fifth volume of the Complete Works of Yoṅs-'dsin Ye-śes-rgyal-mtshan), fols. 333ᵃ 3-335ᵃ 6. Principal dates of his life are also mentioned in the "Chronological Tables".

352. The Tibetan sources differ on the authorship of the *Pad dkar-shal-luṅ*. In the 'chronological table' of the first 'Jam-dbyaṅs-bshad-pa, one Phug-pa Lhun-grub-rgya-mtsho has been named as the author of the *Pad-dkar-shal-luṅ*. The same name is also given in some other sources ; for example, in the *bZo-daṅ-gso-ba skar-rtsis-rnams-las-byuṅ-ba'i-miṅ gi-graṅs* (fol. 17ᵃ 3). But the *Vaiḍūrya-dkar-po* (fol. 13ᵃ 1) mentions the *Pad-dkar-shal-luṅ* as the work of Nor-bzaṅ-rgya-mtsho and Lhun-grub-rgya-mtsho, though a little later, while giving the date of

twelve.[353] This also includes the view which even till now is widely prevalent in

---

this work, its author is again named as Phug-pa-pa only, i.e. Phug-pa Lhun-grub-rgya-mtsho (see *Vaiḍūrya-dkar-po*, fol. 21ᵃ 6). The *Vaiḍūrya-gya'-sel* (fols. 149ᵃ 5-149ᵇ 3) also calls the *Pad-dkar-shal-luṅ* as the work of both these persons but also mentions the name of a third author—some Grwa-chuṅ Yon-tan-rgya-mtsho. As stated in this text, the *Pad-dkar-shal-luṅ* was either written by these "three rgya-mtsho-s" (*rgya-mtsho-rnams-gsum*) or was worked out mainly by Nor-bzaṅ-rgya-mtsho but,—because of the fear that this work by a representative of the dGe-lugs-pa sect, which was not so important at that time, will not be accepted,—was released by Phug-pa Lhun-grub-rgya-mtsho (the representative of the then prevalent Karma-pa sect) in his name.

The 'chronological table' of Sum-pa-mkhan-po states that Nor-bzaṅ-rgya-mtsho started writing *Pad-dkar-shal-luṅ* and that Lhun-grub-rgya-mtsho completed it. But in the text of his "history", Sum-pa-mkhan-po names one more person as the third author of this work. This person who is different from the one mentioned in the *Vaiḍūrya-gya'-sel*, is some Karma Chos-grags-rgya-mtsho, the teacher of Phug-pa Lhun-grub-rgya-mtsho (see *dPag-bsam-ljon-bzaṅ*, fol. 179ᵃ 3-4 ; S. C. Das, *Pag Sam Jon Zang*, p. 277). In the biography of Nor-bzaṅ-rgya-mtsho, the *Pad-dkar-shal-luṅ* is mentioned as one of his works (see *Lam-rim-bla-ma-brgyud-pa'i-rnam-thar*, pt. ii, fol. 335ᵃ 1). In the "List of Rare Books", Phug-pa Lhun-grub-rgya-mtsho is mentioned as the author of the *Pad-dkar-shal-luṅ*, whereas Nor-bzaṅ-rgya-mtsho is named as the author of a secondary derivative text (*bu-yig*) of this work (see *dPe-rgyun-dkon-pa-'ga'-shig-gi-tho-yig*, fol. 52ᵃ 2). These two texts of the *Pad-dkar-shal-luṅ*—the primary or the main text (*ma*) and the secondary or derivative text (*bu*)—are also mentioned in other sources (see, for instance, the *Vaiḍūrya-dkar-po*, fol. 629ᵃ 2, and *dPag-bsam-ljon-bzaṅ*, fol. 179ᵃ 4 ; S. C. Das, *Pag Sam Jon Zang*, p. 277 etc.). All this makes it clear that the compilation of the *Pad-dkar-shal-luṅ* is more firmly connected with the name of Phug-pa Lhun-grub-rgya-mtsho. But there is also a firm tradition attributing the authorship or, at least, the joint authorship to Nor-bzaṅ-rgya-mtsho.

353. See *bsTan-rtsis-'dod-spyin-gter-'bum* ; E. Schlagintweit, *Die Berechnung der Lehre*, S. 662, Zz. 1-2. These trends obviously include the nine trends enumerated in the *'Khrul-sel*, their own opinion by the authors of *Pad-dkar-shal-luṅ* which will be set forth in the next note, the opinion of dbUs-pa bLo-gsal (14th cent.) and the opinion of bLa-ma-dam-pa bSod-nams-rgyal-mtshan (1312-1375). dbUs-pa bLo-gsal dates the birth of Buddha to the Earth-Mouse year (corresponding to 2217 B.C.)—i.e. to a date which is four years earlier than that ascertained by Sa-skya-pa scholars. This means that, according to him, the *nirvāṇa* dates from

Tibet.[354]

Unfortunately, I did not have the possibility of studying either the *'Khrul-sel* or the *Pad-dkar-shal-luṅ*. Both of these works are on the "List of bibliographical rarities".[355] The theses of these texts are briefly set forth in the *bsTan-rtsis-'dod-spyin-gter-'bum*

2138 B.C. (see *bsTan-rtsis-'dod-spyin-gter-'bum, ibid*, S. 663, Zz. 16-17 ; S. 669, Z. 41). bLa-ma-dam-pa bSod-nams-rgyal-mtshan assigns the birth of Buddha to the Fire-Hare year and the *nirvāṇa* to the Fire-Pig year. There is, according to him, a span of 1197 years from this Fire-Pig year to the first year of the era—*me-mkha'-rgya-mtsho*—corresponding to 624 B.C. (see *bsTan-rtsis-'dod-spyin-gter-'bum, ibid.*, S. 665, Zz. 7-10 ff). In this way, on conversion to our calendar, he dated the *nirvāṇa* to 574 B.C. which actually is the Fire-Pig year in Tibetan sexagenary cycle. The period from this date to A.D. 1592 as reckoned by Lha-dbaṅ-blo-gros by following the Tibetan mode of calculation is 2166 years (see *ibid.*, S. 670, Zz. 9-10 and the *table*).

354. From the point of view of the *Pad-dkar-shal-luṅ*, the birth of Buddha dates to Iron-Monkey year and the *nirvāṇa*—to the Iron-Dragon year. The number of years from this last event to the first year of the Tibetan era (i.e. up to A.D. 1027) is generally believed to be 1907 (see *bsTan-rtsis-'dod-spyin-gter-'bum, ibid.*, S. 667, Z. 33-S. 668, Z. 12). From this viewpoint, the *nirvāṇa* dates to 881 B.C. which actually is a Earth-Dragon year, and the birth of Buddha to 961 B.C. which is a Iron-Monkey year. This agrees with the statement of Sum-pa-mkhan-po that, according to the *Pad-dkar-shal-luṅ*, 2707 years had passed from the birth of Buddha to A.D. 1747 (see *dPag-bsam-ljon-bzaṅ*, fol. 28,[b] 3). As regards Lha-dbaṅ-blo-gros, there is a small error in his calculations here. He believes that according to the *Pad-dkar-shal-luṅ*, 2474 years (in Tibetan cycle, *mtsho-ri-rgyal-ba*) had passed from the *nirvāṇa* to A.D. 1592, whereas actually by the Tibetan mode of calculation as followed by this author, he should have mentioned the number of years as 2472 (*mig-ri-rgyal-ba*)—see *bsTan-rtsis-'dod-spyin-gter-'bum, ibid.*, S. 670, Zz. 10-11 and the *table*.

In Tibetan literature, the view of the *Pad-dkar-shal-luṅ* is much more prevalent than even the view of the astronomers of the Jo-naṅ-pa school. This view is accepted, in particular, by the Fifth Dalai Lama in his work *rTsis-skar-nag-las-brtsams-pa'i-dris-lan-ñin-byed-dbaṅ-po'i-snaṅ-ba* (fol. 44[a] 1-2) and in the colophons of his other works, sDe-srid Saṅs-rgyas-rgya-mtsho in his astronomical treatises *Vaiḍūrya-dkar-po* (fol. 18[b] 1 ff.) and *Vaiḍūrya-gya'-sel* (fol. 18[b] 4 ff.) and by many other authors. This view is also accepted as a second possible view (cf. *supra*, note 337) by Ñi-ma-thaṅ-pa Śes-rabs-spyin-pa (see *Ni-thaṅ-dus-tshigs*, fol. 69[a] 1 ff.).

355. *dPe-rgyun-dkon-pa-'ga'-shig-gi-tho-yig*, fol. 52[a] 1-2.

written in 1592 by Lha-dbaṅ-blo-gros.[356] This work quotes—often in the exact words of the authors—all the views expressed by Tibetan writers on the initial dates of Buddhist chronology and cites, besides, the opinion of 'Brug-pa Padma-dkar-po (b. 1527). This last opinion is also shared by Lha-dbaṅ-blo-gros himself.[357] The first scholar to pay attention to this remarkable work was A. Csoma de Koros[358] who, in his

356. In the colophon, the Tibetan name of the author, Lha-dbaṅ-blo-gros-bzaṅ-po, is given after conversion to Sanskrit—Surcśamatibhadra (see *bsTan-rtsis-'dod-spyin-gter-'bum*, E. Schlagintweit, *Die Berechnung der Lehre*, S. 670, Z. 28). The date of composition of this work—the Water-Dragon year of the x cycle corresponding to A. D. 1592—is frequently mentioned in the text itself (*ibid.*, S. 658, Zz. 30-31 ; S. 662, Zz. 9-10 ; S. 667, Zz. 9-10 u.s.w.).

357. As stated in the *bsTan-rtsis-'dod-spyin-gter-'bum* (*ibid.*, S. 670, Zz. 5-8), 'Brug-pa Padma dkar-po first shared the view of the astronomer, gYuṅ-ston rDo-rje-dpal, mentioned earlier (note 336), but later formulated his own views which are followed by Lha-dbaṅ-blo-gros. Continuing to place the birth of Buddha at Earth-Mouse year and the *nirvāṇa* at Water-Sheep year, as before, 'Brug-pa Padma-dkar-po considered it necessary to assign theṣe dates of Tibetan sexagenary cycle to a more remote period than done by gYuṅ-ston rDo-rje-dpal. Proceeding from the calculations made by 'Brug-pa Padma-dkar-po, Lha-bdaṅ-blo-gros says that 2650 years had passed from the *nirvāṇa* to A.D. 1592 (inclusive) —*ibid*, S. 670, Zz. 11-13 and the *table*. As already stated, following the general convention of the Tibetan authors, Lha-dbaṅ-blo-gros included the year of the event itself in the figure for the number of years that had passed. Thus, as converted to our calendar, 'Brug-pa Padma-dkar-po dated the *nirvāṇa* to 1058 B.C. which really bears the cyclic symbol of "Water-Sheep". Lha-dbaṅ-blo-gros gives a detailed exposition of his calculations in the form of an opinion which he himself shares (*ibid.*, S. 649, Z. 8-S. 661, Z. 40). This opinion is not popular in Tibetan literature.

358. The earliest information on the thirteen various views on the date of the *nirvāṇa* as expounded in the *bsTan-rtsis-'dod-spyin-gter-'bum* was published by A. Csoma de Koros in the "Quarterly Oriental Magazine", N VII (Calcutta, 1826). In 1827, E. Burnouf printed, in "Journal Asiatique" (t x, p. 140 ff) a French translation of this report. Though, in this translation, the very dates of the *nirvāṇa* are wrongly given as the dates of birth of Buddha, and the name of the source is also not correctly indicated, the conversion of these dates into European calendar as followed in this translation is generally much more correct—with the exception of two dates (the 5th and 11th serially)—than in the *Grammar* of Csoma de Koros. It is, however, possible that this error is due to a

Grammar, published a free prose rendering, into Tibetan and English, of the concluding parts of the text—which is a short summary in verse of all the opinions contained in it.[359] As regards the text itself, E. Schlagintweit was the first to acquaint the academic world with it by publishing its Tibetan original in Roman transcription along with a German translation.[360] However, I might say frankly that the translation made by E. Schlagintweit requires considerable corrections and even complete revision at many places.[361]

---

simple misprint in the figures for the numbers of years that had passed from the *nirvāṇa* to A.D. 1825 : 3123 instead of 3133, and 2390 for 2399. On subtracting 1825 from 3123 and 2390, one gets respectively 1298 instead of 1308 and 565 instead of 574. There are minor inaccuracies (of one year) in the conversion of some other dates too.

359. See A. Csoma de Koros, *A Grammar of the Tibetan Language*, pp. 199-201. After mentioning the number of years that, according to various theories, had passed from the *nirvāṇa* to the date of composition of the *bsTan-rtsis-'dod-spyin-gter-'bum*, A. Csoma de Koros tries here to find out the year at which various authors placed the *nirvāṇa*. However, the very base of his calculations is defective. First, Csoma de Koros errs in ascertaining the date of composition (1591 instead of 1592) of the *bsTan-rtsis-'dod-spyin-gter-'bum*—up to which the number of years that had passsed from the *nirvāṇa* is calculated. Then, he assumes that this year, viz. the running year is not included in the figure for the number of years that had passed from the time of the *nirvāṇa* as given in the *bsTan-rtsis-'dod-spyin-gter-'bum*. Thus he advances all the dates of the *nirvāṇa* mentioned in this text by two years. Here, he totally ignores the fact that on calculating the date of an event, from which a specific number of years (say *b*) has passed upto a certain year of our era (we shall call it *a*), it is necessary to add "1" to the difference of these two figures (viz. *b-a*)—Cf. W. Wislicenus, *Astronomische Chronologie*. S. 46. Csoma de Koros simply subtracts 1590 years (1591-1) from each figure given in the text, and thus obtains all his dates. However, this error of Csoma de Koros is practically insignificant, for the author of the text includes the year of completion of this event also in the figure given by him for the number of years that had passed from the *nirvāṇa*, and each of these figures should therefore be reduced by 1. To this too, Csoma de Koros does not pay any attention.

360. E. Schlagintweit, *Die Berechnung der Lehre. Eine Streitschrift zur Berichtigung der buddhistisch Chronologie verfasst im Jahre 1591 von Sureśamatibhadra,*—"Abhandlungen der konigl. bayerischen Akademie der Wissenschaften," 1 Cl., xx bd., iii abt., München, 1897, Ss. 589-670.

361. As is clear from the translation itself and from the annotations and introduction to it, E. Schlagintweit simply did not understand many places of the text. It is

The thirteen trends enumerated here do not exhaust the whole diversity of views of the Tibetan writers on the date of *nirvāṇa*. Besides, there also exist other trends.

---

enough to say that he did not even understand which 9 and 12 trends were discussed in the text (see *ibid.*, S. 631, Anm. 274). This work *'Khrul-sel* is ascribed by E. Schlagintweit to Lhun-grub-rgya-mtsho and Nor-bzaṅ-rgya-mtsho (*ibid.*, SS. 591-592) in spite of a clear statement in the text that these two authors have specially criticized the *'Khrul-sel.* The text reads : *De-ltar-bkod-pa'i-bstan-rtsis-thams-cad-daṅ-lhag-par-'khrul-sel-la mkhas-pa-lhun-grub-rgya-mtsho-daṅ-nor-bzaṅ-rgya-mtsho-gñis-kyis-brgal-skiṅ-dpyad-nas raṅ-lugs-bshag-pa* etc. (*ibid.*, S. 667, Zz. 33-35) which literally translated is : "The scholars Lhun-grub-rgya-mtsho and Nor-bzaṅ-rgya-mtsho, having subjected to a critical analysis, all chronologies of the doctrine thus expounded and particularly the "Elimination of Errors" (*'Khrul-sel*), set forth their own opinion" etc. However, E. Schlagintweit translates as : Die solcher Art begründete Berechnung der Lehre beseitigt besser als alle die Fehler. Prüft man die Streitpunkte der zwei Weisen Lhun grub rgya mthso und Nor bzang rgya mthso, so sieht man die eigene Methode geordnet" etc. (S. 635). Though the text leaves no doubt that its author, after 'Brug-pa Padma-dkar-po, places the *nirvāṇa* at 1058 B.C., E. Schlagintweit believes that he dated the *nirvāṇa* to 513 B.C. (*ibid.*, SS. 594-595). Similarly, confused with the various views on the date of *nirvāṇa*, he states that bLa-ma-dam-pa bSod-nams-rgyal-mtshan dated the *nirvāṇa* to 653 B.C. (*ibid.*, SS. 595, 631, Anm. 278), whereas actually he had dated this event to 574 B.C. The information of the text that Atiśa, Bu-ston and Padma-dkar-po equally date the birth of the Buddha to the Wood-Mouse year (*ibid.*, S. 660, Zz. 24-26), has been so distorted in the translation of E. Schlagintweit that it almost means that these three persons themselves were born in the same Wood-Mouse year (*ibid.*, S. 618).

The expression *rṅog-lo* (*ibid.*, S. 662, Z. 36), which is a mere abridgement of the proper name rṄog-lo-tsā-ba bLo-ldan-śes-rab (cf. this place of the text with the original reports of the *Chos-la-'jug-pa'i-sgo*, fol. 316[b] 4, and *bLa-ma-rje-btsun-chen-po'i-rnam-thar*, fol. 298[a] 2) has, in E. Schlagintweit's translation, become *rdog-lo*, which makes no sense. As a result, the simple and clear phrase *de-nas-me-phag-la-rṅog-lo-'das* (which literally means : "Then, Ṅog-lo-tsā-ba died in the Fire-Pig year") acquires, in his translation, an absolutely fantastic form : "Ferner : Das Schlussjahr [this is how he translates *rdog-lo*, regarding *rdog* (a bead of a rosary) as *rdog-'dsin* (Schlusskugel im Rosenkranze, viz. holder of a rosary)] Feuer-Schwein war vorüber" (*ibid.*, S. 625). One could cite numerous examples of such errors and discrepancies, not to speak of the fact that here too

In particular, mKhas-grub dGe-legs-dpal-bzaṅ-po (1385-1438),[362] in his commentary on

(as in all other works of his), E. Schlagintweit wrongly regards, as the first year of the Tibetan era, A.D. 1026 (instead of A.D. 1027), and all dates of Tibetan history quoted by him in European calendar are therefore one year behind the actual ones. However, certain dates, which he has taken from the chronological calculations of the Sa-skya-pa school, have been quoted by him quite correctly. This is explained by the fact that all these dates in the text of the *bsTan-rtsis-'dod-spyin-gter- bum* are based on the numbers of years expired from the *nirvāṇa*,—which also include the year of the *nirvāṇa* itself.

On the other hand, the dates of composition of the *'Khrul-sel* and *bsTan--rtsis-'dod-spyin-gter-'bum* as calculated from the numbers of years that had passed from the *nirvāṇa* do not take into account the year of the *nirvāṇa* itself. In establishing the former dates on the basis of the latter,—which, as calculated by him, are one year behind the actual ones,—and without noticing that the modes of calculation were different in both the cases, E. Schlagintweit arrived at correct results [see *ibid.*, SS. 624-625, Anm. 209, 212-215, 217, 219 (1110 misprinted as 1100) and 223], thus contradicting the table which he had himself compiled for the Tibetan dates (according to the sexagenary cycle) and their corresponding years in our calendar (*ibid.*, S. 644). As a matter of fact, in dating the *'Khrul-sel* to 1491 and not to 1492, E. Schlagintweit does not notice that the difference between the figure 3575—which represents the number of years that had passed from the *nirvāṇa* to this date of composition of the work (inclusive)—and any other figure taken from the chronology of the Sa-skya-pa school as interpreted in the *bsTan-rtsis-'dod-spyin-gter-'bum* is one year less than the actual figure ; and therefore by subtracting this difference from 1441, he unexpectedly arrives at correct results.

362. The biography of mKhas-grub dGe-legs-dpal-bzaṅ-po is available under the title *mKhas-grub-thams-cad-mkhyen-pa'i-rnam-thar-mkhas-pa'i-yid-'phrog* (14 fols.) in the first volume of his Complete Works published by the bKra-śis-lhun-po monastery. The author of this biography was some Svasti (in Tibetan, bDe-legs). Another biography entitled *mKhas-grub-thams-cad-mkhyen-pa-dge-legs-dpal-bzaṅ-po'i-rnam-par-thar-ba* (13 fols.) was written by the second 'Jam-dbyaṅs-bshad-pa dKon-mchog-'jigs-med-dbaṅ-po and is available in the fifth volume (*ca*) of the Collected Works of the latter published in bLa-braṅ. We learn from various bibliographical lists that there also are other biographies of mKhas-grub dGe-legs-dpal-bzaṅ-po by other authors (see *Deb-ther-rgya-mtsho*, vol. i, fol. 11ᵇ 1 ; *dPe-rgyun-dkon-pa-'ga'-shig-gi-tho-yig*, fol. 4ᵃ 1-2). Besides, the biographies of mKhas-grub dGe-legs-bzaṅ-po are also enumerated in the *Lam-rim-bla-ma-rgyud-pa'i-rnam-thar* (pt. i, fols. 439ᵃ 2-461ᵇ 6), *dPag-bsam-ljon-bzaṅ* (fols. 175ᵇ 3-178ᵃ 1) [S. C. Das, *Pag Sam Jon Zang*, pp. 271-275] and in many

the *Kālacakratantra*,[363] includes a chronological calculation (*bstan-rtsis*) which was made in 1051 by Atīśa and repeated in 1257 by mChims Nam-mkha'-grags.[364] This calculation

---

other historical texts. The principal dates of the life of mKhas-grub dGe-legs-bzaṅ-po are given in the "Chronological Tables."

363. The sub-commentary of mKhas-grub dGe-legs-dpal-bzaṅ-po on *Kālacakratantra* bears the title *dPal-dus-kyi-'khor-lo'i-'phrel-chen-dri-ma-med-pa'i-'od-kyi-rgya-cher-bśad pa-de-kho-na-ñid-snaṅ-bar-byed-pa* but is usually cited by its short name *Dus-'khor-ṭīk-chen*. The author could not manage to finish the work himself. He wrote a commentary on the first and second chapters and on the earlier portion of the third chapter of the main text which has five chapters in all. The date of composition of this incomplete commentary—the Wood-Tiger year which, from the point of view of the Sa-skya-pa school, is 3567 years after the *nirvāṇa*—is mentioned in the text itself (part i, fol. 23ᵃ 4). This date, which corresponds to A.D. 1434, is also mentioned in the 'chronological table' of Sum-pa-mkhan-po. This commentary is available in the Collected Works of the author published in bKra-śis-lhun-po monastery. Two more commentaries on the remaining part of the text,—which are written by the pupils of mKhas-grub dGe-legs-dpal-bzaṅ-po and which complete this unfinished work,—are also available at the same place. One of these commentaries was written in 1449 by Shaṅ-shuṅ-pa Chos-dbaṅ-grags-pa (1404-1469) who later (from 1458) was the *Upādhyāya* of the Chab-mdo monastery (he was the second *Upādhyāya*). The second commentary was written in 1455 by bLo-gros-chos-skyoṅ (1389-1463), the fifth Head of the dGa'-ldan-monastery in Tibet. Together with these two versions of its later part, the text of the commentary of mKhas-grub dGe-legs-dpal-bzaṅ-po occupies almost full four volumes (from second to fifth) in the Collected Works of this author published in bKra-śis-lhun-po monastery. A copy of this Collected Works is available in the Institute of Peoples of Asia (*Tsybikov Collection*, No. 2).

364. See *Dus-'khor-ṭīk-chen*, pt. i, fol. 22ᵇ 2-6. The date of Atīśa's calculation as mentioned in this text is available in the "Chronological Tables". According to this calculation, the Buddha was born in the Earth-Ox year and he attained *nirvāṇa* in the Earth-Monkey year. It is believed that from this last event 3187 years had passed up to A.D. 1051 when Atīśa made his calculation and 3393 years up to A.D. 1257 when this calculation was repeated by mChims Nam-mkha'-grags. This calculation places the *nirvāṇa* at 2137 B.C., which actually bears the cyclic symbol of "Earth-Monkey", and the birth of Buddha at 2216 B.C. (Earth-Ox year). These dates mentioned in the *Dus-'khor-ṭīk-chen* agree with the report of Sum-pa-mkhan-po that 3963 years (counting also the current year and the year of the event itself) had passed from the Earth-Ox year (to which Atīśa and mChims Nam-mkha'-grags assigned the birth of Buddha) to A.D. 1747 (see *dPag-bsam-ljon-bzaṅ*, fol. 287ᵇ 3).

which differs from the chronology established by the Sa-skya-pa scholars by only three years is referred to by Bu-ston.[365] Three more trends are indicated by Sum-pa-mkhan-po.[366]

Chronological calculations of this kind seldom constitute independent individual works ; more frequently, these form special sections of other historical or astronomical works.

The historical importance of such calculations does not, of course, lie merely in reckoning the date of the *nirvāṇa* (though this too is their immediate object), for, in this respect, the Tibetan literature gives us no more than more or less unauthentic traditional statements. These chronologies are significant because by giving the numbers of years that had passed from the date of the *nirvāṇa* to various events of the Tibetan history, they enable us to form some idea of the dates of these events themselves by comparing the data furnished. However, all chronologies of this kind (even the ones discussed here) do not possess this advantage, for many of these give nothing more than some unsubstantiated views.

Such chronologies (which continue to be compiled right to the present day) apart, there also exist more advanced works of this kind, which aim not at a study of the narrow question of the dates of birth and death of Buddha but at a comparative study of a more or less broad chronology of the political and particularly ecclesiastical history of Tibet. These works, which also are called "chronologies of the doctrine" (*bstan-rtsis*), again usually quote the dates of the *nirvāṇa*. In these works too—like the works with a narrower scope already surveyed by us—the starting point, viz. the "era" of the chronology is, in a majority of cases, the year of composition of the work itself ; that is, the antiquity of an event is determined by the number of years expired from the date of this event to the date of composition of the chronological work concerned. But unlike the other works,—which quote the results of some successive measurements of the numbers of years expired from the date of one and the same event, viz. from the *nirvāṇa*,—these works give the numbers of years expired from the dates of various events to one single date, viz. to the date of composition of the work itself. For this, the events are arranged according to these numbers of years in strict decreasing order. Quite frequently, the figures for the numbers of years are replaced by symbolic terms which can be deciphered only by following the reverse order, viz. from right to left. Sometimes, the names of the years are mentioned according to the animal cycle prevalent in Tibet. The chronological works in this form are quite prevalent in Tibetan literature ; these exist as independent entities and also as parts of other works. In particular, it is precisely in this form that the chronological calculations are entered in special manuscript almanacs, which were being regularly compiled every year for the

365. See Bu-ston, *Chos-'byuṅ*, fols. 103ᵃ 5-103ᵇ 2-3.

366. See *dPag-bsam-ljon-bzaṅ*, fol. 287ᵇ 3.

Heads of the large monasteries of Tibet and Mongolia, and which contain, besides the usual Tibetan calendar, a prophecy for the new year and a brief chronological report, in verse, on the most important events in the history of Buddhism in general, and on those in the history of a particular monastery.[367]

The chronological reports in this form are also included in the general works on astronomy which, in this respect, show a definite influence of the literature formed in India around the remarkable astronomical and astrological treatise, the *Kālacakratantra*.[368] One such report was published and translated by A. Csoma de Koros in his *Grammar*.[369] His publication essentially is, however, an extremely free prose rendering

---

367. I have, at my disposal, such manuscript almanacs from Aginsky and Tsugol (bKra-śis-chos-'phel-gliṅ) *datsan*-s of Buryatia.
368. A Tibetan translation of the *Kālacakratantra* is available in the *bKa'-'gyur*, rGyud-'bum, vol. i (*ka*), fols. 22ᵇ 1-128ᵇ 7.
369. See A. Csoma de Koros, *A Grammar of the Tibetan Language*, pp. 181-198. One cannot say that Csoma de Koros had absolutely no predecessors in the field of study of the Tibetan chronology. Chronological reports of the Tibetan history appeared in European literature even earlier. As early as 1762, Georgi tried to give such a report in his work *Alphabetum tibetanum missionum apostolicarum commodo editum* (Rome, 1762, pp. 296-341). In 1783, this report was translated—though in an abridged form—into Russian language and published in the article *Izvestiya o geograficheskom, istoricheskom i fizicheskom sostoyanii Tibeta* [Reports on the Geographical, Historical and Physical State of Tibet] by Fedor Haeckman (in "Sobranie sochinenii, vybrannykh iz mesyatseslovov na raznye gody", pt. v, St. Petersburg, 1790, pp. 242-264). However, the dates given by Georgi—like much of the other material in his book—are absolutely fantastic. Fortunately, these were not reproduced in any subsequent work. Then, a small and imperfect chronological table of Tibetan Buddhist history was translated from some unknown Mongolian source and published by Academician P. Pallas (see P. S. Pallas, *Sammlungen historischer Nachrichten*..., ii theil, St. Petersburg, 1801, Ss. 11-16). However, Pallas did not correctly specify the year up to which the figures for the numbers of years expired from a particular event are given in his source. He made no attempt to convert these figures and the accompanying cyclic dates into European calendar. This deficiency was, however, made up by Klaproth who published the same source (on the basis of a German translation in manuscript form, obtained by him in Irkutsk in 1806) in his article *Table chronologique des plus celebres patriarches et des evenements remarquables de la religion bouddhique ; redigee en 1678* (JA, t. vii, 1831, pp. 161-176). By paying special attention to the cyclic dates of the text and following the correct principle of their conversion into European calendar, Klaproth avoided many chronological

of the Tibetan text. In the original, this report is written in verse with the numbers of

---

inaccuracies of the text in his work. Of course, some errors are still there in his work. Besides the wrong identification of the cyclic name of the first date (Wood-Sheep year instead of Earth-Sheep year) as pointed out by P. Pelliot (see P. Pelliot, *Le cycle sexagénaire*, JA, 1913, t. i, p. 638, n. 1), the same error is noticed in ascertaining the cyclic name of A.D. 1012 (Wood-Mouse year in place of "Water-Mouse"). Again, because of the inaccurate calculations in the text itself, A.D. 1290 and A.D. 1374 are wrongly mentioned as 1289 and 1375 [not to speak of another error of the text which dates the birth of the fourth Dalai Lama, Yon-tan-rgya-mtsho, to 1599 (Earth-Pig year) instead of 1589 (Earth-Ox year), and various corruptions of certain names as, for instance, "Kamra" instead of "Kaidub"]. But these minor inaccuracies apart, Klaproth's work can be regarded as a model, though in the history of our scholarship, it has not merited much attention. This is quite understandable because this work contains very few dates and it is based on some anonymous Mongolian source.

A. Csoma de Koros distinguishes himself from his predecessors in that he, for his work, has dependend on the original and hence extremely authoritative Tibetan source. He was the first to publish this Tibetan chronological table (though, unfortunately, not in original but only in a free rendering), and this fact alone explains the decisive influence that his work—particularly his principles of conversion of Tibetan cyclic dates into European calendar—had on the subsequent scholars. For this influence, see P. Pelliot, *Le cycle sexagénaire*..., —JA, 1913, t. i, pp. 639-663 ; B. Laufer, *The Application of the Tibetan Sexagenary Cycle*,—"T'oung Pao", vol. xiv, 1913, pp. 569-596 ; and B. Laufer, *The Sexagenary Cycle*,—"T'oung Pao", vol. xv, 1914, pp. 278-279. It was only many years later that Professor P. Pelliot established that the principle followed by Csoma de Koros for conversion of Tibetan cyclic dates was wrong and that all the dates given by A. Csoma de Koros (and by a number of other scholars after him) were one year behind the actual ones. Professor Pelliot established that the first year of the first Tibetan cycle was 1027 and not 1026 as accepted by A. Csoma de Koros. Besides, Professor Pelliot also showed that on the basis of this false principle, Csoma de Koros, in his chronological table, not only erroneously assumed that the year up to which the numbers of years expired had been calculated in the text was 1686 (instead of 1687) but also eliminated this year as the current year from the numbers of years passed. This is why the dates mentioned in his chronology are two years behind the actual ones. However, Professor Pelliot is not quite right when he says that "toute la chronologie donnée dans la grammaire de Csoma doit donc etre abaissée de deux ans" (*ibid.*, p. 644). This is true only of the dates of our era, which constitute a

years expired written over the lines in figures. It forms the third chapter of the well-known Tibetan astronomical treatise *Vaiḍūrya-dkar*-po (or, as it is called in full : *Phug-lugs-kyi-rtsis-kyi-legs-bśad-mkhas-pa'i-mgul-rgyan-vaiḍūrya-dkar-po'i-do-śal-dpyod-ldan-sñiṅ-nor*) and covers five folios (fols. 18-22).[370] The author of this treatise was the aforementioned scholar and political leader of Tibet, sDe-srid Saṅs-rgyas-rgya-mtsho, who has bequeathed to us many large and interesting works.[371] In this report, the first year of the xii Tibetan cycle (i.e. A.D. 1687) is taken as the starting point for calculating the

---

major—and undoubtedly the most important—part of the chronology. On the other hand, the dates before our era, cited in the beginning of the table, are one year (and not two years) behind the actual ones. This is explained by the fact that Csoma de Koros assumes that the figure obtained after subtracting "1686-1" from the figure for the number of years expired as given in the text gives us the required year before our era. Here, he forgets that in view of the special nature of the chronological system before our era, this difference should be increased by "1". Since, in the table of Csoma de Koros, all the dates before our era are advanced by one year and those of our era by two years (except one date, viz. A.D. 906, which, because of some accidental misprint or slip of the pen, correctly corresponds to the cyclic date of the text), it is not difficult to correct this table in spite of the fact that the cyclic names of years appearing in the original Tibetan text are throughout omitted.

370. See *Old Collection*, No. 473 ; *Tsybikov Collection*, No. 29.

371. Apart from the aforementioned astronomical treatises, *Vaiḍūrya-dkar-po* and *Vaiḍūrya-gya'-sel*, and besides the historical work *Vaiḍūrya-ser-po* which we shall discuss in the next chapter, sDe-srid Saṅs-rgyas-rgya-mtsho has written a very important and authoritative Tibetan work on medicine, which is briefly known as *Vaiḍūrya-sṅon-po*. The full title of this work is *gSo-ba-rig-pa'i-bstan-bcos-sman-bla'i-dgoṅs-rgyan-rgyud-bshi'i-gsal-byed-vaiḍūrya-sṅon-po'i-mllig*. It is a commentary on a fundamental work of Tibetan medicine known under the title *rGyud-bshi*, and like this latter original work, *Vaiḍūrya-sṅon-po* is also available in many editions. Some of these are available in the Institute of Peoples of Asia (see *Old Collection*, No. 486-492 ; *Tsybikov Collection*, No. 27, *Nova*). Other works of this author are : the well-known medical manual, *Lhan-thabs* (see *Old Collection*, No. 475-477 ; *Tsybikov Collection*, No. 49, *Nova*); the work on the history of Tibetan medicine, entitled *dPal-ldan-gso-ba-rig-pa'i-khog-'bugs-legs-bśad-vaiḍūrya'i-me-loṅ-draṅ-sroṅ-dgyes-pa'i-dga'-ston* (see *Tsybikov Collection*, No. 74) ; biographies of the famous physicians gYu-thog-pa Yon-tan-mgon-po (senior and junior), the aforementioned "histories of incarnations" of the Fifth Dalai Lama along with his own, the works on eristics,

numbers of years expired, though the work itself was written a little earlier. It was begun in 1683 and completed in 1685.[372]

One brief chronological report of this type—though in prose—may be found in a small work composed in 1738 in the Co-ne monastery by the Head of this monastery,

---

grammar, etc. A short list of printed works of this Tibetan polyhistor is available in the *bKa'-gdams-pa-dan-dge-lugs-pa-bla-ma-rags-rim-gyi-gsuṅ-'bum-mtshan-tho* (fols. 58ᵇ 6-59ᵇ 6).

372. See *Vaiḍūrya-dkar-po*, colophon, fols. 631ᵃ 5 ff. The date when this work began to be composed—viz. the Water-Pig year of the xi cycle (A.D. 1683)—is given in the 'chronological table' of Sum-pa-mkhan-po. Thus, Professor P. Pelliot is not right in blaming this 'chronological table' for giving wrong date of composition of the *Vaiḍūrya-dkar-po* (see P. Pelliot, *Le cycle sexagénaire* . , p. 652, n. 2). Professor P. Pelliot was misled by the wrong interpretation that A. Csoma de Koros gave to the last paragraph of the Tibetan exposition of the third chapter of this text as published by him in his *Grammar*. This Tibetan rendering printed *en regard* with a translation states : *De-nas-las-so-bshi-'das-pa-rab-byuṅ-bcu-gñis-pa'i-thog- ma-pra- bha-la-shes-me-mo- yos-la-vaiḍūrya-dkar-po'i-rtsis-gshi-mdsad-do*. Csoma de Koros translates as : "Thence thirty-four years being elapsed, in the beginning of the twelfth cycle, in the year (called in Sans.) *Prabhava* (in Tibetan) *Me-mo Yos*, (this) *Bai-'durya dkarpohi rtsis dzhi* (ground work in computation) was written" (see A. Csoma de Koros, *A Grammar of the Tibetan Language*, p. 191). However, what is stated here is not that the work *Vaiḍūrya-dkar-po* itself was written in the Fire-Hare year but that in this year, the calculations of the dates were made and that this year served as the basis—the starting point—for chronological calculations (*rtsis-gshi*) of this work. The original text of the *Vaiḍūrya-dkar-po* (fol. 22ᵇ 3-4), of which the phrase quoted above is an extremely free and imperfect rendering, clearly states that the Fire-Hare year of the xii cycle is the limit to which the years expired are reckoned and which is the beginning (of the era) of calculations of this treatise under the title *Legs-bśad-vaiḍūrya-dkar-po-'di'i rtsis-'go'i-'das-lo-bzuṅ-par-mtshams*. In the Fire-Hare year of the xii cycle, i.e. in A.D. 1687, sDe-srid Saṅs-rgyas-rgya-mtsho started composing his refutations of the objections raised against this treatise (see *Vaiḍūrya-gya'-sel*, fol. 472ᵇ 2).

The odd interpretation which Csoma de Koros gives in this case to the Tibetan rendering of the original as published by him makes us suspect that this rendering was made not by him but by some one of his Tibetan informants. This suspicion is all the more probable because it is otherwise difficult to explain why Csoma de Koros translated and published a free rendering instead of the original text if the latter was available and understandable to him. If, on the other hand, Csoma de Koros himself wrote this rendering, it is impossible to

Grags-pa-bśad-sgrub (1675-1748).[373] This work is entitled *bsTan-rtsis-'phros-don-dań-bcas-pa* and is specially devoted to the problems of chronology and astronomy.[374]

---

understand why he did not pay any attention to the cyclic dates mentioned in the original text for each event and did not notice that these dates did not correspond—even from his point of view—to those dates of the European calendar which he gives.

373. An autobiography of Co-ne Grags-pa-bśad-sgrub, bearing the title *sLob-dpon-bśad-sgrub-mtshan-can-gyi-rnam-thar-rgyu-skar-rnam-par-rtse-ba* (15 folios), is available in the Collected Works of this author published in the Co-ne monastery (Co-ne'i-dgon-pa), vol. 7 (*ja*).. The Institute of Peoples of Asia has two copies (*Old Collection*, No. 312-322 and 446-456)—though both these copies are incomplete—of this "Collected Works" (in 11 volumes). Of these, only the second copy contains this autobiography. Another autobiography (in verse) of Co-ne Grags-pa-bśad-sgrub—entitled *sLob-dpon-bśad-sgrub-miń-can-gyi-rnam-thar-zur-pa-gzur-gnas-dga'-byed* (16 fols.)—is included in the eleventh (*aa*) volume of this "Collected Works". Besides, a short biography of his is available in the *Deb-ther-rgya-mtsho* (vol. iii, fols. 132ᵇ 5-133ᵇ 4). The dates of birth and death of Co-ne Grags-pa-bśad-sgrub are taken by me from this text, which states that he was born in the Wood-Hare year of the xi cycle (1675) and that he died in the Earth-Dragon year (1748) in the 74th year of his life. The date of birth is also mentioned in the first (fol. 2ᵇ 2) of the two autobiographies of his mentioned above. This date fully agrees with the repeated references by Grags-pa-bśad-sgrub to his age in the colophons to his works. See, for example, his works (available in the aforesaid "Collected Works") : *'Dul-ba-rgya-mtsho'i-sñiń-po'i-dgon-rab-tu-snań-bar-byed-pa'i-sgron-me*, vol. 7 (*ja*), fol. 16ᵃ 2 ; *Ri-bo-dga'-ltan-pa'i-bstan-pa-bla-rabs-dań-bcas-pa-chos-'byuń-gsal-bar-ston-pa'i-ston-me*, vol. 10 (ā), fol. 16ᵃ 3-4 ; *rJe-btsun-re-mńa'-bas-rje-la-bskul-nas-rje-ñid-kyis-'jam dbyańs-la-dńos-su-shus-pa'i-sńags-phyogs-kyi-ñams-len-las-brtsams-pa'i-dri-lan-gyi-'grel-pa*, fol. 35ᵃ 3-4, etc. Because of some absurd discrepancy, the date of birth of Co-ne Grags-pa-bśad-sgrub as given in my article *K bibliografii tibetskoi literatury* [On a Bibliography of Tibetan Literature]—in "Bibliografiya vostoka", Nos. 2-4, p: 32, note 1—is absolutely wrong. The year 1675 is misprinted there as 1727. This unfortunate error was also mechanically repeated in the English version of the article (see A. Vostrikov, *Some Corrections and Critical Remarks on Dr. Johan van Manen's Contribution to the Bibliography of Tibet*, BSOS, vol. viii, 1935, p. 75).

374. This work of Co-ne Grags-pa-bśad-sgrub is available in the sixth (*cha*) volume

As is well known, for measuring time in their every-day life, the Tibetans use a 12-year animal cycle, which is quite widely prevalent among the various peoples of Asia. A combination of the twelve animals of this cycle with the five elements—corresponding to the combination of 12 "branches" with ten "stems" followed in the Chinese chronology, in which, in one sexagenary cycle, the ten stems are repeated six times and the twelve branches five times—constitutes a 60-year cycle used for measuring larger spans of time. As frequently and quite specifically mentioned by the Tibetan sources themselves right from the aforementioned *Chos-la-'jug-pa'i-sgo* (A.D. 1167), the Tibetan and Chinese systems of reckoning time are identical, and the years of the Tibetan animal cycle fully coincide with the corresponding years of the Chinese calendar.[375] The erroneous opinion of E. Schlagintweit that, previously, the Tibetan animal cycle did not possibly agree with the Chinese one and that only from the beginning of the 18th century, the years of the Tibetan cycle were, under pressure from the Chinese powers, brought in conformity with those of the Chinese[376] has been fully refuted by P. Pelliot.[377] The Tibetan chronological system differs from that of the Chinese not in that the years bearing the same names in them do not tally with each other—in this respect, on the other hand, complete unity is observed in them—but in that the Tibetans, without changing anything in the sequence of the years of the sexagenary cycle of

---

of the Collected Works of the author. It occupies 7 folios. The date of composition of this work (Earth-Horse year of the xii cycle, corresponding to A.D. 1738) is mentioned in the text itself (fol. 2[a] 1-2 ff.). The chronological table occupies fols. 1[b] 1-2[b] 1 in this work.

375. See *Chos-la-'jug-pa'i-sgo*, fol. 315(53)[a] 5, which states that the Hindus do not reckon time by twelve-year cycles as the Tibetans and the Chinese do (*spyir-rgya-gar-gyi-lugs-las-bod-dan rgya-nag-bshin-lo-skor-bcu-gñis-su-brtsi-ba-ni-med-de*), and that Buddha was conceived in the year which, in the Chinese and Tibetan chronological systems, is called the year of the "Fire-Hare"—*rGya-dan-bod-kyi-lo'i-miṅ-ni-me-mo-yos-la-lhums-su-shugs* (*ibid.*, fol. 315[b] 5). This early evidence of the agreement of the Tibetan and Chinese chronological systems is extremely important, for such early positive statements are wanting in the remarkable article of Professor P. Pelliot (see P. Pelliot, *Le cycle sexagénaire..*) for a more convincing proof of absolutely fantastic nature of the statement of E. Schlagintweit (see E. Schlagintweit, *Buddhism in Tibet*, p. 278) that earlier, the Tibetan system of chronology did not supposedly agree with the Chinese system and that only from the early 18th century, it was brought in conformity with the latter.

376. E. Schlagintweit, *Buddhism in Tibet*, p. 278.

377. P. Pelliot, *Le cycle sexagénaire,...*—JA, 1913, t. 1, pp. 646-648.

animals and elements consider, as the first year of this cycle, not the year of the Wood-Mouse as the Chinese do but the year of the Fire-Hare which, in China, is regarded as the fourth one. This is due to the influence, on Tibetan chronology, of the Indian literature on *Kālacakra* system—which is based on the 60-year cycle of Jupiter and which regards, as the first year of each such cycle (called *prabhava* in Sanskrit and *rab-byuṅ* in Tibetan), the year which in the Chinese sexagenary cycle of animals and elements is the fourth, i.e. the year of the Fire-Hare. From the name of the first year, in the *Kālacakra* system, the Jupiter cycle itself came to be known as *rab-byuṅ*.

Introducing their chronological system on the basis of the *rab-byuṅ*-s, the Tibetans also accepted the numerical order of the latter. As the first *rab-byuṅ* or rather the first year of the first *rab-byuṅ* was taken the year 1027—the year in which, according to the *Kālacakra* system, Kulika Sūrya (Rig-ldan-ñi-ma) ascended the throne in the legendary country of Śambhala. This was the year when, according to some, the *Klacakratantra*[378] was delivered to India, and when, according to others, it was translated into Tibetan by a translator from Gyi-jo.[379]

The adoption of a chronological system in Tibet made it possible for the Tibetan historians to specify the date of a particular event not only by the number of years passed but also by the name of the cycle and the year. This ultimately led to the emergence of a special class of chronological works—namely, that of the so-called "Chronological Tables of the Doctrine" (*bstan-rtsis-re'u-mig*-s), which have a close resemblance to our European chronological tables.

As a specimen of works of this type, we can take the *bsTan-pa'i-gsal-byed-chen-po-bod du-rim-gyis-byuṅ-ba'i-lo-tshig-re'u-mig-tu-bkod-pa'i-tshigs-luṅ-tshigs-chuṅ-rtags-byed-gser-gyi-ñi-ma-'od-zer-bkra-ba*, written by the first 'Jam-dbyaṅs-bshad-pa named Ṅag-dbaṅ-brtson-'grus (1648-1722). This work, already mentioned by me as one of the sources of the present work, was composed in 1716.[380] It is included in the Complete Works of the author published from the monastery of bLa-braṅ (founded by him) in Amdo.[381] This work is in two parts, each having its own pagination. The first part covers 11 Tibetan folios of the usual size and contains, besides an introduction, an exposition of the events prior

---

378. See the 'chronological table' of the first 'Jam-dbyaṅs-bshad-pa.
379. See the 'chronological table' of Sum-pa-mkhan-po.
380. The date of compilation of the 'chronological table' of the first 'Jam-dbyaṅs-bshad-pa (Fire-Monkey year of the xii cycle, corresponding to A.D. 1716) is mentioned in its colophon (fol. 26^b 3) and in the 'chronological table' of Sum-pa-mkhan-po.
381. Unfortunately, the Complete Works of the first 'Jam-dbyaṅs-bshad-pa are not yet available in the Institute of Peoples of Asia. What in the "List of Tibetan works, brought by G. Tsybikov in 1902" (see Musei Asiatici Petropolitani Notitia, iv, no. 22) is mentioned as *'Jam-dbyaṅs-bshad-pa'i-rdo-rje-sku-goṅ-ma'i-gsuṅ-'bum* (i.e. Collected Works of the first 'Jam-dbyaṅs-bshad-pa) is actually a

to A.D. 1027. The second part covers 26 folios and contains, besides six lines of concluding note, the chronological tables beginning from 1027 and ending at 1715. Each year in this table is entered in a separate cage which gives the name of the year according to the Tibetan sexagenary cycle and a list of events that took place in this year. The cages are arranged from left to right along the length of the Tibetan folio and are in two rows. Every time that a new cycle is begun, its ordinal number is given —*rab-byuṅ-daṅ-po, rab-byuṅ-gñis-pa* (*rab-byuṅ* 1st, *rab-byuṅ* 2nd) etc.

A still more complete chronological work is the table included in the frequently quoted work of the well-known Sum-pa-mkhan-po Ye-śes-dpal-'byor on the history of Buddhism.[382] This table occupies 12 folios of large format. Besides, one folio in the beginning gives a short exposition of the events prior to the Tibetan era (i.e. up to A.D. 1027) and the three folios in the end contain critical comments on the chronology followed in other Tibetan historical texts. This table begins from A.D. 1057 and ends at A.D. 1746, i.e. covers full twelve cycles (*rab-byuṅ*-s). The text of this table has not been published so far. It was, however, translated—independently of each other—by Academician V. P. Vasil'ev and S. C. Das. The translation made by V. P. Vasil'ev[383] was not publishxd. As regards S. C. Das, he published his translation in an article entitled *Life of Sum-pa khan-po, also Styled Yeśes-Dpal-'byor, the Author of the Re'umig*

---

collection of text-books (*yig-cha*) used in the sGo-maṅ *datsan* of the 'Bras-spuṅs monastery, in which the chief place is occupied by the works of this author. The 'chronological table', however, is not included in this collection.

382. *dPag-bsam-ljon-bzaṅ*, fols. 272ª 4-287ᵇ 7.

383. The translation of the 'chronological table' of Sum-pa-mkhan-po as made by V. P.Vasil'ev is preserved in manuscript among other works of this author available in the Asiatic Archives of the Institute of Oriental Studies, Academy of Sciences, USSR (see Musei Asiatica Indica III, 665 *Nova* III). Cf. M. I. Tubyansky, *Predvaritel'noe soobshchenie o buddologicheskom rukopisnom nasledii V. P. Vasil'eva i V. V. Gorskogo* [A Preliminary Report on the Manuscript Heritage of V. P. Vasil'ev and V. V. Gorsky on Buddhist Studies],—"Doklady AN SSSR, 1927, pp. 61-62 ; and S. A. Kozin, *Bibliografičeskii obzor izdannykh i neizdannykh rabot Akad. V. P. Vasil'eva po dannym Aziatskogo muzeya Akademii nauk SSSR* [A Bibliographical Review of the Published and Unpublished Works of Acad. V. P. Vasil'ev on the Basis of the Data of the Asiatic Museum, Academy of Sciences, U.S.S.R.],—Izvestiya AN SSSR. Otdelenie obshcestvennykh nauk", 1931, p. 762, no. 12. This translation forms the third and the most important chapter of V. P. Vasil'ev's unpublished work, *Istoriya Buddizma v Tibete* [History of Buddhism in Tibet]. The first chapter of this work contains "some preliminary remarks". The second chapter comprises "extracts from the work of Sum-pa khutuktu", of which some have been

(*Chronological Table*),[384] but this translation is absolutely unsatisfactory. Even limiting himself to a translation of the actual tables only without the introductory and concluding parts, S. C. Das accomplished this task very negligently. Despite the fact that the original text correctly gives the names of the years every time they occur, S. C. Das found it possible to do away with them and was satisfied with his own conversion of these into the European calendar. Not only that the conversions made by him are not correct even from the general principle which he followed in this regard ; he has also digressed from these principles for no reasons whatsoever. Following Csoma de Koros and E. Schlagintweit, S. C. Das regarded the first year of the Tibetan era as 1026 instead of 1027 and therefore, as correctly shown by Prof. P. Pelliot, all the dates cited by S. C. Das should be advanced by one year for obtaining the true dates.[385] But even without

---

translated and others only expounded. These extracts are taken from the section on the political history of Tibet (*rgyal-rabs*) in the same work of Sum-pa-mkhan-po (see *dPag-bsam-ljon-bzaṅ*, fols. 95ᵃ 6-108ᵃ 7 ; S. C. Das, *Pag Sam Jon Zang*, pp. 147-166). V. P. Vasil'ev refers to this work of his in the preface to the first part of his famous work ***Buddizm*** : *ego dogmaty, istoriya i literatura* [Buddhism : Its Dogmas, History and Literatue ; St. Petersburg, 1857, p. iv] However, it was only in 1899 that the Academy of Sciences decided to publish it as a monograph. The responsibility for reading the proofs was, at the request of V. P. Vasil'ev, passed on to Professor A. O. Ivanovsky (see the minutes of the meeting of the Historico-Philological Department of the Academy of Sciences, held on 29th September 1899, p. 150). In the papers of A. O. Ivanovsky in the Asiatic archives of the Institute of Oriental Studies, I could discover the proofs of the first and of the earlier portion of the second chapter of this work (see Musei Asiatica Indica, Sect. iii, 588 *Nova*). As regards the translation of the "Chronological Tables", this too obviously was not finally prepared for the press. A. O. Ivanovsky had compared it with the translation made by S. C. Das,—a tedious and thankless task, because the translation of S. C. Das cannot at all be taken seriously.

A close acquaintance with V. P. Vasil'ev's translation shows that it is not free from errors, but this is quite understandable and pardonable in view of the fact that this translation was made so long ago. Much information expressed laconically in the original text with the use of all possible conventional abbreviations remained obscure to V. P. Vasil'ev and was therefore distorted in his translation. He did not explain these abbreviations and did not give any notes or indices to his translation. Nevertheless, this old and incomplete translation is far better than that published by S. C. Das.

384. JASB, vol. lviii, pt. i, no. 2, 1889, pp. 37-84.

385. P. Pelliot, *Le cyclé sexagenaire*,—JA, 1913, t. 1, pp. 650-652.

comparing the true dates with those mentioned by S. C. Das after conversion, P. Pelliot has pointed out a case when S. C. Das digressed from the actual date not by one but by two years.[386] In fact, there are several such cases in the conversions made by S. C. Das. In particular, the events which he has dated to the years between 1225 and 1253 (yearwise) actually happened from 1227 to 1255. In the same way, the events marked 1269 and 1270 respectively actually took place in 1271 and 1272 etc. The events which, in the original texts, are shown to have taken place in the same year, have been ascribed by S. C. Das to different years, and vice versa.[387] But the matter does not end

386. *Ibid.*, p. 652, no. 1.

387. For example, in the original text, the date of birth of sPyi-po-lhas-pa and that of death of 'Khon-phu-pa is regarded as A.D. 1144, whereas in the translation of S. C. Das, the first of these events is dated as 1143 and the second as 1144. In the original text, both the birth of Mun-me-brag-kha-pa Grags-seṅ and the death of sPyan-sṅa Grags-'byuṅ are dated A.D. 1255 ; in the translation of S. C. Das, the former is dated A.D. 1253 and the latter A.D. 1254. In the original text, both the birth of Bya-yul Saṅs-ston Tshul-khrims seṅge and the death of Chag Chos-rje-dpal are assigned to 1265 whereas in the translation of S. C. Das, these dates are 1263 and 1264 respectively. In the original text, the birth of Bya-yul gShon-nu-smon-lam and the death of sTag-luṅ Saṅs-rgyas-yar-byon are dated 1272 but in the translation of S. C. Das, the former is dated as 1270 and the latter as 1271. In the original text, the death of Śaṅs-ston Tshul-mgon and Tshul-mgon and the death of Grub-chen U-rgyan-pa are assigned to 1309 but in the translation of S. C. Das, the first of these events is assigned to 1308 and the second to 1309 etc. Such errors are found throughout the entire translation of S. C. Das. Of the two events dated as A.D. 1344 in the original, S. C. Das, in his translation, has dated one as A.D. 1343 and the other as A.D. 1344. The erection of the "Red prayer-hall" (*mchod-khaṅ-dmar-po*) in the sTag-luṅ monastery, dated in the original as 1384 has, in the translation of S. C. Das, also been dated to 1384, but all the remaining events of this year have been assigned to 1383. The events which, in the original, are shown against A.D. 1423 have, in the translation of S. C. Das, been assigned partly to 1421 and partly to 1422. The events of A.D. 1620 in the text have been put by S. C. Das against 1619 ; but one of these—the death of Khri Dam-chos-dpal—has been assigned to 1620, etc. On the other hand, the original text dates the death of rNog Jo-bsod to 1145 and the death of rÑog Jo-'od to 1146, but in the translation of S. C. Das, both these events are dated as 1145. In the original text, the death of the Mongolian Khan Huluk has been dated to 1311 and the birth of bLa-ma-dam-pa bSod-nams-rgyal-mtshan and the death of Bya-yul-pa Saṅs-rgyas-jo-ba to 1312 ; but S. C. Das, in his translation,

at these chronological errors only. A considerable portion of the information available in the original text is totally omitted by S. C. Das. In certain cases, S.C. Das translates only half the sentence and omits the remaining part.[388] What is stated in the original

has assigned all these events to A.D. 1310. Again, in the original text, the birth of bLo-gros-rnam-dag and some other events are dated 1322 and the birth of a Mongolian Khan as 1323 ; but in the translation of S. C. Das, all these events are found assigned to A.D. 1321. In the original text, the birth of Kun-spaṅs-chen-po bSod-nams-rgyal-mtshan and Se-skyil-pa Śāk-bsod, and the death of dPal bLo-brtan are all dated to 1342. Again, in the text, the accession of bLa-ma-dam-pa to the headship of the Sa-skya monastery and the death of Dwags-po gShon-smon, rÑiṅ-ma Ku-mar and Jo-naṅ-pa Mun-me-brag-kha-pa are all dated to A.D. 1343. But in the translation of S. C. Das, all these events (except the last one) are dated to 1341, and the last one—the death of Mun-me-brag-kha-pa—is dated to 1342 etc. The events of A.D. 1182 in the original text have, in the translation of S. C. Das, been assigned partly to 1180 and partly to 1181. The birth of gZi-brjid-grags and sPyan-sṅa Rin-chen-ldan, along with some other events, is, in the original text, assigned to 1202 but in the translation of S. C. Das, the first of these events has been included in the events of 1200 and all others in those of A.D. 1201.

388. In the translation of S. C. Das, such omissions are found literally at every step. To be specific, S. C. Das omits, as a rule, the reports of the original text on the accession to the headship of Se-ra, 'Bras-spuṅs, Chab-mdo and other monasteries. These reports are mentioned in the translation of S. C. Das only casually. Again, there are many omissions in the accounts of the accession to the headship of dGa'-ldan monastery (cf, for example, the information of the text under the years 1438, 1450, 1493, 1511, 1516, etc. with the respective portions in the translation). The reports on the heads of the dGon-luṅ and bKra-sis-lhun-po monasteries are the most complete in the translation of S. C. Das, but even these are not without unnecessary omissions (cf. the statements of the text under the years 1404, 1487 and 1516 with the corresponding places in the translation). It is interesting to note that such omissions are more frequent in the middle portion of the table than in the beginning (2nd-3rd cycles) or in the end (9th-12th cycles). The account of the accession of various persons to the headship of the monasteries are, in the original text, often mixed with the account of the death of their predecessors, and set forth in a single sentence. But this does not prevent S. C. Das from omitting the former while he duly translates the latter. Besides, various data on the birth and death of some persons and on other events are also found omitted in the translation of S. C. Das. Such

as a hypothesis or as the view of someone else, of the authenticity of which the author is not quite sure, appears, in the translation of S. C. Das, as a categorical statement of the author.[389] Numerous references by the original authors to the views of other historians are almost invariably omitted by S. C. Das.[390] Finally, in certain cases, even the very facts stated in the text have been distorted by S. C. Das beyond identification.[391] Two names of the same person have been shown by S. C. Das as those of

---

omissions include the reports on the death of the famous rGyal-tshab Dar-ma-rin-chen (1364-1432), the pupil and successor of Tsoṅ-kha-pa, those on the composition of the works *Pad-dkar-shal-luṅ* (1447) and *Deb-ther-sṅon-po* (1476) etc.

389. Many statements in the original text are accompanied by an interrogative particle (*sam* etc.) or by the expression "it is said" (*zer*). See, for instance, the relevant portions of the text against the years 1053, 1064, 1075, 1083 etc. But S. C. Das pays no attention to this.

390. The author of the Tibetan text, frequently enough, refers to the views of other sources or argues against them (see, for example, the portions of the text relevant to the years 1031, 1033, 1039, 1040, 1041, 1051 etc.). However, S. C. Das does not, as a rule, translate such references.

391. It is enough to quote some striking examples. Under A.D. 1044, the Tibetan text states : *ma-cig-sha-ma'i-mdsa'-pho-la-stod pa-rma-lo-tsā-ba-chos-'bar-'khruṅs.* S. C. Das, dating this event to A.D. 1043, translates : "Machig Sha-ma's husband was born. Rma-Lo-chāva Chhos 'bar of La-stod was born". A correct translation would be : "rMa-lo-tsā-ba Chos-'bar, famous as the husband (*mdsa'-pho-la-stod-pa*) of Ma-cig-sha-ma, was born"—for an account of rMa-lo-tsā-ba Chos-'bar (1044-1089) and his "secret wife" (*gsaṅ-yum* or *śakti*) Ma-cig-sha-ma (1062-1149), see *Deb-ther-sṅon-po*, vol. i, fols. 113b 1-117b. In the original text, the portion against A.D. 1052 states : *khams-pa-luṅ-pa-lab-sgron-yu-mo-phyi-dar-gyi-rÑiṅ-ma- sba- sgom- ye- byaṅ- rnams- kyi- slob-ma-'dseṅ- dharma- bodhi-'khruṅs.* S. C. Das, dating this event to 1051, translates : "Machig Lab sgron of Kham-pa Luṅ was born. Machig Yumo became the pupil of Sba-sgom ye-byaṅ and others of the later Rniṅ-ma school. Dharma Bodhi was born". An accurate translation reads : " 'Dseṅ Dharma-bodhi—the pupil of Khams-pa-luṅ-pa (1025-1115 ; different dates are also found), Ma-cig Lab-sgron (1055-1143 ; other dates are also found), Yu-mo and sBa-sgom Ye-śes-byaṅ-chub, the representative of the rÑiṅ-ma sect of the period of later spread (of Buddhism in Tibet)—was born" (About 'Dseṅ Dharma-bodhi (1052-1168), see *Deb-ther-sṅon-po*, vol. i, fols. 91b 3-97a 3 ; his teachers are also named there). Under A.D. 1144, the Tibetan text states : *Sa-paṇ-gsaṅ-ston-spyi-bo-lhas-pa-'khruṅs-zer.* S. C. Das, dating this report to A.D. 1143, translates : "Gsaṅ ston spyipa chaspa, one of the Pan chchen of Sa-skya was born". A correct translation is : "It is said that

two different persons[392] and, on the other hand, the names of two different persons have

sPyi-bo-lhas-pa, 'the secret confessor' (*raho'nuśāsaka*) of Sa-skya-paṇḍita, was born". A "secret confessor" (*gsaṅ-ston*) is one who hears confessions from a person who has taken holy orders (from one ordained to the dGe-tshul or dGe-sloṅ order). In the modern Buddhist order, this person is also called "a teacher" (*slob-dpon*). However, the *Hor-chos-'byuṅ* (G. Huth, *Geschichte des Buddhismus in der Mongolei*, vol. i, p. 76) states that at the time of the ordination of Sa-skya-paṇḍita to the dGe-sloṅ order, the aforementioned sPyi-bo-lhas-pa was the "teacher" and someone else was the "secret confessor". Under A.D. 1160, the Tibetan text states : *rma-lo-tsā-ba-daṅ-ma-cig-sha-ma'i-chos-brgyud-'dsin-pa'i-sprul sku-yaṅ-dben-pa-'khruṅs*. S. C. Das, dating this event to A.D. 1159, translates : Rma Lochāva and Yañ dnenpa, the emanations of Machig S'ama were born". A correct translation reads : "The incarnation Yaṅ-dben-pa, the follower of the teaching of rMa-lo-tsā-ba and Ma-cig-sha-ma, was born". Under A.D, 1201, the Tibetan text states : *lo-bya-yul-gñis-ka-saṅs-rgyas-sgom-pas-bskyaṅs*. S. C. Das, placing this statement against A.D. 1200, translates : "Saṅs rgyas sgom-pa protected the Lochāva of Bya yul". A correct translation reads : "Saṅs-rgyas-sgom-pa took, under his patronage, both (the monasteries) —Lo (Lo-dgon-pa, founded in 1093 or 1095) and Bya-yul (Bya-yul-dgon-pa, founded in 1113)". There are many such distortions in the translation of S. C. Das.

392. Thus, for example, under 1059, the original Tibetan text states : *Dol-buśer-rgya-ma'-rog-dmar-shur-'khruṅs*. S. C. Das, dating this event to A.D. 1058, translates : "Dol bu śer-rgyama was born." Actually, the reference here is to a person called Dol-ba Śes-rab-rgya-mtsho or Rog-dmar-shur-pa (1059-1131). This leader of the bKa'-gdams-pa sect—the author of the Be'u-bum-sṅon-po, the well-known didactic work in verse—is mentioned in the *Deb-ther-sṅon-po* (vol. i, fol. 140[b] 1-5) and in the *dPag-bsam-ljon-bzaṅ* (fol. 133[a] 4 ; S. C. Das, *Pag Sam Jon Zang*, p. 201). Under A.D. 1067, the original text states : *Grub-thob-yu-mor-grags-pa 'i-slob-ma- gñis- kyi-khuṅ- pa-hab- jo-sras- 'jam-dpal- 'khruṅs*. S. C. Das, dating this event to 1066, translates : "H Jam-Dpal and skyi khuṅ pa Hab-jo, the two disciples of the Crubthob Yumo, were born". Actually, the expression gÑos-skyi-khuṅ-pa Hab-jo-sras-'jam-dpal, from which S. C. Das makes out names of two different persons is the name and nick-name of one person (see *Deb-ther-sṅon-pa*, vol. i, fol. 97[a] 1). Under A D. 1077, the Tibetan text states : "*Bya-yul-ba'i-slob-ma-gtsaṅ-ba-rin-po-che-nam-mkha'-rdo-rje-'khruṅs*. S. C. Das, dating this event to 1076, translates : "Gtsaṅ-pa Rin-po chhe, the disciple of Bya-yul-pa, was born. Nam kha rdorje was born". Actually, the expression gTsaṅ-ba-rin-po-che Nam-mkha'-dpal, which S. C. Das breaks up into names of two different persons, is the name of one person. It is interesting

been turned into those of the same person etc.[393] It is no use enumerating and rectifying all the defects of the translation of S. C. Das. It is simply necessary to make a fresh translation of the entire text of the chronological table of Sum-pa-mkhan-po. When the original text is available, it is better not to use at all the translation of S. C.

---

to note that mentioning later about the death of this person (see the text under A.D. 1161, the translation under A.D. 1160), S. C. Das himself correctly translates this expression as the name of one person. Under A.D. 1400, the Tibetan text states : *dGe-'dun-grub-pa'i-slob-ma-'dul-'dsin-blo-gros-spas-pa-grags-pa-dpal-ldan-lo-sna-ma-kha-cig-zer-yan-'dir-'khruns.* S. C. Das, assigning this report to 1399, translates : "Gragspa dpalldan of Sbas and Hdul-hdsin Blo-gras, the disciple of Dge-hdun grub, were born"—A correct translation would read : " 'Dul-'dsin bLo-gros-spas-pa-grags-pa-dpal-ldan, the pupil of dGe-'dun-grub-pa, was born, though some also say (that this event) perhaps (occurred) in the preceding year". This very name occurs again in the text—though in a somewhat abridged form ('Dul-'dsin bLo-spas-grags-dpal)—under A.D. 1475 (the year, to which the death of this pupil of the first Dalai Lama is dated). But this time, S. C. Das correctly understands this name as that of one person. Under A.D. 1455, the original Tibetan text states : *Phyogs-rgyal-skyes-pa-zer-pa'i-ka rñin-dpa'-po-dun-po-chos-dban-lhun-grub-'khruns.* S. C. Das, dating this event to 1454, translates : "Phyogs las rnam rgyal and Chhos dvan Lhun-grub were born". A correct translation reads : "First dPa'-po (by name) Chos-dban-lhun-grub (Lama of the) Karma-pa and rÑin-ma-pa (sects)—also called the incarnation of Phyogs-las-rnam-rgyal—was born". In the translation of S. C. Das, there are many such cases of the names and nicknames of the same person being treated as names of several persons. However, we shall not enumerate all these cases here, for we do not intend to correct the absolutely low-grade work of S. C. Das.

393. Under A.D. 1129, the Tibetan text reads : *rNog-jo bsod-shes-pa-jo-'od gcun-'khruns.* S. C. Das, dating this information to 1128, translates : "Jo hod gchun, also called Rnog jo va-son (sic) was born". A correct translation reads : "The younger brother of Jo-'od, named rNog Jo-bsod, was born". The dates of birth and death of both these brothers are mentioned in the present 'chronological table' and also in the 'chronological table' of the first 'Jam-dbyans bshad-pa. rÑog Jo-'od was born in 1122 and he died in 1146. rÑog Jo-bsod was born in 1129 and he died in 1145. Then, under A.D. 1303, the Tibetan text states : *dPan-lo-blo-brtan-dbon-po-byan-chub-rtse-mo-'khruns.* S. C. Das, dating this information to 1302, translates : "Dvan lo-chāva Byan-chhub rtse-mo, also called Blo-brtan dpon-po was born". However, a correct translation reads : "Byan-chub-rtse-mo, the nephew (*dbon-po*) of dPan-lo-tsā-ba bLo-gros-brtan-pa was born".

Das as it lacks the necessary critical apparatus and does not identify the proper names included. Without the original text, on the other hand, it is risky to use this translation because it is full of errors.

S. C. Das prefaced his translation of the chronological tables with a short biography of their author, Sum-pa-mkhan-po, without, in any way, specifying the sources on which this biography is based.[394] As rightly remarked by Prof. P. Pelliot,[395] S. C. Das errs in this biography too. The date of birth of the author as given in this biography (in European calendar) is different from that given in the text of the chronological table. In his tables, the date of birth of Sum-pa-mkhan-po Ye-śes-dpal-'byor is given as 1702-1703 and in the biography, it is shown as 1702, whereas actually, it is 1704. This error can, however, be easily rectified as S. C. Das gives here the number of the cycle and the name of the year in Tibetan calendar—the Wood-Monkey year of the 12th cycle, corresponding to A.D. 1704. It is much more difficult to verify the remaining dates given in this biography as S. C. Das does not give the Tibetan names of the years. Nonetheless, some of these dates are certainly to be rectified[396]—particularly the date of death of Sum-pa-mkhan-po Ye-śes-dpal-'byor. S. C. Das simply states that Sum-pa-mkhan-po died at the age of 73 whereas he actually died in 1788 (Earth-Monkey year of the 13th cycle), i.e. in the 85th year of his life.[397] In 1782 (Water-Tiger year of the 13th cycle), he compiled his critical and bibliographical work *gSuṅ-rab-rnam-dag-chu'i-dri-ma-sel-byed-nor-bu-ke-ta-ka*.[398]

---

394. S. C. Das, *Life of Sum-pa-khan-po*,—JASB, 1889, pp. 37-40. This biography is repeated by S. C. Das in the form of a preface to the text of *dPag-bsam-ljon-bzaṅ* (see S. C. Das, *Pag Sam Jon Zang*, pp. i-iii).
395. P. Pelliot, *Le cycle sexagenaire...*, —JA, 1913, t. 1, p. 650 *et suiv.*
396. The date of travel of Sum-pa-khan-po to Tsang province—when he received ordination to the highest monastic stage from the second Panchen Lama—as given by S. C. Das is also not correct. These events took place not in 1725 but in 1723 (Water-Hare year of the 12th cycle)—see the aforementioned autobiography, fols. 29^b 7-32^a 3.
397. See the aforementioned autobiography, fols. 242^b 5-243^a 1. See also the *Deb-ther-rgya-mtsho* (vol. i, fol. 76^a 5). S. C. Das erred probably because the main text of the autobiography of Sum-pa-khan-po ends with an account of the 73rd year of his life and the former colophon of this work states that it was written in 1776 (Fire-Monkey year of the 13th cycle) in the 73rd year of the life of the author (see the autobiography, supplement, fol. 34^a 7 ff).
398. See *supra*.

7. *Histories of Religion or Doctrine* (*Chos-'byuṅ-s*)

The so-called "histories of religion or the Doctrine" (*chos-'byuṅ*-s) form an extensive class of Tibetan historical literature. By this name, in Tibet, are meant not only the works on the history of religion proper but also general historical works of reference, which give, besides the exposition of the history of religion, that of the secular history of the country too. Such composite works are usually compiled from materials drawn from various types of Tibetan historical works enumerated above, as well as from biographical, historico-bibliographical and geographical literature. Frequently, these materials are put together so arbitrarily that one can easily take away from the text dynastic and genealogical chronicles, monastic annals and lists of incarnations, biographies of individual persons and sometimes even the chronological tables without any particular damage to the coherence and completeness of the text.

There is a great diversity in the contents of the "histories of religion" (*chos-'byuṅ*-s). Sometimes such works are devoted either to the history of Tibet and of Buddhism in Tibet or to that of the spread of Buddhism in China as a whole, in India, in Mongolia etc., or finally to the exposition of the secular and ecclesiastical history of all or some of the peoples of these countries together. In the last case, the exposition of the history of each people is usually given separately and can essentially be studied independently and irrespective of the remaining text. Besides, the term "history of religion" is also applied to works devoted to the history of the spread of Buddhism in some particular province or locality and also to works expounding the history of some Buddhist sect or monastic school. Finally, by the same title are denoted the numerous works on the history of Buddhist mystic cults.

So far as we can judge from the citations and from the fragmentary references of the later Tibetan authors, the history of Buddhism in Tibet was, to some extent, already expounded inthe *rGyal-rabs sBa-bshed* which by the Tibetan is regarded as one of the earliest works of Tibetan historiography.[399]

We did not have the possibility of seeing personally the historical works written by Khu-ston brTson-'grus-gyuṅ-druṅ (1011-1075)[400] and known under the title *Lo-rgyus-chen-mo* or *Log-gnon-chen-mo*, to which Brag-dgon-shabs-druṅ dKon-mchog-bstan-pa-rab-rgyas refers in his list of Tibetan historical works.[401]

399. About this work, see *supra*.

400. The dates of birth and death of Khu-ston brTson-'grus-gyuṅ-druṅ are given in the "Chronological Tables".

401. *Deb-ther-rgya-mtsho*, vol. i, fol. 4b 1.

Of the texts of which I have first-hand knowledge, the earliest one which—though not being of a nature of special historical study—nevertheless includes a short exposition of the "history of religion" (*chos-'byuṅ*) is the aforesaid work of the famous bSod-nams-rtse-mo (1142-1182)—entitled *Chos-la-'jug-pa'i-sgo* [The Door Leading to the (Buddhist) Faith] written in 1167[402] In this work, after the prefatory verses and a discussion on as to what the doctrine is (fols. 263-266^{b} 5) and how to attain the main tenets of Buddhism (fols. 266^{b} 6-273^{a} 3), the author tells how salvation is attained by this Doctrine and also who expounded this Doctrine. Thereafter, the author describes the twelve deeds of Buddha (fols. 273^{a} 3-301^{a} 3), the three Buddhist Councils (fols. 301^{a} 3-311^{a} 4), further development of Buddhism in India (fols. 311^{a} 4-312^{a} 2) and lastly the spread of Buddhism in Tibet. The work ends up with the aforementioned chronological note on the period of the existence of Buddhism (fols. 314^{b} 6-316^{b} 6) and concluding verses.

Some attention to the "history of religion" is also given by 'Phags-pa-bla-ma bLo-gros-rgyal-mtshan (1235-1280) in his encyclopaedic work entitled *Śes-bya-rab-gsal.* This work, covering 35 folios of usual Tibetan format, was written in 1278 at the orders of Chingim [Jim-gyim], the son of Kublai,[403] and is divided into five chapters which describe : (1) the inanimate world (*snod-kyi-'jig-rten*), fols. 2^{b} 1-8^{b} 6, (2) the animate world (*bcud-kyi-'jig-rten*), fols. 9^{a} 1-26^{b} 3, (3) the path (*lam*), fols. 26^{b} 3-28^{a} 5, (4) the result (*'bras-bu*), fols. 28^{a} 5-34^{a} 5, and (5) the unrevealed elements of existence (*'du-ma-byas'*, fols. 34^{a} 5-34^{b} 5. In this, to the historical problems are devoted about 2½ folios of the second chapter (fols. 17^{b} 4-19^{a} 1),—which expound the genealogy of Śākyamuni from Mahāsammata to Rāhula, a short history of Buddhism in India and in Tibet and a genealogy of the Mongolian Khans from Genghis [Chinghiz] to Kublai and his children.

Of the large historical works of Tibet known to us, the earliest one is that entitled *bDe-par-gśegs-pa'i-bstan-pa'i-gsal-byed-chos-kyi-'byuṅ-gnas-gsuṅ-rab-rin-po-che'i-mdsod* (briefly, *Chos-'byuṅ*) by the famous Bu-ston Rin-chen-grub (1290-1364).[404] This

---

402. See *supra.*
403. This work is available in the Complete Works of the Sa-skya-pa Scholars [see *Sa-skya-bka'-'bum*, vol. xiii (*pa*), fols. 1-35]. The date of its composition—Earth-Tiger year (A.D. 1278)—is mentioned in the colophon (*ibid*, fol. 35^{a} 5-6). The name of the client—Prince Chingim (Jim-gyim)—is also mentioned there.
404. The biography of Bu-ston Rin-chen-grub—entitled *mKhan-chen-thams-cad-mkhyen-pa-ston-lo-tsā-ba'i-rnam-par-thar-pa-brjod-pa'i-me-tog* (55 fols.)—was written in 1366 (Fire-Horse year) by his pupil Rin-chen-rnam-rgyal. This biography was published in bLa-braṅ. A copy of this publication is available in the Institute of Peoples of Asia (*Baradiin Collection*, No. 34). An abridged

Chos-'byuṅ covering 244 folios was written in 1322.[405] It consists of four parts, which expound successively : (1) general introduction to the Buddhist creed (fols. 3ᵃ 3-39ᵃ 2), (2) history of appearance of the Buddhist creed on earth and of its development in India (fols. 39ᵃ 2-137ᵃ 1), (3) spread of Buddhism in Tibet (fols. 137ᵃ 1-159ᵃ 5), and (4) a systematic catalogue of literature translated into Tibetan (fols. 159ᵃ 6-241ᵇ 6). Such contents of this work enable us to compare it with the so-called "catalogues of the Buddhist canon" (*bKa'-daṅ-bstan-'gyur-gyi-dkar-chag*) which we shalll discuss later, since these catalogues are compiled on approximately the same scheme.[406] From these works, however, Bu-ston's work is distinguished in that it discusses the canon in general, and not any one particular collection or redaction of it. That is why it does not contain an account of the compilation of any single specific collection. This historico-bibliographical work of Bu-ston enjoys great fame and authority among the Tibetan historians. References to this work can be found almost in every large historical work of Tibet. In Europe, too, this *Chos-'byuṅ* of Bu-ston has merited repeated attention right from the time of A. Csoma de Koros.[407] This work was used by V. P. Vasil'ev,

---

biography of Bu-ston Rin-chen-grub is also available in the *thob-yig* composed by bLo-bzaṅ-'phreṅ-las (see *Thob-yig-gsal-ba'i-me-loṅ*, Peking edition, vol. iii, fols. 1-13ᵇ 5). This abridged biography is based on the above-mentioned biography compiled by Rin-chen-rnam-rgyal to which it directly refers by the name of its author (*ibid.*, fol. 13ᵇ 5 ; also cf. fol. 12ᵇ 1-2). The colophon of the first detailed biography mentions only the nick-name of the author—Gra-tshan-pa—instead of his full name. In the *Deb-ther-rgya-mtsho* (vol. i, fol. 13ᵇ 3) are mentioned two other biographies of Bu-ston, but I could not find them. Both these are named in the "List of Rare Books" (see *dPe-rgyun-dkon-pa-'ga'-shig-gi-tho-yig*, fol. 6ᵃ 1). The biographical materials on Bu-ston may also be found in many general works on the history of Buddhism in Tibet. The principal dates of his life are, however, given in the "Chronological Tables".

405. The date of composition of the *Chos-'byuṅ* of Bu-ston Rin-chen-grub is given in the colophon (fol. 244ᵃ 4)—Water-Dog year, 3455 years from the *nirvāṇa* (following the method of the Sa-skya-pa scholars), and 33rd year of the life of the author—and in the "Chronological Tables". This work was published in the monastery of bKra-śis-lhun-po. A copy of this publication is available in the Institute of Peoples of Asia (*Old Collection*. No. 368).

406. See, for instance, the catalogue of the Co-ne edition of the *bsTan-'gyur* described below.

407. A. Csoma de Koros, *Enumeration of Historical and Grammatical Works to be met with in Tibet*,—JASB, 1838, p. 149.

who was the first to evaluate it highly.[408] Individual passages from this work were translated by Academician F. I. Shcherbatskoi [Th. Stcherbatsky].[409] Sarat Chandra Das,[410] L. A. Waddell,[411] Charles Bell[412] and other authors referred to it as an important monument of Tibetan historiography. In 1931-32 was published a complete translation of the first three parts of this text as made by E. E. Obermiller.[413] In this translation, one comes across several mistakes.[414] But, on the whole, it gives an accurate idea of

---

408. V. P. Vasil'ev, *O nekotorykh knigakh, otnosyashchikhsya k istorii buddizma, v biblioteke Kazanskogo universiteṭa* [On Some Books Relating to the History of Buddhism in the Library of the University of Kazan],—"Uchenye zapiski Akademii nauk", 1855, vol. iii, No. i, p. 13. See also : V. P. Vasil'ev, *Buddhizm, ego dogmaty, istoriya i literatura* [Buddhism, Its Dogmas, History and Literature], pt. i, p. 319 and pt. iii, p. 5, 10, 11, 42-44, 58, 61, 66, 67 etc. (see the *index* to this part). Almost all the references to Bu-ston in this latter part are reproduced in the German translation of A. Schiefner (see Schiefner, *Tāranātha's Geschichte des Buddhismus in Indien*, St. Petersburg, 1869, SS. 5, 40, 109, 214, 276, 284, u.a ; see *Register* under the word "Bu-ston").
409. F. I. Shcherbatskoi, *Notes de litterature bouddhique. La litterature Yogācāra d'apres Bouston*—"Le Museon", 1905, vol. vi, N 1, pp. 144-155. This apart, Academician Stcherbatsky also translated Bu-ston's communication on the *Abhidharma* literature of the *Sarvāstivāda* school. This translation was published by Takakusu in his articles (see Takakusu, *On the Abhidharma Literature of the Sarvāstivādins*,—"Journal of the Pali Text Society", 1904-1905, pp. 75-77).
410. See S. C. Das, *Indian Pandits in Tibet*,—JBTS, 1893, vol. i, pt. i, pp. 2-7. This article includes a translation of Bu-ston's account of Śāntarakṣita and the first major part of his account of Kamalaśīla (cf. Bu-ston, *Chos-'byuṅ*, fols. 139^{b} 6-143^{b} 5).
411. L. A. Waddell, *Ancient Historical Edicts at Lhasa*,—JRAS, 1909, p. 923, n. 3. See also L. A. Waddell, *The Buddhism of Tibet*, p. 166.
412. C. Bell, *The Religion of Tibet*, pp. 200-201.
413. E. Obermiller, *History of Buddhism*, pp. i-ii. The first part was translated under the direct guidance of Academician F. I. Shcherbatskoi.
414. I take this opportunity of rectifying some errors and discrepancies found in the translation of E. E. Obermiller. In particular, many errors and discrepancies are discovered in the section devoted to the calculation of the period of the existence of Buddhism (E. Obermiller, *History of Buddhism*, pt. ii, pp. 102-108 of the translation). The Tibetan text states that according to the calculations of the scholars of the Sa-skya-pa school, 800 years had passed from the king Nandin (dGa'-byed) to the king Candragupta (Zla-sruṅ)—see

the original text and is a valuable contribution to the study of Tibetan historiography. It is a pity that in the portion concerning the history of Tibet, the translation is almost

---

Bu-ston, *Chos-'byuṅ*, fol. 103ª 6 ff. Though this figure is clearly fantastic, it cannot at all be replaced by the figure "108" (*brgya-brgyad*) as done by E. E. Obermiller (*ibid.*, t. ii, p. 106),—primarily because the original works of the scholars of the Sa-skya-pa school (see *Chos-la-'jug-pa'i-sgo*, fols. 315ᵇ 6-316ª 1, and *bLa-ma-rje-btsun-chen-po'i-rnam-thar*, fol. 297ª 5) and the works of other authors, which quote the chronological calculations of the scholars of the Sa-skya-pa school (see *Dus-'khor-ṭīk-chen*, vol. i, fol. 22ª 6, and *bsTan-rtsis-'dod-spyin-gter-'bum*, E. Schlagintweit, *Die Berechnung der Lehre*, S. 662, Zz. 16-17) throughout mention 800 years (*brgyad-brgya*). Besides, if "800" be replaced by "108", it breaks down the whole chronological notion of this school, for the figure "800" is one of the components of the sum of 2955 years which, in the view of the representatives of this school, had passed from the *nirvāṇa* to the conclusion of a peace treaty between Tibet and China in A.D. 822. Further, the Tibetan text (fol. 103ᵇ 1) has the expression : *De-nas-lo-bdun-brgya-ñi-śu-rtsa-bshi-nas-'phro-bzaṅ-nas lo-brgyad-brgya-bcu-bshi-na-bal-bar rgyal-po-'od-zer-go-cha-byuṅ*. E. E. Obermiller translates : "from 724 to 814 years after him—the king Aṃśuvarman in Nepal" (E. Obermiller, *History of Buddhism*, pt. ii, p. 106). A correct translation would be : "After him, after 724 years (...) and then after another 814 years, there appeared in Nepal the king Aṃśuvarman". This phrase simply wants the information as to what happened "after 724 years"—viz. the appearance in Nepal of the king Dharmavarman (cf. *Dus-'khor-ṭīk-chen*, fol. 22ᵇ 1). The name of mChims Nam-mkha'-grags, which in the Tibetan original (fol. 103ᵇ 2-3) is given in full, has been abridged by E. Obermiller to mChims Nam-mkha' (*ibid.*, p. 106). Again, the Tibetan original (fol. 103ᵇ 4) states : *Du-nas-me-mo-glaṅ-la-chu-mig-chos-'khor-gyi-dus-su-bla ma-chos- rgyal- gyis-brtsis-pas- sum-stoṅ- bshi-brgya-daṅ-bcu-lon-par-brtsis-pas*. E. E. Obermiller (*ibid.*, p. 106) translates : "Thereafter, in the year of the fire-cow, at the time of the installation of the prayer-wheel moved by water, the Lama Cho-rgyal has counted 3410 years". A correct translation would be : "Thereafter, when Lama Dharmarāja (an epithet of the famous 'Phags-pa-bla-ma) made (his) calculation in the year of the Fire-Cow (i.e. in A.D. 1277) at the time of preaching (*dharma-cakra-pravartana*) at the source, (he) reckoned 3410 years (from the *nirvāṇa*)". Information on this famous preaching is given in the *Hor-chos-'byuṅ* (see G. Huth, *Geschichte des Buddhismus in der Mongolei*, vol. i, S. 101, Z. 6, ff.), in the *Dus-'khor-ṭīk-chen* (fol. 23ª 2), in the *rGyal-ba-lṅa-pa'i-deb-ther* (fol. 57ᵇ 1-2), in the "Chronological Tables" and in other texts. Further, the Tibetan original (fol. 103ᵇ 5) contains

absolutely without any annotation. Besides, no attempts have been made to convert

---

a phrase : *Chu-pho-khyi-lo-la-bla-ma-ti-śri-kun-dga'-blo-gros-rgyal-mtshan-dpal-bzaṅ po-bod-du bsñen-rdsogs-la-byon-pa'i-lo-yan-chad-la-sum-stoṅ-bshi-brgya-lṅa-bcu-rtsa-lṅa-'das rtsa-drug-pa'i-steṅ-na-yod-pas*. E. E. Obermiller translates : "Accordingly up to the male-water-dog year, when the Lama Matiśrī Kun-gā-lo-do-gyal-tshan-pal-zan-po came to Tibet in order to become ordained,—3455 years had passed away and the 3456 th year (of the Doctrine) was lasting" (*ibid.*, p. 106). A correct translation would read : "up to the Water-Dog year, when the Lama Ti-śri (Chinese title) Kun-dga'-blo-gros-rgyal-mtshan arrived in Tibet for being finally ordained, 3455 years had passed away ; and now 3456 th year (from the *nirvāṇa*) is running". The Water-Dog year referred to here corresponds to A.D. 1322 and is the same year in which Bu-ston wrote his historical work. As regards Lama Kun-dga'-blo-gros-rgyal-mtshan mentioned in this phrase, apparently he is none other than the elder brother of Sa-skya-pa bSod-nams-rgyal-mtshan (1312-1375)—who is already known to us and who figures in the historical texts under the name of Kun-dga'-blo-gros (1299-1327) and bears the title "Ti-śri" (see *Deb-ther-sṅon-po*,. vol. i, fol. 110^{b} 4 and "Chronological Tables"). He was one of the teachers of Bu-ston (see the aforementioned biography of the latter, compiled by Rin-chen-rnam-rgyal, fol. 10^{b} 1-2). Finally, the original Tibetan text (fol. 104^{b} 2) states : *Des-na-dus-'khor-lugs-kyi-rtse- rgyud-bstan-nas chu-pho- khyi- yan-chad- la-lo-ñis-stoṅ-chig-brgya-dgu-bcu-rtsa-brgyud-'das-par-śes-par-bya'o*. E. E. Obermiller translates : "It is necessary to know that, according to the teaching contained in the chief *tantra* of the *Kālacakra* system, up to the male-water-dog year, 2198 years have passed away" (*ibid.*, p. 108). A correct translation would read : "It is therefore necessary to know that, according to the *Kālacakra* system, from the time of the preaching (by Buddha) of the chief *tantra* of this doctrine" etc. Other errors found in the translation of this special section of the text have already been mentioned (see *supra*). Similar discrepancies are also found in other places of the translation of the historical part. Thus, for instance, in the exposition of the genealogy of Tibetan kings in the original text, (fol. 137^{b} 4-5) there is a phrase : *De'i-sras-lde-snol-gnam-nas-bzuṅ-ste khri-thog-rje-thog-btsan- gyi-bar- yan-chad- rgyal-rabs- ñi- śu-rtsa- drug-na lha-tho-tho-ri-gñan-btsan-byon-pa'i-tshe*. E. E. Obermiller translates : "The son of this one—De-nol-nam. From the time of the latter and up to Ṭhi-thog-je-thog-tsen there was a long succession of kings. As the 26th of this line there appeared the king Tho-tho-ri-ñan-tsen" (*ibid.*, p. 182). A correct translation would be : "The son of this one—sDe-snol-gnam. From him, (the succession of Tibetan kings continues) up to Khri-thog-rje-thog-btsan who was the 26th Tibetan

the Tibetan dates into European calender—not to speak of the critical comparison of the data of the text with those of other historical works of Tibet.

Other subsequent works (chronologically),—which to some extent can be and are classified under the heading "Histories of Religion" (*Chos-'byuṅ*-s), as composite works —are the so-called "Will-book" (*bka'-chems-deb-ther*) which is attributed to Si-tu

---

king (counting from gÑa'-khri-btsan-po). Then appeared Lha-tho-tho-ri-gñan-btsan". Cf. *Bod-kyi-rgyal-rabs* compiled by Grags-pa-rgyal-mtshan, fol. 197ᵃ 4-5 ; *rGyal-rabs-gsal-ba'i-me-loṅ*, fols. 24ᵇ 3-6 and 26ᵃ 6-26ᵇ 3 ; and *Hor-chos-'byuṅ* (see G. Huth, *Geschichte des Buddhismus in der Mongolei*, vol. i, S. 3), where Khri-thog-rje-thog-btsan is regarded as the 26th and his son, Lha-tho-tho-ri-gñan-btsan, as the 27th Tibetan king from gÑa'-khri-btsan-po, their mythical ancestor. (According to another version, they are regarded as the 27th and 28th Tibetan kings respectively—see *Deb-ther-sṅon-po*, vol. i, fols. 20ᵇ 6-21ᵃ 3 ; *dPag-bsam-ljon-bzaṅ*, fols. 97ᵃ 3-97ᵇ 1, S. C. Das, *Pag Sam Jon Zang*, p. 150). Towards the end (fol. 146ᵃ 5-6) of the chapter on the initial spread of Buddhism in Tibet, there is an account of how the elder wife of the king gLaṅ-dar-ma passed the child of someone else for her own new-born child despite the fact that this child already had teeth and how the ministers agreed with her. The text reads : *bLon-po-rnams-na-re mdaṅ-skyes-pa'i-bu-chuṅ-la-so-mi-'byuṅ-ste yum-gyi-bka'-brtan-du-chug-gsuṅs-pas yum-brtan-shes-grags-te*. Considering the text a bit vague, E. E. Obermiller translates : "The ministers said to this : A child born a day before cannot have teeth. Let him carefully preserve the instructions of his mother ! Accordingly the boy became known by the surname of 'Yum-tan' (preserving his mother's word)"—*ibid.*, pp. 199-200. However, the context is clear. A correct translation reads : "The ministers said : A child born yesterday cannot have teeth. But since the mother says so, let him be brought up. And so he was called 'Yum-brtan' (i.e. brought up by the mother)". This account is also repeated in other texts, particularly in the *rGyal-rabs-gsal-ba'i-me-loṅ* (fol. 99ᵃ 4-6). In the Kalmuck translation of this text, the name "Yum-brtan" is correctly translated (see I. J. Schmidt, *Geschichte der Ost-Mongolen* , S. 365, which gives the Kalmuck expression and its correct translation into German : "der von der Mutter Erzogene"). This account is also repeated in the *rGyal-ba-lṅa-pa'i-deb-ther* (fol. 49ᵃ 2-3), from where it has been borrowed and re-told in his own words by S. C. Das (see S. C. Das, *Contributions on* ,—JASB, vol. L, 1881, pt. i, p. 235), who also translates this name as "one upheld by his mother". Such minor errors do not, of course, belittle the general merits of E. E. Obermiller's translation, particularly because Obermiller was a patient suffering from paralysis.

Byaṅ-chub-rgyal-mtshan (1302-1373), the founder of Phag-mo-gru-pa,[415] *Deb-ther-dmar-po*, and *rGyal-rabs-gsal-ba'i-me-loṅ* (which we have already examined). With the exception of the last work, the other works are bibliographical rarities.[416] Other such rare works include the one on "History of Religion" written in 1417 by Kam-kam-pa Don-grub-dpal (b. 1365) and another entitled *Chos-'byuṅ-bstan-pa-rin-po-che'i-gsal-byed*[417] by Nel-pa-paṇḍita sMon-lam-tshul-khrims,[418] etc.

One of the most remarkable works of Tibetan historiography is the so-called "Blue Annals" (*Deb-ther-sṅon-po*). The author of this work is 'Gos-lo-tsā-ba Yid-bzaṅ-rtse-ba gShon-nu-dpal (1392-1481), whom the Fifth Dalai Lama and other Tibetan writers give the epithet of the scholar "not having his equal among the historians" (*lo-rgyus-smra-la-zla-med*).[419] This work was begun in 1476 and finished in 1478. In the text itself, the year before its compilation,—which is the starting point for calculating the numbers of years that have passed from the time of various events—is taken, as usual, as the year of the beginning of the work (i.e. 1476).[420] In spite of the fact that certain data in the *Deb-ther-sṅon-po* have been disputed by later historians,[421] this work, even today, continues to enjoy, in Tibetan historical literature, exceptional fame as one of the works richest in information. The "Blue Annals" was thrice published in

---

415. See *Deb-ther-rgya-mtsho*, vol. i, fol. 4ᵇ 2. The Fifth Dalai Lama also refers to *Si-tu-rin-po-che'i-bka'-chems-deb-ther* (see *rGyal-ba-lṅa-pa'i-deb-ther*, fol. 63ᵇ 5).
416. See *dPe-rgyun-dkon-pa-'ga'-shig-gi-tho-yig*, fols. 3ᵃ 4 and 7ᵇ 2.
417. See *Deb-ther-rgya-mtsho*, vol. i, fol. 4ᵇ 4, and also *dPe-rgyun-dkon-pa-'ga'-shig-gi-tho-yig*, fol. 3ᵃ 2-3. The date of composition of this work is given in the "Chronological Tables".
418. See *Deb-ther-rgya-mtsho*, vol. i, fol. 4ᵇ 3-4, and also *dPe-rgyun-dkon-pa-'ga'-shig-gi-tho-yig*, fol. 3ᵃ 1. This work of Nel-pa-paṇḍita is also refferred to in the *Deb-ther-sṅon-po* (vol. i, fol. 28ᵇ 6).
419. See *rGyal-ba-lṅa-pa'i-deb-ther*, fol. 36ᵇ 4. At another place in the *rGyal-ba-lṅa-pa'i-deb-ther* (fol. 7ᵃ 5-6), Yid-bzaṅ-rtse-ba is called the "ornament of the head of all historians of the sinful period" (*sñigs-dus-kyi-lo-rgyus-smra-pa-kun-gyi-gtsug-rgyun*). The well-known scholar, Lama bSod-nams-grags-pa, says of Yid-bzaṅ-rtse-ba that after the death of Bu-ston, he was the person who expanded the knowledge of history (see *bKa'-gdams-gsar-rñiṅ-gi-chos-'byuṅ-yid-kyi-mdses-rgyan*, fol. 90ᵃ 6-90ᵇ 1). According to Sum-pa-mkhan-po, he is reputed as the "most learned of (all) historians" (*lo-rgyus-smra-mkhas-su-grags-pa*)—see *dPag-bsam-ljon-bzaṅ*, fol. 100ᵃ 3; S. C. Das, *Pag Sam Jon Zang*, p. 154. Similar comments may also be found in the works of other historians.
420. See *supra*, note 239.
421. See *dPag-bsam-ljon-bzaṅ* (fols. 285ᵃ 1-285ᵇ 2), which quotes and repudiates numerous reports of the *Deb-ther-sṅon-po*.

xylograph. The first edition, the blocks of which perished at the time of Tibetan-Nepalese war, was accomplished in the monastery of Yaṅs-pa-can.[422] The second edition was accomplished in the monastery of Kun-bde-gliṅ in Lhasa ; the colophon to this edition was composed by the Head of this monastery, rTa-tshag-pa Ye-śes-blo-bzaṅ bsTan-pa'i-mgon-po, in the 18th century.[423] In this edition, the text consists of 15 separate books corresponding to the main sections of the work—each having separate pagination. In all, they cover 485 folios of large format.[424] Lastly, the third edition was accomplished in the monastery of Ā-mchog dGa'-ldan-chos-'khor-gliṅ in Amdo. The second edition served as the original for this work ; however, as distinct from the former, the text in the third edition is divided into two volumes : the first volume having 297 folios and the second 271 folios of usual format.[425]

In European literature, the first scholar to pay attention to the *Deb-ther-sṅon-po* was A. Csoma de Koros, who borrowed from it the genealogical list of the Tibetan kings published by Prinsep.[426] Besides, this work was referred to by V. P. Vasil'ev,[427] Sarat Chandra Das and B. Baradiin.[428] The "Blue Annals" was used by Charles Bell[429]

---

422. This edition is mentioned in the colophon—see *Deb-ther-sṅon-po*, vol. ii, fol. 270ᵇ 4-5.
423. This colophon is appended to the edition referred to here as a separate folio. It is also repeated in the edition of the Ā-mchog-dgon-pa monastery (see *Deb-ther-sṅon-po*, vol. ii, fol. 270ᵇ 1-6).
424. A copy of this edition is available in the Institute of Peoples of Asia (*Old Collection*, No. 286).
425. Copies of this edition are available in the Institute of Peoples of Asia (*Baradiin Collection*). All our references are to this edition.
426. Prinsep, *Useful Tables, forming an Appendix to the Journal of the Asiatic Society*, pt. ii, Calcutta, 1836, pp. 131-132.
427. V. P. Vasil'ev, *O nekotorykh knigakh, otnosyashchikhsya k istorii buddizma v biblioteke Kazanskogo universiteta*, [On Some Books Relating to the History of Buddhism in the Library of the University of Kazan],—"Uchenye Zapiski Akademii nauk"; vol. iii, No. 1, p. 13.
428. S. C. Das, *Contributions on...*,—JASB, vol. L, 1881, pt. i, p. 212. Also B. Baradiin, *Statuyá Maitrei*...[Statue of Maitreya in the Golden Temple in bLa-braṅ], p. 04 ff. —The place of the latter edition of the *Deb-ther-sṅon-po* as given by B. Baradiin (viz. the monastery of mDsod-dge-dgon-pa) is not correct. The colophon (vol. ii, fol. 271ᵃ 6) mentions Ā-mchog-dgon-pa monastery.
429. C. Bell, *The Religion of Tibet*, pp. 201-207 and *Appendix*.

who expounded its brief table of contents, and by Professor G. Tucci, who published several small passages from it.[430]

In its subject-matter, the *Deb-ther-snon-po* is primarily the history of Tibetan Buddhism. But it also gives a great deal of information on general secular history of the country. The first book of this work expounds : the genealogy of the Buddha and his deeds, brief information from the history of Buddhism in India, the genealogy of the Tibetan kings, brief information from the history of the initial spread of Buddhism in Tibet and the "prophecies" with regard to Tibetan kings, the genealogies of the Chinese dynasties and a chronology of earlier Tibetan history, the genealogy of Mongolian Khans, etc. The second book describes "the later spread of Buddhism" in Tibet (*phyi-dar*). The subsequent books expound the histories of various lineages of sects or schools of Tibetan Buddhism, special secret doctrines, cults, etc.[431]

---

430. G. Tucci, *Indo-Tibetica*, ii : *Rin chen bzan po e la rinascita del buddhismo intorno al mille*, Rome, 1933, pp. 77-84.

431. I do not consider it superfluous to give here the titles of the fifteen books which comprise the *Deb-ther-snon-po*, along with the folio numbers of each of these in the edition of the Kun-bde-gliṅ monastery. Besides, I am also giving, in parentheses, the numbers of the folios which each of these books occupies in the edition of the Ā-mchog-dgon-pa monastery. The translation of these titles as published by C. Bell in his *The Religion of Tibet* (p. 219, *Appendix*) is absolutely unsatisfactory.

1. *Chos-'byuṅ-gi-rtsa-ba rgyal-rabs bstan-pa-dar-gyi-skabs*, 28 fols. (vol. i, fols. 1-32ᵃ 6). Chapter on the origin of the history of (the Buddhist) religion, on the dynasties of kings and on the initial spread of Buddhism in Tibet.

2. *bsTan-pa-phyi-dar-gyi-skabs*, 17 fols. (vol i, fols. 32ᵃ 6-51ᵃ 6). Chapter on the later spread of Buddhism in Tibet.

3. *gSaṅ-sṅags-sṅa-'gyur-gyi-skabs*, 46 fols. (vol. i, fols. 51ᵃ 6-106ᵃ 3). Chapter expounding the history of the tradition of "ancient translations of *mantra*-s" (i.e. of the main trend of the rÑiṅ-ma-pa sect).

4. *gSaṅ-sṅags-gsar-ma lam-'bras-rjes-'braṅ-daṅ bcas-pa'i-skabs*, 16 fols. (vol. i, fols. 106ᵃ 4-124ᵇ 5). Chapter expounding the history of the school of "new translations of *mantra*-s" (i.e. of the second new trend of the rÑiṅ-ma-pa sect) and the history of the "teaching of path and result" (main teaching of Sa-skya-pa sect).

5. *Jo-bo-rje-brgyud-pa-daṅ-bcas-pa'i-skabs*, 38 fols. (vol. i, fols. 124ᵇ 6-171ᵇ 6). Chapter expounding the history of Atiśa and his followers.

6. *rNog-lo-pa-tshab-brgyud-pa-daṅ-dbu-tshad- byams-chos-sogs-ji-ltar-byuṅ ba'i-skabs*, 10 fols. (vol. i, fols. 172ᵃ 1-183ᵇ 5). Chapter expounding the history

The Tibetan sources tell us of some works on the history of Buddhism in Tibet, the appearance of which dates back to the 16th century. These are : *Chos-'byuṅ-mkhas-*

---

of rÑog-lo-tsā-ba bLo-ldan-śes-rab (1059-1109) and his successors, the history of Pa-tshab-lo-tsā-ba Ñi-ma-grags-pa (b. 1055) and his school, and giving an account of the spread of the teaching of the sceptical philosophy (*Mādhyamika*), logic (*Pramāṇavārtika*), and the five treatises of Maitreya etc.

7. *rGyud-sde'i-bśad-srol-ji-ltar-byuṅ-pa'i-skabs*, 20 fols. (vol. i, fols. 183ᵇ 5-206ᵃ 6). Chapter on how the commentaries on the *tantra*-s appeared.

8. *mNa'-bdag-lo-tsā-ba-chen-po-mar-pa-nas-brgyud-de-dwags-po-bka'-brgyud-ces-grags-pa'i-skabs*, 142 fols. (vol. i, fol. 206ᵃ 6-vol. ii, fol. 84ᵇ 6). Chapter expounding the history of the sect known as Dwags-po bKa'-brgyud-pa, beginning from Mar-pa-lo-tsā-ba Chos-kyi-blo-gros (1012-1097).

9. *Ko-brag-pa-daṅ Ni-gu'i-skabs*, 13 fols. (vol. ii, fols. 85ᵃ 1-99ᵇ 2). Chapter expounding the history of Ko-brag-pa bSod-nams-rgyal-mtshan (1182-1261) and his school, and the history of the sect beginning from Ni-gu-ma, the sister of the yogi Nāropa, and her pupil Khyuṅ-po rNal-'byor (b. 990). This sect is known under the name of Śaṅs-pa bKa'-brgyud-pa.

10. *Dus-kyi-'khor-lo'i-skabs*, 41 fols. (vol. ii, fols. 99ᵇ 2-144ᵇ 6). Chapter expounding the history of the *Kālacakra* doctrine.

11. *Phyag-rgya-chen-po'i-skabs*, 13 fols. (vol. ii, fols. 145ᵃ 1-158ᵇ 6). Chapter expounding the history of the *Mahāmudrā* doctrine.

12. *Shi-byed-brgyud-pa-sṅa-phyi-bar-gsum-gyi-skabs*, 50 fols. (vol. ii, fols. 159ᵃ 1-213ᵇ 6). Chapter expounding the history of the ancient, middle and new sect of the Shi-byed-pa sect.

13. *gCod-yul-daṅ-kha-rag-pa'i-skabs*, 12 fols. (vol. ii, fols. 214ᵃ 1-226ᵇ 6). Chapter expounding the history of the gCod doctrine and the history of Kha-rag-pa-sgom-chuṅ.

14. *Thugs-rje-chen-po'i-skor-daṅ-rdo-rje-phreṅ-ba-sogs-kyi-skabs*, 25 fols. (vol. ii, fols. 227ᵃ 1-254ᵇ 6). Chapter expounding the history of the cult of Avalokiteśvara, the history of the *Vajramālā-sādhana* cult, etc.

15. *Tshogs-mde-bshi-sogs-dge-'dun-gyi-sde-ji-ltar-byuṅ-pa-daṅ shu-lan par-du-bsheṅs-pa'i-skabs*, 14 fols. (vol. ii, fols. 255ᵃ 1ff). Chapter which expounds the biography of the Kashmiri scholar, Śakyaśrībhadra—to whom go back two of the four traditions of *Vinaya* existing in Tibet—and which gives replies to the questions which were put to the author, and gives an account of the preparation (undertaken in 1481) of the printing blocks of this work (the latter account comprises largely of genealogies of the Tibetan feudal Bya'i-khri-dpon bKra-śis-dar-rgyas, the patron of this publication). This chapter also

pa'i-dga'-ston written by dPa'-po gTsug-lag-phreṅ-ba (b. 1566),[432] *Chos-'byuṅ-bstan-pa'i-padma-rgyas-pa'i-ñin-byed* written by 'Brug-pa Padma-dkar-po (b. 1527),[433] etc. A. Csoma de Koros[434] knew about the work of 'Brug-pa Padma-dkar-po. A small passage from this work was published by Professor G. Tucci.[435] Unfortunately, these works are not as yet available in our collections.

Of much later works—apart from the afore-mentioned work of the Fifth Dalai Lama,[436] which surveys the secular and ecclesiastical history of Tibet—one ought to mention the work entitled *Dam-pa'i-chos-kyi-byuṅ-tshul-bstan-pa'i-rgya-mtshor-'jug-pa'i-gru-chen*, the author of which was Ṅor-ba dKon-mchog-lhun-grub. The author himself could not manage to finish this work. He only wrote about half of the text, viz. the first introductory part (fols. 2^a 2-44^a 7) and two chapters of the second main part (chapter on Buddha, fols.44^a 7-80^a 7 and chapter on the spread of Buddhism in India, fols. 80^a 7-115^b 7). The third chapter—spread of Buddhism in Tibet—was only begun ; the period of initial spread (*sṅa-dar*) has been described (fols. 116^a 1-126^a 4), but the exposition of the period of later spread (*phyi-dar*) of Buddhism (fols. 126^b 4-129^a 6) has only been begun. The remaining portion—the end of the second part devoted to the history of Buddhism in Tibet (fols. 129^a 6-199^a 6), the third concluding part devoted to the finding out of places and periods of the activity of Buddhist religion (fols. 199^a 7-227^b 6) and also the introductory verses (fols. 1^b 1-2^a 2) and colophon (fols. 227^b 6-228^a 5)—was written by Bya-bral Saṅs-rgyas-phun-tshogs. This supplement (*kha-skoṅ*) bears its own title : *Legs-bśad-nor-bu'i-baṅ-mdsod.* This was compiled in 1692.[437] Both

---

contains a history of the dGe-ldan-pa or dGe-lugs-pa sect (a new sect at that time) and histories of the Nā-landa (Nalanda, founded in 1435) and rTses-thaṅ (f. 1351) monasteries.

432. See *Deb-ther-rgya-mtsho*, vol. i, fol. 4^b 3, and *dPe-rgyun-dkon-pa-'ga'-shig-gi-tho-yig*, fol. 3^a 1-2. This historian is referred to by the Fifth Dalai Lama (see *rGyal-ba-lṅa-pa'i-deb-ther*, fols. 40^b 3 and 41^a 5) and Sum-pa-mkhan-po, who disputes some of his reports (see *dPag-bsam-ljon-bzaṅ*, fol. 286^a 1-3). The date of birth of dPa'-po gTsug-lag-phreṅ-ba is given in the 'chronological table' of Sum-pa-mkhan-po.

433. See *Deb-ther-rgya-mtsho*, vol. i, fol. 4^b 2, and *dPe-rgyun-dkon-pa-'ga'-shig-gi-tho-yig*, fol. 3^a 2. Certain reports made by this author are disputed by Sum-pa-mkhan-po (see *dPag-bsam-ljon-bzaṅ*, fol. 286^a 3-4).

434. A. Csoma de Koros, *Enumeration of Historical and Grammatical Works...*, —JASB, 1838, p. 149.

435. G. Tucci, *Indo-Tibetica*, ii, pp. 84-88. G. Tucci mentions (*ibid.*, p. 93) that the xylograph used by him was printed in the monastery of sPuṅs-thaṅ.

436. See *supra*.

437. The colophon of this supplement (fol. 228^a 2) mentions the cyclic date of the

the works—the beginning and the end—were published together in sDe-dge and cover 228 folios of large format.[438]

After this, one must metion a short work entitled *rGyal-rabs-daṅ-'brel-ba'i-rgya-bod-kyi-chos-'byuṅ-dgos-'dod-kun-'byuṅ*, written by Co-ne Grags-pa-bśad-sgrub (1675-1748). This work is included in the Collected Works of the author published in Co-ne monastery. It covers, in all, 31 folios of usual Tibetan format.[439] In this work, to the history of Buddhism in Tibet has been devoted only one folio (fol. 29ᵇ 5-30ᵇ 4). All the remaining folios are devoted to the history of India and of Buddhism in this country.

Of the works, which besides the secular and ecclesiastical histories of Tibet and India also expound the secular and ecclesiastical history of other countries, it is necessary first of all to mention the oft-quoted work *'Phags-yul-rgya-nag-chen-po-bod-daṅ-sog-yul-du-dam-pa'i-chos-byuṅ-tshul-dpag-bsam-ljon-bzaṅ* (or *dPag-bsam-ljon-bzaṅ*) written in 1748[440] by Sum-pa-mkhan-po Ye-śes-dpal-'byor (1704-1788). This work is included in the Complete Works of the author and contains 317 folios of large farmat.[441] It consists of 4 parts. The first part contains a general introduction (fols. 1ᵇ 1-41ᵃ 4) and recounts the history of Buddhism in India (fols. 41ᵃ 4-95ᵃ 6). The second part expounds the secular (fols. 95ᵃ 6-108ᵃ 7) and ecclesiastical (fols. 108ᵃ 7-287ᵇ 7) history of Tibet. The third part briefly deals with the history of China (fols. 288ᵃ 1-292ᵇ 6) and of Budhism in China (fols. 292ᵇ 7-300ᵇ 2). The fourth part is a short account of the history of the Mongols (fols. 300ᵇ 2-312ᵇ 2) and of the history of the spread of

---

composition of this work—Water-Monkey year—but does not mention the ordinal number of the cycle. Fortunately, the text itself gives us correct indication of this date, for the section on the periods of existence of Buddhist religion sets forth calculations of number of years that had passed from the *nirvāṇa* to this date from the point of view of various schools. In particular, he mentions that, according to the Sa-skya-pa school (which, as is known, dates the *nirvāṇa* to 2134 B.C.), 3825 years had passed up to the year of the Water-Monkey (fol. 218ᵇ 5). Thus, the Water-Monkey year mentioned here corresponds to A.D. 1692.

438. A copy of this edition is available in the Institute of Peoples of Asia (*Baradiin Collection*). Our references are to this edition.

439. It is available in the 8th volume (*ña*) of the complete works of the author.

440. The date of composition of this work—Earth-Dragon year of the xiii cycle—is mentioned in the colophon (see *dPag-bsam-ljon-bzaṅ*, fol. 317ᵃ 2-3).

441. As already stated (note 32), this work comprises the first volume of the Collected Works of Sum-pa-mkhan-po published in Kuku-hoto (?). However, this volume often circulates as a separate work in the same edition. Such a separate volume is available in the Institute of Peoples of Asia (*Old Collection*, No. 286ᵃ).

Buddhism among them (fols. 312b 2-316a 1). The account of the history of Tibet ends with the chronological table (*bstan-rtsis*, fols. 272a 4-287b 7) already described above. To the history of the Mongols are appended the genealogical tables of the descendants of Genghis [Chinghiz], the Dsungar princes Gushi [Gu-śri] Khan and Ho-urlyuk.

In European literature, the first scholar to pay attention to this remarkable work was V. P. Vasil'ev,[442] who gave it an extremely high evaluation and undertook a translation of the chronological table given in it and of the chapter expoundiug the secular history of Tibet. This translation was, however, not printed.[443]

The world of scholarship is indebted to Sarat Chandra Das for its closest acquaintance with this work, for it was he who published the Tibetan text of its first and second parts and translated selected passages from it.[444] Unfortunately, this edition, like many other works of Sarat Chandra Das, is very slipshod.[445] To begin with, one

---

442. V. P. Vasil'ev, *O nekotorykh knigakh,...* [On Some Books Relating to the History of Buddhism in the Library of the University of Kazan],—"Uchenye Zapiski Akademii nauk", vol. iii, No. 1, p. 14.
443. See *supra*, note 383.
444. S. C. Das, *Pag Sam Jon Zang*—pt. i, *History of the Rise, Progress and Down-fall of Buddhism in India*; pt. ii, *History of Tibet from Early Times to 1745 A.D.*, by Sumpa Khan-po Yeśe Pal Jor, Calcutta, 1908.
445. As already stated, an English translation of the 'chronological table' of this text was published by S. C. Das in his article entitled *Life of Sum-pa Khan-po, also styled Yeśes-dpal-'byor, the Author of the Re'umig (Chronological Table)*—JASB, 1889, pp. 37-84. Some other small passages of this text were also translated and expounded by S. C. Das in various articles. Thus, the whole of his article entitled *Tibet, a Dependency of Mongolia* (JASB, 1905, pp. 152-155) is nothing but a translation (with a minor omission) of pages 164 (line 4)-166 (line 2) of the text published by him, though S. C. Das does not disclose his source. In the same way, his article *Tibet under Her Last Kings* (JASB, 1905, pp. 165-167) is a translation (with certain omissions) of the pages 161 (line 26)-164 (line 3) of the text, which, too, S. C. Das does not mention. The article *Some Historical Facts Connected with the Rise and Progress of the Māhāyāna School of Buddhism* (JBTS, 1893, vol. i, pt. iii, pp. 18-21), published anonymously but obviously written by S. C. Das, is a peculiar amalgam of reports given on pages 44 (lines 17-20), 82 (line 19), 83 (lines 15, 24-29), 91 (line 23) and 92 (line 14) of the text. Finally, the article *A Short Note on the Origin of the Tibetans and Their Division into Clans* (JBTS, 1897, vol. v, pt. i, pp. 1-4) is partly a translation and partly an exposition of pages 148 (line 13) and 149 (line 31) of the text, about which, too, S. C. Das mentions nothing. Besides, as S. C. Das himself indicates, his articles *The Hierarchy of the Dalai*

may mention that the publication of the second part is abruptly brought to an end—for no reason whatsoever—in the middle of the survey of the contents of the *bsTan-'gyur.* Again, this edition contains neither the last portion of this survey (though this, in the original, occupies less than one Tibetan folio—fols. 271^a 5-272^a 4) nor the chronological table,—nor even the critical conclusion to it. The text itself as given in this edition abounds in lacunae, misprints and all sorts of mistakes which sometimes totally distort the meaning. Nevertheless, we must be grateful to Sarat Chandra Das, for he, by his work, has made this important monument accessible to the wide circle of Tibetologists, laying thereby the foundation of its study.

To the class of extremely interesting works of Tibetan historiography, there pertains the work entitled *rGya-bod-hor-sog-gi-lo-rgyus-ñuṅ-ṅur-brjod-pa-byis-pa-'jug-pa'i-'bab-stegs* by dPal-maṅ dKon-mchog-rgyal-mtshan (1764-1853). This work often called simply *dPal-maṅ-tshaṅ-gi-deb-ther*, is included in the Collected Works of the author published in Ā-mchog-dga'-ldan monastery in Amdo and covers 93 Tibetan folios of usual format.[446] It is in two main parts—the general and the special. The general part recounts the spread of Buddhism in India (fols. 2^b 2-7^b 2) and in the mythical country of Śambhala (fols. 7^b 3-10^b 2) and gives a brief idea of the history of Tibet (fols. 10^b 2-21^a 6) and of China as a whole (fols. 21^a 6-24^b 2). The special part gives an account of the conquerer of Tibet, Gushi Khan (1582-1654)[447] and of his descendants

Lama (1406-1745) (JASB, 1904, Extra No., pp. 80-93), *The Monasteries of Tibet* (JASB, 1905, pp. 106-116) and *The Origin of Mankind* (JBTS, 1896, vol. iv, pt. ii, pp. 3-5) are also largely based on this text. These articles also, to some extent, have the discrepancies which we pointed out in other works of S. C. Das. In particular, one has invariably to rectify all the dates mentioned by him according to the European calendar and some dates mentioned by him according to the Tibetan sexagenary cycle (for instance, JASB, 1905, p. 165, line 11 from below : Read 'Earth-horse' instead of 'Earth-ox' ; *ibid.*, p. 167, line 12 from above : Read 'Iron-dog' instead of 'Iron-dragon' ; *ibid.*, line 25 from above : Read 'Earth-horse' instead of 'Earth-hare'). About the article *Life of the Author* appended to the edition of the *dPag-bsam-ljon-bzaṅ* in lieu of the preface—which, as already stated, is a literal repetition of the article *Life of Sum-pa Khan-po, also styled Yeśes dpal-'byor, the Author of the Re'umig (Chronological Table)* (JASB, 1889, pp. 37-40)—see *supra*, note 394.

446. This work is included in vol. iv (*ṅa*) of the Complete Works of the author, but is also often found separately.

447. The dates of birth and death of Gu-śri Khan are borrowed from the 'chronological table' of Sum-pa-mkhan-po. These are also available in the work being surveyed here (see *dPal-maṅ-tshaṅ-gi-deb-ther*, fols. 54^b 3 and 68^b 3), but the date of birth of Gu-śri Khan (the sixth year from the time of departure of the

and also states as to how they patronized Buddhism (fols. 24^b 2-52^a 5). This part also expounds the history of Tibet up to the time of—and particularly after Gushi Khan (fols. 52^a 5-92^b 4). Here it ought to be mentioned that dPal-maṅ dKon-mchog-rgyal-mtshan used only the Tibetan sources, for he, as he himself confesses, was weak in Mongolian language and script.[448]

A special place among the Tibetan historical works of analytical type goes to the famous historico-philosophical work *Grub-mtha'-thams-cad-kyi-khuṅs-daṅ-'dod-tshul-ston-pa-legs-bśad-śel-gyi-me-loṅ* (or, in short, *Grub-mtha'-śel-gyi-me-loṅ*), which expounds the history of the origin of various philosophical and religious doctrines of India, China (including Tibet) and of other countries, and the main tenets of these doctrines. The author of this unique work of its kind was Thu'u-bkwan bLo-bzaṅ-chos-kyi-ñi-ma (1737-1802), an incarnation and the Head of the dGon-luṅ (dGon-luṅ-byams-pa-gliṅ) monastery in Amdo.[449] This work was completed by him in the beginning of 1802 in the 65th year of his life. However, he stopped correcting it only two days before his death, which took place on the 10th day of the 6th Mongolian month of Water-Dog year of the xiii cycle.[450]

---

third Dalai Lama to Mongolia) has been mentioned here as Water-Tiger year (*chu-stag*) instead of the Water-Horse year (*chu-rta*). This evidently is a misprint.

448. See *dPal-maṅ-tshaṅ-gi-deb-ther*, fol. 27^b 1, which states : *bDag-sog-po'i-skad-daṅ yi-ge-la-rtul-ba'i-stabs-kyis 'dir-bkod-pa-rnams-bod-yig-tu-bris-pa-'ga'-shig-las-btus-pa-yin-pas*. Translation : "In view of the fact that I am weak in Mongolian language and script, the information given (by me) here is taken from the sources written in Tibetan".

449. A detailed biography of Thu'u-bkwan bLo-bzaṅ-chos-kyi-ñi-ma, entitled *Rigs-daṅ-dkyil-'khor- rgya-mtsho'i- mṅa'-bdag- rje-btsun-blo- bzaṅ-chos-kyi-ñi-ma'i-gsuṅ-gsum-rmad-du-byuṅ-ba'i-rtags-brjod-padma-dkar-po*, was written in 1815 by Guṅ-thaṅ dKon-mchog-bstan-pa'i-sgon-me (1762-1823), a Lama from bLa-braṅ. The biography is appended to the Complete Works of Thu'u-bkwan bLo-bzaṅ-chos-kyi-ñi-ma published in dGon-luṅ monastery and covers two volums—vol. xv (*ba*), 400 fols.; and vol. xvi (*ma*), 350 fols. Besides, this biography is available in the Complete Works of its compiler (Guṅ-thaṅ dKon-mchog-bstan-pa'i-sgon-me) published in bLa-braṅ, where again it occupies two volumes—vol. vi (*cha*), 351 fols.; and vol. vii (*ja*), 315 fols. Stray biographical data on him are also available in the *Deb-ther-rgya-mtsho* (vol. i, fols. 77^a 1-78^a 3).

450. See *Grub-mtha'-śel-gyi-me-loṅ*, dGon-luṅ edition, book 12, fols. 20^b 2-4 and 21^b 1-22^a 2. See also the aforementioned biography of Thu'u-bkwan bLo-bzaṅ-chos-kyi-ñi-ma, bLa-braṅ edition, vol. ii, fol. 262^b 5. The date of composition of the *Grub-mtha'-śel-gyi-me-loṅ* as given in the author's colophon is the 8th day of the bright half of the month of *Pauṣa* (*rgyal-zla*) of the Iron-Hen year.

This work consists of 12 individual chapters. The first chapter expounds the history of origin of philosophical systems (Buddhistic and non-Buddhistic) of ancient India and the main tenets of each of them (29 folios). The second chapter contains the history of the initial and later spread of Buddhism in Tibet and of the origin of the sect of "Ancient *mantra*"—gSaṅ-sṅags-rñiṅ-ma (or, in short, rÑiṅ-ma-pa)—and also the doctrine of this sect (21 folios). The third chapter gives the history of origin of bKa'-gdams-pa sect and its teaching (17 folios). The fourth chapter recounts the history of bKa'-rgyud-pa sect and its teaching (34 folios). The fifth, sixth and seventh chapters give respectively the history of Shi-byed-pa sect and its teaching (11 folios), history of Sa-skya-pa sect and its teaching (24 folios), history of Jo-naṅ-pa sect and its teaching and the history of origin of some ephemeral (*ñe-tshe-ba*) doctrines (15 folios). The eighth chapter contains the history of dGa'-ldan-pa or dGe-lugs-pa sect and its teaching (87 folios). The ninth chapter is an account of the history of Bon religion of ancient Tibet and its literature (8 folios). The tenth chapter gives the history of the philosophical systems of China and the main tenets of these systems (18 folios). The eleventh chapter contains the history of Buddhism in China (17 folios). The twelfth chapter gives the history of Buddhism in Mongolia, in Khotan and in the mythical country of Śambhala, besides including the general concluding note (22 folios).

The *Grub-mtha'-śel-gyi-me-loṅ* enjoys great and fully deserved fame in Tibetan literature as the first attempt at expounding not only the history but also the system of views of various philosophical and religious streams of Tibet and neighbouring countries. It exists in three xylograph editions. The first edition was accomplished in the dGon-luṅ monastery, where were prepared the xylograph cliché of the Complete Works of the author.[451] In this edition, the work is divided into twelve separate books—each chapter of the work comprising a separate book and having separate pagination. Another (the second) edition—in one volume (209 folios)—was accomplished in the

---

This date is the beginning of the year 1802 of our calendar, though the year of the Iron-Hen actually corresponds to A.D. 1801. This is explained by the fact that the bright part of the month of *Pausa* (which is regarded as the last, twelfth month, in the calendar adopted by the Tibetans) generally corresponds to January.

451. The *Grub-mtha'-śel-gyi-me-loṅ* is included in the Complete Works of Thu'u-bkwan bLo-bzaṅ-chos-kyi-ñi-ma published in 16 volumes in dGon-luṅ, where it covers the entire fourth volume (*ṅa*). A copy of the Complete Works is available in the library of the Leningrad State University (xyl. Q 344). In dGon-luṅ, the *Grub-mtha'-śel-gyi-me-loṅ* was also published as a separate monograph.

sDe-dge monastery.[452] Lastly, the third edition—analogous to the first one—was realized in the bKra-śis-chos-'phel *datsan* of the dGa'-ldan monastery in Urga (now Ulan Bator) in Mongolia.[453]

As already stated by B. Ya. Vladimirtsov,[454] a portion of the work—devoted to the history of Buddhism in Mongolia—was translated into Mongolian and published as a separate xylograph.

In European scientific literature, V. P. Vasil'ev[455] was the first to pay attention to the *Grub-mtha'-śel gyi-me-loṅ*. It was, then, taken up by S. C. Das who—independently of V. P. Vasil'ev—published (along with a translation into English) chapter 9 devoted to the history of Bon religion[456] and a portion of chapter 12 touching the history of Buddhism in Mongolia.[457] Besides, he translated chapters 10 and 11 (devoted to Chinese philosophy and to the history of Buddhism in China)[458] and the first half of

452. A copy of the sDe-dge edition of the *Grub-mtha'-śel-gyi-me-loṅ* is available in the Institute of Peoples of Asia (*Nova* ; acquired from B. Baradiin).

453. A copy of the Urgin edition of the *Grub-mtha'-śel-gyi-me-loṅ* is available in the Institute of Peoples of Asia (*Nova*).

454. B. Ya. Vladimirtsov, *Nadpisi na skalakh khalkhaskogo Tsoktutaidzhi. stat'ya pervays*,—"Izvestiya AN SSSR", 1926, pp. 1272-1273.

455. V. P. Vasil'v, *O nekotorykh krigakh*,... [On Some Books Relating to the History of Buddhism in the Library of the University of Kazan],—"Uchenye Zapiski Akademii nauk", 1855, vol. iii, No. 1, p. 7. The information on Tāranātha as quoted by V. P. Vasil'ev in the preface to his translation of Tāranātha's History of Buddhism in India (see *Buddizm, ego dogmaty, istoriya i literatura* [Buddhism : Its Dogmas, History and Literature], pt. iii, pp. xix-xx) is borrowed, in full, from the *Grub-mtha'-śel-gyi-me-loṅ* (chapters 7 and 12).

456. S. C. Das, *Contributions on*..., —JASB, 1881, pp. 187-205. S. C. Das erroneously calls this chapter as the eighth.

457. S. C. Das, *Contributions on*..., JASB, 1882, pp. 58-73. S. C. Das wrongly calls this chapter "eleventh". The translation made by him is lacunar.

458. S. C. Das, *Contributions on* , —JASB, 1882, pp. 87-114. S. C. Das wrongly calls these chapters "ninth" and "tenth". The translation of the last (the eleventh) chapter abruptly stops at the portion where the teachers of the fifth school of Chinese Buddhism (*sñiṅ-po-don-brgyud*) are enumerated ; even this list of teachers has not been completed. The translation is mechanically stopped at the end of the 12th folio of the dGon-luṅ edition of the text. All the subsequent portion (from the beginning of fol 13ª 1 to the end of fol. 17ᵇ 5), which is a continuation of the account of the fifth school and which describes the appearance of Tibetan Buddhism in China, is wanting in the translation. Even in the translated portions, there are omissions and insertions.

chapter 2 (which expounds the history of the spread of Buddhism in Tibet and of the origin of rÑiṅ-ma-pa sect).[459]

However, this work of S. C. Das is not free from mistakes and various inaccuracies. In particular S. C. Das himself erred and put others in confusion in calculating the dates of birth and death of the author and the date of appearance of the work itself. According to his statement, the author was born "in the year of the Fire-Serpent of the xii cycle, i.e. 1674 A.D., and died in the year 1740 A.D." He also dates the work itself to A.D. 1740, affirming—despite the correct information of the colophon—that the author completed his work "about a week before his death."[460] The Tibetan date of birth of the author as given by S. C. Das is absolutely correct ; the author was actually born in the Fire-Serpent year of the xii cycle.[461] But this year does, in no way, correspond to A.D. 1674, because the xii cycle itself began only from 1687. Being the 51st year of the sexagenary cycle, the Fire-Serpent year of the xii cycle corresponds to A.D. 1737. In other words, in converting this Tibetan date into European calendar, S. C. Das has erred not only by 1-2 years (as he usually does) but by a whole cycle of sixty years by dating the death of the author not to A.D. 1802 (as it should have been) but to A.D. 1740.

Strange though it may seem, nobody has hitherto paid any attention to this sharp divergence between the Tibetan date as quoted by by S. C. Das and the *Anno Domini* which, according to him, corresponds to it. It would, however, have been easier to discover this discrepancy, for only a few lines later, while giving a short biography of Thu'u-bkwan bLo-bzaṅ-chos-kyi-ñi-ma, he names, as one of his teachers, the famous lCaṅ-skya Rol-pa'i-rdo-rje (1717-1786), the court Lama of the Chinese emperor (who reigned from 1736 to 1759).[462] Ignoring this fact, B. Laufer, however, not only repeats the mistake of S. C. Das that the *Grub-mtha'-śel-gyi-me-loṅ* was written in 1740, a week before the death of the author, but also draws a further conclusion from this erroneous

459. S. C. Das. *Contributions on...*, JASB, 1882, pp. 1-14. The translation is full of omissions, insertions and transpositions. For example, the report on the rDsogs-chen-pa sect set forth by S. C. Das at the end of the translation is, in the original text, put before the account of the "treasured books (*gter-ma* or *gter-chos*)—see *Grub-mtha'-śel-gyi-me-loṅ*, book ii, fols. 12ᵃ 1-13ᵃ 3. Some Tibetan names have been distorted by S. C. Das in his translation.

460. S. C. Das, *Contributions on...*, JASB, 1881, pp. 187-188.

461. See the detailed biography of Thu'u-bkwan bLo-bzaṅ-chos-kyi-ñi-ma (mentioned *supra*, note 449), bLa-braṅ edition, vol. i, (vi), fol. 11ᵃ 6-11ᵇ 2, and the *Deb-ther-rgya-mtsho*, vol. i, fol. 77ᵃ 1-2.

462. S. C. Das, *Contributions on...*, —JASB, 1881, p. 187.

judgment that the information given in this work about the publication, during the period of Ch'ien-lung, of a Mongolian translation of the *bKa'-'gyur* and *bsTan-'gyur* should be regarded as a later addition because this work was completed, "as is supposed, in A.D. 1741."[463] It is a pity that the mistake of S. C. Das was not noticed even by Prof. P. Pelliot whose works are a model of accuracy. Observing correctly that "toutes les reductions chronologiques effectuées par Sarat Chandra Das sont suspects", Professor P. Pelliot corrected a number of dates quoted by S. C. Das—particularly the date of birth (as erroneously converted by S. C. Das into European calendar) of Thu'u-bkwan bLo-bzaṅ-chos-kyi-ñi-ma. But here, he failed to notice that the mistake committed by S. C. Das in the conversion of this date was not that of three but of sixty-three years. The date as corrected by Professor Pelliot, therefore, differs from the actual date by exactly sixty years. The Fire-Serpent year of the xii cycle, according to him, corresponded to A.D. 1677, whereas it actually corresponds to 1737.[464]

We shall not dwell here on other mistakes in this work of S. C. Das—though they are there in plenty in the field of chronology (as pointed out by Professor P. Pelliot[465]) and even in the translation itself (as already indicated, to some extent, by B. Laufer[466] and B. Ya. Vladimirtsov).[467]

Coming to the Tibetan works on the history of Buddhism in other countries, we must first of all mention the well-known work on the history of Buddhism in India (*rGya-gar-chos-'byuṅ*) composed in 1608 by the famous Tāranātha or, as he is otherwise called, Kun-dga'-sñiṅ-po (b. 1575).[468] This work is entitled *dPal-gyi-'byuṅ-gnas-*

---

463. B. Laufer, *Ocherk mongol'skoi literatury* [Essay on Mongolian Literature], p. 55.
464. P. Pelliot, *Le cycle sexagénaire...*, —JA, 1913, v. i, pp. 648-649.
465. *Ibid.*, pp. 649-650.
466. B. Laufer *Ocherk mongol'skoi literatury*, p. 54, notes 1 & 2.
467. S. Ya. Vladimirtsov, *Nadpisi na skalakh khalkhaskogo Tsoktu-taidzhi. Stat'ya pervaya*,—"Izvestiya Akademii nauk SSR", 1926, p. 1273, note 5.
468. As seen from the table of contents, the first volume of the "Collected Works of Tāranātha contains his detailed autobiography under the title *rGyal-khams-pa-tā-rā-nā-thas-bdug-ñid-kyi-rnam-thar-ṅes-par-brjod-pa'i-deb-gter-śin-tu-shib-ma-ma-bcom-lhug-pa'i-rtogs-brjod* (331 fols.) ; but this autobiography is wanting in the copy of this "Collected Works" available in the Institute of Peoples of Asia (*Tsybikov Collection*, No. 15). Brief biographical data on Tāranātha are given by bLo-bzaṅ-'phrin-las in his *thob-yig* [Peking edition, vol. iv (*ṅa*), fols. 55ᵃ 4 ff]. The date of birth of Tāranātha is also mentioned in the Chronological Tables" ; the table of Sum-pa-mkhan-po gives even the date of composition of the *rGya-gar-chos-'byuṅ*. These dates were mentioned by

dam-pa'i-chos-rin-po-che-'phags-yul-du-ji-ltar-dar-pa'i-tshul-gsal-bar-ston-pa-dgos-'dod-kun-'byuṅ,[469] but is better known in Tibetan literature by its short title *Tāranātha'i-rgya-gar-chos-'byuṅ*. It was translated into the Russian language by V. P. Vasil'ev, who already in 1866 had presented his translation to the Academy of Sciences.[470] By using this translation, Academician A. Schiefner brought out in 1868 an edition of its Tibetan text.[471] In 1869, he translated it into German.[472] Schiefner's translation, however, does not substantially differ from the translation of V. P. Vasil'ev published in the same year, viz. 1869,[473] and agrees with the latter even in individual errors.[474] At present, these translations have of course already become somewhat outdated ; but for the middle of the last century, the translation of such a text as the work of Tāranātha was a task of exceptional difficulty and was brilliantly performed.

Thereafter, we ought to mention another no less known work on the history of Buddhism in Mongolia, the *Hor-chos-'byuṅ*, composed in 1819 by some Gushi [Gu-śri] bLo-bzaṅ-tshe-'phel in the monastery of bKra-śis-dga'-ldan-bśad-sgrub-gliṅ. This work

---

V. P. Vasil'ev in his *Buddizm* : *ego dogmaty, istoriya i literatura* [Buddhism : Its Dogmas, History and Literature ; pt. iii, p. xviii]. After him, these were also mentioned by A. Schiefner (see A. Schiefner, *Tāranātha's Geschichte des Buddhismus in Indien*, St. Petersburg, 1869, p. vi). However, as correctly noticed by B. Laufer (see B. Laufer, *The Application of the Tibetan sexagenary Cycle*,—"T'oung Pao", 1913, pp- 572-73), A. Schiefner wrongly gave the date of birth of Tāranātha as 1573 instead of 1575 repeating the mistake committed by A. Csoma de Koros in the conversion of Tibetan dates into European calendar.

469. This work is available in vol. xvi of the Complete Works of Tāranātha published in the dGa'ldan-phun-tshogs-gliṅ monastery. It covers 143 folios.

470. A. Schiefner himself mentions this in the preface to his translation (see A. Schiefner *Tāranātha's Geschichte des Buddhismus in Indien*, p.v).

471. A. Schiefner, *Tāranāthae de doctrinae Buddhicae in India propagatione narratio*, Petropoli, 1868.

472. A. Schiefner, *Tāranātha's Geschichte des Buddhismus in Indien*. St. Petersburg, 1869.

473. V. P. Vasil'ev, *Buddizm, ego dogmaty, istoriya i literatura* ; pt. iii, *Istoriya Buddizma v Indii,sochinemie Daranaty*, Perevod s tibetskogo [*Buddhism : Its Dogmas, History and Literature* ; pt. iii, *Tāranātha's History of Buddhism in India*, tr. from the Tibetan]- St. Petersburg, 1869.

474. See, for example, A. Grünwedel, *Der Weg nach Śambhala*, München, 1915, p. 91. Here, A. Grünwedel directly states that A. Schiefner "oft nur das Russische übersetzt". Cf. also Th. Stcherbatsky (F. I. Shcherbatskoi), *Buddhist Logic*, vol. i, Leningrad, 1932, p. 45, n. 1.

bears the title *Chen-po-hor-gyi-yul-du-dam-pa'i-chos-ji-ltar-byuṅ-ba'i-tshul-bśad-pa-rgyal-ba'i-bstan pa-rin-po-che-gsal-bar-byed-pa'i-sgron-me* and exists in the form of a separate xylograph consisting of 162 folios of usual Tibetan format.[475] It was published and translated into German by G. Huth.[476]

Unfortunately, G. Huth's translation leaves much to be desired. G. Huth did not even understand who the author of the text was. The colophon explicitly states that the author of this text is the "unworthy monk" (*btsun-gzugs-gyi-na-ba*) Gu-śri-dka'-bcu-su-dhai-a-yu-lwa-rta (sic !) or, as he is otherwise called, dByaṅs-can-sgeg-pa'i-blo-gros-'jigs-med-rig-pa'i-rdo-rje. The first of these names is a bad translation, into Sanskrit, of the Tibetan name bLo-bzaṅ-tshe-'phel.[477] It is by this name and by the short name Gushi [Gu-śri)-tshe-'phel that the author of this work is also known to Tibetan and Mongolian historiography.[478] Gu-śri-tshe-'phel wrote his work, as stated in the same colophon, at the request of a famous Lama from Amdo—Zam-tsha-sku-shabs-rin-po-che 'Jigs-med-nam-mkha' (1768-1821),[479]—who is regarded as the incarnation of Nam-mkha'-bzaṅ-po, the 55th Head of the dGa'-ldan monastery in Tibet

475. Copies of this xylograph are available in the Institute of Peoples of Asia (*Old Collection*, No. 438^{b}), in the Asiatic Department (No. 505) and in the Library of the University of Leningrad. The Leningrad University Library also has a manuscript copy made from the original of this work referred to by V. P. Vasil'ev (*O nekotorykh knigakh, otnosyashchikhsya k istorii buddizma v biblioteke kazanskogo universiteta*,—"Uchenya Zapiski Akademii nauk", 1855, vol. iii, No. 1, pp.13-14).
476. G. Huth, *Geschichte des Buddhismus in der Mongolei* vol. i (text), vol. ii (Ubersetzung), Strassburg, 1892-1896.
477. See the author's and publishers's colophons to a work of this very author entitled *rGyud-thams-cad-kyi-rgyal-po-'phags-pa-'jam-dpal-gyi-mtshan-yaṅ-dag-par-brjod-pa'i-'grel-pa-tshig-don-gsal-ba* (bLa-braṅ edition, fols. 58^{b} 3-59^{b} 6). In the author's colophon, the author calls himself by one of the names mentioned here—'Jigs-med-rig-pa'i-rdo-rje. In the publisher's colophon, he is called by his usual name—Gu-śri dKa'-bcu bLo-bzaṅ-tshe-'phel. Cf. also the translation of the name "Ṅag-dbaṅ-blo-bzaṅ" as "Vā-gi-ndra-ā-yu varta" in the *dPag-bsam-ljon-bzaṅ* (fol. 189^{b} 7) etc...
478. He is mentioned under this name in the "List of historical literature" in the *Deb-ther-rgya-mtsho* (vol. i, fol. 7^{b} 5) where one of his works entitled *Gu-śir-tshe-'phel-gyi-chen-po-hor-gyi-rgyal-rabs* is listed.
479. A short biography of Zam-tsha-sku-shabs-rin-po-che 'Jigs-med-nam-mkha'—also called Zam-tsha-sprul-sku 'Jigs-med-nam-mkha'—is given in the *Deb-ther-rgya-mtsho* (vol. ii, Fols. 170^{b} 6-175^{a} 6), for he is regarded as the previous incarnation of the 53rd Head of the bLa-braṅ monastery, Zam-tsha-sprul-sku

(during the time of Sum-pa-mkhan-po).[480] As is usual in such cases, the author, in his colophon, writes the name of Zam-tsha-sku-shabs-rin-po-che 'Jigs-med-nam-mkha' in full with appropriate honourable titles, calling him Yoṅs-rdsogs-bstan-pa'i-mṅa'-bdag-khri-chen- mchog- sprul- zam-tsha- sku- shabs- rin- po-che- rigs-kun- khyab- bdag-rdo-rje-'chaṅ-chen-po-'jigs-med-nam-mkha'. This long title of one and the same person, the sponsor of the work, was arbitrarily broken into two parts by G. Huth—understanding, by these parts, two different names. By the first part (Yoṅs-rdsogs-bstan-pa'i-mṅa'-bdag-khri-chen-mchog-sprul-zam-tsha-sku-shabs-rin-po-che), he understood the name of the sponsor of the work : "der Fürst der ganzlich vollkommenen Lehre Kri-chen mchog-sprul Zam-tsa Sku-Zabs rin-po-che". By the second part (Rigs-kun-khyab-bdag-rdo-rje-'chaṅ-chen-po-'jigs-med-nam-mkha') he misunderstood the proper name and title of the author, whereas the name Zam-tsha-sku-shabs-rin-po-che or Zam-tsha-sprul-ba'i-sku-rin-po-che is only a common title for all the well-known incarnations from Amdo, one of whom was 'Jigs-med-nam-mkha'. The real name of the author—Gu-śri bLo-bzaṅ-tshe-'phel—was converted by G. Huth into one of the sources of his own work.[481]

'Jigs-med-bsam-'grub-rgya-mtsho (b. 1833). According to this biography, he was born in the Earth-Mouse year (1768) and he died in the Iron-Serpent year (1821). His biography is also given in the *Hor-chos-'byuṅ* (see G. Huth, *Geschichte des Buddhismus in der Mongolei*, vol. i, p. 225, l. 3—p. 228, l. 9 ; the biography of Nam-mkha'-bzaṅ-po, who is regarded as his immediate incarnation, is also given here—p. 225, ll. 6-18). However, G. Huth, in his translation (*ibid.*, pp. xvi, 356), mistakes this biography of Nam-mkha'-bzaṅ-po for that of the author, though the whole context and, above all, the great reverence with which Ram-tsha-sku-shabs-rin-po-che 'Jigs-med-nam-mkha' is spoken of positively contradicts this.

480. See the aforementioned biography (*Deb-ther-rgya-mtsho*, vol. ii, fols. 170ª 3-170ᵇ 6) and *dPag-bsam-ljon-bzaṅ* (fol. 190ª 4-7).

481. The Tibetan original of the colophon reads (see G. Huth, *Geschichte des Buddhismus in der Mongolei*, vol. i, pp. 284-285).—Yoṅs-rdsogs-bstan-pa'i-mṅa'-bdag-khri- chen- mchog- sprul- zam- tsha-sku- shabs-rin-po-che- rigs- kun- khyab-bdag-rdo-rje-'chaṅ-chen-po- 'jigs-med- nam-mkha'i- shal- sṅa-nas-de- ñid-raṅ-re'i-thu-med-śog-gi-bstan-pa'i-spyin-bdag-chen-po-pe'i-se-no-yon-gyi- dgon-par-gdan-'dren-shus-pa- ltar-phebs- pa'i-skabs- su-ṅos- kyis-mjal-bar rje-ñid-kyi-shal-nas-khyod-kyis- hor-yul- du- rgyal-rabs- daṅ-rgyal- ba'i-bstan- pa-ji- ltar-dar- tshul-gyi-rnam-bshag-bod-kyi-yi-ge-daṅ-sog-po'i-yi-ge-gñis- kas-rtsoms- śig-pa'i- gsuṅ-gi- me-tog-spyi-bor-lhuṅ-ba-la ṅos-kyis-de-dag-gi-khuṅs-rtsad-gcod-dka'-bas-mi-thub-pa-'dra-shus-par thub- mod-'bri- dkos-ces-pa'i- gsuṅ-lci- ba-lan- gñis-gnaṅ- ba- daṅ-du-blaṅs-te don-gyi-slad-du-mtshan-nas-smos-te-paṇ-chen-thams-cad-mkhyen-pa-blo-

In spite of the fact that the lobaur spent by G. Huth over the colophon becomes

---

bzaṅ-dpal-ldan-ye-śes-dbaṅ-po'i-shal-sṅa-nas-daṅ 'jams-dbyaṅs-chos-kyi-rgyal-po-rje-btsun-dkon-mchog-'jigs-med-dbaṅ-po-yab-sras- kyi-shabs- rdul-spyi-bo'i- rgyan-du-'dsin-pa'i- btsun- gzugs-gyi- na-ba- gu-śri-bka'- bcu- su- dhī-ā- yu- varta'm- miṅ-gshan-dbyaṅs-can-sgeg-pa'i-blo-gros-'jigs-med-rig-pa'i-rdo-rje-'bod-pas hor-gyi-rgyal-rabs- rnams-ni-hvo- thog-tha'i- se-chen- hvoṅ-tha'i- ci'i- sku- tsha-se- chen-sa-snaṅ-tha'i-cis-mdsad-pa'i-rgyal-brgyud-kyi-gtam-me- tog-gi-tshoms- mthoṅ-ba-don-ldan-sogs-hor- gyi-yig-cha- rnams-la- bshir-bshag bstan-pa-rin- po-che- rgyas-par-mdsad-pa'i-skyes-mchog-rnams-kyi-rnam-par-thar-pa-ni-bod-kyi-mkhas-grub-dam-pa-rnams-kyis-mdsad-pa'i-legs-bśad-dag-las-śin-tu-ñuṅ-bar-bsdus-te rab-byuṅ-bcu-bshi-pa'i-legs-sbyar-gyi-skad-du-pra-mā-dā bsil-ldan-gyi-ljoṅs-su-myos-ldan ma-hā-tsi-na'i-yul-du-gyi-ma'u-shes- pa'i-sa-yos-lo'i- khrums-zla-ba'i- dkar-phyogs-kyi-dga'-ba-gsum-pa'i-ñin-bkra-śis-dga'-ldan-bśad-sgrub-gliṅ-du-rdsogs-par-sbyar- ba'i. G. Huth translates: "Der Fürst der ganzlich volkommenen Lehre Khri-chen mchogs-spul zam-tsha sku-zabs rin-po-che, lud eben jenen Rigs-kun Khyb-bdag rDo-rje chan chen-po Jigs-med nam-mkhai zal-sṅa-nas hoeflich in das Kloster des grossen Gabenspender : der Lehre, des Pei-se Noyon unseres Thümed-sog, ein. Als ich (Jigs-med-nam-mkha') daraufhinkam und ihm meine Aufwahrtung machte, fiel aus dem Munde dieses Herrn folgende Anrede auf mein Haupt : "Verfasse du in gesonderten Abschnitten die Geschichte der verbereitung des Koenigsgeschlechtes und derjenigen der Jina-Lehre in der Mongolei, sowohl in einem tibetischen wie in einem mongolischen Werke". Als ich hierauf erwiderte, ich wurde wegen der Schwierigkeit der Erforschung der Quellen für diese (Werke) wohl nicht imstande dazu sein, wiederholte er seine Rede mit Nachdruck. "Du musst (die Werke) verfassen so gut du es vermagst." Da gab ich denn unterthanen nach. Darauf habe ich im Interesse der Sache einen Mann, den ich mit Namen nennen will : den des Pan-chen thams-cad mkhyen-pa Blo-bzaṅ dpal-ldan ye-śes dbaṅ-poi shal-sṅa-nas und des Jam-dbyaṅs choi-kyi rfyal-po rJe-btsun dKon-mchog jigs-med dbaṅ-po—des Vaters und des Sohnes (i.e. des Meisters und des Jungens)—Fusstaub zum Scheitelschmuck nehmenden, an dem verehrungswürdigen leibe krankenden Guśri dKa-bcu Sudhi Āyuwarta oder, mit anderem Namen, dByaṅs-can sgeg-pai blo-gros Jigs-med rig-pai rdo-rje berufen, die mongolische Koenigsgeschichte auf die von dem Enkel des Hwothogtai Secen Hwon T'aici, verfasste Geschichte des Koenigsgeschlechtes, die dem Zwecke den Blumenhof zu sehen dient, und andere mongolische Geschichtswerke basiert, die Biographieen der Mahāpurusha's, welche das Kleinoed der Lehre zur Blüte gebracht haben, aus den vorzüglichen tibetischen Gelehrten verfassten Subhāṣhita's sehr kurz zusammengefasst und in dem in der Sanskrit sprache Pramādi, in dem kalten Lande (Tibet) Myos-ldan, in

quite obvious even on a preliminary acquaintance with the work, this work has

---

Mahācina-Lande Gyi-mau genannten Erde-Hasen-Jahr des 14. Cyklus (1818), im Monat Bhādrapada, am 3. Tage, dGa-ba, der lichten Haelfte, in bKra-śis dga-ldan bśad-sgrub gliṅ die Abfassung (des vorliegendes Werkes) beendet." (*ibid.*, vol. ii, pp. 446-447).

A correct translation of this text is : "When the sovereign of the most perfect religion, the exalted incarnation of the Head (of the monastery of dGa'-ldan), the precious master Zam-tsha (Zam-tsha-sku-shabs),—the sovereign who embodies in himself all (the five) births (gotra of the Buddhas of contemplation),—Vajradhara named 'Jigs-med-nam-mkha' arrived, on an invitation, at the monastery of our benefactor of religion, Pe'i-se No-yon, I met him, and there fell on my head the following flower of his speech : 'You (he told me) must set forth, in Tibetan and in Mongolian, a genealogy of the kings of Mongolia and an account of how Buddhism was spread in this country.' (To this,) I said, 'It appears that I cannot (do so), because it is difficult to ascertain the sources of both these.' But he said, 'You probably can ! Do write.' On listening to this repeated command and consenting to it, and taking, for the decoration of my head, dust from the feet of the omniscient Paṇ-chen bLo-bzaṅ dPal-ldan-ye śes (the third Panchen Lama) and (the veritable) Mañjughoṣa, the king of the religion, the venerable dKon-mchog-'jigs-med-dbaṅ-po (the second 'Jam-dbyaṅs-bshad-pa) and his pupils (all these called here by name on business), I, the unworthy monk Gu-śri bKa'-bcu Sudhī-āyuvarta (otherwise called dbYaṅs-can-sgeg-pa'i-blo-gros 'Jigs-med-rig-pa'i-rdo-rje), have compiled the genealogies of the Mongolian kings. (For this,) I have depended upon the account of the Mongolian kings written by Se-chen-hwoṅ-tha'i-ci'i, the descendant of Hwo-thog-tha'i Se-chen-hwoṅ-tha'i-ci'i [Secen Hwon Thaici], upon a (work entitled) 'Good-to-look-at Bouquet of Flowers' and upon other Mongolian texts. Besides, I have also made a brief selection of the biographies of great people,—who had spread the (Buddhist) religion,—from the works of distinguished Tibetan scholars. (My work) was completed in the monastery of bKra-śis-dga'-ldan-bśad-sgrub-gliṅ on the third day of the Nanda category (i.e. 11th) of the bright half of the month of Bhādrapada of the Earth-Hare year (1819) which in Sanskrit is called *Pramādi*". Obviously enough, G. Huth did not know that the author could not use the expression *shal-sṅa-nas* for himself. This expression is used only when one has to pronounce the name of one's teacher, which generally a pupil should not. In this connection, the *Gurupañcāśikā* (*bLa-ma-lṅa-bcu-pa*) contains a special

somehow escaped the attention of the scholars. Beginning with L. Feer[482] and A. Grünwedel[483] who, in their time, wrote special reviews of G. Huth's work, and right up to such authors as B. Ya. Vladimirtsov,[484] C. Bell[485] and L. Ligeti,[486] who repeatedly used not only the translation but also the text publised by G. Huth,—all repeat the erroneous statement of G. Huth that the author of the *Hor-chos-'byuṅ was* 'Jigs-med-nam-mkha'.[487]

---

direction which reads: *De-yi-mtshan-smos-brjod-na-ni miṅ-mthar-shal-sṅar-ldan-pas-bya gshan-daṅ-gus-par-bya-ba'i-phyir khyad-par-gyi-ni-tshig-kyaṅ-brjod* [see *bsTan-'gyur*, rGyud-'grel, vol. lxxii (*nu*), fol. 244ª 7, 34th line of the text]. The Sanskrit original of the first 33 verses of this text (which has 50 verses in all) was found in Nepal by S. Lévi and published by him along with a French translation (see Sylvain Lévi, *Autour d' Aśvaghoṣa*,—JA, 1929, pp. 259-263). This direction, when translated, reads: "If it is necessary to call him (i.e. the teacher) by name, one must add the word *shal-sṅa* in the end of the name and also say (a few) words on his outstanding qualities to arouse veneration in others." Thus this direction explains the great abundance of epithets which the author uses in the colophon for his teacher 'Jigs-med-nam-mkha'. Another such expression not understood by G. Huth is *don-gyi-slad-du-mtshan-nas-smos-te* (called by name on business). According to a direction in the *Vinayasūtra* (*'Dul-ba'i-mdo*), which reads: *Don-gyi-slad-du-mtshan-nas-smos-te-shes-bya-ba-daṅ-bcas- par- ma- smras- par- mkhan- po'i- miṅ-mi-gzuṅ-ṅ o* (=the name of an *Upādhyāya* cannot be pronounced without using the expression "called by name on business")—see *bsTan-'gyur*, mDo-'grel, vol. lxxxii (*zu*)—this expression is used when calling an *Upādhyāya* by name. The expression *btsun-gzugs-gyi-na-ba* translated by G. Huth as "an dem verehrungswürdigen leibe krankender", actually means "unworthy", "low", "paltry" (*gyi-na-ba*) monk (*btsun-gzugs*). The expression *me-tog-gi-tshoms-mthoṅ-ba-don-ldan* is a Tibetan translation of the title of a Mongolian chronicle to which Sagan Setsen also refers (see I. J. Schmidt, *Geschichte der Ost-Mongolen...*, p. 298, l. 10).

482. JA, 1893, pp. 367-368; 1897, pp. 159-165.
483. "Wiener Zeitschrift für die kunde des Morgenlandes", xii Bd, 1898, pp. 70-74.
484. B. Ya. Vladimirtsov, *Nadpisi na skalakh khalkhaskogo Tsoktu-taidzhi*,—"Izvestiya Akademii nauk SSSR", 1926, p. 1266, 1271, note 2, 1275.
485. See C. Bell, *Religion of Tibet*, p. 213 and also the notes to pp. 65-66, 97 a.o.
486. See L. Ligeti, *Rapport préliminaire d'un voyage d' exploration fait en Mongolie chinoise* 1928-1931, Budapest, 1933, pp. 55-56. Cf. *idem.*, *Les noms mongols de Wen tsong des Yuan*,—"T'oung Pao", vol. xxvii, 1930, p. 59.
487. For example; B. Laufer, *Application of the Tibetan Cycle*,—"T'oung Pao", 1913, p. 585, n. 1; A. H. Francke, *Antiquities of Indian Tibet*, pt. ii, p. 98 a.o.; G. Schulemann, *Die Geschichte der Dalai-lamas*, p. 209, etc.

In the translation of G. Huth, there are other errors too.[488] In particular, as rightly shown by Professor P. Pelliot,[489] he is throughout committing a mistake of one year in the conversion of Tibetan dates into European calendar. But we shall not examine these mistakes here, and shall only remark that one general defect of the whole work of G. Huth is the complete lack of any explanatory notes and indices.

As already stated by Academician B. Ya. Vladimirtsov,[490] there also exists, in Tibetan language, another work on the history of Buddhism in Mongolia, written in 1889 by some Dam-chos-rgya-mtsho—or, as he is otherwise called, Dharma-tāla. This work which bears the title *Chen-po-hor-kyi-yul-du-dam-pa'i-chos-ji ltar-dar-ba'i-tshul-gsal-bar-brjod-pa-padma-dkar-po'i-phreṅba,* is not available in our collections. However, I could see a copy of this work—though casually—in the Aginsky *datsan* in Buryatia.[491] To

488. See, for instance, section 8 of the present chapter. See also B. Ya. Vladimirtsov, *Nadpisi na skalakh...,*—"Izvestiya Akademii nauk SSSR", 1926, p. 1275.

489. P. Pelliot, *Le cycle sexagénaire...,*—JA, 1913, t. i, pp. 655-657.

490. B. Ya. Vladimirtsov, *Nadpisi na skalakh...*, p. 1279.

491. It was only recently that I was able to have a first-hand acquaintance with the *Dam-chos-rgya-mtsho* through the kindness of B. I. Pankratov. This xylograph (the same as was referred to and used by B. Ya. Vladimirtsov) has 281 folios of large format, and contains :

Introduction, fols. 1ᵇ 1-4ᵇ 1.

General part—On the appearance and spread of Buddhism in the world, fols. 4ᵇ 1-21ᵇ 4.

1. On the appearance of Buddhism in India, fols. 4ᵇ 2-11ᵃ 1.
2. On the appearance of Buddhism in China, fols. 11ᵃ 1-15ᵃ 6.
3. On the appearance of Buddhism in Tibet, fols. 15ᵇ 1-21ᵃ 6.

Special part—On the appearance and spread of Buddhism in Mongolia.

I. General information on the Mongols, fols. 21ᵇ 5-30ᵇ 6.

II. Genealogies of the Chinese and Mongolian dynasties, fols. 30ᵇ 6-80ᵃ 1.

1. Information on dynasties : A brief report on the dynasties of ancient China, fols. 31ᵃ 2-34ᵃ 3 ; A report on Yüan Mongolian dynasty, fols. 34ᵃ 4-47ᵃ 5, and on its Epigoni, fols. 47ᵃ 5-52ᵃ .
   Brief information on Ming dynasty, fols. 52ᵃ 2-54ᵇ 6, and more detailed information on Tsing dynasty, fols. 54ᵇ 6-62ᵃ 3.
2. General view of the princely surnames of the Mongols :
   Princely surnames of individual
   1) princes of 49 internal regions and Khalkha, fols. 62ᵃ 5-65ᵇ 6, and
   2) some Khans and princes, fols. 65ᵇ 6-77ᵇ 3.

the learned Lamas, this work is better known under the title *Gu-śri-tā-la'i-chos-'byuṅ* and the previous *Hor-chos-'byuṅ* under *Gu-śri-tshe-'phel-gyi-chos-'byuṅ*. In common parlance, therefore, these works are often known as the historical treatises of the "two Gu-śri".

Along with the works on the history of Buddhism in Mongolia, there also exists, in Tibetan, a special work devoted to the history of Buddhism in China—*rGya-nag-chos-'byuṅ*. This work, called in full as *rGya-nag-gi-yul-du-dam-pa'i-chos-dar-tshul-gtso-bor-bśad-pa-blo-gsal-kun-dga'-ba'i-rna-rgyan*, was written by mGon-po-skyabs (18th century), a Mongolian prince (*guṅ*), the great translator (*lo-chen*) under the Chinese emperor Ch'ien-lung.[492] This work, published in the sDe-dge monastery, covers

---

An excursus on the titles of the nobility and priesthood, etc., fols. 77ᵇ 3-79ᵇ 2.

III. Spread of Buddhism in Mongolia

1. Beginning of the spread (of Buddhism) and the relevant "prophecies", fols. 80ᵃ 2-88ᵃ 1.
2. History of the spread (of Buddhism).
   a) about the Buddhist Lamas who worked in Mongolia, fols. 88ᵃ 2-227ᵇ 5 ; about the Lamas of Sa-skya-pa and Karma-pa sects, fols. 88ᵃ 3-111ᵇ 4 ; and about the Lamas of dGe-lugs-pa sect : 1) about the advantages of this sect, fols. 111ᵇ 4-119ᵃ 1 ; 2) about the Tibetan Lamas of dGe-lugs-pa sect who worked in Mongolia, fols. 119ᵃ 3-203ᵃ 3 ; and about the Lamas of Mongolia proper, fols. 203ᵃ 4-227ᵃ 6 ;
   b) about the translation of Buddhist works into Mongolian, fols. 227ᵇ 5-247ᵇ 3 ;
   c) about the Buddhist Monasteries of Mongolia, fols. 247ᵇ 3-261ᵃ 5 ;
   d) about the persons who patronized the Buddhist religion, fols. 261ᵃ 5-272ᵇ 6.
3. Conclusion, fols. 272ᵇ 6-279ᵇ 2. Colophon, fols. 279ᵇ 2-281ᵃ 4. The date of composition of the *Dam-chos-rgya-mtsho*—the Earth-Cow year of the xv cycle (1889)—is given in the colophon (fol. 280ᵇ 4-5); the names of this year are also given in Sanskrit, Chinese and Mongolian. Besides, the colophon also mentions the numbers of years that had passed from the dates of various events to the year of composition of this work.

492. See the colophon of the sDe-dge edition of this work, fols. 109ᵇ 5-6 and 110ᵃ 4-5. The author of *rGya-nag-chos-'byuṅ*, dGon-po-skyabs,—whom the Chinese emperor gave the title of "*tai-ji* of first degree" and later that of *guṅ*—was the senior chief (*spyi-dpon*) of the ruling Tibetan school (*bod-kyi-bslab-graw*) and is

110 folios of usual format.[493] It falls into three main sections : the first section gives a general account of the Chinese history (fols. 2^a 3-25^b 5), the second contains a short history of the Chinese philosophy and science (fols. 25^b 5-28^b 1) and a history of Buddhism in China (fols. 28^b 1-73^a 5), and the third section is a catalogue to the Chinese *tripitaka* (fols. 73^a 5-107^b 2); Besides, in Tibetan language was also written a special work on the history of Buddhism in the kingdom of the Tanguts—*Mi-ñag-chos-'byuṅ*. But we know nothing of it so far except a simple reference to it in the "List of Tibetan Historical Literature".[494]

As already indicated by C. Bell,[495] among the Tibetan historical works there also are some on the history of Buddhism in Bhutan and in Sikkim. In the same way, there are works on the history of Buddhism in individual regions, provinces and specific kingdoms.

Of such local historical works, one must, first of all, mention the one on the

---

known for his translation work. In particular, he was one of the most active members of a commission which was engaged, in 1741-42, on a Mongolian translation of a Tibetan dictionary entitled *Dag-yig-mkhas-pa'i-'byuṅ-gnas* (which had just been compiled by lCaṅ-skya Rol-pa'i-rdo-rje, and which was intended for establishing the main principles of translation of the Tibetan *bsTan-'gyur*. Besides, this author, jointly with Tā-bla-ma bsTan-'dsin-chos-dar and others, compiled an extremely important Tibetan-Mongolian dictionary—*Bod-kyi-brta-yig-rtogs-par-sla-ba*—which was revised and published in 1737 by a group of scholars led by Gu-śri Śes-rab-rgya-mtsho (for an account of this person, see B. Ya. Vladimirtsov, *O tibetsko-mongol'skom...* [On the Tibetan-Mongolian dictionary Li-śihi gu-khaṅ],—"Doklady Akademii nauk SSSR",1926, p. 27). Besides, to dGon-po-skyabs is also attributed an extremely interesting work in Mongolian language on the history of Buddhism in Mongolia. This work is dated 1725 ; a manuscript copy of this work is available in the Institute of Peoples of Asia. Finally, to the same author is also ascribed an annotated translation, into Chinese, of a small Tibetan treatise entitled *Saṅs-rgyos-kyi-sku'i-gzugs-brñan-gyi- mtshan- ñid- mtho- bcu-pa- śiṅ-nya- gro-dha- ltar-chu-sheṅ- gab-pa* (*bsTan-'gyur*, mDo-'grel, vol. cxxiii [*go*], fols. 5^a 5-7^a 6). This translation is included in the supplements to the Chinese *Tripiṭaka*, and it also exists as a separate individual work (a copy of such a separate edition is available in the Institute of Peoples of Asia, *Chinese Collection*, D. 891). This translation is dated 1742.

493. A copy of this publication is available in the Institute of Peoples of Asia (*Baradiin Collection*).
494. See *Deb-ther-rgya-mtsho*, vol. i, fol.7^a 1.
495. C. Bell, *Religion of Tibet*, pp. 213-215.

history of Buddhism in Amdo—the *Deb-ther-rgya-mtsho*—which has been frequently quoted by us. The *Deb-ther-rgya-mtsho* was published in the monastery of Ā-mchog-dgon-pa in Amdo[496] and covers three large volumes of usual Tibetan long format. The first volume, which bears a general title *Yul-mdo-smad-kyi-ljoṅs-su-thub-bstan-rin-po-che-ji-ltar-dar-ba'i-tshul-gsal-bar-brjod-pa-deb-ther-rgya-mtsho*, contains a brief history of Amdo and a history of the spread of Buddhism in this region—set forth in the form of a history of individual large monasteries and their leaders (412 fols.).[497] The

---

496. A copy of this work is available in the Institute of Peoples of Asia (*Baradiin Collection*). In European literature, the earliest scholar to mention the existence of *Deb-ther-rgya-mtsho* was B. Baradiin—see his *Statuya Maitrei v Zolotom khrame v Labrame* [Statue of Maitreya in the Golden Temple in bLa-braṅ], p. 05. However, the name of the place of publication of this work (mDsod-dge-dgon-pa) given by B. Baradiin is not correct. The date of birth of the author and that of composition of the work as mentioned by B. Baradiin are also not correct.

497. The contents of the first volume of the *Deb-ther-rgya-mtsho* are:

1) a brief introduction, fols. 1-4ª 5 ;

2) a list of Tibetan historical works—*chos-'byuṅ-rnam-thar-gyi-tho-bkod-pa* (which we have frequently quoted), fols. 4ª 5-19ª 4 ;

3) a general account of the history of Buddhism in Amdo from the earliest times—*spyir-bśad-pa'i-skabs*, fols. 19ª 4-32ª 6 ;

4) the main text of the work, which expounds the history of numerous monasteries (large and small) of Amdo—*gshuṅ-dṅos-'chad-pa*, fols. 32ᵇ 1-412ª 3.

The main text falls into two parts : 'the history of the monasteries located on the left, northern side of the river rMa-chu', fols. 32ᵇ 1-273ª 4 ; and 'the history of the monasteries on the right, southern side of this river', fols. 273ª 4-412ª 3.

The history of the monasteries of the northern group (*byaṅ-rgyud*) includes :

a) the history of the Kokonor princely families and that of the monastery of Grwa-tshaṅ-dgon dGa'-ldan-chos-'khor-gliṅ—*ā-mdo'i-thog-ma-mtsho-sṅon-gyi-skabs*, fols. 32ᵇ 1-64ª 6 ;

b) the history of the monasteries on the left, northern side of the river Tsoṅ-chu—chiefly, such as dMar-gtsaṅ-brag, dGon-luṅ, Chu-bzaṅ-dgon dGa'-ldan-mi-'gyur-gliṅ, gSer-khog-dgon dGa'-ldan-dam-chos-gliṅ, etc.—*tsaṅ-chu-byaṅ-rgyud-dmar-gtsaṅ-brag dgon-luṅ chu-bzaṅ gser-dgon-sogs-kyi-skabs*, fols. 64ᵇ 1-129ª 1 ;

c) the history of the monasteries in the northern and north-eastern region of Amdo—*'Ju-lag-rgyud-daṅ dpa'i-ri-pho-rod kun-luṅ-śus-gsum-sogs-kyi-skabs*, second volume, which bears the sub-title *Chos-sde-chen-po-bkra-śis-'khyil-gyi-dkar-chags-gdan-rabs-kha-skor-daṅ-bcas-pa,* expounds the history of the monastery of bLa-braṅ and its Heads and also of the Heads of its individual *datsan*-s (216 folios).[498] The third

---

fols. 129^{a} 1-181^{a} 4 (these monasteries include Kan-chen-dgon Theg-chen-thar-pa-gliṅ, mChod-rten-thaṅ, etc.) ;

d) the history of the monasteries on the right, southern side of the river Tsoṅ-chu but on the northern side of the Tsoṅ-la range (which serves as the watershed between the rMa-chu and its tributary, the Tsoṅ-chu)—chiefly, the monastery of sKu-'bum—*sku-'bum-dgon-ma-lag-bcas-daṅ gro-tshaṅ-brag thaṅ-riṅ ba'-jo'i stod- du- stoṅ- 'khor- dgon- sogs- tsoṅ- la- byaṅ- rgyud- kyi- skabs,* fols. 181^{a} 4-221^{a} 1 ;

e) the history of the monasteries located on the southern side of the Tsoṅ-la range—chiefly, the monastery of Bya-khyuṅ Theg-chen-yon-tan-dar-rgyas- gliṅ—*bya- khyuṅ- dgon- ma- lag- sogs- tsoṅ- la- lho- rgyud- kyi- skabs,* fols. 221^{a} 1-273^{a} 4.

The history of the monasteries of the southern group includes :

a) the history of the monasteries located on the upper rMa-chu in the province of mGo-log, etc.—*lho-rgyud-kyi-thog-ma-rma-stod-mgo-log-sogs-kyi-skabs,* fols. 273^{a} 4-311^{a} 5 ;

b) the history of the monasteries located on the lower rMa-chu, from the point where this river turns its course to the East (these monasteries include La-mo bDe-chen and the monasteries of the province of Khri-ka)—rma-chu'i-smad-la-mo-daṅ-khri-ka'i-skabs, fols. 311^{a} 5-351^{a} 2 ;

c) the history of the monasteries located on the river dGu-chu (chiefly, the monastery of Roṅ-bo-dgon bDe-chen-chos-'khor-gliṅ) and in the adjoining provinces—*dgu-chu-rgyud-roṅ-bo-dgon- grub-sde-bco- brgyad-daṅ- bcas-pa khri-rtse-bshi'i-dgon-daṅ mgar-rtse-dgon-ma-lag rma-khar-gtogs-pa-mar-naṅ-tsho-lṅa'i-dgon-sgrub-sde-rnams-daṅ bis-mdo-dgon-ma-lag-lṅa gcu-'khor bse-chaṅ-dgon rdo-bis-dgon-ma-lag-bcu-gsum ā-mtsho stag-luṅ-dgon-le-lag-daṅ-bcas-pa'i-skabs,* fols. 351^{a} 2-411^{a} 3.

As seen from this table of contents, the author gives us a great deal of valuable geographical information in addition to the extensive material on the history of the monasteries of Amdo. He also sometimes expounds, though briefly, the general history of individual provinces and the genealogies of their rulers.

498. The contents of the second volume of the *Deb-ther-rgya-mtsho* are :

1. Biography of the first 'Jam-dbyaṅs-bshad-pa Ṅag-dbaṅ-brtson-'grus, and an account of the history of the establishment of the monastery of bLa-braṅ (A.D. 1710), fols. 1-10^{a} 4.

volume having the sub-title *Kha-gya-tsho-drug-nas-rgyal-mo-tsha-ba-roṅ-gi-bar-gyi-dgon-sgrub-sde-phal-che-ba'i-dkar-chags-tho-tsam-bkod-pa* contains a short historical account of the numerous monasteries—large and small—in the province of Amdo (272 fols.).[499]

---

2. Biography of his incarnation dKon-mchog-'jigs-med-dbaṅ-po, who contributed greatly to the development of the bLa-braṅ monastery, and a history of the development and fortification of this monastery, fols. 10ª 4-36ª 1.

3. Biographies of the Heads of bLa-braṅ, beginning with the second Head (the first Head of this monastery was its founder, 'Jam-dbyaṅs-bshad-pa Ṅag-dbaṅ-brtson-'grus) and ending with the 53rd Head ; fols. 36ª 2-181ª 5.

Many of these biographies are also supplemented with the biographies of persons, who are regarded as the previous or successive incarnations of the person concerned.

4. A Chronicle of the faculty of Occult Sciences (*dpal-ldan-smad-rgyud-grwa-tshaṅ*), founded in A.D. 1716, fols. 181ª 5-191ᵇ 5.

5. A chronicle of the faculty of Astrology (*dus-'khor-grwa-tshaṅ-e-va-chos-'khor-gliṅ*), founded in A.D. 1763, fols. 191ᵇ 5-202ª 3.

6. A chronicle of the faculty of Medicine (*sman-pa-grwa-tshaṅ-gso-rig-gshan-phan-gliṅ*), founded in A.D. 1784, fols. 202ª 3-212ᵇ 5.

7. A report on various temples of bLa-braṅ and on the surrounding small monasteries, fols. 212ᵇ 5-216ª 4.

499. The contents of the third volume of the *Deb-ther-rgya-mtsho* are :

1. History of the monasteries located along the river bSaṅ-chu and on its left side (in -the provinces of Kha-gya-tsho-drug and mDsod-dge) ; a list of small monasteries in Hor-tshaṅ etc. ; a history of the monasteries of sGo-mog-bkra-śis-bde-chen-gliṅ and sGaṅ-śul-dgon Chos-'khor-gliṅ, and a list of other small Chinese monasteries—*Kha-gya-tsho-drug-mdsod-dge-śog-pa-lṅa hor-tshaṅ-che-chuṅ-sogs-kyi-sgar-sgrub-sṅa sgo-mog-bkra-śis-bde-chen-gliṅ sgaṅ-śul-ri-dgon-sogs-rgya'i-dgon-phran-du-ma-daṅ-bcas-pa'i-sgabs*, fols. 1-51ª 1.

2. History of the monasteries located on the upper gLu-chu (Chos-'khor-sgar-gsar-dga'-ldan-chos-'khor-gliṅ, etc.) and of the monasteries (large and small) in the vicinity of sṄon-po-thaṅ, sKyis-tshaṅ, rMug-śoṅ and Reb-tsha—*Chos-'khor-sgar-gsar-sogs-glu-śod-ṅos ā-mchog-dgon-sṅon-po-thaṅ rmug-śoṅ rab-tsha-rgyal-mo-dgon-sgrub-sṅe-daṅ-bcas-pa'i-skabs*, fols. 51ª 2-96ª 3.

3. History of the monasteries located on the lower gLu-chu—chiefly, Co-ne-dgon-chen dGa'-ldan-bśad-sgrub-gliṅ—*glu-chu'i-smad-co-ne'i-khul men-ju-chos-sde-chos-rdsoṅ śiṅ-kun-dgon-ma-lag gru-gu-stod-smad mgal spen-le-daṅ-bcas-pa'i-skabs*, fols. 96ª 3-195ª 5.

4. History of the monasteries located on the southern side of the upper gLu-chu—*Lha-mo-ñin-srib the-bo-stod-smad zuṅ-ju-khul dmu-dge-daṅ-bcas-pa'i-skabs*, fols. 195ª 5-240ᵇ 5 ;

The author, Brag-dgon-shabs-druṅ dKon-mchog-bstan-pa-rab-rgyas (b. 1801), the 49th Head of the monastery of bLa-braṅ, worked hard over this work for over 33 years. In 1833, he wrote a work on the history of Buddhism in Amdo at the instance of dKon-mchog-rgyal-mtshan. But this work was considered too inadequate, and the author therefore enlarged it by supplementing it with additional data. The work as revised was completed towards the end of 1865, thus including also the dates and accounts of historical events up to this period.[500]

There also exists an earlier account (though short) of the history of Buddhism in Amdo, compiled partly in verse and partly in prose by some Grub-chen sKal-ldan-rgya-mtsho (1607-1677).[501] Besides, there exist a special work on the history of

---

5. History of the monasteries located in the provinces of rÑa-ba (Rṅa-ba), Rwa-khog and Tsha-ba—*rṅa-ba-stod-smad-bar-gsum rwa-khog tsha-ba-khag-gsum-daṅ-bcas-pa'i-skabs*, fols. 240^b 5-265^a 3.

6. Geographical account of the countries lying on the south of Amdo, fols. 265^a 3-269^b 6.

7. Concluding verses and colophon, fols. 269^b 6-272^a 6.

The third volume, in its exposition, does not substantially differ from the first. It is only somewhat more concise. Like the first volume, this volume, too, expounds the history of the monasteries in Amdo, and gives, besides, much valuable material on the geography of Amdo, historical information on individual provinces and principalities of this country, and sometimes brief chronicles and genealogies of local interest.

500. See *Deb-ther-rgya-mtsho*, vol. iii, colophon, fols. 271^b 4-272^a 6. The date of completion of the work—the Wood-Cow year corresponding to A.D. 1865—is mentioned in the colophon and often in the text itself (cf. vol. ii, fols. 109^a 4, 181^a 4 etc). After the erroneous statement of B. Baradiin (see B. Baradiin, *Statuya Maitrei v Zolotom khrame v Lavrane*, p. 05), I, too, in my article *K bibliografii tibetskoi literatury* [For a Bibliography of Tibetan Literature]—in "Bibliografiya Vostoka", Nos. 2-4, p. 27 (cf. also A. Vostrikov, *Some Corrections and Critical Remarks on Dr. Johan vam Manen's Contribution to the Bibliography of Tibet*,—BSOS, vol. viii, 1935, pt. i, pp. 51-76)—wrongly placed the date of composition of *Deb-ther-rgya-mtsho* at A.D. 1833.

501. A biography of Grub-chen sKal-ldan-rgya-mtsho—entitled *Grub-chen-skal-ldan-rgya mtsho'i-rnam-thar-yid-bshin-dbaṅ-gi-rgyal-po*—was written in 1708 (Earth-Mouse year) by his pupil Byaṅ-chub Ñag-dbaṅ-bsod-nams. It is included in the first volume of the collected Works of Grub-chen-skal-ldan-rgya-mtsho and it covers 74 folios. (A copy of this 'Collected Works' is available in the

Buddhism in the province of Myaṅ (which also includes a description of this province),[502] a work on the history of Buddhism in rGyal-rtse,[503] a work on the history of Buddhism in sTag-luṅ, compiled by sTag-luṅ-shabs-druṅ Ṅag-dbaṅ-rnam-rgyal (b. 1571) in mDo-khams,[504] and various other works mentioned in the Tibetan sources.

Of the works devoted to the history of individual sects of Tibetan Buddhism, the one best known in Tibetan historical literature is that on the history of bKa'-rgyud-pa sect compiled in 1640 by Śā-kya-lha-dbaṅ (1585-1655).[505] Another work—no less known—is that on the history of bKa'-gdams-pa sect written in 1494 by Las-chen Kun-dga'-rgyal-mtshan.[506] This work, in 417 folios,[507] is also sometimes called as the "Great History of the bKa'-gdams-pa Sect" (*bKa'-gdams-chos-'byuṅ-chen-po*).[508] As mentioned by Sum-pa-mkhan-po,[509] this work served as a source for the brief history of

Institute of Peoples of Asia, *Baradiin Collection*, No. 10). Besides, brief biographical data on him are available in the *Deb-ther-rgya-mtsho* (vol. i, fols. 353ᵇ 5-355ᵇ 2). According to these sources, Grub-chen sKal-ldan-rgya-mtsho was born in the Fire-Sheep year of the x cycle (A.D.1607) and he died in the Fire-Serpent year (A.D. 1677) in the 71st year of his life. His work on the history of Buddhism in Amdo is found mentioned in the aforementioned biography (fol. 41ᵃ 1) and in the *Deb-ther-rgya-mtsho* (vol. i, fol. 7ᵇ 1, where two works, one in verse and the other in prose, are mentioned ; and vol. iii, fol. 271ᵇ 5). Unfortunately, this work has not come down to us.

502. See *Deb-ther-rgya-mtsho*, vol. i, fols. 6ᵇ 6-7ᵃ 1. C. Bell was able to obtain a copy of this historico-geographical work (see C. Bell, *The Religion of Tibet*, p. 214).
503. See *Deb-ther-rgya-mtsho*, vol. i, fol. 7ᵃ 1.
504. *Ibid.*, fol. 7ᵃ 6.
505. The dates of birth and death of Śākya-lha-dbaṅ along with the date of composition of his work are given in the "Chronological Tables".
506. The date of composition of this work is given in the "Chronological Tables". It is also mentioned in the *Deb-ther-rgya-mtsho* (vol. i, fol. 4ᵇ 6) and in the *dPe-rgyun-dkon-pa-'ga'-shig-gi-tho-yig* (fol. 3ᵇ 1). Sum-pa-mkhan-po, in his historical work, criticizes some of the reports of this work (see *dPag-bsam-ljon-bzaṅ*, fol. 285ᵇ 2-6).
507. See V. P. Vasil'ev, O nekotorykh knigakh, otnosyashchikhsya k istorii buddizma, b biblioteke kazanskogo universiteta,—"Uchenye zapiski Akademii nauk", 1855, vol. iii, No. 1, p. 13. From the library of the University of Kazan, this text (along with other oriental manuscripts and books) was transferred to the library of the Leningrad University but was apparently lost at the time of the floods of 1924.
508. Such a name has been given to it in the *Deb-ther-rgya-mtsho* (vol. i, fol. 4ᵇ 6).
509. See *dPag-bsam-ljon-bzaṅ*, fol. 186ᵇ 7 (S. C. Das, *Pag Sam Jon Zang*, p. 291).

this sect compiled in 1529 by Paṇ-chen bSod-nams-grags-pa (1478-1554),[510] the fifteenth Head of the dGa'-ldan monastery. This brief history is entitled *bKa'-gdams-gsar-rñiṅ-gi-chos-'byuṅ-yid-kyi-mdses-rgyan*. The first edition of this text is not known to me. The second edition—the xylograph edition—was brought out in Potala (Phyogs-las-rnam par-rgyal-ba'i-pho-braṅ-chen-mo-po-ta-la) in 1762; the colophon (*par-byaṅ*) to this edition was written by the regent of Tibet, De-mo-no-mon-han Ṅag-dbaṅ-'jam-dpal bDe-legs-rgya-mtsho. In this edition, the work has 103 folios of the usual format.[511] Another work that may be mentioned here is that on the history of the sTag-luṅ-pa sect compiled by sTag-luṅ-shabs-druṅ Ṅag-dbaṅ-rnam-rgyal in 1609.[512]

There also exist numerous other works—no less important and interesting than the ones just mentioned—on the history of these and other sects of Tibetan Buddhism, but we shall not enumerate these here for reasons of space. Of course, there is a particularly large number of works devoted to the exposition of the history of the dominant "yellow-cap" sect of Tibet (and of Mongolia)—the dGe-lugs-pa or dGe-ldan-pa sect. In particular, to the history of this sect is devoted an extensive work (in 419 folios) entitled *dPal-mñam-med-ri-bo-dga'-ldan-pa'i-bstan-pa-shwa-ser-cod-pan-'chaṅ-ba'i-riṅ-lugs-chos-thams-cad-kyi-rtsa-ba-gsal-bar-byed-ba-vaiḍūrya-ser-pa'i-me-loṅ*, but better known by its short title *Vaiḍūrya-ser-po*.[513] This work was written in 1698[514] by the

510. The dates of birth and death of bSod-nams-grags-pa along with the date of composition of his work are mentioned by Sum-pa-mkhan-po in his 'Chronological table'. These dates (except the date of birth) are also given in the 'chronological table' of the first 'Jam-dbyaṅs-bshad-pa. Besides, the date of composition of the work is also mentioned in the colophon (fol. 103ᵃ 1).

511. A copy of this edition is available in the books transferred from the Kazan University to the library of the University of Leningrad (xyl. C. 215).

512. See *Deb-ther-rgya-mtsho*, vol. i, fol. 6ᵇ 6. The date of birth of sTag-luṅ-shabs-druṅ Ṅag-dbaṅ-rnam-rgyal is mentioned in the 'chronological table' of the first 'Jam-dbyaṅs-bshad-pa. The date of composition of his historical work is mentioned in the 'chronological table' of Sum-pa-mkhan-po.

513. A copy of this work is available in the Institute of Peoples of Asia (*Tsybikov Collection*, No. 30).

514. The date of composition of the Vaiḍūrya-ser-po is mentioned in the colophon of this text (fol. 417ᵇ 4) and in the 'chronological table' of Sum-pa-mkhan-po. The author worked over this work for about six years (he started writing it in 1692 and completed it in 1698)—see the colophon, fols. 414ᵃ 1-419ᵃ 2, which gives not only the cyclic names of both the dates but also the numbers of years expired till then from the time of various events.

aforementioned sDe-srid Saṅs-rgyas-rgya-mtsho (1653-1705).[516] There is also an

---

515. The contents of the *Vaiḍūrya-ser-po* are :

1. Introduction, fols. 1-5ᵃ 4.

2. Panegyric to the founder of the dGe-lugs-pa sect, Tsoṅ-kha-pa, and to his teaching,—full of various prophecies on this leader of Tibetan Buddhism but very poor in historical and biographical materials, fols. 5ᵃ 4-60ᵃ 3 (sDe-srid Saṅs-rgyas-rgya-mtsho has merited just reproach from the later authors for his fascination for prophecies which he tried to look for even where these were not there—see, for instance, *dGa'-ldan-chos-'byuṅ-nor-bu'i-phreṅ-ba-rtsom-'phro*, fols. 12ᵇ 4-13ᵃ 1).

3. History of the spread of the teaching of Tsoṅ-kha-pa in various provinces of Tibet,—set forth in the form of a list of monasteries (large and small) of the dGe-lugs-pa sect located in these provinces, along with the names of their founders and sometimes (though rarely) the dates of their establishment, the names of their previous and the then Heads, and the number of monks in them at the time of the composition of the text. These lists sometimes also give short biographical data on the founders and the more distinguished Heads of large monasteries. The present section of the text covers folios 60ᵃ 3-271ᵇ 3. The section begins with some historical information on the monasteries of the dGe-lugs-pa sect in the Ui province, located near Lhasa (partly in Lhasa itself) —chiefly, the monasteries of dGa'-ldan (f. 1409), 'Bras-spuṅs (f. 1416), Se-ra (f. 1419), etc. (fols. 60ᵃ 3-127ᵃ 4). This is followed by some historical information on the spread of the "yellow-cap" sect in the provinces of sTod-luṅ (fols. 127ᵃ 4-131ᵇ 6) and sKyid-smad (fols. 131ᵇ 6-132ᵇ 3), in the estate of rGya-ma (fols. 132ᵇ 3-141ᵃ 6), in the province of 'Phan-yul (fols. 141ᵃ 6-143ᵇ 6), in the estate of dbU-stod 'Bri-guṅ (fols. 143ᵇ 6-154ᵇ 6), in the provinces of 'Ol-kha (fols. 154ᵇ 6-162ᵇ 1), Dwags-po (fols. 162ᵇ 1-165ᵃ 3), Ae (fols. 165ᵃ 3-168ᵃ 1), gÑal (fols. 168ᵃ 1-172ᵃ 6) and Lho-brag (fols. 172ᵃ 6-175ᵃ 5), in the district of Yar-kluṅs of the Phag-gru principality (fols. 175ᵃ 5-185ᵃ 5), in the province of Tsang (fols. 185ᵃ 5-218ᵃ 6), in the three districts (*skor-gsum*) of the mÑa'-ris province (fols. 218ᵃ 6-223ᵃ 3), in the province of Maṅ-yul (fols. 223ᵃ 3-226ᵇ 1), in the provinces of Ñaṅ, Loṅ (fols. 226ᵇ 1-230ᵇ 1) and Koṅ (fols. 230ᵇ 1-247ᵃ 6) and finally, in various regions of the mDo-khams province (fols. 247ᵃ 6-271ᵇ 3). The last portion of this section contains, among other things, a historical survey of the monasteries of Amdo (fols. 264ᵇ 6 ff.).

4. Historical account of the activities of the Fifth Dalai Lama, Ñag-dbaṅ bLo-bzaṅ-rgya-mtsho, for the spread of the views of the dGe-lugs-pa sect (fols. 271ᵇ 3-352ᵇ 5). This account is written in a panegyric tone and begins with an explanation as to why the Fifth Dalai Lama is called Avalokiteśvara. Then are

unfinished work on the history of the dGe-lugs-pa sect,—entitled *dGe-ldan-chos-'byuṅ-nor-bu'i-phreṅ-ba-rtsom-'phra* (in 85 folios),—by the second 'Jam-dbyaṅs-bshad-pa dKon-mchog 'Jigs-med-dbaṅ-po (1728-1791).[516] Then, there is a small work by the aforementioned Co-ne Grags-pa-bśad-sgrub (b. 1685). This work, compiled in 1744, is entitled *Ri-bo-dga'-ldan-pa'i-bstan-pa-bla-rabs-daṅ-bcas-pa-chos-'byuṅ-gsal-bar-ston-pa'i-sgron-me* (in 16 folios), and also provides, incidentally, some information on the history of Buddhism in Co-ne.[517] We can mention many other large and small, detailed and

---

given the twelve deeds, of which (as in case of Buddha) his biography is composed. One of these deeds—the eleventh—is the propaganda of the Buddhist doctrine (*dharma-cakra-pravartana*); the author pays his primary attention to the exposition of this deed. This exposition includes, among other things, a list of the monasteries founded by the Fifth Dalai Lama with the dates of their establishment, names of their Heads and the number of monks in each of them (fols. 314ᵃ 5-326ᵃ 6). Besides, a list of various other acts (donations, etc.) of the Fifth Dalai Lama in favour of the Buddhist religion is also given here.

5. Account of the activities of the author of the present work, sDe-srid Saṅs-rgyas-rgya-mtsho, in the field of the spread of the views of the dGe-lugs-pa sect, and a report on the appearance of the new, sixth Dalai Lama bLo-bzaṅ-rin-chen-tshaṅs-dbyaṅs-rgya-mtsho (fols. 352ᵇ 5-402ᵇ 4). This account of the activity of sDe-srid Saṅs-rgyas-rgya mtsho, which also begins with numerous prophecies, gives, among other things, a list of the monasteries established by him (fols. 364ᵃ 5 ff.).

6. Concluding verses, fols. 402ᵇ 5-410ᵃ 4.

7. Colophon, fols. 410ᵃ 4-419ᵃ 5. The contents of the text of the *Vaiḍūrya-ser-po* as given above are not the chapter-headings of the text in the strict sense of the word. The chapters of this text do not have any special titles and cannot be easily demarcated. The entire text is one organic whole, in which only the accounts of the spread of the monasteries of the dGe-lugs-pa sect in various regions of Tibet are separately marked. Incidentally, these accounts were made much use of by Sum-pa-mkhan-po, who reproduced the materials from these accounts in his historical work (see *dPag-bsam-ljon-bzaṅ*, fols. 190ᵃ 7-228ᵃ 5). Some such reports of the *Vaiḍūrya-ser-po* were supplemented with additional information by Sum-pa-mkhan-po in his work; for instance, the report on the monasteries of Amdo.

516. The work *dGe-ldan-chos-'byuṅ-nor-bu'i-phreṅ-ba-rtsom-'phro* mentioned here is available in the fifth volume (*ca*) of the Collected Works of dKon-mchog 'Jigs-med-dbaṅ-po. The account in this work abruptly breaks off at the biographical data on the pupils of Tsoṅ-kha-pa.

517. This text is available in vol. x (*ā*) of the Collected Works of Co-ne Grags-pa-bshad-grub. The date of composition of the text—Wood-Mouse year of the

concise works on the history of this dominant sect of Tibet, but are constrained to stop because of the fear of enlarging the size of our work.[518]

The types of works already described still do not exhaust the vast and extremely branchy class of Tibetan historical literature denoted by the term *chos-'byuṅ* (lit. "history of religion"). This also includes works on the history of individual sciences and philosophical disciplines. In particular, the "List of Historical Literature" repeatedly quoted by us enumerates several works on the history of medicine (*gso-rig-chos-'byuṅ*), as for instance, *gSo-rig-chos-'byuṅ-śes-bya-rab-gsal*, *Gso-rig-chos-'byuṅ-pad-tshal-bshad-pa'i ñin-byed*, written by some Byaṅ-smad-pa bSod-nams-ye-śes-rgyal-mtshan[519] etc. The work entitled *dPal-ldan-gso-pa-rig-pa'i-khog-'bugs-legs-bśad-vaiḍūrya'i-me-loṅ-draṅ-sroṅ-dgyes-pa'i-dga'-ston* (in 293 folios) written in 1702-03 by sDe-srid Saṅs-rgyas-rgya-mtsho[520] is extremely rich in information on the history of Tibetan medicine. This work, known by its short title *sDe-srid-kyi-gso-rig-khog-phub*, is also mentioned in the "List of Historical Literature."[521] The same List indicates the existence of a special work on the history of sceptical philosophy of Mādhyamika (*dBu-ma'i-chos-'byuṅ*), written by Paṇ-chen Śā-kya-mchog-ldan, and of works on the history of Vinaya—*'Dul-ba'i-chos-'byuṅ* composed by Paṇ-chen bSod-nams-grags-pa (1478-1554) and Yoṅs-'dsin Ye-śes-rgyal-mtshan (b. 1713), etc.[522]

The work of Yoṅs-'dsin Ye-śes-rgyal-mtshan is available in the seventh volume

---

xii cycle (A.D. 1744)—is mentioned in the colophon (fol. 16ᵃ 2-4). This work is a simple list of the monasteries of the dGe-lugs-pa sect and gives, besides the names of the Heads of some of the more important ones. The dates are rarely mentioned. The last folios of the text (fols. 13ᵇ 1-15ᵇ 4) give a list of the monasteries of Co-ne kingdom and a short history of the foremost of these—the bSad-sgrub-gliṅ or Tiṅ-'dsin-dar-rgyas-gliṅ monastery [founded in the end of the viii Tibetan sexagenary cycle according to the author of the aforementioned text and in A.D. 1459 (at the place where, according to a legend, the foundation of the monastery was laid in 1295) according to the statement of the *Deb-ther-rgya-mtsho*, vol. iii, fols. 121ᵇ 2-122ᵃ 5].

518. A list of some of these is given in the *Deb-ther-rgya-mtsho*, vol. i, fols. 5ᵃ 1-5, 5ᵇ 2-3 and 7ᵃ 5-6.

519. See *Deb-ther-rgya-mtsho*, vol. i, fol. 7ᵃ 3-4.

520. A copy of this work is available in the Institute of Peoples of Asia (*Tsybikov Collection*, No. 74). The date of composition is mentioned in the colophon (fols. 287ᵃ 1-293ᵃ 5), which states that this work was started in the Water-Horse year of the xii cycle (A.D. 1702) and completed in the Water-Sheep year (A.D. 1703).

521. See *Deb-ther-rgya-mtsho*, vol. i, fol. 7ᵃ 4-5.

522. *Ibid.*, fol. 5ᵇ 3-4.

(*ja*) of the Collected Works of this author (154 folios).[523] It is called : *rGyal-ba'i-bstan-pa'i-nan-mdsod-dam-pa'i-chos-'dul-ba'i-byun-tshul-brjod-pa-rgyal-bstan-rin-po-che'i-gsal-byed-ñin-mor-byed-pa'i-snan-ba* and is dated as 1789.[524]

Lastly, to this class of literature belong the works on the history of individual doctrines and cults. Of these, one may mention the four works of the famous Bu-ston Rin-chen-grub (1290-1364). One of these, bearing the title *rNal-'byor-rgyud-kyi-byun-tshul-gru-bzins* expounds the history of the origin of the Yoga-tantra system ; another entitled *Gsan-'dus-pa'i-chos-'byun-rgyud-kyi-bšad-pa'i-snon-'gro'i-bšad-thabs* is devoted to the history of the origin and spread of mystic teaching (*guhya-samāja*). A third work *bDe-mchog-chos-'byun-don-gsal-zab-don-gsal-byed* is devoted to the history of Samvara (Sambara) system and the fourth one entitled *dPal-dus-kyi-'khor-lo'i-chos-'byun-rgyud-kyi-snon-'gro-'gsal-byed*[525] deals with the history of the famous astrological system

523. See *Tsybikov Collection*, No. 17.

524. This work is divided mainly into four parts.

1. Report on how the teaching of *Vinaya* was preached by Buddha—*ston-pa-thub-pa'i-dban-po'i-sa- dam-pa'i-chos-'dul- ba-ji-ltar- gsuns-tshul-bstan-pa'i-skabs*, fols. 2ª 2-38ᵇ 1.

2. History of spread of this teaching, which includes :

a) a report on the three Buddhist councils—*rGyal-ba-mya-nan-las-'das-pa'i- rjes- su- bka'- bstu- rim- pa- gsum- ji- ltar- byun- tshul- bstan- pa'i- skabs*, fols. 38ᵇ 2-48ᵇ 4 ;

b) a report on the persons who preached the Buddhist doctrine in India —*rGyal- bas- lun- bstan-pa'i- dam- pa-rnams- kyis- rgyal- ba'i- bstan-pa-ji ltar-bzun-tshul-bšad-pa'i-skabs*, fols. 48ᵇ 4-61ª 4 ;

c) a history of the spread of *Vinaya* in Tibet during the period of the initial spread of Buddhism in this country—*Bod-yul-du-bstan-pa-sna-dar-la-dam-pa'i-chos-'dul-ba-ji-ltar-dar-tshul-bšad-pa'i-skabs*, fols. 61ª 5-80ª 3 ; and

d) a history of the spread of *Vinaya* in Tibet during the period of the later spread of Buddhism there—*bsTan-pa-phyi dar-la-dam-pa'i-chos-'dul-ba-ji-ltar-dar-tshul-bšad-pa'i-skabs* ; fols. 80ª 3-108ᵇ 3.

3. a brief exposition of the contents of *Vinaya sūtra—'Dul-ba'i-mdo'i-bsdus-don-bstan-pa*, fols. 108ᵇ 3-137ᵇ 3.

4. Directions as to how to preserve the precepts and behests of Buddhist moral—*Vinaya* (*Lun-las-gsuns-pa'i-bslab-khrims-mtha'-dag-ji-ltar-bsrun-tshul-gyi-man-nag-bstan-pa*) ; fols. 137ᵇ 3-152ª 6.

The date of composition of this work—the Earth-Hen year of the xiii cycle (A.D. 1789)—is mentioned in the colophon (fol. 154ª 2-3). The date of birth of the author is also taken from the colophon (which states that the said year of composition of the work is the 77th year of the life of the author).

525. These works of Bu-ston Rin-chen-grub are mentioned by kLon-rdol-bla-ma in

Kālacakra. Here should also be mentioned similar works by Tāranātha (b. 1575),—particularly on the history of the Kālacakra system, the *dPal-dus-kyi-'khor-lo'i-chos-skor-gyi-'byuṅ-khuṅs-ñer-mkho-bsdus-pa* (22 folios),[526] on the history of Yamantaka teaching, the *rGyod-rgyal-śin-rje-gśed-skor-gyi-chos-'byuṅ-rgyas-pa-yed-ches-ṅo-mtshar* (74 folios, written in 1631)[527] and Tāranātha's work devoted to the exposition of the history of the teaching and cult of Tārā—*sgrol-ma'i-rgyod-gyi-'byuṅ-khuṅs-gsal-bar-byed-pa'i-lo-rgyus-gser phreṅ* (20 folios).[528] It will not be superfluous also to mention the major work on the history of teaching and cult of Bhairava (Yamantaka)—*dPal-rdo-rje-'jigs-byed-kyi-chos-'byuṅ-khams-gsum-las-rnam-par-rgyal-ba-dṅos-grub-kun-kyi-gter-mdsod,* which was written in 1718 by the famous 'Jam-dbyaṅs-bshad-pa'i-rdo-rje-ṅag-dbaṅ-brtson-'grus (1648-1722).[529] This works is available in the Complete Works of the

---

his "Catalogue to the Collected Works of the teachers of bKa'-gdams-pa and dGe-lugs-pa sects"—*bKa'-gdams-pa-daṅ-dge-lugs-pa-bla-ma-rags-rim-gyi-gsuṅ-'bum-mtshan-tho,* fols. 4ᵃ 1, 5ᵃ 2, 5ᵇ 2 and 6ᵃ 2. This catalogue gives the titles of all the texts included in the Complete Works of Bu-ston Rin-chen-grub, which have not come down to us. According to kLoṅ-rdol-bla-ma, the four works mentioned here are included in vols. x, xi, xii and xv respectively of this "Complete Works". These four works are also mentioned in the *Deb-ther-rgya-mtsho* (vol. i, fol. 5ᵇ 4), where they are briefly called *Bu-ston-gyi-bde-gsaṅ-dus-yog gi-chos-'byuṅ-bshi.*

526. This work is included in vol. ii of the Collected Works of Tāranātha available in the Institute of Peoples of Asia (*Tsybikov Collection*, No. 15).

527. This work is available in vol. x of the aforementioned Collected Works of the author. The date of its composition is indicated in the colophon.

528. Available in vol. xii of the aforementioned Collected Works of the author.

529. The contents of this work are :

    Introduction, fols. 1ᵇ 1-3ᵇ 6.

    Chapter I. On how the *Vajrabhairava-tantra* was preached, fols. 3ᵇ 6-44ᵇ 3.

    Chapter II. On the text of the *tantra*-s and commentaries, fols. 44ᵇ 3-46ᵇ 6.

    Chapter III. On the origin of this teaching in Udyāna, fols. 46ᵇ 6-79ᵇ 5.

    Chapter IV. On the appearance of this teaching in Tibet, fols. 79ᵇ 5-81ᵇ 5.

    Chapter V. On the persons who successively passed on this teaching in the treatise of Rwa-lo-tsā-ba rDo-rje-grags, fols. 81ᵇ 5-96ᵃ 5.

    Chapter VI. Biographies of Tsoṅ-kha-pa and his pupils and of the pupils of the latter, fols. 96ᵃ 5-181ᵃ 3 ; a list of persons who passed on this doctrine to 'Jam-dbyaṅs-bshad-pa-*s*, fols. 181ᵃ 2-184ᵃ 1, and their biographies, fols. 184ᵃ 2-334ᵇ 4.

    Chapter VII. On the spread of the doctrine, fols. 334ᵇ 4-401ᵃ 3. This chapter mainly contains a history of the Heads of the 'Bras-spuṅs

author (*gsuṅ-'bum*) published in bLa-braṅ, in Amdo, and occupies a whole volume having 417 folios.[530] There also exist other such works devoted to the history of the same and other teachings and cults,[531] but we shall not dwell on these here.

Such are the general features of the main types of the extensive class of Tibetan historical works called *chos-'byuṅ*. As already stated, such works—particularly those on the general history of Buddhism (*spyi'i-chos-'byuṅ*) in a specific or in many countries—are not stuffed with church-historical material alone ; they also frequently expound, together with the history of Buddhism, the secular political history of the country. Being works of composite or synthetic nature, they sometimes also include —in toto, without any alterations—materials drawn from various individual works of Tibetan historiography. Such composite works on the history of Buddhism in Tibet and her neighbouring countries undoubtedly deserve to be carefully studied, published and translated—more so because the materials from which they are compiled have, in a number of cases, not come down to us in original. But, of course, these when publised and translated should be provided with the necessary critical and reference apparatus—which, unfortunately, many existing European works cannot at present claim to have.

---

monastery, beginning with 'Jam-dbyaṅs-chos-rje-bkra-śis-dpal-ldan (1379-1449), the founder of this monastery.

Concluding verses, fol. 401[a] 3-6 ; author's colophon, fols. 401[a] 6-402[a] 3 ; publisher's colophon (written by dKon-mchog-'jigs-med-dbaṅ-po, the incarnation of the author), fols. 402[a] 4-404[a] 3.

530. As already stated, the Institute of Peoples of Asia does not at present have the Complete Works of 'Jam-dbyaṅs-bshad-pa'i-rdo-rje Ṅag-dbaṅ-brtson-'grus. But there is a stray copy (published in Peking) of this historical work (in 404 folios) among the xylographs which V. P. Vasil'ev had sent to the Academy of Sciences from Peking (See *Old Collection*, No. 436[b]). The date of composition of this work—the Earth-Dog year of the xii cycle (A.D. 1718)—is given in the colophon (fols. 401[b] 3-402[a] 2).

531. Some of these are listed in the *Deb-ther-rgya-mtsho*, vol. i, fols.5[b] 4-6[b] 4.

8. *Biographical Literature*

The numerous biographical works—the so-called *rnam-thar*-s—must also be classed under Tibetan historical literature. The *rnam-thar*-s are biographies either of individuals,—written by their ownselves or by their pupils or even by later authors,—or of groups of persons linked together in a continuous philosophical or religious tradition. The latter complex works (viz. biographies of groups of persons) are usually called *bla-ma-brgyud-pa'i-rnam-thar*-s, i.e. "biographies of successive teachers". In their character, these works are quite closely allied to the *gdan-rabs*-s and *'khruṅs-rabs*-s (described earlier) which also are virtually collections of biographies of various persons. However, unlike the latter, the biographies in the *bla-ma-brgyud-pa'i-rnam-thar*-s are linked not on the basis of the succession to the headship of a monastery (as in the *gdan-rabs*-s) or of the succession of incarnations (as in the *'khruṅs-rabs*-s), but on the basis of the succession in receiving and imparting some doctrine or cult from one tradition to the other (*brgyud*).

One example of a work of this kind is that of the voluminous work entitled *Byaṅ-chub-lam-gyi- rim-pa'i-bla-ma- brgyud- pa'i-rnam-par-thar- pa-rgyal-bstan-mdses-pa'i-rgyan-mchog-phul-byuṅ-nor-bu'i-phreṅ-ba*, which contains biographies of the Indian and Tibetan authors who taught the "stages of the path of enlightenment" (*Bodhimārga—Byaṅ-chub-lam-rim*). This work was written in 1787 in Potala by the well-known author Yoṅs-'dsin Ye-śes-rgyal-mtshan (b. 1713), the teacher of the eighth Dalai Lama 'Jam-dpal-rgya-mtsho.[532] It is included in the Complete Works of this author and occupies only two volumes—the fourth (475 fols.) and the fifth (499 fols.).[533] The canvas for this work was provided by a small work entitled *Byaṅ-chub-lam-gyi-rim-pa'i-brgyud-pa-rnams-la-gsol-ba-'debs-pa'i-rim-pa-lam-mchog-sgo-'byed*,[534]—compiled by the famous Tsoṅ-kha-pa bLo-bzaṅ-grags-pa (1357-1419),[535] the founder of the "yellow cap" dGe-lugs-pa Buddhist sect (the dominant sect of Tibet). Being the author of two (a big one and a small one) treatises "about the stages of path of enlightenment",[536] Tsoṅ-kha-pa, in the

532. The date of composition of this text—Fire-Sheep year of the xiii cycle (A. D. 1787)—is mentioned in the colophon [see vol. ii (5), fol. 497ᵃ 5-6].
533. A copy of the Collected Works of Yoṅs-'dsin Ye-śes-rgyal-mtshan is available in the Institute of Peoples of Asia (*Tsybikov Collection*, No. 17).
534. With this work begins (fols. 1-3ᵇ 4) a collection of small works of Tsoṅ-kha-pa —*bKa'-'bum-thor-bu*—included in the second volume of the Collected Works of Tsoṅ-kha-pa published in bKra-śis-lhun-po (Two copies of this publication are available in the Institute of Peoples of Asia ; *Tsybikov Collection*, No. 1, and *Nova*).
535. About the biographies of Tsoṅ-kha-pa, see *infra*, note 561. The principal dates of his life and work are given in the "Chronological Tables."
536. The big treatise entitled *Byaṅ-chub-lam-gyi-rim-pa-chen-po* (481 fols.) covers

above-mentioned small text, enumerates and eulogizes his predecessors in the propagation of this teaching right from the Buddha Śākyamuni himself. This text is widely known in Tibet and Mongolia and is included in works marked for compulsory mass reading in spiritual schools (*chos-sgra*).[537] Thus, every school adds something to these works, which enumerate, in chronological order, and eulogize the persons expounding the teaching about the "path" in the particular school. The work of Yoṅs-'dsin Ye-śes-rgyal-mtshan, therefore, is like a commentary on such a supplementary text of Tsoṅ-kha-pa and besides giving the biographies of persons enumerated in the text itself and in its supplement, also includes the biographies of other persons right up to the immediate teachers of Yoṅs-'dsin Ye-śes-rgyal-mtshan himself (vol. i, fol. 1-vol. ii, fol. 409b 4).

The author concludes his work with an exposition of the teaching of the path of salvation,—which finds expression in the *'Jam-dpal-shal-luṅ* (fols. 295b 4-409b 4),[538] the

---

the whole of vol. xiii (*pa*) of the Collected Works of Tsoṅ-kha-pa published in bKra-śis-lhun-po, and exists in many separate editions. Besides, some Mongolian translations of this work are also available. The first part of one such translation was published, along with an incomplete Russian translation, by G. Tsybikov (see G. Ts. Tsybikov, *Lam-rim chen-po*, vol. i, nos. i-ii, Vladivostok, 1910-1913). The small treatise entitled *Byaṅ-chub-lam-gyi-rim-pa-chuṅ-ba* (201 fols.) is available in vol. xiv of the Collected Works of Tsoṅ-kha-pa. It is called *sKyes-bu-gsum-gyi-ñams-su-blaṅ-pa'i-lam-gyi-rim-pa-la-blo-spyaṅ-ba'i-tshul-gsal-bar-byed-pa.*

537. These works are called *Chos-spyod-rab-gsal* or simply *Rab-gsal.* Each monastery has its own collection of such works. The Institute of Peoples of Asia has some such collections from various monasteries (see *Old Collection*, No. 437-445). In the catalogue (see I. J. Schmidt und O. Bohtlingk, *Verzeichniss der Tibetischen Handschriften und Holzdrücke im Asiatischen Museum*), all these are wrongly recorded as historical texts. This error is evidently due to the fact that the list of Tibetan books, which Csoma de Koros gave in his *Grammar* (see A. Csoma de Koros, *A Grammar of the Tibetan Language*, p. 180) and which was reproduced in toto in the *Grammar* compiled by Schmidt, mentions a work of encyclopaedic character—*Śes-bya-rab-gsal*, the title of which has been wrongly translated by Csoma de Koros as "very clear science, history". Since the list of Csoma de Koros mostly mentions only the common names, Schmidt obviously mistook this name, too, for a common name for historical works.

538. Its full title is *Byaṅ-chub-lam-gyi-rim-pa'i-khrid-yig-'jam-pa'i-dbyaṅs-kyi-shal-luṅ.* It was composed in 1658 (Earth-Dog year) and it is available in vol. xii of the Collected Works of the Fifth Dalai Lama, where it covers 92 folios.

work of the Fifth Dalai Lama,—and gives, besides, the biographies of persons who had successively expounded the special (*zur-du-bkol-ba*) teaching about the training of mind for the path to *bodhisattva*—the so-called *theg-chen-blo-sbyoṅ* (vol. ii, fols. 409ᵇ 4-479ᵇ 3). Thereafter, he enumerates the names of persons who. had expounded the secret (*gsaṅ-ba*) esoteric (*thun-moṅ-ma-yin-pa*) teaching about the path of enlightenment (the so-called *ñams-len-byin-rlabs*)—especially the teaching of Guhyasamāja, Cakrasaṃvara, Vajrabhairava and the secret teaching of Atīśa and his school known as *bka'-gdams-theg-le-bcu-drug* (vol. ii, fols. 479ᵇ 3-494ᵇ 3).

A similar work—though considerably shorter—was composed still earlier by the second Panchen Lama Paṇ-chen bLo-bzaṅ-ye-śes (1663-1737),[539] the teacher of the aforementioned Yoṅs-'dsin Ye-śes-rgyal-mtshan. This work, called *Byaṅ-chub-lam-gyi-rin-pa'i-bla-ma-brgyud-pa'i-rnam-par-thar-pa-padma-dkar-po'i-'phreṅ-ba*, is available in the third volume of the Complete Works of the author and covers 61 folios.[540] There also exist works by other authors on this subject.

---

539. A detailed autobiography of Paṇ-chen bLo-bzaṅ-ye-śes, entitled *Śā-kya'i-dge-sloṅ-blo-bzaṅ-ye-śes-kyi-spyod-tshul-gsal-bar-byed-pa-'od-dkar-can-gyi-phyeṅ-ba*, is available in his Collected Works published in bKra-śis-lhun-po, where it covers the whole of vol. i (400 fols). This autobiography covers the period up to the beginning of 1732. A copy of the Collected Works of this author is available in the Institute of Peoples of Asia (*Tsybikov Collection*, No. 11). This biography was further continued by the third Pan chen-bla-ma dPal-ldan-ye-śes (1738-1780), and this extended portion is contained in the Collected Works of the latter (vol. iii) under the title *rDo-rje-'chaṅ-chen-po-paṇ-chen-thams-cad-mkhyen-pa-blo-bzaṅ-ye-śes-dpal-bzaṅ-po'i- sku- gsuṅ- thugs- kyi-mdsad- pa-ma-lus- pa-gsal- bar--byed-pa'i-rnam-par-thar-pa-'od-dkar-can-gyi-'phreṅ-ba'i-smad-cha* (138 fols). (A copy of this 'Collected Works' is available in the Institute of Peoples of Asia ; *Tsybikov Collection*, No. 12). The dates of birth and death of Paṇ-chen bLo-bzaṅ-ye-śes are taken by me from this biography. He was born in Water-Hare year of the xi cycle (A.D. 1663)—see the autobiography, fols. 78ᵇ 5-87ᵇ 2. He died in Fire-Serpent year of the xii cycle (A.D. 1737)—see the extended portion of the biography just mentioned, fols. 78ᵇ 5-87ᵇ 2. These dates are also mentioned in a short biography of his given in the *Lam-rim-bla-ma-brgyud-pa'i-rnam-thar* [vol. ii (5), fols. 128ᵃ 6 and 179ᵇ 4]. However, the 'chronological table' of Sum-pa-mkkan-po somehow gives his date of death as 1739 (Earth-Sheep year).

540. The order of arrangement of material in this work is the same as in the aforementioned work of Tsoṅ-kha-pa—*Byaṅ-chub-lam-gyi-rim-pa'i-brgyud-pa-rnams-la-gsol-ba-'debs-pa'i-rim-pa-lam-mchog-sgo-'byed*. The usual introductory verse is followed by a report on Buddha Śākyamuni (fols. 1ᵃ 4-2ᵇ 2), who is regarded

These and other such biographical collections are important because they furnish historical information on persons whose individual biographies have not reached us. Besides, even with regard to persons otherwise known to us, these works frequently give such useful information as is not found in the biographies at our disposal. In particular, the work of Yoṅs-'dsin Ye-śes-rgyal-mtshan referred to above is rich in historically valuable material and gives fairly detailed biographies of many distinguished Buddhist leaders like Nāgārjuna, Āryāsaṅga, Vasubandhu, Candrakīrti and other Indian writers, Atīśa and his pupils, Tsoṅ-kha-pa and his pupils, Dalai Lamas, Panchen Lamas and many other personages of Tibetan history.[541]

---

as the founder of the doctrine of the "stages of path of enlightenment" (*byaṅ-chub-lam-rim*). This is then followed by some information on the representtatives of the so-called "broad active tradition" (*rgya-chen-spyod-rgyud*) in the exposition of this doctrine from the *Bodhisattva* Maitreya and the Indian philosophers Asaṅga and Vasubandhu to Atīśa who carried this tradition from India to Tibet, and from Atīśa and his pupil 'Brom-ston-pa to Lho-brag Nam-mkha'-rgyal-mtshan, the direct teacher of Tsoṅ-kha-pa (fols. 2ª 2-21ᵇ 1). The succeeding 14 folios—from 21ᵇ 2 to 35ª 1—give information on persons who represented the so-called "deep meditative tradition" (*zab-ma-lha-brgyud*) in the exposition of this doctrine from Bodhisattva Mañjughoṣa and the Indian philosophers Nāgārjuna and Candrakīrti to Atīśa and 'Brom-ston-pa. From here, this tradition bifurcates. One trend—the so-called trend of the "protagonists of the principal doctrine of the bKa'-gdams-pa sect" (bKa'-gdams-gshuṅ-pa)—goes from Po-to-ba, the pupil of 'Brom-ston-pa, to Śa-ra-pa and further on to Chos-skyoṅ-bzaṅ-po, the teacher of Tsoṅ-kha-pa (fols. 35ª 1-42ᵇ 5). Another—the so-called trend of the "protagonists of special precepts of the bKa'-gdams-pa sect" (bKa'-gdams-man-ṅag-pa)—goes from sPyan-sṅa Tshul-'khrims-'bar to Bya-yul-pa gShon-nu-'od and further on to the aforementioned Lho-brag Nam-mkha'-rgyal-mtshan (fols. 42ᵇ 5-46ª 1). The brief biographical data on persons enumerated in the aforementioned work of Tsoṅ-kha-pa end here. Then follows a report on persons added to this list by the author himself, the second Panchen Lama, who describes the subsequent representatives of this doctrine from Tsoṅ-kha-pa and his pupils to rDo-rje-'dsin-pa dKon-mchog-rgyal-mtshan, the direct teacher of the author (fols. 46ª 1-60ᵇ 2). Folios 60ᵇ 3-61ª 2 contain a list of the persons who had preached (one after the other) the treatise *Byaṅ-chub-lam-gyi-rim-pa-chen-mo* composed by Tsoṅ-kha-pa, followed by the colophon (fol. 61ª 2-4).

541. The main part of the work of Yoṅs-'dsin Ye-śes-rgyal-mtshan expounds the biographies of the same persons as enumerated in the aforementioned works of Tsoṅ-kha-pa and the second Paṇ-chen-bla-ma bLo-bzaṅ-ye-śes. But these

All collections of this kind do not, of course, have the same historical significance. Even in the same collection, the materials on different persons differ widely in

---

biographies are far more extensive than those given by the aforesaid scholars, and often include not only the life-history of a particular person but also brief biographical information on his pupils. Besides, the list of these biographies has been extended further and also covers the period from the second Paṇ-chen-bla-ma to the immediate teachers of the author—Ṅag-dbaṅ-byams-pa (1638-1762) and the third Paṇ-chen-bla-ma dPal-ldan-ye-śes (1738-1780).

The order of arrangement of material in this work is somewhat different from that adopted in both the works referred to above. Distinguishing the two traditions in the history of *Lam-rim*—the "broad active tradition" and the "deep meditative tradition"—Yoṅs-'dsin Ye-śes-rgyal-mtshan, on the basis of the *bKa'-gdams-glegs-bam* (vol. i, fol. 391ᵇ 4-392ᵃ 2), adds one more special type of "active tradition"—the so-called "violent, active tradition" (*rlabs-chen-spyod-rgyud*) supposed to have been preached by the *Bodhisattva* Mañjughoṣa to the well-known Indian philosopher Śāntideva (see the aforementioned work of Yoṅs-'dsin Ye-śes-rgyal-mtshan, vol. i ; Collected Works, vol. iv, fols 145-146). Considering that all these "three trends" (*chu-po-gsum*) originated from Śākyamuni and merged in Atīśa, whose views were later passed on in Tibet in three different ways (which again merged in Tsoṅ-kha-pa), the author, too, based his exposition accordingly.

The work of Yoṅs-'dsin Ye-śes-rgyal-mtshan first describes the Buddha Śākyamuni (vol. i ; Collected Works, vol. iv, fols. 3ᵇ 1-70ᵇ 6) and then the representatives of the aforementioned three Indian traditions—namely, 1) the representatives of the "broad active tradition" : Maitreya, Asaṅga, Vasubandhu, etc., right up to Suvarnadvīpin Dharmakīrti who taught Atīśa (*ibid.*, fols. 70ᵇ 6-118ᵃ 5) ; 2) the representatives of the "deep, meditative tradition" : Mañjughoṣa, Nāgārjuna, Buddhapālita, Candrakīrti, Vidyākokila (Senior) and Vidyākokila (Junior) from whom, too, Atīśa studied (*ibid.*, fols. 118ᵃ 5-145ᵇ 1) ; and 3) the representatives of the "violent, active tradition" : Śāntideva, etc. right up to Suvarṇadvīpin (*ibid.*, fols. 145ᵇ 1-152ᵇ 2). This portion of the text (covering about 150 folios of the first volume) is of very little historical interest, because most of the legends on the Indian teachers of Buddhism given here are already known to us from the works of Bu-ston and Tāranātha.

Of far greater interest is another portion of the text which expounds the biographies of various Tibetan authors. This portion begins with a biography of Atīśa, in the end of which are given short biographical data on his pupils, Lo-chen Rin-chen-bzaṅ-po (958-1055), Nag-tsho-lo-tsā-ba Tshul-khrims-rgyal-ba (b. 1011) and others (*ibid.*, fols. 152ᵇ 3-192ᵃ 1). Then follows a biography of

quality. The biographies of the earlier—especially the Indian—preachers of Buddhism are so full of legendary material that one has to be very cautious in depending upon them. Generally, the importance of some of these biographical collections, which are typical "life-histories of saints", is more folkloristic than historical. One such well-known work is that by Tāranātha—the *bKa'-babs-bdun-ldan-gyi-rnam-thar*—which expounds the life-histories of the Indian *yogin*-s (*siddha*-s). The full title of this work,

---

'Brom-ston-pa rGyal-ba'i-'byuṅ-gnas (1004-1064), in the end of which is given a short biography of his pupil, Khams-pa-luṅ-pa Śākya-yon-tan (1025-1115)—*ibid.*, fols. 192ᵃ 1-219ᵃ 3. Next come the biographies of the representatives of three various traditions,—namely, 1) representatives of the tradition, which has no special name : dGom-pa-pa dBaṅ-phyug-rgyal-mtshan (1062-1082) and his pupils, sNe'u-zur-pa Ye-śes-'bar (1016-1138) and others (*ibid.*, fols. 219ᵃ 3-238ᵃ 1) ; 2) the so-called "protagonists of the principal teaching of bKa'-gdams-pa (*bKa'-gdams-gshuṅ-pa*) : Po-to-ba Rin-chen-gsal (1027-1105) and his pupils, Śa-ra-pa Yon-tan-grags (1070-1141), gTum-ston bLo-gros-grags (1106-1166), 'Chad-kha-ba Ye-śes-rdo-rje (1101-1175) and others right up to mKhan-chen Chos-skyabs-bzaṅ-po, the teacher of Tsoṅ-kha-pa (*ibid.*, fols. 238ᵃ 1-288ᵇ 2) ; and 3) the so-called "protagonists of the precepts of bKa'-gdams-pa" (*bKa'-gdams-pa-man-ṅag-pa*) : sPyan-sṅa-ba Tshul-khrims-'bar (1033-1103) and his pupils, Bya-yul-pa gShon-nu-'od (1075-1138), rJe sGam-po-pa (1079-1153), dGyer-sgom-pa gShon-nu-grags-pa (1090-1171) and others right up to Lho-brag Nam-mkha'-rgyal-mtshan (1326-1401), the teacher of Tsoṅ-kha-pa (*ibid.*, fols. 288ᵇ 2-325ᵃ 2).

Then follow the biographies of Tsoṅ-kha-pa and his closest pupils, rGyal-tshab Dar-ma-rin-chen (1364-1432), 'Dul-'dsin Grags-pa-rgyal-mtshan (1374-1436 ; the "Chronological Tables" give the date of death as 1434), etc., along with the biographies of his later followers right up to the third Paṇ-chen-bla-ma dPal-ldan-ye-śes (vol. i ; Collected Works, vol. iv, fol. 325ᵃ 2-vol. ii ; Collected Works, vol. v, fol. 295ᵇ 4).

Here, the main part of the text ends. Then, the author gives biographical data on persons, who had expounded the special teaching of training the mind on the path to *bodhisattva* (*theg-chen-blo-sbyoṅ*)—*ibid.*, fols. 409ᵇ 4-479ᵇ 3. Stating briefly that this teaching passed on from the philosopher Śāntideva (in the third Indian tradition) to Atīśa, from Atīśa to 'Brom-ston-pa, Po-to-ba and further (as per second Tibetan tradition) on to Se-spyil-bu-pa, and finally, through a number of persons (of whom the author knows nothing more than mere names), to mKhan-chen bDe-ba-dpal (1231-1297), the author expounds the biography of this person along with the biographies of the subsequent representatives of this tradition right up to Reṅ-mda'-ba gShon-nu-blo-gros (1349-1412),

written in 1600, is *bKa'-babs-bdun-ldan-gyi-brgyud-pa'i-rnam-thar-ṅo-mtshar-rmaṅ-byuṅ-rin-po-che*, and it covers 70 folios[542] in the sixteenth volume of Tāranātha's Complete Works. It was published (though very carelessly) by S. C. Das[543] and translated into German by Professor A. Grünwedel.[544]

As regards the individual biographies, these fall into two main categories : the usual "general" biographies (*thun-moṅ-pa*), in which the authors describe all aspects of their own life or of the life of another person ; and private biographies (*thun-moṅ-ma-yin-pa*)—also called "secret" biographies (*gsaṅ-ba'i-rnam-thar*-s)—in which the authors narrate, generally very briefly, the individual mystic events of their own life or sometimes (though rarely) of the life of another person intimately known to them as, for instance, the perception of some occult doctrine, miraculous dreams and various "supernatural" phenomena. Normally, such works form a special part of the general biographies, but sometimes they do exist independently too. Thus, for instance, there are short "secret" biographies of Tāranātha (written by him himself),[545] "secret" biographies of Tsoṅ-kha-pa[546] and of various other persons.[547] Of course, only the works

---

the teacher of Tsoṅ-kha-pa. The later representatives of this tradition have been simply enumerated by him.

As regards the persons who expounded the esoteric teaching of the path of enlightenment—*tantra*-s and *bka'-gdams-thig-le-bcu-drug*—Yoṅ-'dsin Ye-śes-rgyal-mtshan gives nothing more than their mere names. Short biographical data are given only on Phu-chuṅ-ba gShon-nu-rgyal-mtshan (1031-1106), the pupil of 'Brom-ston-pa (*ibid.*, fols. 479b 3-494b 3).

The work ends, as usual, with concluding verses (*ibid.*, fols. 494b 3-496b 2) and colophon.

542. The date of composition of this work is given in its colophon which states that it was written in the 26th year of the life of the author.

543. S. C. Das, *Kah bab dun dan, the Book of Seven Mystic Revelations*, Bengal Secretariat Press, 1901. For the inadequacies of this publication, see A. Grünwedel, *Tāranātha's Edelsteinmine*, p. 3.

544. A. Grünwedel, *Tāranātha's Edelsteinmine, das Buch von den Vermittern*, der Sieben Inspirationen, Petrograd, 1914 (*Bibliotheca Buddhica*, xviii).

545. See the Collected Works of Tāranātha, vol. i, which contains his three "secret" biographies.

546. See the Collected Works of Tsoṅ-kha-pa mentioned earlier, vol. i.

547. See the Collected Works of the second 'Jam-dbyaṅs-bshad-pa, vol. i ; the Collected Works of rGyal-mkhan-po Grags-pa-rgyal-mtshan (*Baradiin Collection* No. 5), vols. iv and v, which contain the "secret" biographies of dKon-mchog bsTan-pa'i-sgron-me ; the Collected Works of sDe-pa-sprul-sku 'Jam-dbyaṅs-thub-bstan-ñi-ma (*Baradiin Collection*, No. 6), vol. i, which contains

of the first category can be regarded as biographies in the real sense of this word. Usually, such biographies—found in plenty—are simply called *rnam-thar*-s, and occupy one of the most important places in Tibetan literature.

Sometimes, the works of a special nature—the so-called *thob-yig*-s or *gsan-yig*-s, which we shall discuss in the next section of this chapter, are also reckoned as "biographies" (*rnam-thar*-s), in which case we get three types of biographies: 1) the biographies proper which, as distinct from other two types, are called "external biographies"—*phyi'i-rnam-thar*-s; 2) the *thob-yig*-s or *gsan-yig*-s, which are called "internal biographies"—*naṅ-gi-rnam-thar*-s; and 3) the "secret biographies"—*gsan-ba'i-rnam-thar*-s. This division has been followed by sDe-srid Saṅs-rgyas-rgya-mtsho[548] and, after him, by some other Tibetan authors in respect of the life-history (in a number of volumes) of the Fifth Dalai Lama, Ṅag-dbaṅ bLo-bzaṅ-rgya-mtsho (1617-1682).[549] According to the classification of sDe-srid Saṅs-rgyas-rgya-mtsho as adopted in the Complete Works (*gsuṅ-'bum*) of the Fifth Dalai Lama, the life-history of the latter comprises a "secret biography" (*gsan-ba'i-rnam-thar*) which is a "sealed" (*rgya-can*) forbidden book and is therefore not included[550] in the usual Collected Works of the author, an "internal biography" (*naṅ-gi-rnam-thar*), i.e. the *thob-yig* (in four volumes) under the title *Zab-pa-daṅ-rgya-che-pa'i-dam-pa'i-chos-kyi-thab-yig-gaṅgā'i-chu-rgyud* compiled by the Fifth Dalai Lama himself,[551] and a general (*thun-moṅ-pa*) "external biography" (*phyi'i-rnam-thar*). As a matter of fact, only the last one is, properly, a biography. It bears the title *Za-hor-gyi-bande-ṅag-dbaṅ-blo-bzaṅ-rgya-mtsho'i-'di-snaṅ-'khrul-pa'i-rol-rtsod-rtogs-brjod-kyi-tshul-du-bkod-pa-du-kū-la'i-gos-bzaṅ*, but is often briefly called *rGyal-ba-lṅa-ba'i-rnam-thar-du-kū-la'i-gos-bzaṅ*. It consists of six volumes of the usual Tibetan format. Of these, three volumes (having 364, 281 and 246 folios) are written by the Fifth Dalai Lama himself and are included in his Collected

---

the "secret" biographies of the third 'Jam-dbyaṅs-bshad-pa and dKon-mchog bsTan-pa'i-sgron-me etc.

548. See the supplement of sDe-srid Saṅs-rgyas-rgya-mtsho to the biography of the Fifth Dalai Lama (mentioned *infra*), vol. iii (6), fols. 377b 6-378a 1.

549. See *bKa'-gdams-pa-daṅ-dge-lugs-pa-bla-ma-rags-rim-gyi-gsuṅ-'bum-mtshan-tho*, fol. 56a 6-56b 2.

550. See the supplement to the biography of the Fifth Dalai Lama, vol. iii, fols. 377b 6-378a 1, and the table of contents (*dkar-chag*) of volumes i-vii of the aforementioned Collected Works of the Fifth Dalai Lama. The "secret" biography is, however, wanting in this collection and in the table of contents referred to.

551. About this work, see *infra*.

Works.[552] The exposition follows the usual chronological order and ends with an account of the events which took place on the sixth of the ninth Mongolian month of the Iron-Hen year (i.e. 1681). The remaining three volumes (having 360, 338 and 383 folios) are a supplement (*'phros*) to this unfinished (*rtsom-'phro*) autobiography and are written by sDe-srid Saṅs-rgyas-rgya-mtsho. This supplement was started by him in 1692 and completed in 1696.[553] The biography of the Fifth Dalai Lama (including the supplement) is the largest of all the Tibetan biographical works known to us and is, of course, one of the most interesting ones, for it essentially constitutes detailed memoirs of the two well-known leaders of Tibetan history.

There is actually no dearth of biographical works in Tibetan language. There are large biographies, small biographies, detailed or brief biographies and then autobiographies—compiled in Tibetan language by the Tibetan and non-Tibetan scholars. In fact, the number of such works is constantly on the increase, though all these works do not of course have historical importance. Apart from the fact that all the persons described in these works are not equally important, the volume, nature and historical authenticity of the biographical data given also differ widely. The Tibetan authors do not draw any clear line of demarcation in the biographical works. To them, on the other hand, any life-history is *eo ipso* a description of the movement of a person on the path of deliverance (*rnam-par-thar-pa*) from the present or future transitory life, for, from the Buddhistic viewpoint, everything done in this life is directly related to this ultimate deliverance. Therefore, besides the biographical works which are really useful for a knowledge of the personal history of some person and in some cases, for that of the whole period, the term *rnam-thar* (biography) in Tibet is also applied to the "life-histories of saints", which are full of legends and are interesting not from the

552. These constitute the fifth and sixth volumes, and the first part of the seventh volume of the aforementioned Collected Works of the Fifth Dalai Lama. According to the testimony of sDe-srid Saṅs-rgyas-rgya-mtsho (vol. iii, fol. 378ᵃ 1-2), the last portion of this autobiography was written by a pupil of the Fifth Dalai Lama—'Jam-dbyaṅs-grags-pa.

553. This supplement of sDe-srid Saṅs-rgyas-rgya-mtsho was published in the state printing-house at Shol-par-khaṅ in Lhasa. A copy of this publication is available in the Institute of Peoples of Asia (*Tsybikov Collection*, No. 24) and is entitled *Drin-can-rtsa-ba'i-bla-ma-ṅag-dbaṅ-blo-bzaṅ-rgya-mtsho'i-thun-moṅ-phyi'i-rnam-thar-dukūla'i-gos-bzaṅ*. The date of composition of this supplement is mentioned in the colophon (vol. iii, fols. 379ᵇ 5-381ᵇ 4), which gives the cyclic dates of the beginning and completion of the work, and also the numbers of years that had passed from the time of various events up to these dates. The work was started in the Water-Monkey year (1692) and completed in the Fire-Mouse year (1696).

historical but only or almost only from the folkloristic and literary standpoint. The numerous biographies of Buddha and his pupils, the life-histories of the king Sroṅ-btsan-sgam-po (included in the *Ma-ṇi-bka'-'bum*) and Padmasambhava (*Padma-bka'-thaṅ*) and other similar works of apocryphal nature are also of this type. The other works, which also, to a certain extent, are of this kind are : *Jo-bo-rin-po-che-rje-dpal-ldan-a-ti-śa'i-rnam-thar-rgyas-ba-yoṅs-grags* (a detailed biography of Atiśa) included in the *bKa'-gdams-glegs-bam* ;[554] the biography of Mar-pa-lo-tsā-ba Chos-kyi-blo-gros (1012-1097),[555] the founder of the bKa'-rgyud-pa sect ; and the biography of the pupil of the latter—the famous poet Mi-la-ras-pa (1040-1123).[556] In all these, the narrative and didactic material is so dominant over the historical canvas that these works can be (rather must be) regarded not so much as biographies in the proper sense of this word as literary works. But such biographies are comparatively few in number. In a majority of cases, the *rnam-thar*-s can be considered real biographies. It is true that some of these—particularly those which

554. About the *bKa'-gdams-glegs-bam*, see *supra.*

555. I have, in view, a biography of Mar-pa-lo-tsā-ba entitled *sGra-bsgyur-mar-pa-lo-tsā-ba'i-rnam-thar-mthoṅ-ba-don-ldan*, which is extremely popular in Tibet and abroad. This biography (in 101 folios) is published in the monastery of bSam-gtan-chos-'phel-gliṅ in Amdo. A copy of this publication is available in the Institute of Peoples of Asia (*Baradiin Collection*, No. 33, iii).

556. The reference here is to the well-known biography of Mi-la-ras-pa entitled *rNal-'byor-gyi-dbaṅ-phyug-chen-po-rje-btsun-mi-la-ras-pa'i-rnam-par-thar-pa-daṅ-thams-cad-mkhyen-pa'i-lam-ston*. This biography and the "Collection of Songs" (*mgur-'bum*) of this greatest Tibetan poet (entitled *rJe-btsun-mi-la-ras-pa'i-rnam-thar-rgyas-par-phye-ba-mgur-'bum*) exist in many editions and have been translated into Mongolian. These have frequently attracted (and will also attract in future) the attention of the European scholars (see H. A. Jaschke, *Proben aus den tibetischen Legenden-buche* ; *die hundert-tausend Gesange des Milaraspa*—ZDMG, 1869, pp. 543-558 ; W. W. Rockhill, *The Tibetan "Hundred Thousand Songs" of Milaraspa*,—JAOS, 1884, xi, Proc., pp. 207-211 ; B. Laufer, *Zwei Legenden des Milaraspa*, Wien, 1902 ; Graham Sandberg, *Tibet and the Tibetans*, London, 1906, pp. 250-272 ; B. Laufer, *Milaraspa*, 1922 ; B. Ya. Vladimirtsov, *Iz liriki Milaraiby* [From the lyrics of Mi-la-ras-pa],—"Vostok", 1922, i, pp. 45-47 ; J. Bacot, *Le poète tibétaine Milarépa*, Paris, 1925 ; W. Y. Evans-Wentz, *Tibet's Great Yogi Milarepa. A Biography from the Tibetan* ; being the Jetsün-Ka'bum or biographical history of Jetsün-Milarepa according to the late Lama Kazi Dawa-Samdup's English rendering, Oxford, University Press, 1928.

describe the life and work of the earlier and highly honoured teachers of Buddhism—are not without legendary material, but this shortcoming does not prevent them from being basically important and fully authentic historical monuments.

We shall not make any attempt here to enumerate all biographical works existing in Tibetan language, and shall restrict ourselves only to a general statement that one can also find, among these, many biographies of the Tibetan leaders of the 11th-13th centuries—as, for instance, those of individual learned representatives of Sa-skya-pa sect,[557] of scholars like Phywa-pa Chos-kyi-seṅge (1109-1169),[558] the founder of Tibetan eristics and one of the earliest Tibetan writers on logic, the great translator Rin-chen-bzaṅ-po (958-1055),[559] Bu-ston Rin-chen-grub (1290-1364), etc., and numerous biographies of various spiritual and partly secular leaders of the later period.[560] To take a specific case, there are numerous biographies of Tsoṅ-kha-pa (1357-1419).[561]

557. See *supra*. Cf. also *Deb-ther-rgya-mtsho*, vol. i, fols. 12ᵇ 5-13ᵃ 1 which mention the five biographies of Sa-skya-paṇḍita Kun-dga'-rgyal-mtshan and the biographies of 'Phags-pa-bla-ma bLo-gros-rgyal-mtshan.

558. See *Deb-ther-rgya-mtsho*, vol. i, fol. 12ᵇ 1-2.

559. See *Deb-ther-rgya-mtsho*, vol. i, fol. 12ᵇ 2, which mentions the biography of Rin-chen-bzaṅ-po compiled by his pupil, mÑa'-ri-khri sTeṅ-pa Śrī-dsña'n.

560. See the list of biographical literature in the *Deb-ther-rgya-mtsho* (vol. i, fols. 11ᵃ 3-19ᵃ 4). Cf. also *dPe-rgyun-dkon-pa-'ga'-shig-gi-tho-yig* fols. 3ᵇ 2-9ᵃ 1.

561. Of the biographies of Tsoṅ-kha-pa, the following are the most popular :

1. A short autobiography, in verse, known under the title *mDun-legs-ma*. It is available in the second volume (fols. 52ᵇ 3-55ᵇ 1) of the Collected Works of Tsoṅ-kha-pa published in bKra-śis-lhun-po. Besides, it also exists as an independent work in many separate editions and is regarded as one of the so-called *rab-gsal*-s—works meant for mass reading in philosophical schools (*chos-grwa*). One Ṅag-dbaṅ-byams pa (1682-1762) from the small monastery of Phur-bu-lcog wrote a commentary on this autobiography,—which is entitled *rTogs-brjod-rin-po-che-mdun-legs-ma'i-'grel-pa-mkhas-pa'i-gshuṅ-lam* (76 folios) and which comprises the first book (*ka*) in the Collected Works of its author published in Phur-bu-lcog monastery (see *Tsybikov Collection*, No. 23).

2. *rJe-btsun-bla-ma-tsoṅ-kha-pa-chen-po'i-ṅo-mtshar-maṅ-du-byuṅ-ba'i-rnam-par-thar-pa-dad-pa'i-'jug-ṅogs*. This biography is written by mKhas-grub dGe-legs-dpal-bzaṅ-po, a pupil of Tsoṅ-kha-pa, and is available in the first volume of the Collected Works of Tsoṅ-kha-pa (published from bKra-śis-lhun-po). This biography covers 71 folios. Another biography—in 16 folios—is entitled *rJe-rin-po-che'i-gsaṅ-ba'i-rnam-thar-rgya-mtsho-lta-bu-las-cha-śas-ñuṅ-ṅu-shig-yoṅs-su-brjod-pa'i-gtam-rin-po-che'i-sñe-ma*.

3. *rJe-btsun-tsoṅ-kha-pa'i-rnam-thar-chen-ma'i-zur-'debs-rnam-thar-legs-bśad-kun-'dus*. This biography is written by 'Jam-dpal-rgya-mtsho (1356-1428), and

Of the rare books alone, no less than fifteen are specially devoted to

---

is also included in the first volume of the Collected Works of Tsoṅ-kha-pa. It covers 11 folios.

4. *rJe-thams-cad-mkhyen-pa-tsoṅ-kha-pa-chen-po'i-rnam-thar-go-sla-bar-brjod-pa-bde-legs-kun-gyi-'byuṅ-gnas* (in 9 books, with an appendix containing a list of the most important events in the life of Tsoṅ-kha-pa). This biography occupies the whole of the second volume of the Collected Works of its author —Cha-har-dge-bśes bLo-bzaṅ-tshul-khrims—published in Peking. (A copy of this 'Collected Works' is available in the Institute of Peoples of Asia, *Nova*). This biography was composed by its author not only in Tibetan but also in Mongolian.

The Mongolian text was published as a separate xylograph (in 9 books) in the Aginsky *datsan* in Buryatia. (Copies of this Mongolian text are also available in the Institute of Peoples of Asia, Mong. Xyl. H. 328). In Mongolia, this biography is extremely popular. Of its nine books, only the first seven contain the biography of Tsoṅ-kha-pa ; the very first book, however, is not on him but on his previous incarnations. The remaining two books briefly expound the later history of the dGe-lugs-pa sect : the eighth book contains biographies of the pupils of Tsoṅ-kha-pa, rGyal-tshab-dar-ma-rin-chen (1364-1432) and mKhas-grub dGe-legs-dpal-bzaṅ-po (1385-1438), etc and a history of the Heads of the monastery of dGa'-ldan ; the ninth book contains a biography of 'Jam-dbyaṅs-chos-rje bKra-śis-dpal-ldan (1379-1449) and a historical account of the 'Bras-spuṅs monastery founded by him in 1416, a biography of Byams-chen-chos-rje Śākya-ye-śes (1354-1435) and a description of the Se-ra monastery founded by him in 1419, a biography of dGe-'dun-grub (1391-1474) and a description of the bKra-śis-lhun-po monastery founded by him in 1447, a biography of mKhas-grub Śes-rabs-seṅge (d. 1445) and a history of the emergence of the Srad-rgyud and sMad-rgyud tantric schools, a history of the rGyud-stod tantric school, and finally the conclusion.

5. *Khyab-bdag-rje-btsun-bla-ma-dam-pa-thub-dbaṅ-rdo-rje-'chaṅ-daṅ-ṅo-bo-dbyer-ma-mchis-pa-'jam-mgon-chos-kyi-rgyal-po-tsoṅ-kha-pa-chen-po'i-rnam-par-thar-pa-thub-bstan-mdses-pa'i-rgyan-gcig-ṅo-mtshar-nor-bu'i-phreṅ-ba,* written by bLo-bzaṅ-'phrin-las-rnam-rgyal of the Lower *datsan* of the Se-ra monastery (Se-ra-smad-thos-bsam-gliṅ). The compilation of this biography was started in 1843 (Water-Hare year of the xiv cycle) and completed in 1845 (Wood-Serpent year). This biography is known in two editions : one published by the Tibetan Government in Lhasa (in 376 folios), referred to by G. Tsybikov (*Lam-rim chen-po,* vol. i, no. ii, p. *v*) ; and the other from the monastery of gTsos-dgon dGa'-ldan-chos-gliṅ in Amdo (in 406 folios). This latter edition is available in

the life and career of this famous reformer of Tibetan Buddhism.[562] Of

---

the Institute of Peoples of Asia (*Baradiin Collection*, No. 35). This biography is considered extremely authentic and is regarded as the most comprehensive and complete of all the existing biographies.

6. *rJe-thams-cad-mkhyen-pa-tsoṅ-kha-pa-chen-po'i-rnam-thar-gyi-bsdus-don-caṅ-zad-brjod-pa.* A list of the principal events in the life of Tsoṅ-kha-pa, similar to the one appended to the Tibetan version of the biography, written by the aforementioned Cha-har-dge-bśes bLo-bzaṅ-tshul-khrims (but containing lesser information). The author of this biography is Ā-kya-sku-skye bLo-bzaṅ-bstan-pa'i-rgyal-mtshan. It comprises the 12th book (*na*) in the above-mentioned Collected Works of the author, and contains 12 folios.

The biographical data on Tsoṅ-kha-pa have been frequently expounded in the European literature (see, in particular, C. F. Koeppen, *Die Lamaische Hierarchie und Kirche*, pp. 108-112ff ; K. F. Golstunsky, *Mongolo-oiratskie Zakony 1640 goda*, p. 78-94 ; G. Tsybikov, *Lam-rim chen-po*, vol. i, no. ii, p. xii-xxix etc). E. E. Obermiller also set forth the biography of Tsoṅ-kha-pa, mainly from the point of view of his career as a scholar (see E. Obermiller, *Tsoṅ-kha-pa le Pandit*,—"Mélanges chinois et bouddhiques publiés par l' Institute Belge des Hautes Etudes Chinoises", vol. iii, Bruxelles, 1935, pp. 319-338). This last work is based exclusively on the material given in the aforementioned biography of Tsoṅ-kha-pa compiled by his pupil, mKhas-grub dGe-legs-dpal-bzaṅ-po, and is an abridged exposition of the latter.

562. The "List of Rare Books" (*dPe-rgyun-dkon-pa-'ga'-shig-gi-tho-yig*, fols. 3b 2-4a 1) enumerates the following rare biographies of Tsoṅ-kha-pa :

1. *rJe-tsoṅ-kha-pa'i-rnam-thar-gser-gyi-mchod-sdoṅ*, with a supplement (*kha-skoṅ*) under the title *gSer-gyi-myu-gu*. Author : Zaṅ-zin-ne-riṅ-pa 'Chi-med-rab-rgyas.
2. *mKhas-btsun-bzaṅ-gsum-gyi-bstod-pa.* Author *idem*.
3. *'Chad-rtsad-rtsom-gsum-gyi-bstod-pa.* Author *idem*.
4. Biography, written by Legs-bzaṅ-pa.
5. Biography, witten by rJo-gdan bSod-nams-lhun-grub.
6. Biography, written by gNas-rñiṅ Kun-dga'-bde-legs (d. 1469).
7. Biography, written by Ku-cor rTogs-ldan (1386-1445).
8. Biography, written by Brag-sgo-rab-'byams-pa Phun-tshogs-rgyal-mtshan.
9. Biography, written by mÑa'-ris-pa Ṅag-dbaṅ-'jam-dbyaṅs-ñi-ma-bstan-pa'i-rgyal-mtshan.
10. Biography, written by sMar-khams-'od-zer-bla-ma dKon-mchog-rgyal-mtshan.

the biographies of other persons, we can mention those of various Dalai

---

11. *rJe'i-rnam-thar-ṅo-mtshar-ba'i-gtam.* Author : rTa-tshag-rje-druṅ Ṅag-dbaṅ-chos-kyi-dbaṅ-phyug.

12. *rJe'i- rnam- thar- luṅ- rigs- rgya- mtsho.* Author : gSer-khaṅ-chos-rje Gu-ṇa-ma-ti.

13. *rJe'i- rtogs- brjod- thub- bstan- rin- po- che'i- rgyan- me- tog- chun- ma-po.* Author : Ra-roṅ Ṅag-dbaṅ-chos-grags-rgya-mtsho-dkon-mchog-grub-pa'i-sde.

14. Biography under the title *dPag-bsam-'khri-śiṅ*, which the second 'Jam-dbyaṅs-bshad-pa quotes.

15. *rJe'i-rnam-thar-legs-bśad-ñin-moṅ-byed-pa.* Author : Brag-yab bLo-bzaṅ-bstan-pa or Ṅag-dbaṅ-dge-legs-dpal-bzaṅ. Besides, many biographies of the pupils of Tsoṅ-kha-pa are also mentioned.

The *Deb-ther-rgya-mtsho* (vol. i, fol. 11ª 3-6) enumerates mainly the same biographies (except those at S. Nos. 2, 3, 13 and 14 *supra*). The additional biographies named in this work are those by : Lhu-la-dka'-bcu, mKhas-pa Śes-rab-rin-chen, Yoṅs-'dsin Ye-śes-rgyal-mtshan, 'Brug rGyal-dbaṅ-sprul-sku, and Guṅ-ru rGyan-bzaṅ. The last one of these has been named as the author of a commentary on the autobiographical verse of Tsoṅ-kha-pa.

The *bKa'-gdams-pa-daṅ-dge-lugs-pa-bla-ma-rags-rim-gyi-gsuṅ-'bum-mtshan-tho* (fols. 46ᵇ 5-47ᵇ 3) gives the following list of the collection of rare biographies of Tsoṅ-kha-pa (and his pupils) :

ka) Table of contents.

kha) Biography, compiled by 'Jam-dpal-rgya-mtsho, 11 fols.

ga) Biography, compiled by gNas-rñiṅ Kun-dga'-bde-legs, 62 fols.

ṅa) Biography, written by Paṇ-chen bLo-gros-legs-bzaṅ, 19 fols.

ca) Biography, written by mÑa'-ris-shabs-druṅ bsTan-pa'i-rgyal-mtshan, 13 folios.

cha) Biography entitled *gSer-gyi-mchod-stoṅ*, written by Ne-rin-pa 'Chi-med-rab-rgyas, 15 fols.

ja) Supplement to the above biography—entitled *gSer-gyi-myu-gu*, 3 fols.

ña) *mKhas-btsun-bzaṅ-gsum-gyi-bstod-pa*, by the same author, 10 fols.

ta) *'Chad-rtsod-rtsom-gsum-gyi-bstod-pa*, by the same author, 7 fols.

tha) Biography entitled *No-mtshar-smad-du-byuṅ-pa'i-gtam-brgya*, written by rJe-druṅ Ṅag-chos, 36 fols.

da) Commentary on an autobiographical poem of Tsoṅ-kha-pa—*mDun-legs-ma* written by Guṅ-ru rGyal-mtshan-bzaṅ-po (1383-1450), 47 fols.

na) *rJe'i-rnam-thar-btsoṅ-kha-brgyad-cu'i-rtsa-'grel*, 30 fols.

Lamas,[563] Panchen Lamas,[564] Incarnations of the Peking lCaṅ-skya-bla-ma,[565]

[Notes 564-5 : see *infra*]

---

pa) *rGyal-ba-tsoṅ-kha-pa'i-rnam- thar-gsol-'debs-mi-'gyur- mchog-yaṅs-ma'i-'grel-pa*, 28 fols.

pha) Biography written by sMar-khams-'od-zer-bla-ma dKon-mchog-rgyal-mtshan, a pupil of the first Panchen Lama, bLo-bzaṅ-chos-kyi-rgyal-mtshan, 40 fols.

ba) Biography written by bLo-bzaṅ-bstan-pa, 47 fols.

ma) Biography of rGyal-tshab-dar-ma-rin-chen, written by the same author, 30 fols.

tsa) Biography of mKhas-grub dGe-legs-dpal-bzaṅ-po, by the same author, 35 fols.

tsha) Biography of mKhas-grub dGe-legs-dpal-bzaṅ-po, written by gSaṅ-mda'-ba Chos-ldan-rab-'byor, 11 fols.

dsa) History of the Silver *suburgan* (*dṅul-'dus*) of the monastery of dGa'-ldan, and a report on the Head of this monastery, 23 fols.

va) Biography of mKhas-grub dGe-legs-dpal-bzaṅ-po, written by Se-ra-rje-btsun Chos-kyi-rgyal-mtshan (1469-1546) from the words of Kun-dga'-bde-legs-rin-chen-rgyal-mtshan. 22 fols.

sha) *mKhas-grub-pa'i-rtogs-brjod*, 6 fols.

As we have seen, most of the biographies of Tsoṅ-kha-pa mentioned in this list are also repeated in the "List of Rare Books" and in the "List of Historical Literature."

563. Biography of the first Dalai Lama, dGe-'dun-grub (1391-1474), under the title *rJe-thams-cad-mkhyen-pa-dge-'dun-grub-pa-dpal-bzaṅ-po'i-rnam-thar-ṅo-mtshar-rmad-byuṅ-nor-bu'i-phreṅ-ba*, was written by Ye-śes-rtse-mo in 1494. It is included in the fifth volume of the Collected Works of dGe-'dun-grub published in bKra-śis-lhun-po (see the copy of this 'Collected Works' in the Institute of Peoples of Asia—*Tsybikov Collection*, No. 4), and covers 63 folios. Another, more concise biography of dGe-'dun-grub, under the title *bLa-ma-thams-cad-mkhyen-pa'i-rnam-thar-ṅo-mtshar-mdsad-pa-bcu-gñis-pa* (in 22 fols.) was compiled by Kun-dga'-rgyal-mtshan (see *ibid.*).

An autobiography of the second Dalai Lama, dGe-'dun-rgya-mtsho (1476-1542),—entitled *rJe-btsun- thams- cad- mkhyen- pa'i- gsuṅ- 'bum-thor- bu-las- rje-ñid-kyi-rnam-thar* (38 fols.),—is available in the first volume of the Collected Works of dGe-'dun-rgya-mtsho (see *Tsybikov Collection*, No. 5). This autobiography covers the period up to A.D. 1528.

The biography of the third Dalai Lama, bSod-nams-rgya-mtsho (1543-1588), was written in 1646 by the Fifth Dalai Lama. This biography is entitled

'Jam-dbyaṅs-bshad-pa[566] of bLa-braṅ, etc. and also the numerous biographies of various other leaders who played a more or less important role in the history of Tibet and in

[Note 566 : see *infra*]

---

rJe-btsun-thams-cad-mkhyen-pa-bsod-nams-rgya-mtsho'i-rnam-thar-dṅos-grub-rgya-mtsho'i-śiṅ-rta (109 fols.), and is available in the eighth volume of the Collected Works of the Fifth Dalai Lama. Four more biographies, which served as the sources for this work, are mentioned in its colophon (fol. 108^b 5-6).

The biography of the fourth Dalai Lama, Yon-tan-rgya-mtsho (1589-1616), is also written by the Fifth Dalai Lama, and is available in the Collected Works of the latter. This biography bears the title : *'Jig-rten-dbaṅ-phyug-thams-cad-mkhyen-pa-yon-tan-rgya-mtsho-dpal-bzaṅ-po'i-rnam-par-thar-pa-nor-bu'i-phreṅ-ba* (52 fols.). Two more biographies, which served as its sources, are mentioned in its colophon (fol. 52^a 1-2).

The biographies of the Fifth Dalai Lama have already been referred to (see *supra*).

The biographies of the sixth Dalai Lama, Tshaṅs-dbyaṅs-rgya-mtsho (b. 1683), written by sDe-srid Saṅs-rgyas-rgya-mtsho and Dar-rgyas No-mon-han—referred to in the *Deb-ther-rgya-mtsho*, vol. i, fol. 12^a 2 (see also *dPe-rgyun-dkon-pa-'ga'-shig-gi-tho-yig*, fol. 8^a 5-6)—have not come down to us.

The biography of the seventh Dalai Lama, sKal-bzaṅ-rgya-mtsho (1708-1757), entitled *rGyal-ba'i-dbaṅ-po-thams-cad-mkhyen-gzigs-rdo-rje-'chaṅ-blo-bzaṅ-skal-bzaṅ-rgya-mtsho-dpal-bzaṅ-po'i-shal-sṅa-nas-kyi-rnam-par-thar-pa-mdo-tsam-brjod-pa-dpag-gsam-rin-po-che'i-sñi-ma* is attributed to the famous lCaṅ-skya Rol-pa'i-rdo-rje (1717-1786). This biography was taken up for compilation in 1758 and completed in 1759. It is included in the first volume of the Collected Works of lCaṅ-skya Rol-pa'i-rdo-rje published in Peking, and covers 588 folios (see the copy of this 'Collected Works' in the Institute of Peoples of Asia ; *Old Collection*, No. 311^a). This biography is also available in the Collected Works (vol. 9, 588 fols.) of the seventh Dalai Lama (a copy of this 'Collected Works' is also available in the Institute of Peoples of Asia ; *Tsybikov Collection*, No. 7).

Besides, the "List of Historical Literature" in the *Deb-ther-rgya-mtsho* (vol. i, fol. 12^a 2-4) mentions :

A biography of the eighth Dalai Lama, 'Jam-dpal-rgya-mtsho (1758-1804), written by rTa-tshag-rje-druṅ and entitled *rGyal-ba-'jam-dpal-rgya-mtsho'i-rnam-thar-'dsam-gliṅ-mtha'-gru-yaṅs-pa'i-rgyan*.

A biography of the ninth Dalai Lama, Luṅ-rtogs-rgya-mtsho (1805-1815), written by De-mo bLo-bzaṅ-thub-bstan-'jigs-med-rgya-mtsho and entitled *rGyal-ba-luṅ-rtogs-rgya-mtsho'i-rnam-thar-dad-pa'i-yid-'phrog*.

the development of her science, philosophy, religion and literature. Besides, there also are, in Tibetan language, many biographies of the Mongolian Lamas. There also

---

However, these last two biographies are not available in our collections. Besides, I could not so far find the biographies of the subsequent Dalai Lamas, though these do exist. The list of the biographies of the Dalai Lamas given by me here is in no way exhaustive. The biography of the tenth Dalai Lama, Tshul-khrims-rgya-mtsho (1816-1837), is given by L. A. Waddell (see L. A. Waddell, *Tibetan Manuscripts and Books etc. Collected during the Young Husband Mission to Lhasa*,—"The Imperial and Asiatic Quarterly Review and Oriental Colonial Record", 3rd series, vol. xxxiv, July-October 1912, p. 112, N 439).

The biographies of the Dalai Lamas have been frequently set forth in European literature. Of the greatest interest are : the history of the Dalai Lamas set forth in Koeppen's work (see Koeppen, *Die lamaische Hierarchie und Kirche*, pp. 130-236) ; very valuable (for the accuracy of dates) but brief biographies of the Dalai Lamas expounded by Tsybikov on the basis of the Tibetan sources (G. Tsybikov, *Buddist-palomnik u svyatyn' Tibeta*, p. 251-272) ; and a long article written by Rockhill on the basis of the Chinese sources (see W. W. Rockhill, *The Dalai Lamas of Lhasa and Their Relations with the Manchu Emperors of China*, 1644-1908,—"T'oung Pao", vol. xi, 1910, pp. 1-104). Besides, a work of Schulemann (see G. Schulemann, *Die Geschichte der Dalai-Lamas*, Heidelberg, 1911) is exclusively devoted to this subject, though this work, based on European sources and translations, repeats the errors of the previous scholars (especially, in respect of the chronological dates).

564. The autobiography of the first Panchen Lama, bLo-bzaṅ-chos-kyi-rgyal-mtshan (1570-1662), entitled *Chos-smra-ba'i-dge-sloṅ-blo-bzaṅ-chos-kyi-rgyal-mtshan-gyi-spyod-tshul-gsal-bar-ston-pa-nor-bu'i-'phreṅ-ba*,—along with its last portion written in 1720 by the second Panchen Lama, bLo-bzaṅ-ye-śes (1663-1737)—is included in the first volume of the Collected Works of Pan-chen bLo-bzaṅ-chos-kyi-rgyal-mtshan, and covers 225 folios (see the copy of this 'Collected Works' in the Institute of Peoples of Asia ; *Tsybikov Collection*, No. 10). Its last portion, covering fols. 191a 1-225, is also available separately in the third volume of the works of the second Panchen Lama, under the title *Paṇ-chen-blo-bzaṅ-chos-kyi-rgyal-mtshan-gyi-rnam-thar-gsal-bar-ston-pa-nor-bu'i-'phreṅ-ba'i-smad-cha* (35 fols.)—see *Tsybikov Collection*, No. 11.

The biography of the second Panchen Lama has already been referred to (see *supra*).

The biography of the third Panchen Lama, bLo-bzaṅ-dpal-ldan-ye-śes (1740-1780), was written by his pupil, the second 'Jam-dbyaṅs-bshad-pa dKon-mchog-'jigs-med-dbaṅ-po (1728-1791). It is entitled *rJe-bla-ma-srid-shi'i-gtsug-*

exist Tibetan biographies of some important Lamas from Buryatia, as for instance : the biographies of the first *paṇḍita* (*mkhan-po*) of the Buddhist Order of Eastern Siberia,

---

rgyan-paṇ-chen-thams-cad-mkhyen-pa-blo- bzaṅ-dpal-ldan-ye- śes-dpal-bzaṅ-po'i-shal-sṅa-nas-kyi-rnam-par-thar-pa-ñi-ma'i-'od-zer, and is dated 1786. This biography covers two volumes—the third (358 folios) and the fourth (291 folios)—in the Collected Works of its author. Besides, it is also available in the Collected Works of the third Panchen Lama (in the copy of this 'Collected Works' available in the Institute of Peoples of Asia—*Tsybikov Collection*, No. 12—only the first part of this biography is given).

The biography of the fourth Panchen Lama, bLo-bzaṅ-bstan-pa'i-ñi-ma-phyogs-las-rnam-rgyal (1781-1854), was written by bLo-bzaṅ-spyin-pa in 1883. This biography bears the title *Rab-'byams-rgyal-ba'i-spyi-gzugs-skyabs-mgon-paṇ-chen-thams-cad-mkhyen-pa-rje-btsun-blo-bzaṅ- dpal-ldan- bstan-pa'i-ñi-ma-phyogs-las-rnam-rgyal-dpal- bzaṅ-pa'i- shal-sṅa-nas- kyi-sku- gsuṅ- thugs- kyi- rnam- par- thar-pa-'dsam-gliṅ-mdses-rgyan* (414 fols.), and is available in the first volume of the Collected Works of the fourth Panchen Lama (see *Tsybikov Collection*, No. 13).

The biography of the fifth Panchen Lama, bLo-bzaṅ-dpal-ldan-chos-kyi-grags-pa-bstan-pa'i-dbaṅ-phyug (1855-1881), is attributed to bLo-bzaṅ-bstan-'dsin-dbaṅ-rgyal, and is called *rJe-btsun-blo-bzaṅ-dpal-ldan-chos-kyi-grags-pa-bstan-pa'i-dbaṅ-phyug-dpal- bzaṅ-po'i-rnam- thar-dad-ldan- pad- tshal- bshad- pa'i-ñin-byed-snaṅ-ba*. It was begun in 1888 and completed in 1889. The biography is available in the first volume of the Collected Works of the fifth Panchen Lama (see *Tsybikov Collection*, No. 14), and covers 303 folios.

The biographies of Panchen Lamas have been frequently set forth in European literature. In particular, the biographies of the first three Panchen Lamas along with those of ten persons regarded as their previous incarnations were set forth by S. C. Das (see S. C. Das, *Contributions on...*,—JASB, 1882, pp. 15-52. Most of the dates given by S. C. Das according to the European calendar, however, require rectification). A short exposition of the biographies of all the five Panchen Lamas mentioned here may also be found in Tsybikov's work (see G. Tsybikov, *Buddist-palomnik u svyatyn' Tibeta*, pp. 370-74).

565. The autobiography of the first lCaṅ-skya-bla-ma Ṅag-dbaṅ-blo-bzaṅ-chos-ldan (1642-1714)—under the title *rJe-btsum-bla-ma-ṅag-dbaṅ-blo-bzaṅ-chos-ldan-dpal-bzaṅ-po'i-rnam-par-thar-pa-dad-pa'i-rol-mtsho*—is published in the fifth volume of his Collected Works (see *Tsybikov Collection*, No. 35).

The biographies of the second lCaṅ-skya-bla-ma—Rol-pa'i-rdo-rje—have been mentioned earlier. There is no doubt that the biographies of subsequent incarnations are also existing, but I have not seen these.

bsTan-pa-dar-rgyas (Zayaev) (1711-1776);[567] the interesting autobiography entitled *Raṅ-spyod-raṅ-gsal-raṅ-gi-thems-yig* (in six separate volumes) written in 1864-1872 by the Head of the small bKra-śis-chos-'phel-gliṅ monastery, Ṅag-dbaṅ bLo-bzaṅ sKal-bzaṅ-spyin-pa Dylgirov (b. 1816),[568] who is known for his Mongolian translations of various Tibetan works; and the biography of the teacher of the latter, the well-known founder of the Tsugol *datsan*, bLo-bzaṅ Lhun-grub Dandarov (1781-1859),[569] etc.

566. The biographies of the first three 'Jam-dbyaṅs-bshad-pa-s have already been mentioned. I have not come across any biographies of the subsequent incarnations.

567. A short biography of bsTan-pa-dar-rgyas (Zayaev), written on the basis of his autobiography, is attributed to the Buryat Lama bLo-bzaṅ-rgya-mtsho (Batszaron). This biography is entitled *dBaṅ-phyogs-po-riṅ-kyi-yul-du-dgon-sde-dpal-ldan-'bras-spuṅs-btab-nas-'jam-mgon-rgyal-ba-gñis-pa'i-rin-lugs-spel-bar-mdsad-pa-po-rgyal-ba'i-sras-mchog-mkhan-chen-paṇḍita-bstan-pa-dar-rgyas-dpal-bzaṅ-po'i-rnam-thar-mdor-bsdus*. It was written in 1891 in bLa-braṅ. The Institute of Peoples of Asia has a copy made by B. B. Baradiin from the manuscript of the author himself [see "Musei Asiatici Petropolitani Notitia", vii, No. 11 (3)]. This copy is written on letter-paper and it covers 6 pages (without counting the title-page).

Besides, the Institute of Peoples of Asia also has a manuscript copy of the interesting autobiographical account of bsTan-pa-dar-rgyas (Zayaev) himself on the construction of the Tsugol *datsan* in Buryatia. This manuscript is entitled *Ti-phu-thad-paṇḍita-mkhan-po'i-bka'-stsal*, and is written on European paper (6 folios).

568. This autobiography is published in the Tsugol *datsan* in Buryatia.

569. The biography is entitled *rNam-'dren-bstan-pa'i-rtsa-lag-mtshuṅs-zla-med-pa-rje-btsun-blo-bzaṅ-lhun-grub-dpal-bzaṅ-po'i-rtogs-pa-brjod-pa-dad-pa'i-'khri-śiṅ*. Its author is the fourth 'Jam-dbyaṅs-bshad-pa sKal-bzaṅ-thub-bstan-dbaṅ-phyug (b. 1856). It is published in the Tsugol *datsan* in Buryatia and it covers 21 folios. A copy of this publication is available in the Institute of Peoples of Asia—see "Musei Asiatici Petropolitani Notitia", vii, No. 11 (33).

9. *Thob-yig*-s *or gSan-yig*-s

A quite distinctive class of Tibetan works is that of the so-called *thob-yig*-s or *gsan-yig*-s. Although these works, as we have already seen, are sometimes classed under biographical literature, they essentially comprise a special and highly extensive class of Tibetan works.

In their simplest and most prevalent form, these works are more or less systematized lists of disciplines, precepts, directions and consecrations of all types taken by the author and indicate as to from whom exactly these were taken. In this sense, they are like special supplements to autobiographies. However, these works do not only indicate the name of the person from whom these disciplines, directions or consecrations were taken ; they endeavour to establish a more or less complete succession of persons giving these precepts or directions, beginning with the founder himself and ending with the author of the *yig*-s. Being typical historico-literary works or records of oral and written traditions (*rgyud-rim*), grouped on an autobiographical basis (in a systematic though not chronological order), these works are, of course, far beyond the framework of autobiographies.

These works, in their simplest form, are nothing more than bare lists of disciplines, directions and consecrations taken and of the persons giving them. Such, for instance, are the *gsan-yig*-s compiled by 'Phags-pa-bla-ma bLo-gros-rgyal-mtshan (about 22 folios),[570] Tsoṅ-kha-pa (27 folios)[571] and his pupil mKhas-grub dGe-legs-dpal-bzaṅ-po (44 folios)[572] and some others. But this concise form apart, there also exist more extensive forms, in which the lists of traditions are supplemented by various data of literary and historical nature.

One of the largest works of this type is the aforementioned *thob-yig* of the Fifth Dalai Lama—*Zab-pa-daṅ-rgya-che-pa'i-dam-pa'i-chos-kyi-thob-yig-gaṅgā'i-chu-rgyun*—consisting of four large volumes (of 418, 385, 366 and 367 folios of usual format).[573] This work, started by the author in 1665 and completed in 1670,[574] follows a strict

570. This work, under the title *Luṅ-daṅ-brgyud-pa-sna-tshogs-thob-pa'i-gsan-yig*, is included among other works of 'Phags-pa-bla-ma bLo-gros-rgyal-mtshan in the Collected Works of Sa-skya scholars. See *Sa-skya-bka'-'bum*, vol. xv (*ba*), fols. 361^{b} 4-383^{a} 5.
571. This work, under the title *rJe-rin-po-che-blo-bzaṅ-grags-pa'i-dpal-gyi-gsan-yig*, is available in the first volume of the Collected Works of Tsoṅ-kha-pa bLo-bzaṅ-grags-pa.
572. This work, under the title *mKhas-grub-thams-cad-mkhyen-pa-dge-legs-dpal-bzaṅ-po'i-gsan-yig*, is included in the first volume of the Collected Works of mKhas-grub dGe-legs-dpal-bzaṅ-po.
573. See the Collected Works of the Fifth Dalai Lama, vols. i-iv.
574. See *Thob-yig-gaṅgā'i-chu-rgyun*, vol. iv, colophon (fols. 366^{b} 4-367^{a} 5), which

systematic order. After a small introduction (vol. i, fols. 1-8ᵇ 6), this work describes when and by whom the Fifth Dalai Lama took orders first in dGe-tshul and then in dGe-sloṅ and gives the traditional succession of the person who consecrated him—the first Panchen Lama, Paṇ-chen bLo-bzaṅ-chos-kyi-rgyal-mtshan (1570-1662)[575]—right upto Buddha himself. Besides, this work contains an account of the tradition of the orders taken by him up to Vinaya etc. (vol. i, fols. 9ᵃ 1-12ᵇ 3), the genaral sciences studied by him and the respective tradition of each of them (vol. i, fols. 12ᵇ 3-20ᵇ 6). The rest of the text sets forth the main content of the work, viz. the traditions of Buddhist doctrines, directions and orders accepted by the author. It falls into an account of the traditions of various teachings of philosophy (*mtshan-ñid-gyi-theg-pa*—vol. i, fols. 21ᵃ 1-50ᵃ 6), of Tantrism (*sṅags-gyi-theg-pa*—vol. i, fol. 50ᵃ 6-vol. iv, fol. 143ᵇ 4), and of individual texts of the *bKa'-'gyur* (vol. iv, fols. 143ᵇ 4-362ᵇ 4). The second section—the largest and the most important—includes *inter alia* an exposition of the traditions of the study of the texts written by various Tibetan philosophers and religious leaders (vol. ii, fols. 42ᵇ 3-156ᵇ 4). However, despite the large number of historical personages mentioned, this extensive work has little historical significance, for it gives nothing more than mere names of these persons. This work nonetheless has some bibliographical importance as it gives the titles of a very large number of works along with the names of their authors and sometimes even the circumstances under which they were compiled. In particular, we find, in this work, materials on the history of compilation of the catalogues of the *bKa'-'gyur*[576] and of 100 treatises of Atīśa[577] (vol. i, fols. 44ᵃ 1-49ᵇ 5) and other data of similar nature.

Another equally large work of this type is the *thob-yig* bearing the title *Zab-pa-daṅ-rgya-che-pa'i-dam-pa'i-chos-kyi-thob-yig-gsal-ba'i-me-loṅ* (or *Thob-yig-gsal-ba'i-me-loṅ*), which is also in four volumes (having 297, 315, 319 and 303 folios).[578] The author

---

states that this work was started by the author in the 49th year of his life in the Wood-Serpent year (1665) and completed in the 54th year of his life in the Iron-Dog year (1670).

575. The autobiography of Paṇ-chen bLo-bzaṅ-chos-gyi-rgyal-mtshan, and its supplement written by his incarnation, the second Paṇ-chen-bla-ma bLo-bzaṅ-ye-śes, are mentioned earlier (note 564). Besides, his biography is also given in the *Lam-rim-bla-ma-brgyud-pa'i-rnam-thar* (pt. ii, fols. 44ᵇ 1-118ᵃ 6). The dates of his birth and death are also given in the "Chronological Tables".

576. See *Thob-yig-gaṅgā'i-chu-rgyun*, vol. iv, fols. 143ᵇ 4-146ᵃ 5.

577. *Ibid.*, vol. i, fols. 44ᵃ 1-49ᵇ 5, where 103 treatises are enumerated. Of these, only the first 26 are the works of Atīśa himself (see *ibid.*, fol 45ᵃ 1-2).

578. This work is published in Peking. Its full title is *Śākya'i-btsun-pa-blo-bzaṅ-'phrin-las-kyi-zab-pa-daṅ-rgya-che-ba'i-dam-pa'i-chos-kyi-thob-yig-gsal-ba'i-me-loṅ*. Copies of this publication are available in the Institute of Peoples of Asia (*Old Collection*, No. 287-290) and in the library of the University of Leningrad.

of this work was bLo-bzaṅ-'phrin-las (b. 1642), the pupil of the Fifth Dalai Lama ; the latter had given him the rank of Dsa-ya-paṇḍi-ta-khu-thug-thu (see vol.iv, fols. 298ᵇ 6-299ᵃ 1).[579] This work, compiled by bLo-bzaṅ-'phrin-las in 1702,[580] was first taken up in Europe by Academician V. P. Vasil'ev[581] who rated it very highly—though not without sufficient grounds. In its structure, the *Thob-yig-gsal-ba'i-me-loṅ* is almost fully identical to the aforementioned *thob-yig* of the Fifth Dalai Lama. Here, too, the introductory part (vol. i, fols. 1-57ᵃ 1) is followed by an account of the consecration of the author in dGe-sloṅ-s etc. (vol. i, fols. 57ᵃ 1-60ᵇ 1). Then follow the section on general information (vol. i, fols. 60ᵇ 1-122ᵇ 3) and that on specially Buddhistic disciplines,—which covers the entire remaining part of the text (vol. i, fols. 122ᵇ 3-vol. iv, fol. 289) except the Conclusion and Colophon (vol. iv, fols. 289-303). The main section, i.e. the section on Buddhist disciplines, also falls into an account of the traditions of various philosophical doctrines (vol. i, fols. 122ᵇ 3-174ᵇ 3), of Tantrism (vol. i, fol. 174ᵇ 3-vol. iv, fol. 175ᵃ 3) and of various texts in the *bKa'-'gyur* (vol. iv, fols. 175ᵃ 3-289). Besides, as in the *thob-yig* of the Fifth Dalai Lama, the section on Tantrism also expounds the traditions of the study of original Tibetan texts (vol. ii, fol. 259ᵃ 5-vol. iv, fol. 175ᵃ 3). However, the present work is distinguished from the previous one,—which has served not only as a model but also as a source for our author,[582]—primarily in that here the original Tibetan literature has been given a more important place. In this work, the Tibetan literature has been divided into two periods : the literature before Tsoṅ-kha-pa and that after him. The work gives first a brief biography of a Tibetan author and then a list of his works and that of the persons, through whom the knowledge of these works reached the compiler of the *thob-yig*. Sometimes, bLo-bzaṅ-'phrin-las does not limit himself to the biographies of authors only and also gives

---

579. See *Thob-yig-gsal-ba'i-me-loṅ*, vol. iv, colophon. The date of birth of bLo-bzaṅ--'phrin-las has been established on the basis of his own statement that he composed his work in the 61st year of his life (A.D. 1702).

580. See *Thob-yig-gsal-ba'i-me-loṅ*, vol. iv, colophon (fols. 299ᵇ 4-303ᵃ 4), which gives not only the cyclic date of the composition of the work—Water-Horse year (A.D. 1702)—but also the numbers of years that had expired up to this date from the time of various events.

581. V. P. Vasil'ev, *O nekotorykh knigakh, otnosyashchikhsya k istorii buddizma, v biblioteke kazanskogo universiteta*, [On Some Books, Relating to the History of Buddhism, in the Library of the University of Kazan]—"Uchenye zapiski Akademii nauk", vol. iii, no. 1, pp. 7-8.

582. See *Thob-yig-gsal-ba'i-me-loṅ*, vol. iv, colophon (fol. 299ᵇ 2), which mentions the work of the Fifth Dalai Lama (*Thob-yig-gaṅgā'i-chu-rgyun*) as one of the sources of the present text.

short biographical data on persons who are regarded as their previous incarnations.[583] The biographical materials given by bLo-bzaṅ-'phrin-las do not always have the same importance. Sometimes, as he has himself confessed, he could not search out the biographies required by him and had, therefore, to be satisfied with the most superficial data.[584] But somehow or the other, he does manage to give biographical data on about hundred persons. And this undoubtedly imparts to his work no small significance as a bio-bibliographical reference work of its kind. The tendency of bLo-bzaṅ-'phrin-las to fill his work with various historical data is also manifest in the brief account of the history of Buddhism, with which he has prefaced the section on the texts in the *bKa'-'gyur*.[585] Generally speaking, however, this work also cannot be assigned to Tibetan historical literature without certain reservations, for it gives almost no information on general history. The biographical data given are also limited to the minimum necessary for a historical survey of Tibetan literature. Other *thob-yig*-s do not contain even this much of data and one can therefore assume that the *thob-yig*-s are not usually given proper place in the Tibetan bibliographies of historical literature. Nevertheless, it would be unfair to ignore completely the historical importance of *thob-yig*-s, for they contain much interesting material not only for characterizing the academic activity of their compilers but also for a history of Tibetan literature and Tibetan traditions in general.

10. Reference Works

Apart from all the genres of Tibetan literature just surveyed by us, there are two extremely useful works of reference from the pen of kLoṅ-rdol-bla-ma Ṅag-dbaṅ-blo-bzaṅ (b. 1719)—the author of a number of remarkable reference books. Like other reference works of this author, both these works are known by a common name *miṅ-gi-graṅs* (i.e. "List of Names") or *mtshan-tho* (i.e. "List of Titles").

One of these works, entitled *bsTan-'dsin-gyi-skyes-bu-rgya-bod-du-byon-ba'i-miṅ-gi-graṅs*, contains a list of the teachers of bKa'-gdams-pa sect (fols. 1ᵃ 6-4ᵃ 6), a list of the incarnations of Bu-ston Rin-chen-grub (fols. 4ᵃ 6-4ᵇ 4) and Tsoṅ-kha-pa (fols. 4ᵇ 4-5ᵇ 5), a list of the teachers and pupils of Tsoṅ-kha-pa (fols. 5ᵇ 5-9ᵃ 3) and the pupils of these latter (fols. 9ᵃ 3-11ᵃ 5), a list of the incarnations of Panchen Lamas (fols. 11ᵃ 5-11ᵇ 4) and Heads of the dGa'-ldan monastery (fols. 11ᵇ 4-13ᵇ 4), lists of the distinguished

583. See *Thob-yig-gsal-ba'i-me-loṅ*, vol. iii, fols. 248ᵇ 1-253ᵃ 5, and vol. iv, fols. 10ᵃ 3-21ᵃ 6, 21ᵃ 6-30ᵇ 3 and 30ᵇ 3-78ᵇ 3.

584. See *ibid.*, vol. iii, fols. 26ᵇ 1-4, 148ᵇ 1-3 etc.

585. See *ibid.*, vol. iv, fols. 175ᵃ 2-196ᵃ 6.

leaders of the most important Tibetan monasteries of dGa'-ldan, bKra-śis-lhun-po, 'Bras-spuṅs, Se-ra and others according to their *datsans*, (fols. 13^{b} 4-19^{b} 1), a list of the incarnations of Dalai Lamas (fols. 19^{b} 1-21^{a} 4) and a number of other hierarchs of the Tibetan Buddhism (fols. 21^{a} 4-25^{b} 6), a list of the Heads of Chab-mdo monastery (fols. 26^{a} 1-27^{b} 6), lists of most important leaders of the bKa'-rgyud-pa sect according to its sub-sects—'Bri-guṅ-pa, 'Brug-pa, sTag-luṅ-pa and Ka-rma-pa—and particularly, the lists of incarnations of both the "black-cap" (*shwa-nag-pa*) and "red-cap" (*shwa-dmar-pa*) hierarchs of Ka-rma-pa (fols. 27^{b} 6-30^{b} 2), a genealogy of the famous dynasty of rulers and scholars from Sa-skya monastery (fols. 30^{b} 2-31^{b} 6), a list of the incarnations of Tshar-chen bLo-gsal (fols. 31^{b} 6-32^{a} 4), a list of the seven successive representatives of the Śaṅs-pa-bka'-rgyud tradition (fols. 32^{a} 4-32^{b} 5) and lastly, a list of the 25 pupils of Padmasambhava (fols. 32^{b} 5-33^{a} 4). In many cases, along with the names of the leaders of the Buddhist Order, the dates of their birth and death, the names of their parents, the places of their births, etc. are also mentioned. This work comprises the 22nd book (*za*) of the Complete Works of kLoṅ-rdol-bla-ma published in Kun-bde-gliṅ monastery in Lhasa and also in Peking. In the Lhasa edition it occupies 33 folios, and in the Peking edition it covers 31 folios of the usual Tibetan format.[586]

The other work entitled *bsTan-pa'i-spyin-bdag-byuṅ-tshul-gyi-miṅ-gi-graṅs* contains brief information on Indian and somewhat more detailed information on ancient Tibetan kings who had patronized Buddhism (fols. 1^{b} 3-9^{b} 4), brief information on the Chinese emperors including the Mongolian dynasty (fols. 9^{b} 4-12^{b} 2), a list of the representatives of the largest feudal dynasties which had ruled Tibet—Sa-skya-pa, sNe-gdoṅ-pa or Phag-mo-gru-pa, and Rin-spuṅs-pa (fols. 12^{b} 2-15^{b} 2)—and finally a report on the transition of power to the palace of the Dalai Lama (dGa'-ldan-pho-braṅ) and a list of the regents, which indicates the work done by them for the welfare of the Buddhist Order (fols. 15^{b} 2-19^{a} 1). In the end is given the traditional division of the Buddhist era into cycles of five-hundred years ; the number of years expired from this era to the Fire-Hen year of the xiii cycle (i.e. up to 1777) when this work was begun is also mentioned (fols. 19^{a} 1-20^{a} 4). This work forms the 23rd book (*'a*) in the Complete Works of kLoṅ-rdol-bla-ma, and occupies 20 folios in the Kun-bde-gliṅ edition and 19 folios in the Peking edition.

---

586. The Institute of Peoples of Asia has both the editions of the Collected Works of kLoṅ-rdol-bla-ma : the Kun-bde-gliṅ edition in the *Tsybikov Collection* (No. 20) and in the *Nova* collection (the former is an incomplete copy ; both the works surveyed here are wanting in it) ; and the Peking edition in the *Old Collection* (No. 311^{B}). All our references are to the Kun-bde-gliṅ edition.

Both these works were probably compiled from individual notes and extracts of chronological and genealogical order, which the author might have made in the course of his study of Tibetan historical literature. Such notes made for one's memory are called *brjed-tho* in Tibetan and consist of most diverse topics including the historical ones. As an example, one may mention the collection of such notes entitled *brJed-tho-sna-tshogs*, i.e. "Various Notes" available in the 5th volume of the Complete Works of Cha-har-dge-bśes bLo-bzaṅ-tshul-khrims.[587] In this collection, which covers 15 folios, we find, in addition to the notes on individual problems of philosophy and religion, a short list of the principal dates of the life of Atīśa (fol. 4^b 2-6), information on the seventeen most important feudal dynasties of Tibet (fols. 6^b 6-9^a 2), information on the conquest of Tibet by Gushi [Gu-śri] Khan and on the dynasty founded by the latter (fols. 9^a 2-10^a 2), information on the ancestors of Genghiz, on the principal dates of his life and on his descendants, on the Mongolian rulers in China (fols. 10^a 2-12^b 3), various historical notes (fols. 12^b 3-13^a 3) and finally, the chronological lists of the emperors of the Ming and Tsing dynasties of China (fols. 13^a 3-14^a 6). Such notes may also be found in the works of other authors.

11. Works on Various Individual Topics

Lastly, in Tibetan language, one also comes across works devoted to the exposition of individual historical events—the so-called *lo-rgyus* ("history" or "historical account"), *gdam-rgyud* (legend), etc. However, we shall not take these up here, and shall only remark that under precisely these names, there figure in Tibetan language, numerous works which are purely narrative in character and which have either no relation or a very distant relation to history.

587. See the copy of the Peking edition of the Collected Works of Cha-har-dge-bśes bLo-bzaṅ-tshul-khrims available in the Institute of Peoples of Asia (*Nova*).

Chapter Four

HISTORICO-BIBLIOGRAPHICAL SURVEYS OF THE TIBETAN BUDDHIST CANON

The descriptions of both the Tibetan canonical collections of translated literature,—viz., the catalogues of the *bKa'-'gyur* (*bKa'-'gyur-ro-cog-gi-dkar-chag*) and *bsTan-'gyur* (*bsTan-'gyur-ro-cog-gi-dkar-chag*)—should also, to a certain extent, be regarded as historical works of Tibet.

The earliest catalogues of this type date back to the period of the initial spread of Buddhism in Tibet. But since these are not extant, it is difficult to say as to what extent these early works contained any historical information.

We learn from the Tibetan sources that during the reign of the king Sad-na-legs (son of the king Khri-sroṅ-lde'u-btsan), the translator Ka-pa dPal-brtsegs, jointly with Chos-kyi-sñiṅ-po and others, compiled the earliest[588] catalogue of the canonical literature. This catalogue lists the texts available in the palace of 'Phaṅ-thaṅ-ka-med, and has accordingly come to be known as the *dKar-chags 'Phaṅ-thaṅ-ma*. This work has, however, not come down to us. This was soon followed by another catalogue, known as *dKar-chag lDan-dkar-ma*,[589]—a catalogue of the texts in the palace of sToṅ-thaṅ ldan-dkar—compiled by the same translator (dPal-brtsegs) jointly with 'Khon gLu'i-dbaṅ-po

---

588. The Tibetan writers differ on this point. A great majority of tnem regards the *dKar-chags 'Phaṅ-thaṅ-ma* as the earliest catalogue of the Tibetan Canon—see *Thob-yig-gaṅgā'i-chu-rgyun*, vol. iv, fol. 145ᵃ 1-2 ; the catalogue to the sNar-thaṅ edition of the *bKa'-'gyur*, fol. 24ᵃ 1-2 ; the catalogue to the sDe-dge edition of *bKa'-'gyur*, fol. 107ᵃ 3-6 ; and also the aforementioned work of Sum-pa-mkhan-po entitled *gSuṅ-rab-rnam-grags-chu'i-dri-ma-sel-byed-nor-bu-ke-ta-ka*, fol. 3ᵃ 2-3. According to others, however, the earliest catalogue is the *dKar-chag lDan-dkar-ma* (also sometimes written as *Lhan-dkar-ma*). One representative of this latter view is Bu-ston Rin-chen-grub. According to him, the catalogue was first compiled in the castle of sToṅ-thaṅ-ldan-dkar, then in bSam-yas-'chiṅ-bu, and thereafter in 'Phaṅ-thaṅ-ka-med (see Bu-ston, *Chos-'byuṅ*, fol. 241ᵇ 1-3). The former point of view being more prevalent, I stick to it.

589. See *Thob-yig-gaṅgā'i-chu-rgyun*, vol. iv, fol. 145ᵃ 2-3 ; the catalogue to the sNar-thaṅ edition of *bKa'-'gyur*, fol. 24ᵃ 3-4 ; the catalogue to the sDe-dge edition of the *bKa'-'gyur*, fol. 107ᵃ 6-7 ; *gSuṅ-rab-rnam-grags-chu'i-dri-ma-sel-byed-nor-bu-ke-ta-ka*, fols. 3-4. Cf. also Bu-ston, *Chos-'byuṅ*, fol. 142ᵃ 4-5.

and others. This catalogue is preserved in the *bsTan-'gyur*[590] under the title *Pho-brań-stoń-thań-ldan-dkar-gyi-bka'-dań-bstan-bcos-ro-cog-gi-dkar-chag*, but it is nothing more than a mere list of books (with the volume of work of their authors). Later, during the reign of Ral-pa-can (9th cent.), son of Sad-na-legs, a new catalogue was compiled. It was a résumé of the grand work of the special commission of Indian and Tibetan scholars engaged in editing and unifying (in respect of language) the then existing translations.[591] This catalogue, again, is not extant. It is possible that some more catalogues may also have appeared during this period, but we know nothing of these at present.

Many catalogues of the still later period, mentioned by the Tibetan authors, have also not come down to us—for instance, the catalogue of the collection of canonical literature of the sNar-thań monastery, compiled by bCom-ldan Rig-pa'i-ral-gri[592] (or bCom-ldan-rig-ral, as he is briefly called—or simply Rig-ral—who lived in the second half of the 13th and the beginning of the 14th century[593]); the catalogue of the *bKa'-'gyur* of the monastery of Tshal-guń-thań, compiled by the scholar-historiographer,

---

590. See *bsTan-'gyur*, Peking edition, mDo-'grel, vol. cxxvi (cho), fols. 352b 5-373a 8. The catalogue is dated 'Dragon year'.

591. See Bu-ston, *Chos-'byuń*, fols. 144b 6-145a 4 (for a translation, see E. Obermiller, *History of Buddhism*, pp. ii, pp. 196-197), the catalogue of the sDe-dge edition of the *bKa'-'gyur*, fols. 107a 7-107b 2, *gSuń-rab-rnam-grags-chu'i-dri-ma-sel-byed-nor-bu-ke-ta-ka*, fol. 3a 4-5.

592. The *Deb-ther-rgya-mtsho* (vol. i, fol. 9b 1) and *dPe-rgyun-dkon-pa-'ga'-shig-gi-tho-yig* (fol. 3a 5-6) mention two catalogues of the Tibetan Canon compiled by bCom-ldan Rig-pa'i-ral-gri—namely, the catalogue to the *bKa'-'gyur* entitled *bKa'-'gyur-dkar-chag-ñi-ma'i-'od-zer*, and the catalogue to both the *bKa'-'gyur* and *bsTan-'gyur* entitled *bKa'-bstan-dkar-chag-bstan-pa-rgyas-pa*. Besides, the first of these two catalogues is mentioned in the *Thob-yig-gańgā'i-chu-rgyun* (vol. iv, fol. 146a 1), in the catalogue of the sNar-thań edition of the *bKa'-'gyur* (fol. 26a 3-4) and in the *gSuń-rab-rnam-grags-chu'i-dri-ma-sel-byed-nor-bu-ke-ta-ka* (fol. 3b 1). The other is referred to in the *Deb-ther-sńon-po* (vol. i, fol. 177a 5).

593. Brief biographical data on bCom-ldan Rig-pa'i-ral-gri are given in the *Deb-ther-sńon-po* (vol. i, fols. 176b 3-177a 5). His pupil, 'Jams-pa'i-dbyańs, was at one time a Lama in the court of Buyantu Khan (reigned 1312-20). From there, 'Jams-pa'i-dbayńs despatched to his teacher various materials required for preparing a manuscript copy of the Canon, thus reconciling with his teacher who was displeased with him. See *Deb-ther-sńon-po*, vol. i, fol. 177a 1-4; cf. also *Grub-mtha'-śel-gyi-me-loń*, book 12, fol. 5a 4-5 (this passage was published and translated by S. C. Das; see S. C. Das, *Contributious on ...*, —JASB, vol. li, pt. i, 1882, pp. 61, 69); and *Hor-chos-'byuń* (G. Huth, *Geschichte des Buddhismus*

Tshal-pa Si-tu dGe-ba'i-blo-gros ; the catalogue of both the collections (*bsTan-'gyur* and *bKa'-'gyur*), compiled by one dbUs-pa bLo-gsal,[594] the catalogue of the *bsTan-'gyur*, compiled by some Thugs-sras-rin-chen-rnam-rgyal,[595] and published in sNe-gdoṅ by the order of Tā'i Si-tu Byaṅ-chub-rgyal-mtshan (b. 1302) ; the catalogue of the *bKa'-'gyur*, compiled by one Thugs-rje-dpal[596] jointly with other scholars and issued in rGyal-rtse by the ruler of this province, Rab-brtan-kun-bzaṅ-'phags (end of 14th-beginning of 15th cent.).[597]

---

in der Mongolei, vol. i, p. 105 [text], and vol. ii, p. 165 [translation]). This means that bCom-ldan Rig-pa'i-ral-gri worked in the second decade of the 14th century. On the other hand, the Tibetan sources indicate that he composed his epigram on 'Phags-pa-bla-ma about A.D. 1267 (see *Hor-chos-'byuṅ*, *ibid.*, vol. i, pp. 98-99, where this epigram has been quoted along with 'Phags-pa-bla-ma'*s* reply to it).

In the translation made by G. Huth (*ibid.*, vol. ii, p. 155), the first line of the epigram is distorted. A correct translation on the basis of the Mongolian translation was, however, given by B. Ya. Vladimirtsov (B. Ya. Vladimirtsov, *Nadpisi na skalakh khalkhaskogo Tsoktu-taidzhi*. Stat'ya vtoraya,—"Izvestiya AN SSSR", 1927, p. 238). Thus, bCom-ldan Rig-pa'i-ral-gri worked from the second half of the 13th century to early 14th century.

594. According to the *Deb-ther-sṅon-po* (vol. i, fol. 177^a 4ff.), dbUs-pa bLo-gsal was a pupil of bCon-ldan Rig-pa'i-ral-gri and 'Jams-pa'i-dbyaṅs, and was one of the most active builders of the sNar-thaṅ collection of translations of the Buddhist Canon. The catalogue compiled by him is mentioned in the catalogue of the Co-ne edition of the *bsTan-'gyur* (fol. 238^a 2-4), in the *Deb-ther-rgya-mtsho* (vol. i, fol. 9^b 3), and in the *dPe-rgyun-dkon-pa-'ga'-shig-gi-tho-yig* (fol. 3^a 5).
595. This catalogue is mentioned in the *Deb-ther-rgya-mtsho* (fol. 9^b 2).
596. This catalogue is mentioned in the catalogue of the sNar-thaṅ edition of the *bKa'-'gyur* (fol. 26^b 1-2) and in the *gSuṅ-rab-rnam-grags-chu'i-dri-ma-sel-byed-nor-bu-ke-ta-ka* (fol. 3^b 3).
597. Some information on prince Rab-brtan-kum-bzaṅ-'phags, the ruler of the principality of rGyal-rtse, is given in the *rGyal-ba-lṅa-pa'i-deb-ther* (fol. 100^b 4-6; S. C. Das, *Contributions on* ,—JASB, vol. l, pt. i, 1881, p. 249). The author of this text, the Fifth Dalai Lama, opines that this prince had rendered greater services to Buddhism than all other princes of both the central provinces of Tibet. In particular, he was the admirer of the famous mKhas-grub dGe-legs-dpal-bzaṅ-po (1385-1438), the pupil of Tsoṅ-kha-pa, and he established the dPal-'khor-bde-chen monastery where he built the famous *suburgan* of bKra-śis-sgo-maṅ having many doors. (For a description of this monastery and *suburgan*, see G. Tsybikov, *Buddist-palomnik u svyatyn' Tibeta*, p. 380ff.).

There is, however, little doubt that in at least some of these old catalogues,—as in those of the modern times,—the systematic list of the canonical texts translated was accompanied by a more or less detailed historical, religious and philosophical introduction. In particular, the two catalogues *bKa'-'gyur-dkar-chag-ni-ma'i-'od-zer* and *bKa'-bstan-dkar-chag bstan-pa-rgyas-pa* compiled by bCom-ldan Rig-pa'i-ral-gri[598] are obviously of such type, for Bu-ston Rin-chen-grub, in his historical and bibliographical work, has frequently cited and reproduced the views of this author on the history of Buddhism in Tibet.[599] Both these catalogues—like those compiled by dbUs-pa bLo-gsal and Thugs-sras-rin-chen-rnam-rgyal, and like the catalogue of the *bsTan-'gyur* of the Sha-lu monastery compiled by the famous Bu-ston Rin-chen-grub—mention the *Brag-dgon-shabs-druṅ-dgon-mchog-bstan-pa-rab-rgyas*[600] among the Tibetan historical works. It is highly probable that many such catalogues were extant in Tibet, for some of these have served, in the eighteenth century, as handbooks for the compilation of new catalogues of various editions of the Canon.[601] The "List of Rare Books" mentions only the catalogues compiled by bCom-ldan Rig-pa'i-ral-gri and dbUs-pa bLo-gsal[602] in addition, however, to the earliest works mentioned above.

The Institute of Peoples of Asia, U.S.S.R., has, at present, four Tibetan catalogues ; namely, the catalogues of the sNar-thaṅ and sDe-dge editions of *bKa'-'gyur* and those of the Peking and Co-ne (or Co-ni) editions of the *bsTan-'gyur*.[603] The last one is, of course, in the same form in which it is included in the Complete Works of its author, i.e. in the form of an extensive historical and philosophical introduction to the Co-ne edition of *bsTan-'gyur* without the list of the texts included in this edition.

Of these, the most interesting from the historical point of view is the catalogue of

---

According to the *Vaiḍūrya-dkar-po* (fol. 21ᵃ 6), this *suburgan* was constructed in A.D. 1439.

598. See *supra* (note 593).

599. See Bu-ston, *Chos-'byuṅ*, fols. 151ᵇ 5 ff and 152ᵃ 2 ff (E. Obermiller, *History of Buddhism*, pt. ii, p. 211 ff).

600. See *Deb-ther-rgya-mtsho*, vol. i, fols. 9ᵃ 6-9ᵇ 5.

601. Thus, for instance, the catalogue of the Co-ne edition of the *bsTan-'gyur* contains many quotations (in verse) from the catalogue compiled by dbUs-pa bLo-gsal (fols. 238ᵃ 4-238ᵇ 1) and from the catalogue of the *bsTan-'gyur* of the Sha-lu monastery compiled by Bu-ston Rin-chen-grub (fols. 238ᵇ 5-240ᵃ 6).

602. See *dPe-rgyun-dkon-pa-'ga'-shig-gi-tho-yig*, fol. 3ᵃ 5-6.

603. Various indexes of the *bKa'-'gyur* and *bsTan-'gyur* enumerated from the catalogue (see I. J. Schmidt und Böhtlingk, *Verzeichniss der tibetischen Handschriften und Holzdrücke im Asiatischen Museum*, N 262-284) are catalogues on the European model, prepared in the *datsan*-s of Buryatia in 1830-1831 at the instance of P. L. Schilling von Constadt. These do not contain any historical introductions.

the Co-ne edition of *bsTan-'gyur*, bearing the title *bDe-bar-gśegs-pa'i-bka'i-dgoṅs-'grel-bstan-bcom-'gyur-ro-cog-par-du-sgrub-pa'i-tshul- las-ne-bar-brtsams- pa'i-gtam- yan-dag-par-brjod-pa-dkar-chag-yid-bshin-nor-bu'i-phriṅ-pa.* It was compiled in 1773 by the second 'Jam-dbyaṅs-bshad-pa, already known to us as dKon-mchog-'jigs-med-dbaṅ-po (1728-1791).[604] As has just been stated, this catalogue, without the list of the texts themselves, is included in the Complete Works of the author published at bLa-braṅ in Amdo, and covers 264 folios of the Tibetan format.[605] It is divided into six chapters (*le'u*), of which the first three form the general and the remaining three the special part. The contents of the general part are :

Chapter 1—On Buddha (fols. 4^a 1-20^b 6) ;

Chapter 2—On the Buddhist Doctrine (fols. 21^a 4-52^b 6) ; and

Chapter 3—On the history of Buddhism in India (fols. 53^a 5-108^b 5), Tibet (fols. 108^b 5-164^b 1), Śambhala (fols. 164^b 2-167^b 5), Khotan (fols. 167^b 5-170^a 3), Central provinces of China (fols. 170^a 3-182^a 2), and Mongolia (fols. 182^a 3-187^b 6).

The second, special part contains :

Chapter 4—On the founder of the Co-ne edition of *bsTan-'gyur*, the princess Rin-chen-dpal-'dsom [the widow of the Co-ne prince, 'Jam-dbyaṅs-nor-bu (1703-1751)],[606] on the grandson of the last bsTan-sruṅ-tshe-riṅ (b. 1744),[607] including a brief description of the province of Co-ne (fols. 188^b 5-189^b 3), information on the origin of Co-ne

604. See colophon, fol. 264^a 4-6.

605. See the copy of the Collected Works of dKon-mchog-'jigs-med-dbaṅ-po available in the Institute of Peoples of Asia (*Baradiin Collection*, No. 1), vol. v (*ca*).

606. The biography of prince 'Jam-dbyaṅs-nor-bu occupies folios 218^b 3-225^a 6 in the text surveyed here. According to this biography, 'Jam-dbyaṅs-nor-bu was born in the Water-Sheep year (A.D. 1703) during the reign of the emperor K'ang-hsi, and he died in the Iron-Sheep year (A.D. 1751) or about the same time. These very dates are given in the *Deb-ther-rgya-mtsho* (vol. iii, fols. 141^a 3 and 141^b 6), which gives short information on him and on other princes of Co-ne. Besides, the date of birth of 'Jam-dbyaṅs-nor-bu (the year of the reign of K'ang-hsi), which is not correctly given in the catalogue of the Co-ne *bsTan-'gyur*, has been rectified in the *Deb-ther-rgya-mtsho*. Cf. the report of the catalogue of the Co-ne *bsTan-'gyur* that the younger brother of 'Jam-dbyaṅs-nor-bu, bLo-bzaṅ-bstan-pa'i-rgyal-mtshan, was born in the 47th year of the reign of K'ang-hsi, in the Earth-mouse year (1708)—fol. 226^b 6.

607. Brief biographical data on bsTan-sruṅ-tshe-riṅ are given in the catalogue being surveyed here (fols. 234^a 4-234^b 5) and in the *Deb-ther-rgya-mtsho* (vol. iii, fols. 142^a 2-142^b 4). The *Deb-ther-rgya-mtsho* mentions the existence of a biography

princes (fols. 189b 3-190a 6), dynastic history of Co-ne kingdom (fols. 190a 6-231a 1), an account of the virtues of the founders and sponsors of the publication, the princess Rin-chen-dpal-'dsom and the prince bsTan-sruṅ-tshe-riṅ (fols. 231a 1-236a 2) ;

Chapter 5—A description of the publication itself—establishment of the date of its publication [according to our calendar, it was started in 1753 and completed in 1773 (fols. 236a 3-237b 4)],[608] information on the sources of the publication including a brief history of the compilation of the Tibetan *bsTan-'gyur* (fols. 237b 4-241a 3), an account of the work done on the Co-ne edition of *bsTan-'gyur* (fols. 241a 3-243b 2), and a detailed list of all the texts included in this work, i.e. a catalogue in the real sense of this word, from which only the Introduction and Concluding verses have been left out in the Complete Works of the author (fols. 243b 2-244b 5) ; and

Chapter 6—Concluding words about the necessity and use of the publication, good wishes (*smon-lam*) and desires (*bsṅo-ba*) (fols. 245a 2-263b 6).

In its character, this work essentially is very close to the *chos-'byuṅ-s* ("histories of religion") which, too, often contain, as we have seen, surveys of canonical literature.[609] But unlike the *chos-'byuṅ-s*, it contains not a survey of the Canon in general, but a study of one specific edition of the Canon along with a history of this edition. This work is particularly interesting and important because it gives us the dynastic history of the Co-ne kingdom ; there being very few sources for a history of this region.

The introduction to the catalogue of the sDe-dge edition of *bKa'-'gyur* also contains extremely interesting historical information in spite of the fact that this introduction is, on the whole, more religious and philosophical in nature than historical. As stated in this introduction, the publication of the *bKa'-'gyur* in sDe-dge was taken up in

---

of this prince and a history of the princely family, compiled by one Mu-ṇe-dpon-slob Saṅs-rgyas-dpal-bzaṅ under the title *dBon-rab-rtogs-brjod-mkhas-pa'i-mdses-rgyan* (*ibid.*, fol. 142b 4-5). This work has, however, not come down to us. The date of birth of bsTan-sruṅ-tshe-riṅ—the Wood-Mouse year of the xii cycle (A.D. 1744)—is given in both the texts.

608. The publication was undertaken in the 17th year of (the reign of) Ch'ien-lung in the Water-Hen year, 336 years after the death of Tsoṅ-kha-pa (A.D. 1419, Earth-Pig year)—fols. 236b 6-237a 2. Besides, the catalogue indicates the numbers of years that had passed from the various eras of *nirvāṇa*. Thus, on conversion to our calendar, it comes out that the catalogue was taken up for publication in A.D. 1753. The year of composition of the catalogue, i.e. A.D. 1773, should be regarded as the date of its completion.

609. See *supra*.

1729[610] under the orders of the sDe-dge prince, bsTan-pa-tshe-riṅ (b. 1678)[611] and was completed in five years (in 1733).[612] A catalogue to this edition was compiled in 1733[613] by Si-tu gTsug-lag-chos-kyi-snaṅ-ba (b. 1700),[614] the celebrated author of an extensive and most authoritative Tibetan grammar. This catalogue bears a long title: *bDe-bar-gśegs-pa'i-bka'-gaṅs-can-gyi-brdas-draṅs-pa'i- phyi- mo'i- tshogs-ji-sñid-pa-bar- du- bsgrubs-pa'i-tshul-las-ñe-bar-brtsams-pa'i-gtam-bzaṅ- po-blo-ldan-mos-pa'i-kunda-yoṅs-su- kha-byed-ba'i-zla-'od-gshon-nu'i-'khri-śin,*[615] and covers 171 folios of large format. It is divided

---

610. See the catalogue referred to (fol. 106[b] 1-2),—which states that the publication of the sDe-dge edition of the *bKa'-'gyur* was started in the year of the Earth-Hen. This year, which in Sanskrit is called *Saumya* and which is the 7th year of the reign of Yung-cheng, is the 52nd year of life of the patron of the publication, the sDe-dge prince bsTan-pa-tshe-riṅ. On conversion to our calendar, this date comes to A.D. 1729.
611. The date of birth of bsTan-pa-tshe-riṅ is based on a reference in the text (quoted in the previous note) that the 7th year of the reign of Yung-cheng [reigned from 1723 to 1735] is the 52nd year of the life of this prince.
612. See the catalogue referred to (fol. 112[a] 1),—which directly states that the publication of the *bKa'-'gyur* in sDe-dge took five years from the Earth-Hen year (1729) to the Water-Ox year (1733).
613. See the colophon of the catalogue (fol. 171[a] 1-3),—which states that it was compiled in the year of the Water-Ox, 2613 years after the *nirvāṇa* of Buddha (which, according to the *Pad-dkar-shal-luṅ*, is dated 881 B.C.). On conversion to our calendar, this date comes to A,D. 1733.
614. The date of birth of Si-tu gTsug-lag-chos-kyi-snaṅ-ba is taken from the colophon of his grammar, entitled *Yul-gaṅs-can-pa'i-brda-yaṅ-dag-par-spyor-ba'i-bstan-bcos-kyi-bye-brag-sum-cu-pa-daṅ-rtags-kyi-'jug-pa'i-gshuṅ- gi-rnam-par- bśad-pa- mkhas-pa'i-mgul-rgyan-mu-tig-phreṅ-mdses* (better known by its short title, *Si-tu'i-sum-rtags*). This grammar was published (unfortunately, with numerous misprints) by S. C. Das in his *An Introduction to the Grammar of the Tibetan Language with the Texts of Situhi Sum-rtags, Dag-je sal-wai me-long and Situhi shal-lung* (Darjeeling, 1915). The colophon of this grammar states that it was written in the Wood-Mouse year of the xii cycle (i.e. in A.D. 1744) in the 45th year of the life of the author (see *Si-tu'i-sum-rtags*, fol. 119[a] 3; S. C. Das, *An Introduction...*, p. 88, 1.13). This implies that the author was born in 1700.
615. This catalogue forms a special, supplementary volume of the sDe-dge edition of the *bKa'-'gyur*. A copy of this edition of the *bKa'-'gyur* is available in the

into five chapters (without taking into account the introductory verses and colophon). The first chapter gives a survey of the Buddhist doctrine, in general, and of its main trends or cycles—*chos-'khor* (*dharmacakra*)—and also narrates the legends as to how the Buddhist Canon of *Hīnayāna* and *Mahāyāna* was compiled (fols. 4^a 2-50^a 5). The second chapter gives a brief history of Buddhism in India and Tibet (fols 50^b 1-98^a 7). Chapter 3 tells us about the founder and sponsor of this publication—the sDe-dge prince, bsTan-pa-tshe-riṅ—and also as to how this publication was accomplished by him (fols. 98^b 1-112^b 7). The story of bsTan-pa-tshe-riṅ includes a short account of the sDe-dge region (fols. 99^a 5-101^a 5), information on the lineage of the royal family of this region (fols. 101^a 5-103^a 4), and a description of the virtues of the prince bsTan-pa-tshe-riṅ (fols. 103^a 4-105^b 7). The description of the publication itself tells us about the date when it was begun (fols. 106^a 1-107^a 2), its sources, history of Tibetan *bKa'-'gyur* (fols. 107^a 2-111^a 6), and how the *bKa'-'gyur* was published in sDe-dge (fols. 111^a 6-112^a 6). The fourth chapter contains the catalogue itself (fols. 113^a 1-157^a 7). The fifth chapter contains the concluding words about the necessity and use of the publication of *bKa'-'gyur* and expresses good wishes and desires (fols. 157^b 1-170^b 5). Of the greater interest from the historical standpoint is the third chapter which gives separate—though very brief—data on the history of sDe-dge and an exposition of the history of the Tibetan *bKa'-'gyur*.

Interesting historical material, especially on the history of *bKa'-'gyur*, may be found in the catalogue to the sNar-thaṅ edition of *bKa'-'gyur*, which was brought out in 1730[616] by the order of the well-known regent of Tibet, Mi-dbaṅ Pho-lha-pa bSod-nams-stobs-rgyas (reigned from 1728 to 1748).[617] This catalogue is entitled : *bKa'-'gyur-*

Institute of Peoples of Asia (*Old Collection*, Nos. 1-101). The catalogue is available under No. 101.

616. See the catalogue referred to, fols. 55^b 4 ff and 62^a 3-4. The entire voluminous publication was brought out in an unusually short period—in one-and-a-half year, from the 26th day of the 8th month of the Iron-Dog year (A.D. 1730) to the 26th day of the 1st month of the Water-Mouse year (A.D. 1732). This is why this publication has come to be known as the "Magic Vehicle" (*rJu-'phrul-gyi-śiṅ-rta*)—see *ibid.*, fols. 59^b 6-60^a 1.

The *gSuṅ-rabs- rnam- dag- chu'i-dri-ma- sel-byed- nor-bu- ke-ta-ka* (fol. 3^b 6) mentions the year of the beginning of the publication as Iron-Hen year (*lcags-bya*) instead of the Iron-Dog year (*lcags-khyi*), which, in all probability, is a simple misprint.

617. The dates of the reign of Pho-lha-pa bSod-nams-stobs-rgyas along with brief information on his work are given by Sum-pa-mkhan-po (see *dPag-bsam-ljon-bzaṅ*, fol. 108^a 3-7 ; S. C. Das, *Pag Sam Jon Zang*, p. 166),—who states that he

rin-po-che'i-gsuṅ-bar-srid-gsum-rgyan-gcig-rdsu-'phrul- śiṅ-rta'i-dkar-chag-ṅo-mtshar- bkod-pa-rgya-mtsho'i-lde-mig.[618] Leaving aside the supplements which have separate pagination, it covers 124 folios of broad format. This catalogue is incomplete; the fourth, concluding section and the colophon are wanting.[619] No definite information is available on its author. As regards the three sections available of the catalogue, the first section states the necessity of the edition (fols. 3^a 2-5^a 6), the second section deals with the deeds of Buddha and the history of the spread of Buddhism in India and Tibet (fols. 5^a 6-22^a 4), and the third (the largest) section gives the history of the formation of the Tibetan *bKa'-'gyur* (fols. 22^a 6-26^b 6), information on the founder of its sNar-thaṅ edition, Mi-dbaṅ-bsod-nams-rgyal (fols. 26^b 6-50^a 4), the history of this edition (fols. 50^a -81^b 7), the catalogue of the edition (fols. 82^a 1-117^a 6), concluding words on the use of the edition (fols. 117^a 6-121^b 7) and good wishes (121^b 7-124^a 2).

As regards the catalogue to the Peking edition of the *bsTan-'gyur*, we shall not discuss its contents here because it is a catalogue only in the narrow sense of this word.

---

was the regent of Tibet for 21 years from the Earth-Monkey year (A.D. 1728) to the year of his death, viz. the Earth-Dragon year of the xiii cycle (A.D. 1748). In European literature, information on him may be found in the writings of Rockhill (see W. W. Rockhill, *The Dalai Lamas of Lhasa and Their Relations with the Manchu Emperors of China*, 1644-1908,—"T'oung Pao", vol. xi, 1910, pp. 42-44) and Tsybikov (see G. Tsybikov, *Buddist-palomnik u svyatyn' Tibeta*, 241-242). He has also been mentioned by Georgi (see Georgi, *Alphabetum Tibetanum*, 1762, pp. 338-339; also quoted in : F. Hackmann, *Izvestiya o geograficheskom, istoricheskom...*—"Sobranie sochinenii vybrannykh iz mesyatseslovov na raznye gody", pt. v, St. Petersburg, 1790, pp. 262-263). Bogle, too, had heard of him (see C. R. Markham, *Narratives of the Mission of George Bogle to Tibet and of the Journey of Thomas Manning to Lhasa*, London, 1879, p. 194).

618. This catalogue forms a special volume of the sNar-thaṅ edition of *bKa'-'gyur*. A copy of this edition of the *bKa'-'gyur* is also available in the Institute of Peoples of Asia.

619. Like many other Tibetan works, the entire text of this catalogue is divided into subjects (*sa-bcad*). One folio in the beginning (fol. 3^a 1) gives the most general division into four parts or chapters, namely : 1. *dgos-pa-brjod-pa* (an exposition of the need [of the publication]), 2. *spyir-bstan-pa* (general remarks), 3. *bye-brag-tu-bśad-pa* (special exposition), and 4. *mjug-bsdu-pa* (conclusion). This last, fourth part is wanting in the text. It is, however, difficult to understand what this "conclusion" might have contained, for the purpose of the "conclusion"

Besides, a fine description of its contents has already been given by P. Cordier.[620] We shall restrict ourselves only to a few remarks on the author of this catalogue and on the date of its compilation. As is well known, the catalogue of the Peking edition of *bsTan-'gyur* was published under the title *bsTan-bcos-'gyur-ro-cog-gi-dkar-chag-'jig-rten-gsum-gyi-bde-skyid-pad-tshal-bshad-pa'i-ñin-byed* (145 fols.)[621] in 1724,[622] but this was a simple reproduction of a much earlier Tibetan work. The colophon of the catalogue indicates that its author was Za-hor-gyi-ban-rgan-gdoṅ-drug-sñems-pa'i-laṅ-tsho, who wrote this work under the orders of sDe-srid Saṅs-rgyas-rgya-mtsho (1653-1703) in the Earth-Dragon year, 2648 years after the birth of Buddha (i.e. in A.D. 1688).[623] P. Cordier[624] does not elucidate this information of the colophon any further. Nonetheless, some clarification is certainly required, for the colophon gives only the conventional nick-name of the author and not his full name. In fact, the nick-name "Za-hor-ban-rgan" (The Old Monk from Za-hor) or simply "Za-hor-bande" (The Monk from Za-hor) is a special name (*gdoṅ-drug-sñems-pa'i-laṅ-tsho*)—one of the names given to the scholars of grammar and poetics. This clearly shows that the author of this catalogue is the Fifth Dalai Lama, bLo-bzaṅ-rgya-mtsho (1617-1682), for both these names are from among those attributed to this famous writer and are incidentally found in the colophons of his works.[625] In Tibetan literature, this catalogue is even known as the work of the Fifth Dalai Lama. This is also quite clear from the supplement to this catalogue itself, written by some Ṅag-dbaṅ-chos-rgya-mtsho in the temple of the sandal-wood Buddha in Peking,[626] and from the aforementioned catalogue of the Co-ne edition of *bsTan-'gyur*, which directly states that the catalogue entitled *'Jig-rten-gsum-gyi-bde-skyid-pad-tshal-'byed-pa'i-ñin-byed* was compiled by the Fifth Dalai Lama and that the Peking edition was based on it.[627] The Fifth Dalai Lama is, however, known to have died in 1682, i.e. six years before the date mentioned in

---

has been fully served by the last paragraph of the third part. It is possible that during the course of his work, the author might have changed the original plan of the work without incorporating the necessary changes on folio 3ᵃ 1.

620. P. Cordier, *Catalogue du fonds tibétain de la Bibliothique Nationale, IIème et IIIème parties. Index du bsTan-'gyur.* Paris, 1909-1915.

621. Appended in the form of a special volume to the Peking edition of the *bsTan-'gyur*, a copy of which is available in the Institute of Peoples of Asia.

622. See P. Cordier, *Catalogue du fonds tibétain...*, pt. iii, p. 534 et suiv.

623. See the catalogue referred to, fol. 145ᵃ 5-7.

624. See P. Cordier, *Catalogue du fonds tibétain...*, pt. iii, p. 536.

625. See *supra*, note 117.

626. See the supplement referred to, fol. 9ᵇ 2-3.

627. See the catalogue of the Co-ne edition of the *bsTan-'gyur*, fol. 240ᵇ 2-6.

the colophon of this catalogue. Therefore, if he really was its author,—as stated in the colophon and other sources,—one has only to surmise that the date of the colophon is not correct. It is possible that this date may have been distorted deliberately by the client of the work—sDe-srid Saṅs-rgyas-rgya-mtsho—who, as is known, tried to conceal the death of the Fifth Dalai Lama[628] for a long time from the Peking court.

628. See W. W. Rockhill, *The Dalai Lamas of Lhasa*,—"T'oung Pao", vol. xi, 1910, pp. 21-30. The fact that sDe-srid Saṅs-rgyas-rgya-mtsho concealed the death of the Fifth Dalai Lama for many years, has been known to the European scholars right from the time of Georgi (see Georgi, *Alphabetum Tibetanum*, p. 329). However, the date of this event as given by Georgi is, as usual, not correct. This fact is also stated by Koeppen (see C. F. Koeppen, *Die lamaische Hierarchie und Kirche*, SS. 173-174), G. Schulemann (see G. Schulemann, *Die Geschichte der Dalai Lamas*, S. 163), G. Ts. Tsybikov (see G. Ts. Tsybikov, *Buddist-palomnik u svyatyn' Tibeta* [A Buddhist Pilgrim in the Holy Places of Tibet], p. 261), and many other authors.

Chapter Five

HISTORICO-GEOGRAPHICAL LITERATURE

In surveying the various genres of Tibetan historical literature we simply cannot ignore the geographical literature of Tibet,—not because the Tibetan authors themselves classify geographical works under historical literature but because these works do, sometimes, give much useful historical information.

Like all other countries at a similar stage of development, Tibet too has, in fact, no geographical literature in the modern sense of this word. What is conventionally termed as Tibetan "geographical" literature, consists either of the descriptions of monasteries or temples and other holy places, or of more or less brief and primitive works on geography in general, or, finally, of the accounts of the routes to various countries. Of all these, the works of the first type, viz. the special descriptions of the monasteries, temples, sacred statues, *stūpa*-s, etc.—which, like the descriptions of the Buddhist Canon, are usually called "catalogues" (*dkar-chag*-s)—are the least geographical and most historical in importance. These works contain a list of the most important objects, worthy of attention, located at the place described,—particularly, a complete list of those objects which are immured inside a statue, *stūpa* or any other sacred structure. But such a list is normally accompanied by a more or less comprehensive account of the history of the building-up of the particular monastery, temple, statue etc—sometimes, even by an account of the earliest history of this monastery, or accordingly an account of the whole history of the cult to which the temple, statue, etc. is dedicated.

There are many such works devoted to a description of either one particular monastery, temple, statue, etc. or to that of a whole group of them. With the latter we are quite familiar, for we have already[629] surveyed a work on the history of Buddhism in Amdo—*Deb-ther-rgya-mtsho*—written by Brag-dgon-shabs-druṅ dKon-mchog-bstan-pa-rab-rgyas. The third volume of this voluminous work—*Deb-ther-rgya-mtsho-las Kha-gya-tsho-drug-nas-rgyal-mo-tsha-ba-roṅ-gi-bar-gyi-dgon- sgrub-sde-phal-che-ba'i- dkar-chag-tho-tsam-bkod-pa* (272 fols.)—is, as already stated, a brief historical description of a number of monasteries in Amdo. The second volume of this work,—which mostly contains the history of the Heads (*gdan-rabs*) of the bLa-braṅ monastery and of its individual *datsan*-s (*grwa-tshaṅ*-s)—is also regarded as a description (*dkar-chag*) of this monastery; this is why the folios of this volume mention both the titles : *dkar-chag* and *gdan-rabs*.

629. See *supra*.

Another instance of such a description of a group of monasteries is that of *Grwa-sa-chen-po-bshi-daṅ-rgyud-pa-stod-smad-kyi-dkar-chag-pad-dkar-phreṅ-pa*[630],—which is a brief account of the four largest monasteries of Tibet (Se-ra, dGa'-ldan, 'Bras-spuṅs, and bKra-śis-lhun-po) and of the two Tantric schools, rGyud-pa-stod and rGyud-pa-smad. This work, which is extremely popular in Tibet, was written by Ṅag-dbaṅ-byams-pa (1682-1762)[631]—otherwise known as Byams-pa-rin-po-che—from the small monastery of Phur-bu-lcog. This work is dated 1744[632], and is included in the Complete Works of its author published from Phur-bu-lcog, where it covers 62 folios of usual format.[633]

---

630. The work begins, as usual, with the introductory verses (fols. 1ᵇ 1-2ᵃ 1) followed by :

1. a description of the monastery of dGa'-ldan, which includes a history of its establishment (fols. 2ᵃ 1-8ᵃ 1), a brief report on its Heads (fols. 8ᵃ 1-10ᵃ 1) and a description of its sacred places (fols. 10ᵃ 1-18ᵇ 4).

2. a description of the monastery of 'Bras-spuṅs, which includes a history of its establishment (fols. 18ᵇ 4-24ᵃ 4) and a description of its sacred places (fol. 24ᵃ 4-29ᵃ 2).

3. a description of the monastery of Se-ra, which includes a history of the establishment of this monastery and of its *datsan*-s (fols. 29ᵃ 2-36ᵃ 6) and a description of its sacred places (fols. 36ᵇ 1-43ᵃ 5).

4. a description of the monastery of bKra-śis-lhun-po, which includes a history of the establishment of this monastery (beginning, as usual, with a biography of its founder, dGe-'dun-grub)—fols. 43ᵃ 5-52ᵃ 5—and a description of the sacred places of this monastery (fols. 52ᵃ 5-55ᵃ 6).

5. a history of the establishment of the monastery of Srad-rgyud and of its first, "lower" faculty of occult sciences (*rgyud-smad*)—fols. 52ᵃ 5-59ᵃ 6.

6. a history of the establishment of the second, "upper" faculty of occult sciences (*rgyud-stod*)—fols. 59ᵃ 6-61ᵃ 5.

7. the concluding verses (fols. 61ᵃ 5-62ᵃ 1), and

8. the colophon (fol. 62ᵃ 2-3).

631. The biography of Ṅag-dbaṅ-byams-pa is set forth by his pupil, the aforementioned Yoṅs-'dsin Ye-śes-rgyal-mtshan, in the *Lam-rim-bla-ma-rgyud-pa'i-rnam-thar* (pt. 2, vol. vi, fols. 235ᵃ 3-272ᵇ 6). According to this biography, he was born in the Water-Dog year (A.D. 1682), and he died in the 81st year of his life, viz. in the Water-Horse year (A.D. 1762).

632. See the colophon, fol. 62ᵃ 3, which states that this work was composed on the 5th day of the 8th month of the Wood-Mouse year (A.D. 1744).

633. This work of Nag-dbaṅ-byams-pa forms the 45th (*be*) book in the Collected Works of the author published from the small monastery of Phur-bu-lcog. A copy of this 'Collected Works' is available in the Institute of Peoples of

The number of texts devoted to the description of individual monasteries, temples, statues, etc. is unusually large. These descriptions of individual monasteries often include more or less detailed histories of their Heads, and are thus, in their subject-matter, quite close to the aforementioned monastery chronicles—*gdan-rabs*-s—in which the histories of the monasteries and their Heads are also accompanied by the descriptions of various holy places. An example of such a work is that of the work of Thu'u-bkwan bLo-bzaṅ chos-kyi-ñi-ma (1737-1802), the incarnation and the Head of dGon-luṅ monastery—*bŚad-sgrub-bstan-pa'i-'byuṅ-gnas-chos-sde-chen-po-dgon-luṅ- byams-pa-gliṅ-gi-dkar-chag-dpyod-ldan-yid-dbaṅ-'gugs-pa'i-pho-ña.*[634] This work, written in 1775,[635] gives an account of how the dGon-luṅ monastery was founded (fols. 3ª 6-10ª 6), a history of its thirty-nine successive Heads (fols. 10ª 6-69ª 2), a description (i.e. *dkar-chag* in the real sense of the word) of its holy places (fols. 69ª 2-76ᵇ 5), and information on the personages, who patronised the monastery (fols. 76ᵇ 5-78ª 6). This work (along with its *appendix*) is available in the third volume of the Complete Works of Thu'u-bkwan bLo-bzaṅ-chos-kyi-ñi-ma published in dGon-luṅ, and covers 88 folios. The *appendix* is entitled *sBas-yul-dkar-po-ljoṅs-kyi-gnas-bstod-ka-la-biṅ-ka'i-sgra-dbyaṅs* (fols. 79ᵇ 3-88ª 2), and is a description of the place in verse, composed by rGyal-sras-sprul-sku bLo-bzaṅ-bstan-'dsin (17th century).[636]

Asia (*Tsybikov Collection*, No. 23). The work discussed here is extremely popular and is also often printed separately from other works in the same Collection. One such separate copy is available in the collections of the Institute of Peoples of Asia (*Old Collection*, No. 438ᶜ).

634. This work is included in vol. iii of the Collected Works of Thu'u-bkwan bLo-bzaṅ-chos-kyi-ñi-ma published in the monastery of dGon-luṅ (see the copy of this 'Collected Works' in the library of the Leningrad University, xyl. Q. 344).

635. This date of composition of the text—Wood-Sheep year (A.D. 1775)—is mentioned in the colophon (fol. 79ᵇ 2).

636. rGyal sras-sprul-sku bLo-bzaṅ-bstan-'dsin, the incarnation of the founder of the dGon-luṅ monastery, rGyal-sras Don-yod-chos-kyi-rgya-mtsho, arrived at dGon-luṅ in 1665 (see *Deb-ther-rgya-mtsho*, vol. i, fol. 68ᵇ 1-2, and the 'chronological table' of Sum-pa-mkhan-po). He died in the early 90's of the 17th century (in 1696) when, according to the 'chronological table' of Sum-pa-mkhan-po, his incarnation, bLo-bzaṅ Ñag-dbaṅ 'Jigs-med-ye-śes-grags-pa, was born. A list of the incarnations of rGyal-sras-rin-po-che is given by kLoṅ-rdol-bla-ma in his reference work, *bsTan-'dsin-kyi-skyes-bu-rgya-bod-du-byon-pa'i-miṅ-gi-graṅs* (fol. 21ª 4-21ᵇ 2). Cf. also *Deb-ther-rgya-mtsho*, vol. i,

Of similar nature is the description of the sKu-'bum monastery—*Phyogs-thams-cad-las-rnam-par-rgyal-ba'i-chos-sde-chen-po-sku-'bum-byams-pa-gliṅ-gi-rten-daṅ-brten-par-bcas-pa'i-dkar-chag-ched-du-brjod-pa'i-gtam-sñan-rna-pa'i-bcud-len*—written in 1832[637] by the forty-seventh Head of this monastery, gSer-tog-mkhan-po (also, gSer-tog-ho-thog-thu) Ye-śes-thub-bstan-rgya-mtsho (b. 1786).[638] It was published in sKu-'bum in one volume along with the aforesaid[639] chronicle of this monastery compiled by the second 'Jam-dbyaṅs-bshad-pa. This volume bears a composite title, *gDan-sa-chen-po-sku-'bum-byams-pa-gliṅ-gi-gdan-rabs-mu-tig-'phreṅ-ba-daṅ-rten-daṅ-brten-par-bcas-pa'i-dkar-chag-ched-du-brjod-pa-rna-ba'i-bcud-len*, and covers 105 folios.[640] Of these, folios 1-42ᵃ 6 contain the chronicle of the second 'Jam-dbyaṅs-bshad-pa, and the rest the description proper. The latter which, in its structure, is not much different from the former is divided into four parts (apart from the introductory and concluding verses and the colophon). The first part (fols. 45ᵃ 6-59ᵇ 3) gives a brief history of the rise of sKu-'bum and of its development under the first thirty-three Heads whose particulars are given in the chronicle. The second part (fols. 59ᵇ 3-86ᵃ 6) contains the biographies of the next eighteen Heads. The third part (fols. 86ᵃ 6-103ᵇ 2) contains the description proper of the sacred places of sKu-'bum. The fourth part (fols. 103ᵇ 2-104ᵇ 3) dwells on the use of worshipping them. As a matter of fact, this description can be and is regarded as a continuation of the chronicle of the second 'Jam-dbyaṅs-bshad-pa—a continuation which by itself is independent and complete. At the same time, a further continuation of this work may be seen in the chronicle of sKu-'bum, compiled by gSer-tog-ho-thog-thu bLo-bzaṅ-tshul khrims-rgya-mtsho,—which contains the biographies of the Heads of the monastery from the fifty-second Head onwards. The first fifty-one Heads, who have been dealt with in the two earlier works, are only casually mentioned.[641]

Such descriptions (*dkar-chag*-s) which not only enumerate the appanages of a monastery but also expound the biograpies of its successive Heads are, however, rare.

fol. 68ᵇ 1-4. Of these incarnations, the Indian philosopher, Śāntideva, the son of a king (*rgyal-sras*), was the foremost (see the work of kLoṅ-rdol-bla-ma referred to here, fol. 21ᵃ 4).

637. See the colophon, fol. 105ᵃ 4-6, which states that this work was written in the Water-Dragon year, 475 years after the birth of Tsoṅ-kha-pa (A.D. 1357) and 249 years after the establishment of sKu-'bum (A.D. 1583)—viz., in A.D. 1832.

638. The author himself gives his bio-data in the work discussed here (fols. 79ᵇ 3-81ᵃ 6). According to this report, he was born in the Fire-Horse year of the xiii cycle (A.D. 1786).

639. See *supra*.

640. A copy of this work is available in the Institute of Peoples of Asia, *Nova*, 1914.

641. See *supra*.

In most cases, the historical part of the *dkar-chag*-s is restricted to an exposition of the history of the building-up of a particular object and to some most general information on its future fate ; the whole attention is paid to its description and glorification.

Of the various *dkar-chag*-s of monasteries, the one which gives a detailed description of the old Tibetan monastery of bSam-yas, erected after the earthquake, deserves special attention. This work, entitled *Rab-'byams-dag-pa'i-shiṅ-gi-yon-tan-kun-tshaṅ-lugs-gsum-mi-'gyur-lhun-gyis-grub-pa'i-gtsug-lag-khaṅ-rten-daṅ-brten-par-bcas-pa-legs-gso'i-sri-shu-ji-ltar-bsgrubs-pa'i-tshul-gyi-khyad-par-brjod-pa'i-dkar-chag-skal-bzaṅ-daṅ-pa'i-sko-'byed-ṅo-mtshar-rgya-mtsho'i-le'u-mig*[642] (in 247 folios of usual format), was written in 1854 by the eminent Tibetan statesman, dBaṅ-phyug-rgyal-po,[643] a prince (*guṅ*) from the family of bŚad-sgra-pa and one of the ministers (*bka'-blon*) of Tibet. Another description (*dkar-chag*) that can be mentioned here is that of Utaishan composed by the aforementioned lCaṅ-skya Rol-pa'i-rdo-rje. This description, known under the title *Ri-bo-dwaṅs-bsil-gyi-dkar-chag-mjug-ma-tshaṅ-ba*, is included in the seventh volume of the Collected Works of the author,—where it covers 28 folios.[644]

Besides, the Tibetan historians refer to the existence of two different descriptions of the monastery of Rwa-sgreṅs, of a description of Pha-boṅ-kha written by 'Khon-ston dPal-'byor-lhun-grub (1561-1637),[645] and of various descriptions of gNas-chuṅ, Guṅ-thaṅ, Thaṅ-bo-che and various other places,[646] but these descriptions have not yet been available to me.

---

642. A copy of this work is available in the Institute of Peoples of Asia (*Tsybikov Collection*, No. 46).
643. See the colophon.
644. A copy of this description is available in the Institute of Peoples of Asia. It is included in the Collected Works of lCaṅ-skya Rol-pa'i-rdo-rje (*Old Collection*, No. 311^a). It is also available as a separate monograph (B. 1953).
645. The biography of 'Khon-ston dPal-'byor-lhun-grub is given in the aforementioned (note 311) collection of the biographies of incarnations of lCaṅ-skya Rol-pa'i-rdo-rje and in the *Lam-rim-bla-ma-rgyud-pa'i-rnam-thar* (pt. 2, vol. vi, fols. 362^a 4-364^a 4). The dates of birth and death of 'Khon-ston dPal-'byor-lhun-grub are also given in the "Chronological Tables".
646. See *Deb-ther-rgya-mtsho* (vol. i, fols. 9^b 6-10^b 3), where a list of some such descriptions (*dkar-chag*-s) is given. As regards the description of Lhasa written by 'Jam-dbyaṅs-dga'-ba'i-bśes-gñen,—which, A. Grünwedel assumed (see A. Grünwedel *Die Temple von Lhasa*, p. 5), was some special work that had not come down to us,—it is actually the well-known (translated and published, in

Of the numerous *dkar-chag*-s of individual temples and holy places, mention may first be made of that of the main temple of Lhasa,—bearing the title *Lha-ldan-sprul-ba'i-gtsug-lag-khaṅ-gi-dkar-chag-śel-dkar-me-loṅ*,[647]—which was composed in 1644 by the Fifth Dalai Lama, Ṅag-dbaṅ bLo-bzaṅ-rgya-mtsho 'Jigs-med-go-cha-thub-bstan-laṅ-'tsho. This work is a brilliant account in verses, each verse being followed by a detailed exposition of the same theme in prose. It is included in the Complete Works of the Fifth Dalai Lama,[648] where it occupies 21 folios of the usual format. The prose part of this work, which is widely known in the Tibetan world, was first translated (though, unfortunately, with omissions and errors) by Waddell[649] in 1895. In 1919, Professor

---

part, by A. Grünwedel himself) description of the Lhasa temple written by the Fifth Dalai Lama ; for, " 'Jam-dbyaṅs-dga'-ba'i-bśes-gñen" is one of the many names of this Dalai Lama (see *supra*, note 117). This description is mentioned by sMin-grol-bla-ma in his geographical work (see V. P. Vasil'ev, *Geografiya Tibeta*..., St. Petersburg, 1895, p. 26), where the name of the Fifth Dalai Lama is preceded by the usual epithet of the Dalai Lamas : *thams-cad-mkhyen-pa* (=omniscient).

647. This work is included in vol. xix of the aforementioned Collected Works of the Fifth Dalai Lama. The date of its composition—*sa-skyoṅ* (*Pārthiva*) year, which is the 19th year in the *Bṛhaspaticakra* and which corresponds to the Wood-Hen year (A.D. 1645) of the Tibetan sexagenary cycle—is mentioned in the colophon (fol. 21ᵃ 6). The same Wood-Hen year as the year of the composition of the work discussed here is mentioned in the autobiography of the Fifth Dalai Lama [vol. i (6), fol. 131ᵇ 3-4]. In the introduction to his translation, A. Grünwedel wrongly states that this work was composed "Im Jahre 1647 nach der Rück-kehr vom chine-sischen Hofe" (see A. Grünwedel, *Die Temple von Lhasa*, p. 9). As is known from the Tibetan and Chinese sources, the Fifth Dalai Lama, Ṅag-dbaṅ bLo-bzaṅ-rgya-mtsho, left for the Chinese court only in 1652 and came back in 1653 (see W. W. Rockhill, *The Dalai Lamas of Lhasa*,—"T'oung Pao", vol. xi, 1910, pp. 14-18). Cf. also the "Chronological Tables".

648. A. Grünwedel—according to his own statement—heard from somewhere that only the prose part of this work had been written by the Fifth Dalai Lama and that the verses had been composed by others. But this report is not well founded. The colophon of this work and the autobiography of the Fifth Dalai Lama (pt. 1, vol. vi, fol. 131ᵇ 3-4) mention this description as the Fifth Dalai Lama's own work.

649. See L. A. Waddell, *Description of Lhasa Cathedral*, translated from Tibetan,—JASB, vol. xiv, pt. i, 1895, pp. 259-283.

A. Grünwedel published *en regard* the full Tibetan text (in transliteration) along with a German translation of the entire work.[650]

---

650. A. Grünwedel, *Die Temple von Lhasa. Gedicht des ersten Dalai-lama, für Pilger bestimmt*,—"Sitzungs-berichte der Heidelberger Akademie der Wissenschaften, Philosophisch-historische Klasse, Heidelberg, 1919, 14 Abh. [Like some other European authors, A. Grünwedel calls the Fifth Dalai Lama the first, for this Dalai Lama was the first to rise to the position of the supreme sovereign of Tibet—a position, which was also retained by his successors].

This work of A. Grünwedel is much better than the work of Waddell, though it is not absolutely free fiom mistakes. The prose portion of the text which separates the first four lines in verse from the subsequent ones, has been turned by A. Grünwedel into a verse. Besides, A. Grünwedel did not properly read many words. In place of the expression *lus-chan-kum-la-ris-su-ma-chad* in the beginning of these verses, A Grünwedel has wrongly published *lus-can-kun-rigs-sum-chad*, which has distorted the meaning. In the third line, he has interpolated an extra word—*bdag*. Again, in the last but one of these verses, A. Grünwedel reads *zabs* in place of *za-bas*. The translation of the colophon as made by Grünwedel is worse than the one made by Waddell. The Tibetan text of the colophon reads :

'Di-yaṅ gtsug-lag-khaṅ-rten-brten-pa-la-rim-gro-daṅ-sri-shur-bgyid-pa'i-dkon-gñer-rnams-kyi-bskul-ba'i-ṅor gnam-bskos-kyi-rgyal-po-phag-mo-gru-pa'i-blon-po rgya-gar-gyi-rgyal-rigs-sā-la-pa-chen-po za-hor-gyi-rigs-las-son-pa'i-lo-rgyus-smra-pa'i-btsun-pa-ṅag-dbaṅ-blo-bzaṅ- rgya- mtsho- 'jigs- med- go- cha- thub- bstan- laṅ-tsho'i-sdes sa-skyoṅ-gi-lo-rgya-nag-gi-rgyal-khab-chen-por-lo-'go- gsar- du- chis- pa ñin-byed-dbaṅ-po-gshu-khyim-du-ñe-bar-spyod-pa'i-phyogs-sṅa-ma'i-bzaṅ-po-daṅ-po dbyaṅs-ai-'chaṅ-ba'i-tshes-la-dga'-ldan-phyogs-thams- cad-las-rnam- par-rgyal-ba'i-pho-braṅ-du-sbyar-ba'i-yi-ge-ba-ni-vāgindra-śrī-ya'o.

Waddell translates : "This catatogue...has been written by Ṅag-dbaṅ-blo-bzaṅ-rgya-mtsho, the fearless one armed with the doctrine, who is descended from the race of Zahor and once (in a former birth) the minister of Phag-mo-gru-pa the king of gNam-bskos and (formerly) the great Sahlapa of the Indian royal race, at the palace of dGa'-ldan-phyogs-thams-cad-las-rnam-par-rgyal-ba, at the request of the stewards in charge of the images of the *Vihāra*, at the beginning of the year of Sa-skyoṅ, in the Chinese court, on a most auspicious day of the first glorious part of the course of the Zodiac around the constellation Ñe, Vagendras' seyo !" A. Grünwedel translates : "Dieser Katalog... ist vom Dalai bla-ma Ṅag-dbaṅ-blo-bzaṅ Abhayavarmā, dem Lehrer der Jügend über Buddhas Religion, dem wir sein Vorgeburtslegenden erwahnen, den Erwürdigen, da er, um zu opfern und seine Verehrung zu bezeugen, von den fungierenden

Then, one may mention a number of works devoted to the description of the various temples and holy places of bLa-brañ. These include, in particular, the descrip-

---

Tempelpriestern aufgefordert, den Tempel gekehrt hat und dafür als Kaiser von China, als Ratsherr in Phag-mo-gru, als Mahāśālī aus indischem Kṣatriyageschlechte und endlich im Geschlechte von Za-hor erschienen ist, verfasst worden am ersten Tage des Neujahrs Bhûpāla nach Palastverfügung des chinesischen Kaisers, am ersten günstigen Tag der nach dem Bogenhaus des Sūryarājā inklinierenden Region, an einem Tage, wo es mit dem Laute i regnete, da er ja schriftstellert im Tempelpalast dGa'-ldan, der alle Welt übertrifft".

Both these translations are wrong. A correct translation of the Tibetan text would be : "This description has been written at the instance of the stewards (*dkon-gñer-s*) engaged in the service and worship of the images of the temple, by the monk-historiographer, Ñag-dbañ bLo-bzañ-rgya-mtsho 'Jigs-med-go-cha-thub-bstan-lañ-tsho'i-sde [the full name of the Fifth Dalai Lama], the descendant from the race of Za-hor—the Indian *kṣatriya* race like the great *Śāla* tree and the race of the ministers of the heaven-appointed king, Phag-mo-gru-pa. (It has been written) in the *Pārthiva* year (A.D. 1645)—when a new year began in China—on the first day of the category of "the good ones" (i.e. on the second day), denoted by the vowel "i", of the first half of the month in which the sun entered the sign of Sagittarius, in the castle of dGa'-ldan-phyogs-thams-cad-las-rnam-par-rgyal-ba'i-pho-brañ [full name of the castle of Dalai Lama in 'Bras-spuñs]. The scribe is Vāgindra-śrī".

About his descent from Hor gShon-nu-bzañ-po—the minister to the founder of the Tibetan Phag-mo-gru-pa dynasty, Tā'i Si-tu Byañ-chub-rgyal-mtshan—the Fifth Dalai Lama speaks in details in his biography (see the Collected Works, vol. v, pt. i, fols. 11^{a} 5-22^{b} 3), where he traces his lineage right to the Indian kings, Aśoka and Daśaratha. The expression *rgya-gar-gyi-rgyal-rigs-sā-la-pa-chen-po*, which we have translated as the "Indian *kṣatriya* race like the great *Śāla* tree", is a simple corruption of the expression *rgyal-rigs-śiñ-sā-la-lta-bu* which is an exact translation of the Sanskrit expression *kṣatriya-mahā-śāla-kulam*. This Sanskrit expression is found in the *Mahāvyutpatti* (N 3862), *Lalitavistara* (See the Sanskrit text in : S. Lefmann, *Lalita Vistara*, vol. i, S. 117, Z. 17 ; and the Tibetan text in : P. E. Foucaux, *Rgya tch'er rolpa ou Développement des Jeux*, p. 104, l.2) and other texts. This is also mentioned by the Fifth Dalai Lama in his autobiography (pt. i, fol. 11^{a} 2). The expression *gnam-bskos* (=the heaven-appointed) is a title of honour, which was earlier used for the Chinese emperor and is now also employed for others. This title can also be and is used for Tibetan kings.

tion of the temple (*suburgan*) in bLa-brañ composed in 1804[651] by the twenty-first Head of this monastery, the well-known scholar Guñ-thañ dKon-mchog-bstan-pa'i-sgron-me (1762-1823).[652] This work (in 35 folios) is entitled *bDe-bar-gśegs-pa'i-sku-gsuñ-thugs-kyi-rten-bsheñs-pa-dañ-phyag-mchod-skor-pa'i-phan-yon-bstan-pa-rnam-dkar-las-la-skul-byed-dkar-chag-lha'i-rña-chen*,[653] and is included in the Complete Works of its author. However,

---

651. See the colophon (fols. 34ᵇ 6-35ᵃ 3), which mentions the cyclic date of the composition of this description—Wood-Ox year of the xiii cycle (A.D. 1805)—and the numbers of years expired up to this date from the dates of various events.

652. A comprehensive biography of Guñ-thañ dKon-mchog-bstan-pa'i-sgron-me was written in 1831 by the aforementioned dPal-mañ dKon-mchog-rgyal-mtshan (1764-1853). This biography (entitled *'Jam-dbyañs-bla-ma-rje-btsun-dkon-mchog-bstan-pa'i-sgron-me'i-rnam-par- thar-pa- brjod-pa'i-gtam-dad- pa'i- padma- bshad-pa'i-ñin-byed*) is included in vol. vi of the Collected Works of its author, where it covers 205 folios.

 A short biography (in verse) of Guñ-thañ dKon-mchog-bstan-pa'i-sgron-me was written by rGyal-mkhan-po Grags-pa-rgyal-mtshan (1762-1837). This biography (entitled *rJe-bla-ma-mtshan-brjod-par-dga'-ba-dkon-mchog-bstan-pa'i-sgron-me-dpal- bzañ- po'i-rtogs- pa-brjod-pa- ño-mtshar- lha'i- rol-mo- mkhas- pa'i-yid-'phrog*) is included in vol. v of the Collected Works of its author, where it covers 11 folios (see the copy of this 'Collected Works' in the Institute of Peoples of Asia, *Baradiin Collection*, No. 5). To the same author (viz. to rGyal-mkhan-po Grags-pa-rgyal-mtshan) are also attributed two "secret" biographies of this scholar. One of these, entitled *rJe-btsun-dkon-mchog-bstan-pa'i-sgron-me-dpal-bzañ-po'i-shal-sña-nas-kyi-gsañ-ba'i-rnam-thar-dños-grub-kyi-sñe-ma* (in 9 folios), is dated A.D. 1825, and is available in vol. v of the author's Collected Works. The other, entitled *rJe-btsun-bla-ma-dkon-mchog-bstan-pa'i-sgron-me-dpal-bzañ-po'i-gsañ-ba'i-rnam-par-thar-pa-nor-bu'i-do-śal* (in 3 folios), is available in vol. iv of the author's Collected Works.

 Another, third "secret" biography of Guñ-thañ dKon-mchog-bstan-pa'i-sgron-me—entitled *rJe-btsun-dkon-mchog-bstan-pa'i-sgron-me-dpal-bzañ-po'i-gsañ-ba'i-rnam-par-thar-pa-rdsogs-ldan-spyin-gyi-sgra-dbyañs* (in 5 folios)—was written by sDe-khri 'Jam-dbyañs-thub-bstan-ñi-ma (1779-1 62). [See the bLa-brañ edition of the Collected Works of this author in the Institute of Peoples of Asia, *Baradiin Collection*, No. 9, vol. i].

 It is possible that there may also be some more biographies of Guñ-thañ dKon-mchog-bstan-pa'i-sgron-me.

653. This description is, however, wanting in the copy of the Collected Works of Guñ-thañ dKon-mchog-bstan-pa'i-sgron-me available in the Institute of Peoples

half the text in this work is simply a discourse on the use of the buildinging and worshiping of the *suburgan*. To the history proper of the construction of the *suburgan* are devoted only eight folios (fols. 4ᵃ 3-11ᵇ 2), half of which, again, contain some legends on the origin of the *stūpa* cult itself. To the same author is ascribed a brief description of the statue of Maitreya, which bears the title *Luṅ-ston-byams-pa'i-dkar-chag-gdaṅs-sñan-chos-kyi-gaṇḍi*. This small work (in 12 folios)[654] is also included in the fifth volume of the Collected Works of the author.

Another such *dkar-chag* is that of the so-called Golden temple of bLa-braṅ. A major portion of this work, which is entitled *gSer-khaṅ-chen-mo-rten-daṅ-rten-par-bcas-pa'i-dkar-chag-byaṅ-chen-thar-lam-'grod-pa'i-them-skas* (51 folios in all), was translated into Russian by B. Baradiin.[655] It was composed in 1825 by the twenty-third Head of the bLa-braṅ monastery, rGyal-mkhan-chen Grags-pa-rgyal-mtshan (1762-1837),[656] and is included in the Complete Works of this author.[657] To the same author is also attributed the description of the temple of Amitābha Buddha—entitled *'Od-dpag-med-kyi-lha-khaṅ-rten-daṅ-rten-par-bcas-pa'i-dkar-chag-nor-bu'i-'khri-śiṅ*—which is found mentioned in the

---

of Asia (*Baradiin Collection*, No. 4) despite B. Baradiin's statement (in his work, *Statuya Maitrei*..., pp. 08 and 10) that he had brought this work and had even prepared a translation of it for the press.

654. A copy of this work is available in the Institute of Peoples of Asia (*Baradiin Collection*, No. 4).

655. B. Baradiin, *Statuya Maitrei v Zolotom khrame v Lavrane*, Leningrad, 1924 (*Bibliotheca Buddhica*, xxii).

656. The biography of rGyal-mkhan-po Grags-pa-rgyal-mtshan is set forth in the *Deb-ther-rgya-mtsho* (vol. ii, fols. 44ᵃ 1-49ᵇ 6). According to this biography, he was born in the Water-Horse year of the xii cycle (A.D. 1762), and he died in the Fire-Hen year in the 76th year of his life (A.D. 1837). Some information on him—apparently, on the basis of this biography—has also been given by B. Baradiin in the introduction to his work (see B. Baradiin, *Statuya, Maitrei*..., pp. 11-12).

657. I have not been able to trace this work so far in spite of a specific report by B. Baradiin that it is available in the Asiatic Museum (now Institute of Peoples of Asia) of the Academy of Sciences, U.S.S.R. amidst the books brought by him from Amdo (see B. Baradiin, *Statuya Maitrei* .., p. 10). According to the 'Table of Contents' appended to the copy of the Collected Works of rGyal-mkhan-po Grags-pa-rgyal-mtshan (bLa-braṅ edition) in the Institute of Peoples of Asia (*Baradiin Collection*, No. 5), this work should be available in vol. vi (*cha*) of this 'Collected Works', but it is not found there. I could not, therefore, compare B. Baradiin's translation with the original.

table of contents of the fourth volume of the Collected Works of the author.[658] Besides, rGyal-mkhan-chen Grags-pa-rgyal-mtshan is also the author of *Grub-pa'i-slob-dpon-chen-po-mtsho-skyes-rdo-rje'i-sku-brñan-mthoṅ-ba-don-ldan-rten-daṅ-brten-par-bcas-pa'i-dkar-chag-mkhas-pa'i-yid-'phrog* (17 fols.),[659] a description of the statue of Padmasambhava in the bKra-śis-byams-brtse-lha-khaṅ temple in bLa-braṅ, and of a collection of various small descriptions entitled *dKar-chag-dad-pa'i-sgo-byed* (14 fols.).[660]

Of all such texts available in our collections, one more that can be mentioned here is the *dkar-chag* of the *suburgan* having the remains of the seventh Dalai Lama at Potala in Lhasa. This work composed by the third Panchen Lama, dPal-ldan-ye-śes (1738-1780), is available in the third volume of the Collected Works of the author, and is entitled *Rigs-daṅ-dkyil-'khor-kun-gyi-bdag-po-rdo-rje-'chaṅ-khams-gsum-'gro-ba'i-bla-ma-mchog-gi-sku-gduṅ-yid-bshin-nor-bu-sñiṅ-por-bshugs-pa'i-lhar-bcas-skye-dgu'i-mchod-sdoṅ-chen-po'i-thog-mtha'-bar-gsum-gyi-che-ba'i-yon-tan-brjod-par-bya-ba'i-gtam-rdsu-'phrul-'od-zer-phyogs-brgyar-'byed-pa'i-snaṅ-byed* (usually cited by its short title, *rGyal-dbaṅ-bskal-bzaṅ-rgya-mtsho'i-gser-gduṅ-dkar-chag*) and covers 79 folios.[661] From the historical standpoint, however, it is of little interest. There are many more works of this type, which, however, we shall not enumerate here. It may, however, be observed that such works are not restricted to the holy places of Tibet alone. There are similar works in Tibetan language, which give the descriptions of various holy places or objects in China, Mongolia and even Buryatia—as, for instance, the description of the statue of Maitreya in the Aginsky *datsan* (dGa'-ldan bśad-sgrub-gliṅ) in Buryatia. This

658. This description is wanting in the copy of the Collected Works of the author available in the Institute of Peoples of Asia, though B. Baradiin states that he had brought the text (*ibid.*, p. 10). Thus, none of the three descriptions mentioned by B. Baradiin could be located in the collections of the Institute. According to the 'Table of Contents' appended to the Collected Works, the present text should be available in vol. iv (*ṅa*).

659. Included in vol. iv of the Collected Works of the author available in the Institute of Peoples of Asia (*Baradiin Collection*, No. 5). A major portion of the text (fols. 3^b 3-10^a 5)' is occupied by the biography of the builder of the temple, bLo-bzaṅ-bstan-pa'i-rgyal-mtshan, along with a history of the construction of this temple.

660. See *Baradiin Collection*, No. 5, vol. vi. As such collections of minor descriptions are not important from historical standpoint, we shall not discuss these here (though many authors do have such collections of their minor works).

661. See the Collected Works of Paṇ-chen dPal-ldan-ye-śes in the Institute of Peoples of Asia (*Tsybikov Collection*, No. 12).

description, entitled *Ā-nā-byams-chen-gyi-dkar-chag-rab-gsal-me-loṅ*,[662] was composed in 1915 by one of the Lamas of this *datsan* (*grwa-tshaṅ*), bLo-brtan.

Apart from such descriptions which are intended to serve as subject-indexes or catalogues to a particular place or temple and are accordingly called *dkar-chag*-s, there also are certain descriptions of a more general geographical nature, usually known as *gnas-bśad*-s (=Descriptions of a Place). These works, too, frequently contain useful historical material. These are normally written with a view to glorify some monastery—big or small—and also contain therefore an account of the leading personages of these places in addition to the description of the place itself. One example of a work of this type is the description of the famous monastery of Jo-naṅ—entitled *Jo-naṅ-gi-gnas-bśad* (in 13 folios)[663]—available in the Complete Works of Lama Tāranātha. This work contains a description of nature (fols. 2^b 1-5^a 4), a list of those distinguished persons who "blessed" (*byin-gyis-brlabs*) this cloister with their presence (fols. 5^a 4-8^b 4) and an exposition of the continuous tradition of meditaters of the cloister (fols. 8^b 4-12^a 6). Such works also include Lama Tāranātha's brief description of 'Khyog-po, a small monastery—entitled *'Khyog-po-ri-khrod-gyi-gnas-bśad* (3 fols.)[664] —and a still shorter description of sKyid-phug bDe-ldan, a place of meditation (entitled *sGrub-gnas-skyid-phug-bde-ldan-gyi-gnas-bśad*).[665] However, the historical material available in all these three works is highly insignificant in quality as well as quantity. Of interest from historical standpoint is another work,—included in Tāranātha's Complete Works,—which is devoted to a description of the well-known monastery, rTag-brtan-dam-chos-gliṅ. [This monastery was a stronghold of the Jo-naṅ-pa sect, but was later turned by the Fifth Dalai Lama into a monastery of the dGe-lugs-pa sect (the dominant sect of Tibet) and renamed as dGa'-ldan-phun-tshogs-gliṅ].[666] This work,—which, in

662. See the manuscript of this work brought in 1935 by S. D. Dylykov—available in the Institute of Peoples of Asia.
663. See the Collected Works of Tāranātha available in the Institute of Peoples of Asia—*Tsybikov Collection*, No. 15, vol. xiv (*pha*).
664. See *ibid.*
665. See *ibid.*
666. This is also mentioned in the *Vaiḍūrya-ser-po* (fol. 319^b 4), where the date of this event—Earth-Dog year (A.D. 1658)—is also recorded. The former name of the monastery has been given in this text in a short form : "rTag-brtan". The *Grub-mtha'-śel-gyi-me-loṅ* (book vii, fol. 4^a 36), which also refers to the conversion of this monastery, gives its former name as rTag-brtan-phun-tshogs-gliṅ. This name as the old name of the monastery is also mentioned by sMin-grol-bla-ma in his "Geography of Tibet". But the text of the description being surveyed here specifically and repeatedly calls this monastery as rTag-brtan-dam-chos-gliṅ (see fols. 4^b 1-2 and 19^a 2). Here, it is interesting to note that this

xylograph edition of Tāranātha's works, is entitled *dGa'-ldan-phun-tshogs-gliṅ-gi-gnas-bśad* (19 fols.),[667]—is very much similar to the descriptions of the special catalogues described above, viz. *dkar-chag*-s. Like the *dkar-chag*-s, it first expounds the history of the rise of the monastery and then enumerates its most important temples along with the objects and images centered in them. Besides these specific works of Tibetan geographical literature, there also are, in Tibetan language, works on general geography —the so-called "General Descriptions of Jambudvīpa" (*'Dsam-gliṅ-spyi-bśad*). Two such works are known to me. One, which is comparatively older and shorter, is called *'Dsam-gliṅ-spyi-bśad-ṅo-mtshar-gtam-sñan*. It was written in 1777[668] by the well-known scholar, Sum-pa-mkhan-po Ye-śes-dpal-'byor (1704-1788)—whose historical work has already been discussed above—and is included in his Complete Works. This work, which covers 14 folios of large Tibetan format,[669] does not contain any historical material. It is a collection of bits of information on the geography of the world known to the author ; one-third of this work is devoted to India (fols. 3^b 6-7^b 5). This work did not remain the only expression of the views of the author on the geography of the world. The reply of Sum-pa-mkhan-po Ye-śes-dpal-'byor sent in 1779 to the third Panchen Lama, dPal-ldan-ye-śes (1738-1780),—who had posed some questions and raised certain objections against the historical and geographical views of the author,—

---

description was published before the re-naming of the monastery, for it gives many indications to this effect. The title given to the text is different : *dGa'-ldan-phun-tshogs-gliṅ-gi-gnas-bśad.* The same new name of the monastery figures on the first folio of the text (see the text, fol. 1^b 5), for which the earlier block of the xylograph has been clearly tampered with. A longer expression—"dGa'-ldan-phun-tshogs"—is found carved in place of the earlier expression, "rTag-brtan-dam-chos". At all other places—in the body of the text and at the end—the old, original name of the monastery is preserved. The margins of the folios also carry the word "rTag", which conclusively shows that the earlier title of this xylograph was *rTag-brtan-dam-chos-gliṅ-gi-gnas-bśad.*

667. This text is available in vol. xiv (*pha*) of the Collected Works of the author cited here.

668. See the colophon, fol. 14^a 2, which states that this work was written by Sum-pa-mkhan-po in the Fire-Hen year (A.D. 1777).

669. This text is available in vol. ii (*kha*) of the Collected Works of Sum-pa-mkhan-po. Since this text is extremely popular, it is also frequently found as a separate monograph. A copy of such a monograph is available in the Institute of Peoples of Asia (*Old Collection,* No. 445^B).

is included in the collection entitled *Naṅ-don-tha-sñad-rig-gnas-kyi-gshuṅ-gi-dogs-gnas-'ga'-shig-dris-pa'i-lan-phyogs-gcig-tu-bris-pa-rab-dkar-pa-saṅs* (100 fols.),[670] among other replies of his to various questions and objections. In this reply which covers 6 folios of large format (fols. 5^b 1-11^a 2), Sum-pa-mkhan-po Ye-śes-dpal-'byor also quotes some historical data, though even here the main emphasis generally is on the list of peoples inhabiting the earth in various directions from India and Tibet.

Considerably more interesting from historical as well as geographical standpoint is another, much more detailed work entitled *'Dsam-gliṅ-spyi-bśad-me-loṅ* which was written half a century later by sMin-grol-sprul-sku 'Jam-dpal Chos-kyi-bstan-'dsin-'phrin-las (1789-1838).[671] We were able to examine—though cursorily—a manuscript copy of this work in Aginsky *datsan* in Buryatia. Like the previous work, it is an essay on general geography. However, what is important for us in this work is only the geography of Tibet and partly that of India, written on the basis of true Tibetan notions, for a great deal of interesting historical references and local legends is scattered in the description of these countries. Besides, the geographical data on Tibet as given in this work are also fairly important. As regards the remaining part of this work, it is almost unimportant, for,—as already pointed out by V. P. Vasil'ev,[672]—it is written on the basis of European and mainly Russian sources. That this work has greatly depended on the Russian works on geography is clear from the fact that many geographical names given in the Tibetan text have not even been translated ; these are mere transliterations of the corresponding Russian names (for instance, "Kuril'skie ostrova" [Kuril islands] etc). However, to supplement the materials taken from the Russian and other European works on geography, the author gives some totally fantastic reports.[673] This leads us to believe that he was directly acquainted only with the maps and that for everything else, he depended upon the most fantastic accounts and rumours.

---

670. This text is available in vol. viii (*ña*) of the Collected Works of Sum-pa-mkhan-po. The date of composition of the text—Earth-Pig year (A.D. 1779)—is mentioned in its concluding note (fol. 11^a 1).
671. A biography of sMin-grol-sprul-sku 'Jam-dpal Chos-kyi-bstan-'dsin-'phrin-las is set forth in the *Deb-ther-rgya-mtsho* (vol. i, fol. 126^a 1-6). This biography also mentions *inter alia* the geographical work surveyed here (*ibid.*, fol. 126^a 5). The dates of birth and death of this author as given by me are borrowed from here. He was born in the Earth-Hen year (1789), and he died in the 50th year of his life, viz. in the Earth-Dog year (1838). V. P. Vasil'ev, possibly by mistake, gives the date of death as A.D. 1839 (see V. P. Vasil'ev, *Geografiya Tibeta*, p. 11).
672. V. P. Vasil'ev, *Geografiya Tibeta* [Geography of Tibet], p. ii.
673. See C. Bell, *The People of Tibet*, Oxford, 1928, p. 8. The fantastic accounts of Corsica and Sicily given by C. Bell are, I think, taken from this work.

A portion of this work (which is of comparatively greater interest and is certainly worthy of being published and studied) devoted to the geography of Tibet was translated into English by Sarat Chandra Das[674] and into Russian by V. P. Vasil'ev.[675] The latter also supplemented his translation of the portion concerning the geography of Tibet with that of relatively more interesting and important extracts from this work relating to the georaphy of Nepal and India. Though V. P. Vasil'ev's translation, made mainly in the forties of the last century, does have certain discrepancies, it is nevertheless,—as rightly remarked by Professor A. Grünwedel,[676]—much better than the above-mentioned translation of S. C. Das. Unfortunately, neither the chapter on the geography of Tibet nor that on the geography of India has been published in Tibetan original. A manuscript copy of both these chapters made in Peking by V. P. Vasil'ev, is available in the library of the Leningrad University.[677] A copy made from it is also there in the Institute of Peoples of Asia of the Academy of Sciences, U.S.S.R.[678]

One may also often find some more or less interesting historical materials in the so-called "travel notes"—*lam-yig*-s. Tibetan sources mention some such works, namely : "Description of a route to India" (*rGya-gar-lam-yig*) written by Chag-lo-chos-rje ; "Description of a route to Nepal" (*bLa-yul-gyi-lam-yig*) by Lha-mthoṅ-lo-tsā-ba bŚes-gñen-rnam-rgyal ; the *rDo-rje-gdan-lam-yig* ; *O-rgyan-lam-yig*, etc.[679] However, I could not see these works and am, therefore, not in a position to say anything definite about their contents and historical importance.

The only work of this kind that I have been able to examine personally, is the famous "Description of the route to (the country of) Śambhala (*Śa-mbha-la'i-lam-yig*) written in 1775 by the third Panchen Lama, dPal-ldan-ye-śes (1738-1780).[680] The full title of this work is *Grub-pa'i-gnas-chen-po-śa-mbha-la'i-rnam-bśad-'phags-yul-gyi-rtogs-brjod-daṅ-bcas-pa-ṅo-mtshar-bye-ba'i-'byuṅ-gnas*. It is included in the Collected Works of the author and covers 50 folios of usual Tibetan format.[681] As is clearly seen from the

---

674. S. C. Das, *A Brief Account of Tibet from "Dsam Ling Gyeshe", the Well-known Geographical Work of Lama Tsanpo Noman-khan of Amdo*,—JASB, vol. lvi, 1887, pt. i, pp. 1-30.
675. V. P. Vasil'ev, *Geografiya Tibeta...*, St. Petersburg, 1895.
676. A. Grünwedel, *Der Weg nach Sambhala*, S. 91.
677. *Tibetan Collection*, Nos. 875 and 876.
678. *Old Collection.*
679. See the *Deb-ther-rgya-mtsho* (vol. i, fol. 10^b 4-5), which mentions some *lam-yig*-s ("travel notes").
680. The date of composition of this text—Wood-Sheep year (A.D. 1775)—is mentioned in the colophon (fol. 50^a 3).
681. This text is available in vol. viii (*ña*) of the aforementioned Collected Works of

full title of this work and especially from the study of its contents, the short title *Śa-mbha-la'i-lam-yig* is too narrow. Actually, the text consists not only of a description of Śambhala but also of that of India. In fact, the latter—the historico-geographical account of India—occupies more space in this text than the account of the mythical country of Śambhala, though Śambhala does form the main theme of the whole work. Besides the introductory verses (fols. 1-5ᵇ 4) and brief remarks on general geography (fols. 6ᵃ 1-8ᵇ 4), this text contains : 1) a description of India which falls into a description of the country (fols. 8ᵃ 5-20ᵇ 4), a short history of the Indian kings (fols. 20ᵇ 4-27ᵇ 4) and a brief historical account of the philosophical and religious teachings of India (fols. 27ᵇ 4-34ᵃ 2) ; and 2) a description of Śambhala which again falls into a description of the route to this country (fols. 34ᵃ 2-41ᵇ 5), a description of the country itself (fols. 41ᵇ 5-44ᵃ 5) and a short essay on the history of her kings and of the Buddhist religion in this legendary kingdom (fols. 44ᵃ 5-49ᵇ 1). As rightly observed by Professor A. Grünwedel,[682] the description of India given in this work is largely based on the reports of G. Bogle,[683] the British Ambassador to Tibet, and his companion, A. Hamilton, who were in the court of the third Panchen Lama[684] from November, 1774 to 1775, and on the accounts of the pilgrims, who had been sent to India by this famous Tibetan hierarch. However, the chief sources for this work on the whole have undoubtedly been the various Tibetan literary masterpieces—original as well as translations from Sanskrit. Professor Grünwedel[685] published this work in Latin transcription along with his annotations and a parallel German translation.

---

the third Panchen Lama. Besides, copies of this text (in the same edition) are also often found separately. One such separate copy is available in the Institute of Peoples of Asia (*Collection of the Asiatic Department*, No. 516). The Institute also has a manuscript copy of this text (*Old Collection*, No. 445C).

682. A. Grünwedel, *Der Weg nach Śambhala*, S. 5.

683. See C. R. Markham, *Narratives of the Mission of George Bogle to Tibet and of the Journey of Thomas Manning to Lhasa*, London, 1879.

684. The author himself refers to *Abhidharmakośa*, *Kālacakra-tantra* and its commentary (fol. 6ᵃ 1-2), the biography of the first Dalai Lama (*ibid*, fol. 17ᵇ 5), the *lam-yig*-s written by 'Phags-pa Don-yod-lcags-kyu, the commentaries on the *Kālacakra* system, written by the Tibetan authors, mKhas-grub dGe-legs-dpal-bzaṅ-po and the first Dalai Lama, the history of India from Aśoka to Pratīta-sena (*ibid.*, fol. 50ᵃ 1-2), and other texts.

685. A Grünwedel, *Der Weg nach Śambhala des dritten Gross-Lama von bKra-śis-lhun-po bLo-bzaṅ dPal-ldan-ye-śes*,—"Abhandlungen der konigl bayerischen Akademie der Wissenschaften", Philosophisch-philologische und historische Klasse,—xxix Bd, 3 Abhandlung, München, 1915.

CONCLUSION

Such are the most common features of the main genres of Tibetan historical literature and allied works of historico-bibliographical and historico-geographical nature.

As we see, there are a great number of various types of works written by the Tibetan authors. These works, in spite of certain shortcomings,—entirely explained by the fact that Tibetan historical literature emerged and developed in the conditions of feudal Middle Ages,—are the most important source for a study of the history of the Tibetan peoples and partly also of the other peoples.

The ever increasing interest in Tibet, her history and culture, and the need for taking up the study of the historical texts in Tibetan language for knowing the history of the Tibetan people themselves and also for a knowledge of various details of the history of the other peoples are, I think, enough to justify the time spent on and attention given to the study of the monumental works of Tibetan historical literature. In the present account, our object was merely to find out what had already been done in this direction, to eliminate certain obvious discrepancies and errors found in the opinions expressed by various scholars and to chart out—though most roughly—the outline of the vast material awaiting investigation.

POSTSCRIPT

In resuming the publication of the *Bibliotheca Buddhica* series, the editors have decided to bring out the works, which have been lying unpublished in the archives of the editorial office of the series. Professor A. I. Vostrikov's work, completed in 1937 and now passed on to the editors by N. P. Vostrikova, is an exceptionally brilliant contribution to the Tibetan studies. If this work has not lost its importance till this day, this is because the author has drawn upon extremely rich material, which hithertofore had remained either obscure or totally unknown. In fact, a work of such a magnitude could be prepared only on the basis of the rich *Tibetica* of the Institute of Peoples of Asia, Academy of Sciences, U.S.S.R.

Since the completion of this work by A. I. Vostrikov, the Tibetan studies have made a further advance. Many written monuments—particularly those of the early medieval (11th-14th centuries) and ancient (7th-9th centuries) periods of the history of Tibet—have since been published and made available to the academic world. Thus, the yearwise chronicles presently preserved in the libraries of London and Paris have been published and translated (J. Bacot, F. W. Thomas, et C. Toussaint, *Documents de Touen-houang rélatifs a l'histoire du Tibet*, Paris, P. Geuthner, 1940). The Tibetan text of the chronicle, *sBa-bshed*, has been prepared for publication (along with a brief synopsis of the text) by Professor Stein. So far as we know, there are, at present, two versions of this chronicle—the original or the so-called "pure" (*gtsaṅ-ma*); and the revised or the one with interpolations (*shabs-btags-ma*). (See G. Roerich, *The Blue Annals*, p. i, Calcutta, 1949). The publication of the epigraphic monuments of Central Tibet has also made a considerable progress. Richardson has published and translated the so-called "Lhasa edicts" and many other inscriptions on the stone obelisks in the Ui province (H. E. Richardson, *Ancient Historical Edicts at Lhasa*, London, 1952 ; *Idem.*, *Three Ancient Inscriptions from Tibet*,—JASB, Letter, vol. xv, No. 1, 1949).

The text of the Sino-Tibetan peace treaty of A.D. 821-22 has again attracted the attention of the learned scholars (Hisashi Sata, A *Study of the Sino-Tibetan Treaty of the T'ang Dynasty*,—"Toyoshi Ken-Kyu", x, 4, 1949, pp. 1-45 ; Fang-kuei Li, *The Inscription of the Sino-Tibetan Treaty of 821/22*,—"T'oung Pao", xliv, 1-3, Leiden, 1956, pp. 1-99 ; H. E. Richardson, *Ancient Historical Edicts at Lhasa*, London, 1952).

We know now that the *Deb-ther-dmar-po* [Red Annals] exists in two versions : the original (*mtshal-pa-kun-dga'-rdo-rje*), dated A.D. 1346 (Fire-Dog year) ; and the later one (*gsar-ma*) revised by the Tibetan scholar, bSod-nams-grags-pa (1478-1554), dated A.D. 1538 (Earth-Dog year). This work is being edited and translated by Professor Tucci (See Yu. N. Rerikh [G. Roerich], *Mongolo-tibetskie otnosheniya* 13-14 vv,—"Filologiya i istoriya mongol'skikh narodov", Moscow, 1958).

Tucci has also published his monumental work, *Tibetan Painted Scrolls* (Rome, 1949), where the historical literature of Tibet has been discussed in the chapter on chronicles (*chos-'byuṅ-s*) and on the history of monasteries.

Professor A. I. Vostrikov has, in his work, elucidated that the well-known chronicle, *rGyal-rabs-gsal-ba'i-me-loṅ*, was published in 1478 by Legs-pa'i-śes-rab.

The *rGya-nag-chos-'byuṅ* is now also available in a new xylograph edition from Lhasa.

Many catalogues of the Tibetan xylographs have also been published after 1937 : Shyiki Yoshimura, *The Denkar-ma, an Oldest Catalogue of the Tibetan Buddhist Canon*, Kyoto, 1950 ; *A Catalogue of the Tohoku University Collection of Tibetan Works on Buddhism*, Tohoku University, Sendai, 1953 ; Lokesh Chandra, *Tibetan Works Printed by the Shol-par-khaṅ of the Potala*, New Delhi, 1959.

Of the historico-geographical works discussed by A. I. Vostrikov, some texts have since been published and translated by Ferrari and Professor Tucci (G. Tucci, *Travels of Tibetan Pilgrims in the Swat Valley*, Calcutta, 1940 ; Ferrari, *Mkhyen-brtse's Guide to the Holy Places of Central Tibet*, Serie Orientale Roma, xvi, Rome, 1958). The text of the "Travels of Chag-lo-tsā-ba in India", mentioned by Vostrikov, has also been published and translated (G. Roerich, *The Life of Chag-lo-tsā-ba*, with an introduction by Dr. A. S. Altekar. Patna, K. Jaisawal Research Institute, 1960).

A. I. Vostrikov was the first to discover the error of G. Huth and ascertain the real name of the author of the *Hor-chos-'byuṅ*—Rig-pa'i-rdo-rje (tshe-'phel). (See also G. Roerich, *The Author of Hor-chos-'byuṅ*,—JRAS, 1946, pp. 192-196).

Yu. Rerikh*

December 7, 1959.

* Yurii Nikolaevich Rerikh [George Roerich],—the late editor of the revived *Bibliotheca Buddhica* series, in which the present work of A. I. Vostrikov was originally published.

CONVERSION TABLE

	FIRE	EARTH		IRON		WATER		WOOD		FIRE	
	f Hare	*m* Dragon	*f* Serpent	*m* Horse	*f* Sheep	*m* Monkey	*f* Hen	*m* Dog	*f* Pig	*m* Mouse	
I	1027	1028	1029	1030	1031	1032	1033	1034	1035	1036	I
II	1087	1088	1089	1090	1091	1092	1093	1094	1095	1096	II
III	1147	1148	1149	1150	1151	1152	1153	1154	1155	1156	III
IV	1207	1208	1209	1210	1211	1212	1213	1214	1215	1216	IV
V	1267	1268	1269	1270	1271	1272	1273	1274	1275	1276	V
VI	1327	1328	1329	1330	1331	1332	1333	1334	1335	1336	VI
VII	1387	1388	1389	1390	1391	1392	1393	1394	1395	1396	VII
VIII	1447	1448	1449	1450	1451	1452	1453	1454	1455	1456	VIII
IX	1507	1508	1509	1510	1511	1512	1513	1514	1515	1516	IX
X	1567	1568	1569	1570	1571	1572	1573	1574	1575	1576	X
XI	1627	1628	1629	1630	1631	1632	1633	1634	1635	1636	XI
XII	1687	1688	1689	1690	1691	1692	1693	1694	1695	1696	XII
XIII	1747	1748	1749	1750	1751	1752	1753	1754	1755	1756	XIII
XIV	1807	1808	1809	1810	1811	1812	1813	1814	1815	1816	XIV
XV	1867	1868	1869	1870	1871	1872	1873	1874	1875	1876	XV

	FIRE	EARTH		IRON		WATER		WOOD		FIRE	
	f Ox	*m* Tiger	*f* Hare	*m* Dragon	*f* Serpent	*m* Horse	*f* Sheep	*m* Monkey	*f* Hen	*m* Dog	
I	1037	1038	1039	1040	1041	1042	1043	1044	1045	1046	I
II	1097	1098	1099	1100	1101	1102	1103	1104	1105	1106	II
III	1157	1158	1159	1160	1161	1162	1163	1164	1165	1166	III
IV	1217	1218	1219	1220	1221	1222	1223	1224	1225	1226	IV
V	1277	1278	1279	1280	1281	1282	1283	1284	1285	1286	V
VI	1337	1338	1339	1340	1341	1342	1343	1344	1345	1346	VI
VII	1397	1398	1399	1400	1401	1402	1403	1404	1405	1406	VII
VIII	1457	1458	1459	1460	1461	1462	1463	1464	1465	1466	VIII
IX	1517	1518	1519	1520	1521	1522	1523	1524	1525	1526	IX
X	1577	1578	1579	1580	1581	1582	1583	1584	1585	1586	X
XI	1637	1638	1639	1640	1641	1642	1643	1644	1645	1646	XI
XII	1697	1698	1699	1700	1701	1702	1703	1704	1705	1706	XII
XIII	1757	1758	1759	1760	1761	1762	1763	1764	1765	1766	XIII
XIV	1817	1818	1819	1820	1821	1822	1823	1824	1825	1826	XIV
XV	1877	1878	1879	1880	1881	1882	1883	1884	1885	1886	XV

	FIRE	EARTH		IRON		WATER		WOOD		FIRE	
	f Pig	*m* Mouse	*f* Ox	*m* Tiger	*f* Hare	*m* Dragon	*f* Serpent	*m* Horse	*f* Sheep	*m* Monkey	
I	1047	1048	1049	1050	1051	1052	1053	1054	1055	1056	I
II	1107	1108	1109	1110	1111	1112	1113	1114	1115	1116	II
III	1167	1168	1169	1170	1171	1172	1173	1174	1175	1176	III
IV	1227	1228	1229	1230	1231	1232	1233	1234	1235	1236	IV
V	1287	1288	1289	1290	1291	1292	1293	1294	1295	1296	V
VI	1347	1348	1349	1350	1351	1352	1353	1354	1355	1356	VI
VII	1407	1408	1409	1410	1411	1412	1413	1414	1415	1416	VII
VIII	1467	1468	1469	1470	1471	1472	1473	1474	1475	1476	VIII
IX	1527	1528	1529	1530	1531	1532	1533	1534	1535	1536	IX
X	1587	1588	1589	1590	1591	1592	1593	1594	1595	1596	X
XI	1647	1648	1649	1650	1651	1652	1653	1654	1655	1656	XI
XII	1707	1708	1709	1710	1711	1712	1713	1714	1715	1716	XII
XIII	1767	1768	1769	1770	1771	1772	1773	1774	1775	1776	XIII
XIV	1827	1828	1829	1830	1831	1832	1833	1834	1835	1836	XIV
XV	1887	1888	1889	1890	1891	1892	1893	1894	1895	1896	XV

	FIRE	EARTH		IRON		WATER		WOOD		FIRE	
	f Hen	*m* Dog	*f* Pig	*m* Mouse	*f* Ox	*m* Tiger	*f* Hare	*m* Dragon	*f* Serpent	*m* Horse	
I	1057	1058	1059	1060	1061	1062	1063	1064	1065	1066	I
II	1117	1118	1119	1120	1121	1122	1123	1124	1125	1126	II
III	1177	1178	1179	1180	1181	1182	1183	1184	1185	1186	III
IV	1237	1238	1239	1240	1241	1242	1243	1244	1245	1246	IV
V	1297	1298	1299	1300	1301	1302	1303	1304	1305	1306	V
VI	1357	1358	1359	1360	1361	1362	1363	1364	1365	1366	VI
VII	1417	1418	1419	1420	1421	1422	1423	1424	1425	1426	VII
VIII	1477	1478	1479	1480	1481	1482	1483	1484	1485	1486	VIII
IX	1537	1538	1539	1540	1541	1542	1543	1544	1545	1546	IX
X	1597	1598	1599	1600	1601	1602	1603	1604	1605	1606	X
XI	1657	1658	1659	1660	1661	1662	1663	1664	1665	1666	XI
XII	1717	1718	1719	1720	1721	1722	1723	1724	1725	1726	XII
XIII	1777	1778	1779	1780	1781	1782	1783	1784	1785	1786	XIII
XIV	1837	1838	1839	1840	1841	1842	1843	1844	1845	1846	XIV
XV	1897	1898	1899	1900	1901	1902	1903	1904	1905	1906	XV

	FIRE	EARTH		IRON		WATER		WOOD		FIRE	
	f Sheep	*m* Monkey	*f* Hen	*m* Dog	*f* Pig	*m* Mouse	*f* Ox	*m* Tiger	*f* Hare	*m* Dragon	
I	1067	1068	1069	1070	1071	1072	1073	1074	1075	1076	I
II	1127	1128	1129	1130	1131	1132	1133	1134	1135	1136	II
III	1187	1188	1189	1190	1191	1192	1193	1194	1195	1196	III
IV	1247	1248	1249	1250	1251	1252	1253	1254	1255	1256	IV
V	1307	1308	1309	1310	1311	1312	1313	1314	1315	1316	V
VI	1367	1368	1369	1370	1371	1372	1373	1374	1375	1376	VI
VII	1427	1428	1429	1430	1431	1432	1433	1434	1435	1436	VII
VIII	1487	1488	1489	1490	1491	1492	1493	1494	1495	1496	VIII
IX	1547	1548	1549	1550	1551	1552	1553	1554	1555	1556	IX
X	1607	1608	1609	1610	1611	1612	1613	1614	1615	1616	X
XI	1667	1668	1669	1670	1671	1672	1673	1674	1675	1676	XI
XII	1727	1728	1729	1730	1731	1732	1733	1734	1735	1736	XII
XIII	1787	1788	1789	1790	1791	1792	1793	1794	1795	1796	XIII
XIV	1847	1848	1849	1850	1851	1852	1853	1854	1855	1856	XIV
XV	1907	1908	1909	1910	1911	1912	1913	1914	1915	1916	XV

	FIRE	EARTH		IRON		WATER		WOOD		FIRE	
	f Serpent	*m* Horse	*f* Sheep	*m* Monkey	*f* Hen	*m* Dog	*f* Pig	*m* Mouse	*f* Ox	*m* Tiger	
I	1077	1078	1079	1080	1081	1082	1083	1084	1085	1086	I
II	1137	1138	1139	1140	1141	1142	1143	1144	1145	1146	II
III	1197	1198	1199	1200	1201	1202	1203	1204	1205	1206	III
IV	1257	1258	1259	1260	1261	1262	1263	1264	1265	1266	IV
V	1317	1318	1319	1320	1321	1322	1323	1324	1325	1326	V
VI	1377	1378	1379	1380	1381	1382	1383	1384	1385	1386	VI
VII	1437	1438	1439	1440	1441	1442	1443	1444	1445	1446	VII
VIII	1497	1498	1499	1500	1501	1502	1503	1504	1505	1506	VIII
IX	1557	1558	1559	1560	1561	1562	1563	1564	1565	1566	IX
X	1617	1618	1619	1620	1621	1622	1623	1624	1625	1626	X
XI	1677	1678	1679	1680	1681	1682	1683	1684	1685	1686	XI
XII	1737	1738	1739	1740	1741	1742	1743	1744	1745	1746	XII
XIII	1797	1798	1799	1800	1801	1802	1803	1804	1805	1806	XIII
XIV	1857	1858	1859	1860	1861	1862	1863	1864	1865	1866	XIV
XV	1917	1918	1919	1920	1921	1922	1923	1924	1925	1926	XV

Bibliography

Baradiin B., *Statuya Maitrei v Zolotom khrame v Lavrane* [Statue of Maitreya in the Golden Temple in bLa-brañ], Leningrad, 1924 (*Bibliotheca Buddhica*, xxii).

Bichurin I., *Istoriya Tibeta i khukhunora* [History of Tibet and Kokonor], pts. l, ii, St. Petersburg, 1831.

Golstunskii K.F., *Mongolo-oiratskie zakony 1640 goda* [Mongolian and Oirat Laws of 1640], St. Petersburg, 1880.

Hackmann F., *Izvestiya o geograficheskom, istoricheskom i fizicheskom sostoyanii Tibeta* [On the History, Geography and Topography of Tibet],—"Sobranie sochinenii, vybrannykh iz mesyatsoslovov na raznye gody", pt. v, St. Petersburg, 1790.

Katalog knig i rukopisei na kitaiskom, manchzhurskom, mongol'skom, tibetskom i sanskritskom yazyke v biblioteke Aziatskogo departamenta [A Catalogue of the Books and Manuscripts in the Chinese, Manchurian, Mongolian, Tibetan and Sanskrit Languages in the Library of the Asiatic Department], St. Petersburg, 1884.

Kozin S.A., *Bibliograficheskii obzor izdannykh i neizdannykh rabot akad. V. P. Vasil'eva po dannym Aziatskogo muzeya AN SSSR* [A Bibliographical Survey of the Published and Unpublished Works of Academician V. P. Vasil'ev in the Asiatic Museum of the Academy of Sciences, U.S.S.R.],—"Izvestiya Akademii nauk SSSR", seriya 7 (otd. obshch. nauk), 1931, No. 6.

Kozlov P.K., *Mongolia i Kam* [Mongolia and Kham],—"Trudy ekspeditsii imperatorskogo russkogo geograficheskogo obshchestva, sovershennoi v 1899-1901 gg.", vol. i, pt. i, St. Petersburg, 1905.

Laufer B., *Ocherk mongol'skoi literatury* [An Outline of Mongolian Literature], 1927.

Potanin G.N., *Ocherki Severo-Zapadnoi Mongolii* [On North-Western Mongolia], St. Petersburg, 1881. no. i.

Schmidt Ya., *Grammatika tibetskogo yazyka* [Grammar of Tibetan Language], St. Petersburg, 1839.

Shcherbatskoi F.I., *Tibetskii perevod sochinenii 'Santānāntarasiddhi' Dharmakīrti i 'Santānāntarasiddhiṭīkā' Vinītadeva vmeste s tibetskim tolkovaniem, sostavlennym Agvan Dandarlkharamboi* [Tibetan Translation of Dharmakīrti's *Santānāntarasiddhi* and Vinītadeva's *Santānāntarasiddhitīka*, with a Tibetan Commentary by Dandar Lha-rampa], Petrograd, 1916 (*Bibliotheca Buddhica*, xix).

Tsybikov G., *Buddist-palomnik u svyatyn' Tibeta. Po dnevnikam, vedennym v 1889-1902 gg.* [A Buddhist Pilgrim in the Holy Places of Tibet...], Petrograd, 1919. *Lam-rim-chen-po*, vol. i, nos. i, ii, Vladivostok, 1910-1913.

Tsybikov G., *Spisok tibetskim izdaniyam, privezennym Gonbozhapom Tsybikovym v 1902 g. i pozhertvovannym muzeyu imperatorskim russkim geograficheskim obshchestvom* [A List of Tibetan Publications Brought by G. Tsybikov in 1902, and Donated to the Museum by the Imperial Russian Geographical Society], "Musei Asiatici Petropolitani Notitiae", iv, v, vi. Curante C. Salemann,—"Izvestiya Imperatorskoi Akademii nauk", seriya v, St. Petersburg, 1904, vol. xxi.

Tubyanskii M.I., *Nekotorye problemy mongol'skoi literatury dorevolyutsionnogo perioda* [Some Problems of Mongolian Literature of the Pre-revolutionary Period], —"Sovremennaya Mongoliya", Ulan Bator, 1935, no. 5 (12).

— *Predvaritel'noe soobshchenie o buddologicheskom rukopisnom nasledii V. P. Vasil'eva i V. V. Gorskogo* [V. P. Vasil'ev and V. V. Gorskii : A Preliminary Survey of Their Unpublished Writings on Buddhist Studies],—"Doklady AN SSSR", seriya B, 1927.

Vasil'ev V.P., *Geografiya Tibeta. Perevod iz tibetskogo sochineniya sMin-grol-sprul-sku'a* [Geography of Tibet. Translation of a Tibetan Work by sMin-grol-sprul-sku], St. Petersburg, 1895.

— *O nekotorykh knigakh, otnosyashchikhsya k istorii buddizma, v biblioteke Kazanskogo universiteta,*—[On Some Books, Relating to the History of Buddhism, in the Library of the University of Kazan],—"Uchenye zapiski Akademii nauk po pervomu i tret'emu otdeleniyam, vol. iii, St. Petersburg, 1855.

— *Perevod khronologicheskoi tablitsy Sum-pa-khutukhty* (*Sum-pa-mkhan-po*) ; *rukopis'* [Translation of the Chronological Table of Sum-pa-khutukhta (Sum-pa-mkhan-po) ; manuscript],—Arkhiv AN SSSR, No. 775, 1, No. 3/2.

Vladimirtsov B. Ya., *Iz liriki Milaraiby* [From the Lyrics of Mi-la-ras-pa],—"Vostok", 1, 1922.

— *Mongol'skii sbornik rasskazov iz 'Pañcatantra'* [Mongolian Collection of the Tales of *Pañcatantra*], Petrograd, 1921.

— *Obshchestvennyi stroi mongolov* [Social Order of the Mongols], Leningrad, 1934.

— *O tibetsko-mongol'skom slovare Li-śihi gur-khan* [On a Tibetan-Mongolian Dictionary], —"Doklady AN SSSR", seriya B, 1926

Vostrikov A.I., *K bibliografii tibetskoi literatury* [On a Bibliography of Tibetan Literature],—"Bibliografiya Vostoka", Nos. 2-4 (1933), Leningrad, 1934.

Bacot J., *La collection tibétaine Schilling von Canstadt a la Bibliothéque de l'Institut*, —JA, t. ccv, 1924.

— *Le poétaine Milarépa*, Paris, 1925.

Bell C., *The People of Tibet*, Oxford, 1928.

— *The Religion of Tibet*, Oxford, 1931.

Burnouf E., *Sur la littérature du Tibet*, extrait du no. vii du Quarterly Oriental magazine de Calcutta,—JA t. x. 1827.

Bushell S. W., *The Early History of Tibet*, from chinese sources,—JRAS, 1880.

Cordier P., *Catalogue du fonds tibétaine de la Bibliothéque Nationale*, Partie II, III. *Index du bsTan-'gyur*, Paris, 1909-1915.

Csoma de Koros A., *Enumeration of Historical and Grammatical Works to be Met with in Tibet*,—JASB, 1938.

— *A Grammar of the Tibetan Language in English*, Calcutta, 1834.

— *Kings of Tibet, to the Subdivision of the Country in the Tenth Century*,—JASB, 1834.

Cunninghan A., *Ladak, Physical, Statistical and Historical with Notices of the Surrounding Countries*, London, 1814.

Das S. C., *A Brief Account of Tibet from "Dsam Ling Gyeshe", the Well-Known Geographical Work of Lama Tsanpo Nomankhan of Amdo*,—JRAS, 1887.

— *Buddhist and Other Legends about Khoten*,—JASB, 1886.

— *Contributions on the Religion, History* etc. *of Tibet*,—JASB, 1881, 1 82.

— *The Hierarchy of the Dalai Lama (1406-1745)*,—JASB, 1904.

— *Indian Paṇḍits in the Land of Snow*, Calcutta, 1893,—JBTS, 1893.

— *An Introduction to the Grammar of the Tibetan Language, with the Texts of 'Situhi sumrtags, Dag-je-sal-wai me-long and Sitahi shal-lung*, Darjeeling, 1915.

— *Kah bab dun dan, the Book of Seven Mystic Revelations*, Calcutta, 1901.

— *The Lamaic Hierarchy of Tibet*,—JBTS, 1893.

— *Life of Sum-pa-khan-po, also Styled Yeśes-dpal'byor, the Author of the Re'u-mig (Chronological Table)*,—JASB, 1889.

— *The Monasteries of Tibet*,—JASB, New series. 1905.

— *The Origine of Mankind, Compiled from the Legendary History of Tibet*,—JBTS, 1896.

— *Pag Sam Jon Zang*, i, ii, Calcutta,1908.

— *Rgyal-rabs-bon-gyi-'byuṅ-gnas*, Darjeeling, 1915.

— *A Short History of the House of Phagdu, which Ruled over Tibet on the Decline of Sakya till 1432 A.D.*,—JASB, New series, 1905.

— *A Short Note on the Origine of the Tibetans and Their Division into Clans*,—JBTS, 1897.

Das S. C., *Some Historical Facts Connected with the Rise and Progress of the Mahāyāna School of Buddhism*,—JBTS, 1893.

— *Tibet, a Dependency of Mongolia (1643-1716 A.D.)*,—JASB, New series, 1905.

— *Tibet under Her Last Kings (1434-1642 A.D.)*,—JASB. New series, 1905.

— *Tibet under the Tartar Emperors of China in the 10th Century A.D.*,—JASB, 1904.

— *The Tibetan Chronological Table Re'u-mig) from the Mss. Original Work, Choos-Jonsang*,—JASB, 1886.

— *A Tibetan-English Dictionary with Sanskrit Synonyms*, Calcutta, 1902.

— Vidyābhūṣana Hari Mohan and Satīsa Candra Vidyābhūṣaṇa, eds. *Kṣemendra. Rtogs brjod Dpag Basam Hkhri Sin or Avadāna Kalpalata/Sanskr. and Tibetan/*, vol. I-II (1889-1917), (Bibliotheca Indica, N 124, 130).

Evans-Wentz W.Y., *Tibet's Great Yogi Milarepa*, Oxford, 1928.

Feer M.L., *Cinca-mānavikā Sundarī*—JA, 9-me série, t. ix, 1897.

— *L'enfer indien (suite et fin)*. ii Brahmanisme,—JA, 9-me série, t. l. 1893.

Foucaux Ph. Ed., *Rgya tch'er rol-ba ou Dévelopment des yeux, contenant l'histoire du Bouddha Śakya-mouni*, traduit sur la version tibétaine du *bKa'-'gyur* et revu sur l'original sanscrit (*Lalitavistara*), pt. i, ii, Paris, 1847-1848.

Francke A., *Antiquities of Indian Tibet*, pt. i, ii, Calcutta, 1914-1926.

— *Achaeological Notes on Bàlu-mkhar in Western Tibet*,—"Indian Antiquary", vol. xxxiv, 1905.

— *Archaeology in Western Tibet*,—"Indian Antiquary", vol. xxxv, 1906; vol. xxxvi, 1907.

— *Dritte sammlung von Felszeichnungen aus Unter-Ladakh*, Leh, 1902 (lithogr.).

— *Ein Dokument aus Turfan in tibetischer Schrift, aber unbekannter Sprache*,—"Sitzungsberichte der Preussischen Akademie der Wissenschaften", Philos-hist. Kl. 1927.

— *Erste and Zweite Sammlung tibetischer historischer Inschriften*, Leipzig, 1906.

— *Felsinschriften in Ladakh*—"Sitzungsberichte der Preussischen Akademie der Wissenschaften", Philos.-hist. Kl., 1925.

— *Die Geschichte des Dogra-Krieges. Nach dem Manuscript C des Ladvags rgyalrabs*,—ZDMG, Bd lxiv, 1910.

— *Historical Documents from the Borders of Tibet*,—"Archaeological Survey of India", Annual Report 1909/10, Calcutta, 1914.

— *Historische Dokumente von Khalaste in West Tibet (Ladakh)*,—ZDMG, Bd lxi, 1907.

— *Die historischen und mythologischen Erinnerungen der Lahouler, Kye-lang/S.a./.*

— *History of Western Tibet. One of the Unknown Empires*, London, 1907.

Francke A., *The Kingdom of gNya khri bstanpo, the First King of Tibet,*—JASB, vol. vi, 1910.

— *Kleine archaeologische Ertrage einer Missionsreise nach Zangskar in West-Tibet,*—ZDMG., Bd lx, 1906 ; Bd lxi, 1907.

— *Konigsnamen von Khotan (A-ma-ca) auf tibetischen Documenten der Turkistan Sammlungen von London und Berlin,*—"Sitzungsberichte der Preussischen Akademie der Wissenschaften, Philos-hist. Kl., 1928.

— *Ladakhi Stone-Implements,*—"Indian Antiquary", xxxiii, 1904.

— *List of Minister's Names Found in the Tibetan Inscription in Front of the Ta-chao-ssu temple (Jokhang) in Lhasa,* 822 A.D.,—"Epigraphia Indica", vol. xi, 1912, pt. vi.

— *Notes on Rock-Carvings from Lower Ladakh,*—"Indian Antiquary", vol. xxxi, 1902.

— *Notes on Sir Aurel Stein's Collection of Tibetan Documents from Chinese Turkestan,*—JRAS, 1914.

— *References to the Bhottas in the Rājataranginī,*—"Indian Antiquary", vol. xxxvii, 1908.

— *Remarks on a Photograph, near Atlng, Taken by the Hon. Eric Upton, During a Tour in Zangskar in 1907,*—"Indian Antiquary", vol. xxxvii, 1908.

— *The Rock Inscriptions at Mul-bhe,*—"Indian Antiquary", vol. xxxv, 1906.

— *Some More Rock-Carvings from Lower Ladakh,*—"Indian Antiquary", vol. xxxii, 1903.

— *Ten Ancient Historical Songs from Western Tibet,*—"Indian Antiquary", vol. xxxviii, 1909.

— *Tibetan Documents, Brought from Chinese Turkestan by Sir Aurel Stein in 1915* (in : A. Stein, *Serindia*, and in : *Innermost Asia*).

— *Tibetan Inscription on the Stone Monument in Front of the Ta-chao-ssu Temple in Lhasa, 822 A.D.*—' Epigraphia Indica", vol. x, 1909/10, pt. iv.

— *Tibetan Inscription on the Darkot Pass.* (in : A. Stein, *Innermost Asia*, vol. ii, 1925).

— *Tibetische Handschriftenfunde aus Turfan,*—"Sitzungsberichte der Preussuschen Akademie der Wissenschaften", Philos.-hist. Kl. 1924.

— *Vorbuddhistische religion Tibets.* Allgemeine Mission,—ZDMG, xxxviii, 1874.

Georgi, *Alphabetum tibetanum missionum apostolicorum commodo editum*, Rome, 1762.

Ginzel Fr. Karl., *Handbuch der Mathematischen und technischen chronologie. Das Zeitrechnungswesen der Volker*, Bd l, Leipzig, 1906.

Grünwedel A., *Buddhistische Studien. Excurs : Das Supparadskhataka in Padmasambhava's Legendenbuch,*—"Veroffentlichungen aus dem koniglichen Museum für Volkerkunde", Bd v, Berlin, 1895.

Grünwedel A., *Drei Leptscha Texte mit Auszügen aus dem Padma-thaṅ-yig und Glossar*,—"T'oung Pao", vol. vii, 1896.
— *Ein kapitel des Ta-sche-sung*,—"Festschrift für Adolf Bastian", Berlin, 1896.
— in his review of : Huth Georg. *Geschichte des Buddhismus inder Mongolei aus dem Tibetischen des 'Jigs-med-nam-mkha'*, Theil 1, 2, Strassburg, 1893-1896.—"Wiener Zeitschrift für die Kunde des Morgenlandes", Bd xii, Wien, 1898.
— *Mythologie des Buddhismus in Tibet und der Mongolei*, Leipzig, 1900.
— *Padmasambhava und Verwandtes*,—"Baessler-Archiv", Bd iii, Heft 1, Leipzig-Berlin, 1912.
— *Padmasambhava vnd Mandārava*,—ZDMG, Bd lii, 1898.
— *Tāranātha's Edelsteinmine, das Buch von der Vermittlern der sieben Inspirationen*, Petrograd, 1914 (*Bibliotheca Buddhica*, xviii).
— *Die Temple von Lhasa. Gedicht der ersten Dalailama*,—"Sitzungsberichte der Heidelberger Akademie der Wissenschaften, Philos. hist. KI., Abh. 14, 1919.
— *Der Weg nach Śambhala des dritten Gross-Lama von bKra-śis-lhun-poblobzan dpal ldan Yeśes*,—Abhand, der konig. bayerischen Akad. der Wissenschaften". cl. I, Bd xxix, Abh. 3, München. 1915.
Hackin J., *Formulaire sanscrit-tibétain du X-e siécle*, Paris, 1924.
Huth G., *Geschichte des Buddhismus in det Mongolei, aus dem Tibetischen des 'Jigs-med nam-mkha'*, Theil 1, 2, Strassburg, 1892-1896.
— *Nachtragliche Ergebnisse bezüglich der chronologischen Ansetzung der Werke im tibetischen Tanjur, Abtheilung mdo* (*sūtra*)—ZDMG, Bd xlix, 1895.
Jaschke H. A., *Proben aus den tibetischen Legendenbuche, die hunderttausend Gesange des Milaraspa*,—ZDMG, 1869.
Klaproth, *Table chronologique des plus célebres patrciarches et des évènements remarquables de la religion bouddhique, redigée en 1678* (*traduite de mongol*), —JA, t. vii, Paris, 1831.
Koeppen, *Die lamaische Hierarchie und Kirche*, Berlin, 1859.
Lassen C., *Indische Altertumskunde*, Bd ii, Leipzig, 1874.
Laufer B., *The Application of the Tibetan Sexagenary Cycle*,—"Toung Pao", vol. xiv, 1913.
— *Aus den Geschichten und Liedern des Milaraspa*, Wien, 1902.
— *Die Bru-za Sprache und historische Stellúng des Padmasambhava*,—T'oung Pao", Série ii, vol. ix, 1908.
— *Milaraspa*. London, 1922.
— *Der Roman einer tbetischen konigin*, Leipzig. 1911.
— *The Sexagenary cycle, Once More*,—"T'oung Pao", vol. xv, 1914.

Laufer B., *Skizze der mongolischen Literatur.*—',Keleti Szemle-Revue Orientale" vii, 1907.

— *Studien zur Sprachwissenschaft der Tibeter Zamatag,*—"Sitzungsberichte der Koenig Bayerischen Akad. der Wissenchaften", der philos.-philol. und hist. KI. 1898.

— *Ueber ein tibetisches Geschichtswerk der Bonpo,*—"T'oung Pao", série 2, vol. ii, 1910.

— *Zwei Legenden des Milaraspa*, Wien, 1901.

Lefmann S., *Lalita-Vistara*, Teil I, II, Halle am Saale, 1902-1908.

Levi Sylvain., *Author d'Aśvaghoṣa*, JA., 1929.

Ligeti L., *Les noms mongols de Wen Tsong des Yuan,*—"T'oung Pao", vol. xxvii (1930).

— *Rapport préliminaire d'un voyage d'exploration fait en Mongolie chinoise*, 1928-1931. Budapest, 1933.

van Manen, Johan, *A Contribution to the Bibliography of Tibet.,*—JASB, New series, vol. xviii, 1922.

Markham C.R., *Narratives of the mission of George Bogle to Tibet and of journey of Thomas Manning to Lhasa*, London, 1879.

Marx K., *Three documents relating to the history of Ladakh. Tibetan text, translation and Potes* —JASB, vol, lx, 1891, pt. 1, N3 ; vol. lxiii, 1894, pt. 1, N2 ; vol. lxxi, 1902, pt. 1, N 1.

Mitra Rajendralala , *Lalita-Vistara or memoirs of the life and doctrines of Śākya Siṃha*, Calcutta, 1853-1877 ; 1881-1886 (*Bibliotheca Indica* N15, N90).

Müller Herbet, *Tibet in seiner geschichtlichen Entwicklung*—"Zeitschrift für vergleichende Rechtswissenschaft", Bd xx, 1907.

Nanjio B.A., *A Catalogue of the Chinese Translation of the Buddhist Tripiṭaka*, Oxford, 1883.

Obermiller E., '*History of Buddhism (chos-'byuṅ)' by Bu-ston*, pt. i, ii, Heidelberg, 1931-1932.

— *Tsoṅ-kha-pa le Pandit,*—"Mélanges chinois et bouddhiques publiés par L'Institut Belge des Hautes Etudes chinoises", vol. iii, Bruxelles, 1935.

Pallas P.S., *Sammlungen historischer Nachrichten über die Mongolischen Voelkerschaften*, Theil ii, St. Petersburg, 1801.

Parker E.H., *Manchu Relations with Tibet or Si-tsong,*—"Journal of the North China Branch of the Royal Asiatic Society", vol. 19, 1886, pt. 2.

Pelliot P., *Le cycle sexagénaire dans la chronologie tibétaine,*—JA Mai-Juin, 1913.

Prinsep J., *Useful Tables forming an Appendix to the Journal of the Asiatic Society,*—JAS, 1836.

Rockhill W.W., *The Dalai Lamas of Lhasa and Their Relations with the Manchu Emperors of China 1644-1908,*—"T'oung Pao", vol. xi 1910.

Rockhill W. W., *The Land of the Lamas*, London, 1891.

— *The Life of the Buddha and the Early History of His Order*, London, 1907.

— *The Tibetan ' Hundred Thousand Songs" of Milaraspa*,—JASB, 1884.

Sandberg G., *Tibet and the Tibetans*, London, 1906.

Schiefner A., *Bericht über die neueste Büchersendung aus Peking*,—"Büll. hist.-philol. de l'Acad. imp. de sciences de St. Pétersbourg", t. viii, N1,2, St. Petersbourg, 1847.

— *Nachtrage zu den O. Boehtlingk und I. J. Schmidt verfassten Verzeichnissen der auf Indien und Tibet bezüglichen Handschriften und Holzdrücke im Asiatischen Museum der Kaiser. Akademie der Wissenschaften.*—"Büll. his.-philol., de l'Akad. imp. de sciences de St. Pétersbourg", t. v, N 10, St. Petersbourg, 1848.

— *Tāranāthae de doctrinae buddhicae in India propagatione narratio*, Petropoli. 1868.

— *Tāranāthas Geschichte des Buddhismus in Indien*, St. Petersbourg, 1869.

Schlagintweit E., *Buddhism in Tibet*, Leipzig-London, 1863.

— *Die Berechnung der Lehre. Eine Streitschrift Berichtigung der buddhistischen Chronologie verfasst im Jahre 1591 von Sureśamatibhadra*,—"Abhand. der koenig, bayerischen Akad. der Wissenschaften", cl. i, Bd xx, Abt. iii, München, 1897.

— *Die Lebensbeschreibung von Padma Sambhava dem Begründer des Lamaismus*, Teil i, ii,—"Abhand. der koenig. bayerischen Akad. der Wissenschaften", cl. i, Bd xxi, Abt. ii ; Bd xxii, Abt. iii, München, 1899-1905.

— *Die Koenige von Tibet von der Entstehung koeniglicher Macht in Yarlung bis zum Erloschen in Ladak*,—"Abhand. der koenig. bayerischen Akad. der Wissenschaften", cl. i, Bd x, Abt. iii, München, 1866.

Schmidt I.J., *Geschichte der Ost-Mongolen und ihres Fürstenhauses, verfasst von Ssanang Ssetseng Chungtaidschi der Ordus*, St. Petersburg, 1829.

— *Grammatik der tibetischen Sprache*, St. Petersburg, 1839.

— *Forschungen im Gebiete der aeltern religiosen, politischen und literarischen Bildungsgeschichte der Voelker Mittel-Asiens, vorzüglich der Mongolen und Tibeter*, St. Petersburg, 1824.

—und Boehtlingk O., *Verzeicheiss der tibetischen Handschriften und Holzdrucke im Asiatischen Museum*,—"Bull. hist.-philol. de l'Acad. imp. de sciences de St. Pétersburg", t. iv, N 6 ; 7 ; 8 ; 31 ; St. Petersburg, 1847.

Stcherbatsky Th. [Shcherbatskoi, F.I.], *Buddhist Logic*, vol. 1, Leningrad, 1932.

— *Notes de littérature bouddhique. La littérature Yogācāra d'apres Buston*—"Le Muséon", vol. vi, N. 1, 1905.

— *On the Abhidharma Literature of the Sarvāstivādins*,—JPTS, 1904-1905.

Schulemann G., *Die Geschichte der Dalai-lamas*, Heidelberg, 1911.

Stein A., *Innermost Asia*, vol. ii, 1925.

Thomas F. W., *The Language of Ancient Khotan*,—"Asia Major", vol. ii, 1925.

— *Law of Theft in Chinese Kan-su : A ixth-xth century Fragment from Tun-huang*,—"Reitschrift für vergleichende Rechtswissenschaft", Band L, Heft 3, 1936.

— *Note on the Tibetan Collections of the India Office Library*,—JASB, New series, vol. xviii, 1922.

— *Tibetan Documents Concerning Chinese Turkestan*,—JRAS, 1927, 1928.

— *Tibetan Literary Texts and Documents Concerning Chinese Turkestan*, pt. i, London, 1935.

—& Sten Konow, *Two Medieval Documents from Tun-huang*,—"Royal Frederik University Publications of the Indian Institute", 1, 3, Oslo. 1929.

Toussaint G. Ch., *Le dict de Padma. Padma thaṅ yig, MS. de Lithang*, Paris, 1933.

— *Le Padma Thaṅ Yig*,—JA, ccii, 1923.

— *Le Padma Thaṅ Yig*,—"Etudes Asiatiques", t. ii, 1925.

Tucci G., *Indo-Tibetica II : Rin c'en bzan po e la rinascita del Buddhismo nel Tibet intorno al mille, Roma*, 1933 (*Reale Academia d'Italia. Studi e documenti*, I).

Vostrikov A., *Some Corrections and Critical Remarks on Dr. Johan von Manen's Contribution to the Bibliography of Tibet*,—BSOS, vol. viii, 1935, pt. i.

Waddell L. A., *Ancient Historical Edicts at Lhasa*—JRAS, 1909-1911.

— *The Buddhism of Tibet or Lamaism*, London, 1895.

— *Chinese Imperial Edict of 1808 A.D. of the origin and Transmigrations of the Grand Lamas of Tibet*,—JRAS, 1910.

— *Description of Lhasa Cathedral* translated from Tibetan—JASB, vol. lxiv, 1895, pt. i.

— *Lhasa and its Mysteries with a Record of the Expedition of 1903-1904*, London, 1905.

— *Note on the Tibetan Collections of the India Office Library*,—JASB, 1904.

— *Tibetan Invasion of India in 647 A.D. and its Results*,—The Imperial and Asiatic Quarterly and Oriental and Colonial Record", vol. xxxi, 1911.

— *Tibetan Manuscripts and Books, etc. Collected During the Younghusband Mission to Lhasa*,—"The Imperial and Asiatic Quarterly and Oriental colonial Record, vol. xxxiv, 1912".

Walsh E. H. C., *A List of Tibetan Books brought from Lhasa by the Japanese Monk, Mr. Ekai Kawa Gochi*,—JASB, vol. lxxiii, 1904.

Wislicenus W., *Astronomische Chronologie*, Leipzig, 1895.

WORKS PUBLISHED AFTER 1936

Aoki B., *Study on Early Tibetan Chronicles Regarding Discrepancies of Dates and their Adjustments.* Tokyo, Nippon Gakujutsu shiukokai, 1955.

Bacot Y., *Réconnaissance en Haut Asie Septentrionale par cinq envoyés ouigours an VIII e siécle*, Paris, JA, 1957.

Bacot J., Thomas F. W. et Toussaint C., *Documents de Touen-houang relatifs a l'histoire du Tibet*, Paris, P. Geuthner, 1940.

Camman Schnyler, *The Panchen Lama's Visit to China in 1780, An Episode in Anglo-Tibetan Relations*,—"Far Eastern quarterly", N. Y., 1949, Nov., vol. 9, N 1, p. 3-12.

A Catalogue of the Tohoku University Collection of Tibetan Works on Buddhism, Tohoku University, Sendai, 1953.

Chandra Lokesh, *Tibetan Works Printed by the Sholpar-Khaṅ of the Potala*, New Delhi, 1959

— *Mkhas-pa'i dga'-ston bo dPa'-bo gtsug-lag,also known as Lho-brag-chos-'byuṅ*, Part i, Intern. Academy of Indian Culture, New Delhi, 1959.

Chattopadhyaya A., *Atīśa and Tibet*, Calcutta, 1967.*

Chattopadhyaya D. (ed.), *Tāranātha's History of Buddhism in India*, tr. by Lama Chimpa and A. Chattopadhyaya, Simla, 1970.*

Demieville P., *Le Concile de Lhasa. Une controverse sur le quiétisme entre bouddhistes de l'Inde et de la Chine au VIII-e siécle de l'ére chretiénne*, Paris, Presses University de France, 1952.

Filliozat J., *Catalogue de Manuscrits Sanskrits et Tibétains de la Société Asiatique*,—JA, 1941-1942, p. 1-81.

Ferrari A., *Mkhyen-brtse's Guide to the Holy Places of Central Tibet*, Roma, 1958 (Serie Oriental Roma, xvi).

Hisashi Sata, *A Study of the Sino-Tibetan Treaty of the T'ang Dynasty*,—"Toyoshi Kenkyû", x, 4, 1949.

Hoffman A., *Zur Literatur der Bon-po*,—"Zeit. d.Deut. Morgen. Gesell", Neue folge, Bd. 19. S. 169-188, 1940.

— *Tibets Eintritt in die Universalgeschichte*,—"Speculum" München, 1950, Bd. 1, Hf. 2, S. 258-279.

— *Die Graeber der tibetischen Koenige in Distrikt 'P' yonsrgyas*, Goettingen, Vandenhoeck Ruprecht, 1950. (Nachrichten der Akad. der wiss. in Goettingen. I Philol-hist. Klasse, 1950, N 1).

— *Die Religionen Tibets. Bon und Lamaismus in ihrer geschichtlichen Entwicklung*, Freiburg, München, 1956.

---

* Added by the translator.

Kuznetsov B.I. (tr.), *Tibetskaya letopis' "Svetloe zertsalo tsarskikh rodoslovnykh* [Tibetan Chronicle "A clear Mirror of Royal Genealogies"], with Introduction and Commentary, Leningrad, 1961.

Lalou M., *Inventaire des Manuscrits tibétains de Touen-huang, conserves a la Bibliothéque nationale (Fonds Pelliot tibétain)*, vols. i-ii, Paris, Libraire d'Amérique et d'Orient, 1939-1950.

— *Documents de Touen-Huang*,—"Mélanges chinois et buddhiques", vol. 8, 1946-1947, Bruxelles, 1947, p. 217-226.

— *Revendicafious des fonctionnaires de Grand Tibet au viii Siecle*,—JA, 1955, N 2.

— *Rituel bon-pa der funerailess royales*,—JA, 1952, F. 240, Fasc 3, p. 339-362.

— *Les textes bouddhiques au temps de Khri-sroṅ-lde-btsan*,—JA, 1953, T. 141, N 3, p. 313-354.

— *Les plus anciens roubaux tibetains trouves a Touenhouang*,—"Rocznie orientalistyczñy", T. 21, Warszawa, 1957, s. 149-152.

Li An che., *Rñiṅ-ma-pa : the Early Form of Lamaism*,—JRAS, 1948, pts. 3-4, p. 142-163.

Li Fang-kuei, The Inscription of the Sino-Tibetan Treaty of 821- 22,—"T'oung Pao", Leiden, 1956, vol. 44, Livr. 1-3, p. 1-99.

— *Notes on Tibetan Sog*,—"Central Asiatic Journal", Hague-Wiesbaden, 1957, vol. 3, N 2, p. 139-142.

Meisezahl R. O., *Tibetica der Pelliot und Stein Tun-huang MSS*,—"Ural-altaische Jahrbucher", Hrsg. von J. von Farkas, Bd. 27, Hf. 3-4, Wiesbaden, 1955, S. 209-221.

Pelliot P., *Histoire du Tibet ancien d'aprés les documents chinois de l'epoque des T'ang*, Paris, 1958, in 8, br. (Oeuvres posthumes de Paul Pelliot, vol vi).

Petech L., *A Study on the Chronicles of Ladakh*, Calcutta, 1939.

— *China and Tibet in the Early 18th Century. History of the Establishment of Chinese Protectorate in Tibet*, Leiden, Brill, 1950.

— *The missions of Bogle and Turner according to the Tibetan texts*,—"T'oung Pao", Leiden, 1950, vol. 39, Livr. 4-5, p. 330-346.

Quellen zur Geschichte der tibetischen Bon-Religion. Hrsg. und übers von H. Hoffmann, Wiesbaden, Akad der Wissenschaften, 1950.

Richardson H. E., *A Tibetan Inscription from Rgyal Lha-Khan and a Note on Tibetan Chronology From A.D. 841 to A.D. 1942*,—JRAS, 1951, pt. 1-2, p. 57-78.

— *Tibetan Inscriptions of Shva-hi Lha-Khan*, pt. i—JRAS, 1952, pt. 3-4. p. 133-154.

— *Tibetan Inscription of Shva-hi Lha-Khan*,—JRAS, 1953, pt. 1-2, p. 1-12.

— *Three Ancient Inscriptions from Tibet*,—JASB, Letter, vol. xv,, N 1, 1949, p. 54-64.

Richardson H.E., *A Ninth Century Inscription from rKon-po*,—JRAS, 1954, pt. 3-4, p. 157-173.
— *Ancient Historical Edicts at Lhasa*, London, 1952.

Roerich G., *The Blue Annals* (*Deb-ther-sṅon-po*). 2 vols., Calcutta, 1949-1953.
— *The Life of Chag-lo-tsā-ba*. With an Introduction by Dr. A. S. Altekar, Publ. by the K. Jayaswal Research Institute, Patna, 1960.

Rona Tas A., *Social Terms in the List of Grants of the Tibetan Tun-Huang Chronicle*,—"Acta Orientalia", Bud., 1955, vol. 5, facs. 3.
— *Tally-stick and Divination-Dice in the Iconography of Lha-mo*,—"Acta Orientalia", Bud., 1956, vol. vi, facs. 1-3.

Schubert J., *Das Wünschgebet um Sambhala* (*Ein tibetischer Kālacakra-Text mit einer mongolischen Uebertragung*),—"Mitteilungen des Inst. fur Orientforschung", Berlin, 1953, Bd. i. Hf. 3, S. 424-473.

Stein R. A., *L'épopée tibétaine de Gesar dans sa version lamaique de Ling*, Paris, 1956. (*Annales du Musée Guimet, Bibliotheque d'études*, tome soixante et uniéme).

Tibetan Literary Texts and Documents Concerning Chinese Turkestan. Selected and Translated by F. W. Thomas, Pt. 2, Documents.—London, Luzac, 1951, vii. (*Oriental translation fund*. N. Ser. vol. 37). Pt. 3, Addenda and corrigenda, with Tibetan vocabulary, concordance of document numbers, plates, 199 pp., London, 1955.

Tucci G., *Travels of Tibetan Piligrims in the Swat Valley*, Calcutta, 1960.
— *Indo-Tibetica*, 7 vols. 1932.
— *On the Validity of the Tibetan Historical Tradition*,—"India Antiqua", Leiden, 1947, p. 309-322.
— *Tibetan Painted Scrolls*, Roma, 1949
— *Tibetan Notes*,—"Harvard Journal of Asiatic Studies", Cambridge, Mass. 1949, Dec., vol. 12, N 3-4, p. 477-496.
— *The Tombs of the Tibetan Kings*, Roma, Ist. italiano per il Medio ed Estremo Oriente, 1950, viii, *Serie Orientale Roma* i.
— *The Tombs of the Tibetans Kings*,—"Journal of the Royal Central Asian Society ", L., 1952, Jan., vol. 39, pt. i, p. 42-44.
— *The Secret Characters of the Kings of Ancient Tibet*.—"East and West", Roma, 1955, Oct., year 6, N 3, p. 197-205.
— *La regalita sacra nell 'antico Tibet. Congresso intern. di storia delle religioui*, 8. (Roma, 1955), Atti Firenze 1956, p. 128-132.
— (tr.), *Deb-ther-dmar-po*. Roma, 1959.*

Turrell, V. Wylie, *A Place Name Index to George N. Roerich's Translation of the 'Blue Annals'*—Serie Orientale. Roma, xv, Roma, 1957.

Yoshimura Shyuki, *The Denkar-ma, An Oldest Catalogue of the Tibetan Buddhist Canon*, Kyoto, 1950.

* Added by the translator.

Sum-pa-mkhan-po Ye-śes-dpal-'byor, *dPag-bsam-ljon-bzaṅ*; pt. iii. "History of Buddhism in China and Mongolia", and 'chronological tables'. Tibetan text, ed. by Lokesh Chandra, New Delhi, 1959.

Dalai Lama V, *Gaṅs-can-yul-gyi-sa-la-spyod-pa'i-mtho-ris-kyi-gyal-blon-gtso-brjod-pa'i-deb-ther-rjogs-ldan-gshon-nu'i-dga'-ston-dbyed-kyi-rgyal-mo'i-glu-dbyaṅs-shes-bya-ba-bshugs-so*, Peking, 1957 (a reprint of the Lhasa edition).

Hor-chos-'byuṅ. Tibetan text, ed. by Hashimoto. Tokyo.

Abbreviations

BSOS—Bulletin of the School of Oriental Studies.
JA—Journal Asitique.
JAOS—Journal of the American Oriental Society.
JASB—Journal of the Asiatic Society of Bengal.
JBTS—Journal of the Buddhist Texts Society of India.
JRAS—Journal of the Royal Asiatic Society.
ZDMG—Zeitschrift der Deutschen Morgenlandischen Gesellschaft.

INDEX

Vos. 38

ERRATA

(incomplete)

Page	*line*	*as printed*	*should be*
12	9, 12, 17, 21	1.	fol.
15	27-8	Sea-book	Book-sea [*Grantha-sāgara*]
18, 64 87, 109	33, 17, 4, 1	belongs to	is attributed to
25	15	*'Bans-bshed*	*'Baṅs-bshed*
34	22	*mṅa'-gdag-...*	*mṅa'-bdag-...*
35	3	Yellow	Golden
70	10-11	who, in the notes to his history of the Mongols-*Sagan Setsen* -	who, in his notes to Sagan Setsen's history of the Mongols,
75	3	Jo-po'i-...	Jo-bo'i-...
	11	bSod-nams-rgyal	bSod-nams-rnam-rgyal
88, 89	33, 10-11	A-mchog-dkon-pa	Ā-mchog-dgon-pa
89, 93	3, 10	belonging to	attributed to
90	24	*...-dkon-mchogs-med-...*	*...-dkon-mchog-'jigs-med-...*
97	34	dKon-luṅ	dGon-luṅ
99	35	dBu-ma-pa	dbU-ma-pa
101	25	'Jyams-dpal-...	'Jam-dpal-...
	27	Saṅs-rgyas	lCaṅ-skya
114	2	*rTsi-kyi-...*	*rTsis-kyi-...*
130	13	1057	1027
136	12	dGe-'dun-grub-pa	dGe-'dun-grub
139	27	Tibetan	Tibetans
155	12	dGa'-ldan-pa	dGe-ldan-pa
160	8	dByaṅs-can-...	dbYaṅs-can-...
	34	*Gu-śir-...*	*Gu-śri-...*
166	last line	*...-bslab-graw*	*...-bslab-grwa*
174	9	*dGa'-ldan-chos-'byuṅ-...*	*dGe-ldan-chos-'byuṅ-...*
175	2	*...rtsom-'phra*	*...rtsom-'phro*
	last line	...-bshad-grub	...-bśad-grub
178	11	works	work

185	35	Se-spyil-bu-pa	Se-skyil-bu-pa
207	21	bCon-ldan	bCom-ldan
208	10-11	mention the Brag-dgon- .. ...among the Tibetan historical works	are mentioned by Brag-dgon-shabs-druṅ dKon-mchog-bstan-pa-rab-rgyas in his list of Tibetan historical works
231	18	bLa-yul-...	Bal-yul-...

("...-Snake year" and "...-Cow year", wherever occurring, should be uniformly read as "...-Serpent year" and .."-Ox year" respectively)

For Product Safety Concerns and Information please contact our EU representative GPSR@taylorandfrancis.com
Taylor & Francis Verlag GmbH, Kaufingerstraße 24, 80331 München, Germany

www.ingramcontent.com/pod-product-compliance
Lightning Source LLC
Chambersburg PA
CBHW060246100726
47907CB00003B/787

* 9 7 8 1 1 3 8 8 6 2 2 7 2 *